10

Edited by David Bates

ROYAL ARMOURIES

CONFERENCE PROCEEDINGS

Published by Royal Armouries Museum, Armouries Drive, Leeds LS10 1LT, United Kingdom

www.royalarmouries.org

ISBN 978 0 948092 84 8

Series edited by Martyn Lawrence

Typesetting by Out Of House Publishing

10 9 8 7 6 5 4 3 2 1

A CIP record for this book is available from the British Library.

Contents

List of contributors

David Bates, University of East Anglia

Pierre Bauduin, CRAHAM, Université de Caen Normandie, IUF

Stephen Baxter, St Peter's College, University of Oxford

Oliver H. Creighton, University of Exeter

Eric Fernie, Courtauld Institute of Art

John Gillingham, Emeritus Professor, London School of Economics and
    Political Science

Judith A. Green, University of Edinburgh

T. A. Heslop, University of East Anglia

Elisabeth van Houts, Emmanuel College, University of Cambridge

Edward Impey, Director General and Master, Royal Armouries Museum

Michael Lewis, British Museum

Tom Licence, University of East Anglia

Rory Naismith, Kings College, London

Thom Richardson, Curator Emeritus, Royal Armouries Museum

Ann Williams, Independent Scholar

Robert C. Woosnam-Savage, Curator of Armour and Edged Weapons,
    Royal Armouries Museum

Acknowledgements

The genesis of this volume, a conference held at the Tower of London on 14–16 October 2016, is fully explained in the Introduction. Its publication is therefore a tribute to all who took part in that event, as organisers, speakers, and audience, as well as to others who have sub-sequently joined the project. Special thanks are due to Edward Impey and the staff of the Royal Armouries for their central organising role in the conference and also to Historic Royal Palaces. Equally warm thanks are due to Royal Armouries for agreeing to publish this volume and to the Series Editor, Martyn Lawrence, who has been an outstandingly efficient and skilful guide and for his work as an editor. Catherine Dunn has been an excellent copy-editor who has tidied up inconsistences and infelicities that I, as editor, overlooked. Zeba Talkhani has carefully and sympathetically overseen the final stages of production and been very helpful to me in preparing the volume for publication. Finally, all images from the Bayeux Tapestry are published with special permission from the City of Bayeux.

Abbreviations

Acts of William I	Bates, D. (ed.) 1998, *Regesta Regum Anglo-Normannorum: The Acta of William I (1066–1087)*, Oxford
AN	*Annales de Normandie*
ANS	*Anglo-Norman Studies: Proceedings of the Battle Conference*
ASC	Anglo-Saxon Chronicle, cited by year (corrected in square brackets if necessary) and manuscript; unless otherwise stated the edition is Plummer, C. (ed.) 1892–9, *Two of the Saxon Chronicles Parallel*, 2 vols., Oxford. For a convenient modern translation, Swanton, M. J. (ed. and trans.) 1996, *The Anglo-Saxon Chronicle*, London
ASE	*Anglo-Saxon England*
BAR	British Archaeological Reports
Breuis Relatio	van Houts, E. (ed. and trans.), 1999, 'The *Breuis Relatio de Guillelmo nobilissimo comite Normannorum*, written by a Monk of Battle Abbey', in van Houts, E., *History and Family Traditions in England and the Continent, 1000–1200*, Aldershot and Burlington, Vermont, chapter VII; reprinted with a translation added from van Houts, E., 1997, in *Camden Miscellany*, 5th ser., x, Cambridge, 1–48
Carmen	Barlow, F. (ed. and trans.), 1999, *The Carmen de Hastingae Proelio of Guy Bishop of Amiens*, OMT, Oxford
CS	Whitelock, D., Brett, M. and Brooke, C. N. L., 1981, *Councils and Synods with other Documents relating to the English Church, 1066–1204*, 2 vols., Oxford
DP	Keats-Rohan, K. S. B., 1999, *Domesday People. A Prosopography of Persons occurring in English*

	Documents, 1066–1166. 1. Domesday Book, Woodbridge
EHD I	Whitelock, D. (ed.), 1979 (2nd ed.), *English Historical Documents, vol. I, c.500–1042,* London
EHD II	Douglas, D. C. and Greenaway, G. W. (eds.), 1981 (2nd ed.), *English Historical Documents, vol. II: 1042–1189,* London
EHR	*English Historical Review*
EME	*Early Medieval Europe*
GDB	References to Domesday Book are given for both the Alecto and the Phillimore editions: GDB = Erskine, R. W. H. (ed.), 1986, *Great Domesday Book,* London; *DB (county)* = the individual volumes in Morris, J. et al. (eds.), 1975–92. *Domesday Book,* Chichester
GG	Davis, R. H. C. and Chibnall, M. (ed. and trans.), 1998, *The Gesta Guillelmi of William of Poitiers,* OMT, Oxford
GND	van Houts, E. M. C. (ed. and trans.), 1992–5, *The Gesta Normannorum Ducum of William of Jumièges, Orderic Vitalis, and Robert of Torigni,* 2 vols., OMT, Oxford
GP	Winterbottom, M. and Thomson, R. M. (ed. and trans.), 2007, William of Malmesbury, *Gesta pontificum Anglorum: The History of the English Bishops,* 2 vols., OMT, Oxford
GR	Mynors, R. A. B., Winterbottom, M. and Thomson, R. M. (eds. and trans.), 1998–9, William of Malmesbury, *Gesta regum Anglorum: The History of the English Kings,* 2 vols., OMT, Oxford
HH	Greenway, D. (ed. and trans.), 1996, Henry, Archdeacon of Huntingdon, *Historia Anglorum: The History of the English People,* OMT, Oxford
HR	*Historical Research*
JMH	*Journal of Medieval History*
JW	Darlington, R. R. and McGurk, P. (ed. and trans.), 1995–8, *The Chronicle of John of Worcester,* 2 vols. (vols. ii and iii), OMT, Oxford
Lanfranc Letters	Clover, H. and Gibson, M. (eds. and trans.), 1979, *The Letters of Lanfranc, Archbishop of Canterbury,* OMT, Oxford

LDB	References to Domesday Book are given for both the Alecto and the Phillimore editions: LDB = Williams, A. and G. Martin (eds.), 2000, *Little Domesday Book*, 3 vols., London; *DB (county)* = the individual volumes in Morris, J. et al. (eds.), 1975–92. *Domesday Book*, Chichester
ODNB	*Oxford Dictionary of National Biography*
OMT	Oxford Medieval Texts
OV	Chibnall, M. (ed. and trans.), 1969–80, *The Ecclesiastical History of Orderic Vitalis*, 6 vols., OMT, Oxford
RADN	Fauroux, M. (ed.), 1961, *Recueil des actes des ducs de Normandie de 911 à 1066*, Mémoires de la Société des Antiquaires de Normandie, vol. xxxvi, Caen
Roman de Rou	Burgess, G.S and Holden, A.J., (eds. and trans.), 2002, *The History of the Norman People: Wace's Roman de Rou*, translated by Glyn S. Burgess with the text of Anthony J. Holden and notes by Glyn S. Burgess and Elisabeth van Houts, Société Jersiaise, St Helier
TNA	The National Archives
TRHS	*Transactions of the Royal Historical Society*
VCH	*The Victoria County History of the Counties of England* [with county name], in progress
VEdR	Barlow, F. (ed. and trans.), 1992 (2nd ed.), *The Life of King Edward who Rests at Westminster, Attributed to a Monk of Saint-Bertin*, OMT, Oxford

Family tree of William the Conqueror

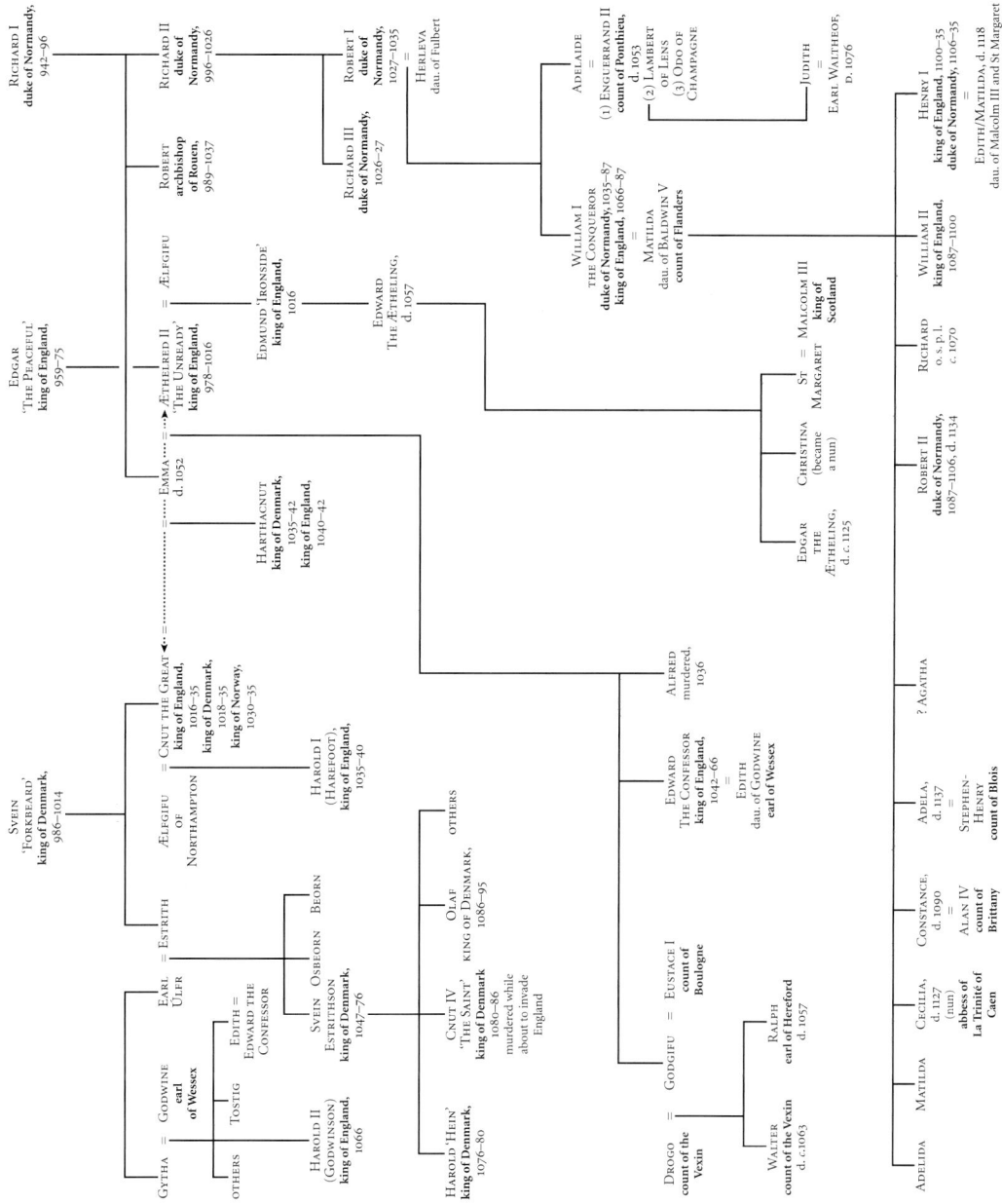

RICHARD I
**duke of Normandy,
942–96**

RICHARD II
**duke of
Normandy,
996–1026**

ROBERT
**archbishop
of Rouen,
989–1037**

ROBERT I
**duke of
Normandy,
1027–1035**
=
HERLEVA
dau. of Fulbert

RICHARD III
**duke of Normandy,
1026–27**

ADELAIDE
=
(1) ENGUERRAND II
count of Ponthieu,
d. 1053
(2) LAMBERT
OF LENS
(3) ODO OF
CHAMPAGNE

JUDITH
=
EARL WALTHEOF,
d. 1076

WILLIAM I
**THE CONQUEROR
duke of Normandy, 1035–87
king of England, 1066–87**
=
MATILDA
dau. of BALDWIN V
count of Flanders

HENRY I
**king of England, 1100–35
duke of Normandy, 1106–35**
=
EDITH/MATILDA, d. 1118
dau. of Malcolm III and St Margaret

WILLIAM II
**king of England,
1087–1100**

EDGAR
'THE PEACEFUL'
**king of England,
959–75**

ÆTHELRED II
'THE UNREADY'
**king of England,
978–1016**
=
EMMA
d. 1052

EDMUND 'IRONSIDE'
king of England,
1016

EDWARD
THE ÆTHELING,
d. 1057

St = MALCOLM III
MARGARET **king of
Scotland**

CHRISTINA
(became
a nun)

RICHARD
o. s. p. l.
c. 1070

EDGAR
THE
ÆTHELING,
d. c. 1125

ROBERT II
duke of Normandy,
1087–1106, d. 1134

? AGATHA

HARTHACNUT
**king of Denmark,
1035–42
king of England,
1040–42**

SVEIN
'FORKBEARD'
**king of Denmark,
986–1014**

ÆLFGIFU = CNUT THE GREAT
OF
NORTHAMPTON
**king of England,
1016–35
king of Denmark,
1018–35
king of Norway,
1030–35**

HAROLD I
(HAREFOOT),
**king of England,
1035–40**

ALFRED
murdered,
1036

EDWARD
THE CONFESSOR
**king of England,
1042–66**
=
EDITH
dau. of GODWINE
earl of Wessex

ADELA, d. 1137
=
STEPHEN-
HENRY
count of Blois

CONSTANCE,
d. 1090
=
ALAN IV
**count of
Brittany**

CECILIA,
d. 1127
(nun)
**abbess of
La Trinité of
Caen**

MATILDA

ADELIDA

GYTHA = GODWINE
**earl
of Wessex**

EARL = ESTRITH
ULFR

OTHERS

TOSTIG

HAROLD II
(GODWINSON)
king of England,
1066

EDITH = EDWARD THE
CONFESSOR

SVEIN OSBEORN BEORN
ESTRITHSON
king of Denmark,
1047–76

CNUT IV
'THE SAINT'
king of Denmark,
1080–86
murdered while
about to invade
England

OLAF
KING OF DENMARK,
1086–95

OTHERS

HAROLD 'HEIN'
king of Denmark,
1076–80

GODGIFU = EUSTACE I
**count of
Boulogne**

DROGO
**count of the
Vexin**

WALTER
count of the Vexin
d. c.1063

RALPH
earl of Hereford
d. 1057

Courtesy of Yale University Press

Introduction

David Bates

This volume is a follow-on from the conference held at the Tower of London on 14–16 October 2016 to mark the 950th anniversary of the Battle of Hastings. The objective of the conference and of this book was to assemble a group of distinguished scholars who were briefed to reflect on a central aspect of the conference's theme. The genesis of both was discussions among the group of British scholars who are members of the committee in France advising on the creation of a new museum at Bayeux for the Bayeux Tapestry, namely myself, Stephen Baxter, Richard Gameson, Lindy Grant and Michael Lewis, expanded to form a conference committee that included representatives of English Heritage (Jeremy Ashbee) and Royal Armouries (Edward Impey and Emma Carver).

Although some of the speakers at the conference were unable to contribute to this volume and others have joined in who were not on the programme, the spirit that animated the conference – and indeed the decision to hold it – is very much present in this volume. In taking on the editorial responsibilities, I was very aware of just how weighty they were. I was also aware that neither the conference nor this book can cover every aspect of the subject. Putting 1066 into perspective in 2016 and 2018 is a complex, multidimensional and multidisciplinary task. With approaches to the study of the past having diversified hugely since the novocentenary of 1966, an event that I am old enough to remember, a volume dedicated to 1066 following on from a conference aimed at the interested general public represents an indispensable element in commemorating a major date in English, British, French, European and even world history.

The 15 essays in this volume largely speak for themselves. They make contributions to specific topics, with Michael Lewis critically and cogently assessing many aspects of current discussions of the Bayeux Tapestry, John Gillingham having new things to say about the site of the Battle of Hastings, Edward Impey looking again at the crucial period between the battle and William's coronation on 25 December 1066, and my own article looking at elements in supposedly familiar narratives that need to be re-examined. While they and all the other articles are designed to be read as self-contained articles, my strongly held wish – and that of all others involved in the project – is that readers will range across all of them and form from them their own impression of the so-called Norman Conquest, of its place in England's history and of how its story should be told. There are inevitably differences of emphasis in the authors' approaches. There are even disagreements between them. Such a situation is not only part of the subject's fascination, it is inherent to it; as I emphasise in my own essay, that there were disagreements at the time and in the generation afterwards makes disagreement germane to everything. The ultimate responsibility for all with an interest in putting 1066 into perspective is only partly to try to create convincing narratives and interpretations; it is also to understand why these disagreements exist and perhaps to recognise that reconciling them is ultimately not fully possible.

Because of the disagreements in the written record, there are arguments for thinking that artefacts rather than the written word constitute a better route to balance and objectivity. A debateable proposition, it is worthy of examination and debate. All forms of evidence can, however, become the foci of debate. To cite three well-known illustrations: firstly there would not have been a Battle of Hastings if all alive in 1065 had understood whatever oath Harold had sworn to William during his visit to Normandy in the same way; secondly that it is clear from those two key texts, the 'D' version of the Anglo-Saxon Chronicle and the *Gesta Guillelmi* of William of Poitiers, that diametrically opposed opinions about William's rule were forming within days of his coronation as king of the English on 25 December 1066 and that they have remained ever-present thereafter; and thirdly that the surviving castles and churches convey very mixed messages. The first of these results from flexible and imprecise customs and norms in relation to succession to kingdoms; the second from diametrically opposed opinions resulting in what for was many necessities required to guarantee security and, for many others, instruments of oppression; the third from what could be seen as a controversial form of modernisation and the cause of destruction and excessive expenditure.

Arguably the main change that has taken place since the 900th anniversary is the way in which the old debates about the backwardness of either Normandy or England in relation to the other have been sidelined. This is a statement that applies as much to the Church on both sides of the Channel as to the state, a term that, while controversial for this period, I am using because it is convenient. William the Conqueror and those associated with him took over a kingdom that was, by the standards of the time, prosperous and well-organised and within which the – for some anomalous – position of Archbishop

Stigand of Canterbury did not detract from the general picture of a well-established and thriving Church.

Since 1966, the late James Campbell and the late Patrick Wormald have been central to bringing about this change in perspective, with, it must be added, the earlier work of Frank Barlow and Henry Loyn also being very important. In France, great changes were brought about by the generation of Lucien Musset, Michel de Boüard and Jean Yver. The result is that England's and Normandy's history and histories must not only be located within the history of Europe and of the North Sea world; they must also start from the widely accepted conclusion that the cultures and structures of rule and society in Normandy and England were ones in which both were participants in the political and religious culture that was prevalent throughout the post-Carolingian medieval West, albeit with significant differences in the way in which it was applied and evolved. Intriguingly, one result has been to make Normandy's and England's institutional and social development look remarkably similar. These themes can be traced in detail in the essays by Pierre Bauduin, Rory Naismith, Stephen Baxter, and the jointly-authored article by Tom Licence and T. A. Heslop. Thom Richardson and Robert Woosnam-Savage perform a similar task in their magisterial essay on armour and weapons.

The multidisciplinary analyses of the last 50 years arguably also mean that terms such as 'continuity' and 'change' have become utterly inadequate for analysing the multiplicity of forces at work in relation to the historical significance of the so-called Norman Conquest of England. Massive change there undoubtedly was, with the essays by Stephen Baxter, Oliver Creighton, Eric Fernie, John Gillingham and Judith Green making this very clear. However, what is also obvious from all of them is that change has frequently to be viewed as taking place over a long historical period, that it often cannot be labelled with the word 'Norman', and that some of it was not necessarily a direct result of the Conquest at all. As these essays show, debates around subjects such as chivalry and ecclesiastical and secular architecture raise issues of the transfer of cultural values across the lands that William and his successors ruled and about their relevance to Normandy's and England's place within broader European changes. And as Judith Green points out, words and phrases like 'feudalism' and 'the feudal system' have largely disappeared from the discussion because they have been replaced by different societal and cultural modes of analysis.

One key to open many doors is provided by Robert Bartlett's summation of his *The Making of Europe* that 'This book then tells both how a more uniform cultural pattern was created and extended on the continent of Europe and also how that same process produced a ring of linguistically and ethnically divided societies'.[1] For all that it can be pointed out that almost endless locally and regionally shaped variations on the theme are possible and that levels of uniformity were already present long before the 11th century, the statement must indubitably be kept in the analytical mix.[2] It prompts questions that, albeit that they are counter-factual, are also surely historically valid, such as, for example, whether castles, Romanesque architecture and the full apparatus of so-called Gregorian Reform would have arrived in England and the British Isles if Harold had won the Battle of Hastings or if the English had instead chosen to support Edgar the Ætheling.

An answer that starts from the uncontroversial statement that all of the above appeared in many places to which William the Conqueror and the Normans did not go indicates that the answer must surely be that they would have done. They are part of the 'more uniform cultural pattern'. But then the qualification has to be made that they might well not have appeared in England and the British Isles in the form in which they did appear if William had lost the Battle of Hastings. As Eric Fernie's article suggests, the size and stylistic originality of some of the great churches built in England surely make them the product of unique circumstances and of an ideological statement; intriguingly, however, and very importantly, there are features of them that have no precedent in Normandy. John Gillingham's and Judith Green's articles suggest differences in warfare and aristocratic culture that were specific consequences of the Conquest, and Stephen Baxter argues that government in England would not have evolved in the way it did if there had not been a conquest. Although mainly focused on London, Edward Impey's third chapter raises analogous issues in relation to the building of castles in towns. Arguments of a similar kind apply to the making of that truly remarkable document that came to be called Domesday Book. There are no precedents for a survey on this scale in either Normandy or England. Yet it did have precedents within the traditions and practices of medieval and classical Europe that were many centuries old. Even the apparently unique cannot be taken in isolation.

While concentrating mostly on the defeated people of England, the articles by Ann Williams and Elisabeth van Houts tackle issues that foreground the fates of English men and women within the new societies created by 1066, and sometimes those of the Normans and the French. Ann Williams, by focusing on 'the middling sort', prompts thoughts about the dynamic that the English must have brought to local and regional societies once the cataclysmic upheavals that followed 1066 had begun to pass; the evidence, above all that of Domesday Book, is deployed to show how the lives of those who are recorded can be used to develop perspectives on those who are not. Elisabeth van Houts focuses on women's history and also on the history of fear. In doing so, she raises issues about the violence of the conquest and about all medieval violence, as well as the issues of adaption and integration into the new societies that emerged. My own essay also comments on some of these issues, and specifically on attitudes towards non-combatants.

The perspectives on which all these articles require us to focus are universal ones within the history of humanity and the impact of war on people's and communities' lives, with it being possible through them to tackle subjects relating to exile, flight, refugees and the resilience needed to rebuild shattered lives. In such an analysis, archaeology has a central role to play, with recent publications illuminating the possibilities and work that is currently ongoing and likely to develop further.[3] All this, I would suggest, could lead to a study of how people experienced victory and defeat in the aftermath of 1066. To make the distinction between the Noman Conquest as an event and the Norman Conquest as a process makes the subject very different. This approach is also centrally relevant to how we must now think about things feudal and also the histories of law, language and education. The sheer scale of the takeover of England's land and resources that took place in the years after 1066 meant that multiple new relationships and new means to support power and to sustain communities were inevitably created.

It is irresistible for me not to include here my comment in a book published in 2018 that the chronological perspective necessary to understanding William the Conqueror's life and place in history must encompass the period from about 900 to about 1250, a reflection that was also included in the address with which I opened the conference.[4] To this comment I will add that it is gratifying to be able to mention that several recently published books share this philosophy. To set 1066 into perspective, it is crucial never to forget that it was an event within contexts and processes, albeit that it was dramatic and, for many, the bringer of great fortune or disaster. It is also important never to forget that the 11th century is a unique century in England's history in that the country was conquered not just once but twice, in 1016 as well as in 1066. A full analysis of 1066 in perspective requires that we consider Cnut's conquest alongside William's. This is also a topic to which a lot more attention is being devoted than previously. One undoubted result will be to emphasise the diversity of English and British history and the impossibility of detaching both of them from the history of Europe.

The conference and this volume have shown just how much the task of putting 1066 into perspective has become a collaborative exercise. They are a tribute to all who have done so much to deepen understanding of matters related to 1066 and who have the responsibility of teaching the subject. Three very enjoyable days have been channelled directly and indirectly into this volume and so too has the scholarship and enthusiasm of an almost infinite number of people. As I and others observe in our contributions, the exercise has made all of us reflect on what still needs to be done. As I have already said, when the conference was planned, I and others involved were only too aware that we could not cover everything. The lives of those who we can call 'ordinary people' and the histories of law, towns, libraries and education, and the English language are obvious omissions. As the book's Select Bibliography shows, there are places where the reader can go for authoritative statements. This *apologia* notwithstanding, this book is offered to the reader as a means to assess where we are and then to think of where we can go, thereby illuminating the importance of putting 1066 into perspective. It also shows just how important and exciting the study of the Middle Ages is and always will be.

1

Normandy before 1066

Pierre Bauduin

By way of introduction I will go back some 50 years. In the Norman bibliography of the *Annales de Normandie* published in 1967, Michel Nortier noted that a large number of works on William the Conqueror and his time were being published, but that the French ones were mainly in fairly basic collective publications, while 'several scholarly studies and sometimes passionate ones' had been produced by the English side.[1] Looking at this mid-1960s bibliography brings back to mind the research led by that period's historians into Normandy's history: Lucien Musset, Michel de Boüard and Jean Yver on the French side; David Douglas, Frank Barlow and Marjorie Chibnall on the British side, to mention only a few. We are much indebted to them, but perspectives and analytical approaches have evolved since those times. This brief retrospective sets out to present several features of how Normandy's history was addressed up until the Norman conquest of England. While it is not possible to mention all of these scholars' publications here, it is notable that there were two papers given in 1966, and published in 1967, which announced important books published several years later.[2]

A comprehensive presentation devoted to Normandy before 1066 would be quite a task, and I have chosen to present some points that show both the evolution of our knowledge and questions that have recently been asked.[3] For the sake of convenience, I have focused my article on a number of key words, put together under two major points that bring together, I believe, an important part of the debates they have stimulated: I will, therefore, speak successively of 'continuity, discontinuity, heritages or legacy, and identities' and then of 'evolution, mutation, evolution and reform'. All this will, in conclusion, be complemented by the outline of a European perspective on the subject.

A fundamental aspect of the topic, the sources, will not be discussed in detail here. It is nonetheless important to remember that our knowledge of pre-1066 Normandy has developed because many written sources have been published or reprinted.[4] While a new edition of Dudo of Saint-Quentin is long overdue, study of his *Historia* has produced an astonishing amount of work that has led to a revision of the very negative assessment levelled at his work a century ago.[5] New thinking has emerged in relation to documentary production, whether literary or diplomatic. A major research theme has been that of 'documentary mutation' (la 'mutation documentaire'), whose major questions, among others, ask to what extent the changes observed during the 11th century reflect the political, religious or social evolutions in the duchy, or are the result of a change in practices and documentary forms.[6] The transmission of memory; the recent use of the concept of 'cultural memory'; the use of obituary documentation; intellectual networks; the movement of people, books, ideas, literary models and borrowings; manuscripts and the history of libraries (such as Mont Saint-Michel and Fécamp)[7] have become research fields that have witnessed remarkable developments in recent years. Our knowledge of these developments should benefit greatly from the creation of digital corpuses and the digitising of charters and manuscripts.[8] The 1960s were also an important time for the development of medieval archeology in Normandy.[9] Castles and places of power were among the first beneficiaries of this research, which could in turn be associated with reflection on the evolution of power.

Continuity, discontinuity, legacy, identities

The Norman experience: sitting on the fence between continuity and discontinuity

This is a recurring issue. The thesis of continuity emphasises continuities between the Carolingian Neustria and ducal Normandy; the discontinuity approach highlights the disruption caused by the Viking invasions. It is important to note, however, that they have been regarded as not necessarily being contradictory, in so far as the Scandinavian contribution was seen as an element capable of making the Carolingian state structures more dynamic. This debate is still ongoing, but it is not possible to reduce discussion to a straightforward confrontation between two opinions. The foundation of what became the Norman duchy was for a long time located within the chronology of the Viking movement, and it had been seen, for the Frankish kingdom, as a sort of culmination of it. We must, however, also seek to understand it by examining the secular relations between the Frankish world and the Scandinavians and also by seeing it as occurring within a period within the internal history of the regnum Francorum when the latter was undergoing profound political changes that witnessed, among other things, the affirmation of the power of major aristocratic families and the emergence of the first territorial principalities. Rollo was not the first Viking chief to reach an agreement with the Frankish authorities, and the 'treaty' of Saint-Clair-sur-Epte (911) was part of the long-standing practice of making deals and of compromises, developments whose history can be followed from Louis the Pious' reign onwards, or even from the end of Charlemagne's.[10] The Norman dynasty played the card of integration into the Frankish kingdom, and its success is explained in part by the ties it managed to establish with the elites of the kingdom through alliances, kinship and friendship.[11] The Treaty of Saint-Clair-sur-Epte not only marked the recognition of the Normans settled on the lower Seine, but it also established a compromise between the various actors (the king, the Frankish princes and Rollo), as well as the Norman chief's entry into the community of the magnates of the kingdom. These initial choices were not contradicted later, even if sources do provide echoes of opposition to the Frankish orientation driven by the Norman rulers.

Normandy was the only sustainable political foundation established by the Scandinavians on the Continent, but the paradoxes raised by its history are numerous. It was apparently one of the principalities where Carolingian institutions were most vigorously maintained, in spite – or because of? – the (supposed) disappearance of the Frankish elite. Available sources show a clear discrepancy between historiographical texts and linguistic or onomastic data, which show that Scandinavians were present there, but archaeological evidence to date is practically non-existent, which casts doubts on the extent and sustainability of the Viking influence. While the establishment of Vikings in that part of Neustria has never been seriously denied, its timing, form, and the density of this settlement and its social make-up have produced divergent interpretations. Was the colonisation that took place mostly that of an elite taking control of the native population? Or was it colonisation via more or less sizeable farming settlements? What about the presence, or not, of women and families, as well as its ethnic composition or, more recently, its 'diasporic' nature? Opinions range from the 'invisible Viking' theory of Vincent Carpentier,[12] arguing that their presence has been overestimated or is 'mythical', to the idea developed by Lesley Abrams of a settlement involving the local presence of a significant Norse-speaking community and cultural traits which are not just anecdotal survivals.[13] I will illustrate these with two examples covered in recent discussions. The study of a sector such as the lower Dives river-valley since the Neolithic period makes it much less obvious that the Scandinavians had an actual impact on a river–sea space that had been exploited for a long time.[14] On the other hand, Éric van Torhoudt has stressed the significance of the Frankish military structures in the Cotentin region, which emerge again when the written material is more abundant in an area that was once thought to have been abandoned to the Bretons and then to the Scandinavians.[15]

The inventory of the evidence for the Frankish and Viking legacies was completed a long time ago by inquiring into their respective importance, their cohabitation and, during the early decades of the 11th century, the gradual blurring of the former in favour of the latter. Assessments of their significance were, however, eventually altered over time by comparing it with other Viking experiments in Europe and by reassessing the Carolingians' power and their institutions, which were less monolithic and powerful than previously believed, as well as through the emergence of the concept of a 'Viking diaspora'.[16] The matter of their legacy and contributions has in fact been misconceived because it involves considering 'objects' (in the broad sense of the term; both material artefacts and intangible elements such as legal concepts, beliefs, languages or patterns of thought) as elements that are immutable over time and unchanging in their form. Current research on exchanges and cultural transfers insists instead on the adoption, appropriation or, conversely, rejection of these objects when the populations interacted; on imitation or the reformulation of cultural facts as well as their integration in a new social context. Studies of the first Norman coinage are interesting from this point of view because, in the absence of written documents, they bear witness to the early days of the Norman duchy.[17] From the beginning of the Norman period, the coins issued in what became Normandy belonged to the Frankish tradition, but William Longsword was one of the earliest princes of the Frankish kingdom who minted coins in his name. Norman coins imitated the Carolingian kings' coinage, but it was not a slavish imitation. The disappearance of the Carolingian monogram, replaced by Temple-type imitation coins, may have been hastened by the conflicts between the Normans and the Carolingian Louis IV in the middle of the tenth century or may have been a reference to the Scandinavian world, where these coins were known. Norman princes were quick to recognise the role of currency as both a symbol of power and a means of propaganda.

Identities

The descendants of the Vikings who settled in Normandy felt no need to express forms of identity with the Viking world. A person's name is a vector of identity; it is even one of its functions, but it is actually very difficult to know whether the use of a Scandinavian anthroponym refers to the expression of ethnic, social or family identity.[18] What is the significance of being called *Turstin* or *Torquetil* in Normandy in the first half of the 11th century? To date in Normandy, hardly any artefacts or decorative elements have been unearthed that were influenced by shapes or patterns found elsewhere in the Viking world.[19] It does not mean these elements were unknown, even less that Norse communities never existed there, but simply that these elements were not acting as vectors of cultural affiliation, as can be seen, for example, in some parts of England, from women's costume elements or from equestrian equipment.[20] Not that these Scandinavian origins were unknown or rejected; rather, they were largely rewritten from cultural facts emanating from the Frankish world. Such reformulation is more visible at the turn of the tenth and eleventh centuries, through the first texts of Norman historiography, but the process was likely to have been initiated earlier, probably as an aspect of the Normans' conversion and acculturation. Highlighting the Trojan origins of the Normans, as borrowed from classical literature and the historiographical tradition of the Early Middle Ages, clearly makes sense here, because it made it possible to link the *Daci* (now called *Dani*) and their Norman descendants to the illustrious ancient peoples, thus placing them on an equal footing with the Franks.[21] The 'Scandinavian' origins of the Normans could thereby clearly be assumed, but they had been 'cobbled together' (in the anthropological sense) using materials from Antiquity and early medieval ethnographic traditions.

Throughout the *Historia*, Dudo's narrative presents us with the essential components of a Norman identity around the year 1000.[22] An ethnic component, which confers on the Normans a Trojan origin but also claims the settlement of Normandy, results from populations intermingling after the first duke had brought people from other regions into the country. There was a religious component, which asserts that the establishment of Rollo and his family was ordained by Divine Providence and pictures Rollo as a new Constantine;[23] a political and dynastic component around the Norman ducal line, which alone can claim to exercise power over the principality; and finally a territorial component, which portrays land given to Rollo as a deserted land – thus legitimising its occupation by its new inhabitants – and a territory whose boundaries were defined as early as Rollo's time. This does not mean that all the Normans fitted into this representation, as several items were only relevant to the elite.

There were several factors that were central to defining a Norman identity.[24] Originating from the Norman principality or dwelling on the Norman territory were not the sole criteria. Being under the authority or at the service of the Norman prince was undoubtedly essential in defining who was truly Norman. Such Norman identity was also supported by a clearer awareness of legal distinctiveness, which may have been felt by the second third of the 11th century in the expression of the principality's own customary law or in the cult of a number of saints already revered in the region. This does not mean that these are in any way immutable facts. Identities are social constructs, which individuals or groups adapt to a given situation or their strategies, as later emphasised in research works on the Norman identity (or Norman identities) in other contexts in England and Italy.[25]

Modern analysis of this Norman identity resides for a large part in further developments related to conquests outside the duchy, in reflections on the 'Norman myth' as discussed by Ralph Davis and in debates over the *gens Normannorum*.[26] The concept of a *gens Normannorum*, endowed with special qualities singled out by military prowess and successes, united around a common awareness of its successes, was possibly a 12th-century creation, articulated in particular by Orderic Vitalis. The controversies that the activities of the Normans stirred up, however, led him to revise this model by minimising the unity of the *gens Normannorum* in ways which emphasised conceptual diversity. Moreover, it is perhaps not so much a sense of unity as a result of the conquests, but rather the *gens'* special qualities, as set out as early as the 11th century by taking up patterns found in ancient and early medieval traditions, that are the most important element in defining the identity of the Normans.

Revolution, mutation, evolution, reform

Revolution, mutation

The interpretation of the conquest of England and its consequences for the country are based in part on the assessment made by historians on society and power in pre-1066 Normandy. The interpretation of the evolution of the duchy during decades before the Conquest was influenced in the 1980s and 1990s by the debates on a 'revolution' or a 'mutation' around the year 1000 and by the refutations of these mutationist arguments by some historians, first and foremost by Dominique Barthélemy.[27] This wide-ranging debate is also available as a series of more focused approaches, often intended to qualify the overall scheme, concerning, for example, the 'documentary mutation' that I have already mentioned; 'family mutation', which we will return to; and more recently 'chivalrous mutation',[28] as Normandy seems to have embodied even before 1066. The idea is that the changes that occurred in the 11th century, and particularly during the second quarter of that century in Normandy, were seen as evidence of a deep and sudden crisis, as seen elsewhere in France with the fragmentation and privatisation of public authority, the appropriation of public fortresses and the building of castles, and the increasing militarisation of society as well as the unleashing of violence.

In an article published in 2000, David Bates recalled that his interpretation of the 11th-century period in his *Normandy Before 1066* had been influenced by the model proposed by Georges Duby on the basis of his famous thesis on the region of the Mâconnais.[29] He suggested then that changes, real and observed ones, could be described more truly as an evolution, not a revolution; as a dynamic change, rather than as fundamentally breaking away from the pre-feudal past; as a reaction to the instability of princely power, rather than as an attempt to overthrow it. Later, he put forward a new analysis of the years during William's minority and supported relinquishing the arguments in favour of a '*mutation de l'an mil*'.[30] Let us remember now that a great number of Normandy's historians were trained in this school of thought and, on this side of the Channel, set great store by the theme of the castle and castellan lordship.[31]

Other events or processes have also been analysed within a mutationist framework. However, they have also been interpreted in terms of resistance, both by ducal power and by a fraction of society, against increasing demands made by the ruling elite. That is why the 996 peasants' revolt has been reinterpreted by Mathieu Arnoux as a movement stirred up by an uprising of the aristocracy leading to the semi-victory of the peasantry 'against the undoubtedly arrant abuses of the noble class', resulting in the strengthening of ducal power and eventually a happy ending for farmers, since they managed to safeguard their freedom and a substantial part of their rights.[32] In fact, it is the rather incoherent nature of the mutationist model as it was put forward, stressing resistance to ducal prerogatives, which made it easier for the duke to recover his power after a few stormy periods and to take advantage of social change for his own benefit. The incomplete nature of lordly domination is alleged to have incited the aristocracy to opt for other forms of exploitation, or even for daring ventures outside the duchy.[33] The Conquest could then be construed as a 'distraction' from the thwarted ambitions of the aristocratic group, which would seek expansion opportunities elsewhere because it could not find enough within the duchy, and, in England, it turned into an opportunity for the Norman ruler to channel and direct for his own benefit this dominant group's appetite for power.

Approaches via the social sciences and groups

More generally, interpretations of Norman society have been influenced by the social sciences, sociology, anthropology, study of cultural exchanges, discussions on conflict resolution, gift, norms (whether written or not), forms of political communication – including symbolic ones – rituals, kinship, friendship, alliances, gender studies and the issue of women. Some of these have been developed in recent years – but probably unevenly – according to the objects of study and historiographical traditions. They have also influenced discussions about the beginnings of the Norman principality, perhaps because a greater familiarity with the period was felt by historians of the Carolingian and post-Carolingian worlds, who were among the first to have adopted these approaches.

Régine Le Jan recalled a few years ago that 'Society in the early Middle Ages is a competitive society where social positions are constantly renegotiated'.[34] Is the history of Normandy before 1066 a different case from this? The concepts of competition (for functions, land and women as well as for all symbols of prestige and power) and of competitive exchange and consensus are useful tools to understand what Norman society was like. Can we not understand the decades prior to 1066 as a time of great fluctuations in the terms of competitive exchange? This was obviously favourable to the duke under Richard II, as he was able to maintain the duchy's stability without having to resort to external conquests, in part because it possessed sufficient resources (including through the ducal domain) to establish the members of the ruling dynasty and aristocratic elite in positions of influence and power.

Duke William's policy after 1042/1043 was to restore a power relation-ship favourable to the duke. The consensus, as an ideal for balanced negotiated relationships between prince and elites, grounded in the rec-ognition of the legitimacy of the former and of his ability to ensure the advancement of the latter, is also a factor to be considered and may offer an interesting framework for interpreting the events of 1066 as well as for post-Conquest events.[35]

There are many other examples that support a more anthropological reading of Norman society and how it enhances the perspectives avail-able to us. Here are a few examples, starting with rituals and symbols of a kind that abound in the sources. Thus, William of Jumièges provides accurate descriptions of the *harmiscara*, a punishment ritual through humiliation, a way for the offended party's honour to be restored while the offender was thereby able to recover the grace he had lost.[36] Hermann Kamp showed the importance of symbolic communication when studying the 'strength of signs and gestures' in Norman princes' public behaviour in Dudo's work.[37] Obviously, these are probably reconstructed scenes, intended to illustrate the dukes' powers and postures as well as their ability to impose them, and to be offered as a model. They demonstrate, however, how important such attitudes were within the political culture at the time that the canon of Saint-Quentin was writing. As a result, Geoffrey Koziol has described Dudo as an author obsessed with ritual and especially with supplication, a theme that might have been emblematic of his view of good lordship, of the right way to express one's subjection to one's lord, of the good faith essential to maintaining peace.[38] It could also be said that the *petitio* formulas that appear in the acta of Norman dukes, as well as the decline in the number of these expressions during the 11th century, may be associated with changes in ducal government and political culture, unless, of course, they simply betray changes in documentary forms.[39]

In another area, much has been written about kinship structures and this provides a lot of opportunities for discussion. I have tried else-where to show how the early Norman dukes used their kinship and friendship networks to consolidate their integration into the Frankish world.[40] Over two generations, the Norman princes built up a net-work of alliances with extensive ramifications which enabled them to become associated with the magnates of the *regnum Francorum*, but which also aroused rivalry caused by the enduring competition among the northern kingdom's major aristocratic families. Possibly – though this is controversial – this policy was initiated very early on, even before Rollo was acknowledged in Rouen. The adoption of Frankish marriage customs is also a way to understand their integration. In addition, it can be surmised that the *more danico* marriage practice, stigmatised by William of Jumièges, was the retrospective invention of a cleric condemning Norman princes' concubinage practices, as these were not so different from what was previously accepted in the Frankish world.[41]

It had been suggested that changes in family structures – simply put, the changeover from broad kinship to lineage – were one of the main springs of the turbulence rampant in aristocratic circles.[42] For all that, what has been called the 'family mutation' probably never took, neither in Normandy nor elsewhere, the radical nature allegedly found in the 1970s and the 1980s. The forms of family organisation, as well as matrimonial strategies and inheritance practices, were apparently more varied before 1066 than is suggested by the paradigm of switching from cousinship to lineage.[43] It is regrettable that women have not been the subject of a synthesis for Normandy. But their influence can be grasped more precisely through studies of Gunnor, her daughter Queen Emma, Herleva, and Adelaide of Aumale,[44] or thanks to research on particular aspects, such as property transfers between spouses, the role of women in transmitting family memory, and their contribution to miracle stories and to religious or literary patronage.[45]

There is insufficient space in this article to develop other examples, but we now indisputably have at our disposal broader views on the social bonds, practices and representations that made up the context in which government and human behaviour operated. This comment also applies to groups, though works on this topic are as yet unequally completed when dealing with laity on one hand and the prosopography of the clergy on the other. Regarding the aristocracy, Lucien Musset published a seminal paper 40 years ago on the Norman aristocracy in the eleventh century, advocating that, between the tenth and eleventh centuries, a 'radical renewal' occurred in the ruling class, which could be interpreted in terms of it being a ducal creation, endowed as it was with systematically dispersed lands in order to guarantee that these families would prove submissive, but also as a group open to *homines novi*, which could involve great social mobility, particularly through service to the duke or to churches.[46] Many works have been published since then, in the form of monographs on themes relating to families and regions (on borders, for example), or to the study of some groups or functions (ducal chaplains or vicomtes). Yet a new synthesis needs to be made about the aristocratic group in the 11th century. I cannot sketch one here, but let me emphasise a few points. I am leaving aside any attempts to try and go back beyond the tenth century: cases are too anecdotal (for example, on the Vernon or Nigellide families)[47] to draw a reliable conclusion. One senses, for example, on reading the account of the preliminaries to the restoration of the abbey of Saint-Evroult, the existence of a locally well-established aristocratic group that constituted the framework of a lesser or middle-ranking local aristocracy, sometimes at the limit of the upper margin of free peasants.[48] Regarding Western Normandy, Eric Van Torhoudt speaks about a '*bajocasso-cotentinaise*' aristocracy that does not emerge until the mid-11th century, but whose structure appears to date back to earlier, to Richard II's reign and probably even before. The duke had to compromise with a previously established local elite, and the pattern of the colonisation of elites from Upper to Lower Normandy probably needs to be revisited.[49] Aristocratic families at the borders have been further investigated and they show the strength of the influence of local issues that were largely independent of political domination from the centre.[50] More generally, the development of these monographs has resulted in a major scale change in our assessment of the relations between duke and aristocracy, and leads us to consider why it was so necessary for the ducal power (but also for the magnates) to compromise and cope with local elites.

Ecclesiastical dignitaries and church personnel have benefited from more systematic prosopographical investigation.[51] We now have an overview of the Norman episcopate in the 11th century, which was the subject of the 1993 Cerisy symposium and of Richard Allen's PhD in 2009.[52] The latter noted how deeply coordinated the episcopal milieu and its actions were before the mid-11th century in a pre-Gregorian context: this related to its closeness to the ducal family, to the exercise of secular power, to family responsibilities (at least 12 of them had fathered children), but also to the reconstruction of cathedrals and the restoration of the chapters. These studies on the episcopate were a welcome complement to the research on cathedral personnel published by David Spear, which, for the period under consideration, managed to measure the timing and pace of the rebuilding of cathedral chapters. Véronique Gazeau's research on the Norman Benedictine abbots helps us understand abbots and their role comprehensively, and not only through a few major figures such as William of Volpiano, John of Fécamp, Herluin or Lanfranc, the prior of Le Bec and then the abbot of Saint-Etienne in Caen (though these personalities have also continued to inspire remarkable research).[53] What was thereby more thoroughly investigated was the way in which abbots were elected, their careers, their social and geographical origins, their training and their relationships with ducal power. In the tenth and early eleventh centuries, abbots were chosen by the duke and the prince's influence remained predominant. Except for Herluin of Le Bec, Robert the Magnificent's hand can be seen behind almost every abbey designation during his reign.[54] His son William did not hesitate to exile the abbot of Saint-Evroult, Robert of Grandmesnil, and imposed twice (in 1061 and 1066) a candidate of his choice on the monks of this house.[55] Abbots came from the aristocracy, but were rarely related to the ducal dynasty, and several of them came from outer lands in Normandy, Italy, the Empire or other regions in France. We know that the abbots coming from outside the Norman principality stimulated the tenth-century revival and the reform impetus of the early eleventh century.[56]

Religious reform

This discussion of the clergy leads me on to one final point: religious reform. William of Volpiano has long been seen as the embodiment of the monastic revival in the ecclesiastical province of Rouen and as the initiator of the reform of Norman monasticism. The characteristics of his actions that have been highlighted include the multiple patronage of monasteries (where the houses concerned were allowed to keep their autonomy), the focus on teaching and liturgy, and the care devoted to the management of the house's property. But the scope of his actions was also minimised by Neithard Bulst and Véronique Gazeau.[57] While the Abbot William had considerable authority, the reform relied on a few institutions and not on those in the entire province. On the other hand, the future abbot of Fécamp did not arrive in an area in which initiatives had not already been taken. In the mid-tenth century, Martin, abbot of Saint-Cyprien of Poitiers, at Jumièges, and soon after him Mainard, a disciple of the reformer Gérard of Brogne at Fontenelle/Saint-Wandrille, had initiated the movement in the province. In William's lifetime, Richard II turned towards another reformer, Gérard, abbot of Crépy-en-Valois, to reform Saint-Wandrille, where the customs of Saint-Père of Chartres and Fleury were introduced.[58] Later, Richard of Saint-Vanne of Verdun benefited from the same ducal favour, and he influenced Thierry, the future abbot of St Evroult, and perhaps also Mauger, archbishop of Rouen.[59] Similarly, other abbots' careers, spirituality, and religious or intellectual orientations have been communicated more accurately, such as those of John of Fécamp or Herluin of Le Bec.[60] The sources and channels of monastic reform have thus been found to have been more diverse than was for a long time thought.

As for the so-called Gregorian reform, we currently know that reviewing the early stages of the movement in the duchy requires a reassessment of the action taken by Archbishop Mauger, whose portrait was deliberately blackened by 11th- and 12th-century writers, and afterwards by modern historiography.[61] Far from being the archetypal bad prelate, he has been proven to have been concerned with his political and religious responsibilities. With Duke William and Abbot Nicholas of Saint-Ouen of Rouen, he seems to have played a role in the introduction of the Peace of God in Normandy in 1047. Mauger welcomed the reformer Richard de Saint-Vanne in 1041–1042 and, before 1046, summoned the first reforming council in Normandy. He proved attentive to his Church and supported the young abbey of Le Bec, founded by Herluin, which Lanfranc of Pavia entered in 1042. Two important biographies and a recent symposium have been dedicated to the latter, who was a leading figure in the Anglo-Norman world's reform movement with Archbishop Maurilius, Anselm – who began his career at the Bec along with Lanfranc – and John of Ravenna, a papal legate from 1050 to 1054 and probably responsible for promoting the reform with the duke.[62] In 1965, Frank Barlow emphasised that Lanfranc's reform program for England was inspired by the Norman model.[63] And yet Lanfranc has been passed off as a traditionalist or even a pre-Gregorian, in that his model was Carolingian, and could accommodate quite well the royal tutelage.

In conclusion: a European history

Maurilius's career took the future archbishop of Rouen from the Lotharingia (Liège) to Saxony (Halberstadt) and to Fécamp, then into Umbria, to Florence and again to Fécamp, where he was chosen to become the duchy's metropolitan.[64] Built after 1017, the abbey of Bernay borrowed much from St Bénigne of Dijon, starting with the wall passage that was then found in many Norman churches: Norman architecture, which flourished in the mid-11th century, borrowed a number of elements whose synthesis, first at Jumièges and then at Caen, helped to shape an architecture that can be characterised as typically 'Norman'.[65] Embarking on the study of a European perspective on the history of Normandy and the Normans involves knowing about people's mobility, cultural transfer processes and the networks at work at that time. In this respect, the comprehensive study of the links between the Fécamp Trinity brotherhood and what Stéphane Lecouteux has called the 'volpianian network' supplies an innovative methodological perspective.[66] William established a Europe-wide network that stretched across northern Italy, Burgundy, Normandy, the Île de France and the region of Lorraine. This network enjoyed a previously unsuspected sustainability; its scope spilled over to Normandy under John of Ravenna, and then to England under his successors. Reviewing it, as well as the first two Benedictine abbots of Fécamp personal relations, has contributed to a demonstration of the different influences on spirituality and the various religious organisational modes that were implemented there. That influence came not only from Cluny and Dijon but was steeped in the work of contemporary Italian reformers, including romuladian hermitism, which strongly tinged John's spirituality. Confraternity networks were the foundations of the movement of people, but also of books, ideas and architectural influences. The oldest surviving manuscript of the Burgundian monk Ralph Glaber's *Vita domni Willelmi* was kept in the Fécamp library. The oldest-known copy of the *Confessio fidei* of John of Fécamp comes from Saint-Bénigne of Dijon.[67] William of Volpiano's liturgical cursus was introduced into 16 institutions in this network and disseminated across England after the conquest, via Mont-Saint-Michel and St Peter's, Gloucester.[68]

I conclude with some comments on Normandy's place in European history. Let us remember that one century after the publication by Charles Homer Haskins of *The Normans in European History*, our current concerns are obviously not new ones. The American historian claimed it was through the Norman Conquest that England was Europeanised and this thesis still needs to be discussed.[69] Relations and exchanges with different parts of Europe were also one of Lucien Musset's concerns. He highlighted the cosmopolitanism of the ducal court under Richard II's reign, and noted that the 'English contribution' was to be found in Normandy before 1066.[70] The 1990s marked a milestone in addressing Norman history from a European perspective, as confirmed by the great interest demonstrated by the public in the great exhibition held at Rome in 1994 entitled 'Les Normands, peuple d'Europe'.[71] Debates over the year 1000 and the significance of 1066 have inevitably raised questions about the similarities, differences and developments found in England and on the Continent during the decades preceding the Conquest. Anyway, the time has come for me to conclude and I shall leave it to others to discuss the relations between England and Normandy before 1066.

2

England before 1066

Rory Naismith

Introduction: England on the eve of the Conquest

On 28 December 1065 the great and the good of England gathered near London for the consecration of the new abbey church at Westminster. Patronage of this church had become a personal project of the king, Edward (only known as 'the Confessor' after his canonisation as a saint in the mid-12th century).[1] But Edward's death just a week later, probably on the night of 4/5 January 1066, was to set in motion a chain of events which would lead to three new kings before the year was out, the last of them being his Norman cousin William I. Edward was buried in the freshly consecrated church on which he had lavished such generosity.

Post-1066 apologists for William's conquest depended heavily on Edward's legitimacy and Harold II's supposed perfidy,[2] giving rise to a general sense of Edward's reign as the end of an era. There was some truth to this view given the sweeping changes that followed the Norman Conquest, but the English worthies assembled at Westminster in the New Year chill of 1065/6 would also have recognised Edward's death as the climax of a turbulent life and a troubled reign. One more conquest would not in itself have been surprising, and neither, by 1066, would the direction from which it came. Edward was the son of a king of impeccable English royal stock, Æthelred II (978–1013, 1014–16), and a Norman queen of the ducal house, Emma. But after his father's reign ended in military defeat and the takeover of England by Cnut (1016–35), Edward had spent much of his early life as an exile in Normandy. His winding path to the throne led through a maze of two kings and two mothers in three different combinations, spread between England, Normandy and Denmark [see the Family Tree]. These decades provided a harsh lesson in the game of snakes and ladders that was 11th-century politics. At one point in 1036, in the wake of Cnut's death, Edward and his brother Alfred had tried their luck for the throne. The adventure ended in disaster: Edward barely escaped and Alfred was captured and mutilated, allegedly at the hands of the powerful Earl Godwine, possibly with the connivance of his own mother. When in 1041 Edward did become king, it was not because of his credentials in the male line, but through Emma and her son by Cnut: Edward's half-brother Harthacnut, who had inherited Denmark but lost out in England in 1035–40 to Harold I, Cnut's son by another woman, Ælfgifu of Northampton.

These experiences seem to have influenced Edward's actions once he became king after Harthacnut's death in 1042. Emma was divested of her property and shunted off the political stage into obscurity, and relations with Earl Godwine remained fraught. Politicking between the king and Godwine would, along with the question of who was to succeed the childless Edward, be one of the defining issues of the reign. Matters came to a head in 1051. An attack at Dover on one of the growing number of French nobles who frequented Edward's court spir-alled into a confrontation between king and earl. Godwine and his sons fled to Flanders and Ireland before anyone actually came to blows, and his daughter Edith, Edward's queen, was taken into custody by being placed in a nunnery. William of Normandy probably paid a visit to the king at this time, for reasons left unclear by the one version of the Anglo-Saxon Chronicle to mention it, while Norman writers claimed that around this time the newly appointed archbishop of Canterbury, Robert of Jumièges (a Norman), visited William and communicated Edward's wish that he should be his heir.[3] For a moment, Edward appeared to be victorious and taking a new direction, but the earl and his sons returned in 1052 and forced the king to restore their power and position. The death of Godwine the following year changed the game again, and paved the way for somewhat improved relations between his surviving sons, especially Harold and Tostig, and the king. Harold took on the role of right-hand man to the king, leading English forces against Gruffydd ap Llewelyn, Prince of North Wales, in the 1060s. Harold would also, of course, eventually follow Edward as king, appar-ently as the result of a deathbed nomination.[4] By this time, however, the Godwinesons' unity had fractured. When Tostig's position as earl of Northumbria was thrown into jeopardy by a revolt in 1065, Harold and the king both eventually sided with the rebels and acquiesced in his dismissal and exile. Tostig's failed attempt to force his way back into power, in alliance with Harald Hardrada of Norway, was one of the pivotal events in 1066.

The Norman Conquest of 1066 was thus by no means the first sudden jolt in English political fortunes since the millennium, or even the first military takeover. Events of these decades had also set the scene in other ways. Gone, for instance, was any expectation that a single dynasty should enjoy a unique claim to legitimacy. The lack of an obvious heir to Edward prompted a wide range of potential claimants to weigh up their chances over the course of his reign.[5] Prior experience showed that almost anything was now possible. Æthelred had been supplanted by a Danish king, Edward had allegedly sworn to uphold the laws of Cnut and his sons in 1041,[6] and in 1066 power passed to Harold Godwineson, who was brother-in-law to Edward but numbered no kings among his ancestors. This was a significant change from the tenth century: there had been disputes between rival candidates for the throne in 924, 957 and 975, but all of these had involved brothers or half-brothers from the same dynasty. The geographical scope of England's connections in Europe was also transforming. On the one hand, there were still strong links to Scandinavia, political and otherwise, including a substantial number of Scandinavians who had settled in England under Cnut and Harthacnut; on the other, France and Lotharingia, which had long been familiar from economic and ecclesiastical connections, were becoming more prominent in political terms. The primary catalysts for this realignment were Edward the Confessor's Norman background and family connections, as a result of which more and more French nobles and clergy grew familiar with England and its elite.

It should not be thought that the complex history of 11th-century England had rendered it weak or especially prone to conquest. On the contrary, England's greatest strength by the middle of the 11th century lay not so much in the prestige or ability of any individual king, but in a society and set of institutions which held the kingdom tightly together. Both had been honed through more than a century and a half of external buffeting and progressive integration into an efficient framework overseen by ambitious kings. These conditions fostered the generation of great wealth, and also enabled rulers to harness that wealth to a degree unique in 11th-century western Europe. In 1066, William thus had strong incentives to pursue the claim to England which political circumstances dealt him.

Making a kingdom: the emergence of England in the tenth and eleventh centuries

England owes its name to the Angles: one of several peoples from northern Europe thought, at least by the time of the Venerable Bede (d.734), to have come across the North Sea in the fifth century and taken over much of the Roman province of Britain. In time, the Angles, Saxons, Jutes and others established a number of kingdoms. Since the 11th and 12th centuries these have traditionally been schematised into a 'Heptarchy' of seven, though in practice the situation was much more fluid. While Bede stressed ecclesiastical and cultural factors which united the Anglo-Saxon kingdoms,[7] wide-ranging political supremacy was rare and short-lived in his day. Smaller units over time came into the orbit of a few larger kingdoms, which by the ninth century consisted of East Anglia, Mercia, Northumbria and Wessex. No united Anglo-Saxon kingdom existed before the tenth century.

It was Viking invasions in the later ninth century which galvanised political transformation across Britain and led to the creation of the polity that would evolve into the medieval kingdom of England. Its roots lay in Wessex, which by the mid-ninth century effectively meant England south of the Thames (plus Essex). Northumbria, East Anglia and the eastern part of Mercia were defeated and later settled by the Vikings between the 860s and 880s, while Wessex came under severe pressure. The defining personality of this period was Alfred the Great (871–99), king of the West Saxons. Alfred maintained an alliance with Mercia established under his predecessors, and came to be accepted as overlord of the surviving western portion of Mercia as well as Wessex. Upon his death he was recognised in the Anglo-Saxon Chronicle as 'king over the whole English people except for that part which was under Danish rule'.[8] This new entity which combined Wessex and Mercia was referred to as the kingdom of the Anglo-Saxons.[9]

In the first two generations of the tenth century this kingdom took on a whole new shape, as military conquests led by Alfred's son and daughter Edward the Elder (899–924) and Æthelflæd, lady of the Mercians (911–18), and latterly by his grandson Æthelstan (924–39), brought East Anglia, the Midlands and eventually York under English supremacy. These rulers and their supporters were well aware that they were crafting a polity without precedent. A poem written to celebrate Æthelstan's takeover of York in 927 referred to him as ruler of 'this England [now] made whole',[10] and charters, coins and other sources from his reign constructed a dual role for him as 'king of the English, elevated by the right hand of the almighty … to the throne of the whole kingdom of Britain'.[11] This assertion of pan-British overlordship was prompted by a ceremonial submission of other kings from what are now Scotland and Wales at Eamont Bridge, Cumbria, in 927. Some of these rulers even attested Æthelstan's charters in subsequent years.[12]

The reign of Æthelstan was a high point of English ambition in many respects, reflected in a burst of innovative charters, coins and legislation.[13] But redrawing the political map of Britain so dramatically was bound to prompt challenges. Æthelstan's hard-won supremacy was successfully defended against an alliance of Vikings with the men of Alba and Strathclyde in 937, but in the wake of his death two years later the Vikings returned and seized Yorkshire and the East Midlands, wiping out most gains made by the English since about 917. Æthelstan's unusual decision not to marry or produce children bore fruit at this point, since the two half-brothers who followed him, Edmund (939–46) and Eadred (946–55), were both mature and militarily effective on succeeding. After a series of repeated losses and reconquests, York was brought under English control for good in 954.

The next generation of kings oversaw consolidation of the gains that earlier rulers had fought to achieve. Eadwig (955–9) tried to establish a whole new power bloc based on his wife's family, but resistance from other factions among the elite led to the kingdom being divided between him and his brother Edgar. Edgar would eventually inherit

Eadwig's portion and hold the combined kingdom for 16 years (959–75). Ruling in a time of relative peace, and being the patron of a series of monastic reformers who produced a rich literary legacy, Edgar attained an enviable reputation in later times.[14] Indeed, in the words of Sir Frank Stenton, 'it is a sign of Edgar's competence as a ruler that his reign is singularly devoid of recorded incident'.[15] There is reason to believe, however, that a lot was going on behind the scenes in terms of administrative developments,[16] and in Edgar's last few years there was a renewed emphasis placed on the symbolic power of the English king, through a coronation at the Roman city of Bath and a ceremony involving other British kings rowing their English overlord along the Dee.

At the time of Edgar's death in 975 England was in a commanding position. But the long reign of his son Æthelred II would show the kingdom's strengths and weaknesses in sharp relief. Æthelred came to the throne under a cloud, his accession marred by the murder of his half-brother Edward the Martyr in 978.[17] This deep sin was later viewed as the cause of renewed Viking incursions, which took on apocalyptic overtones in sermons of the day. Beginning on a small scale in the 980s, these attacks escalated from the 990s. Attempts to stop the Vikings with local and hired mercenary armies proved unsuccessful, as did a policy of buying them off with gold and silver. When, in 1013, King Swein Forkbeard led an army to England bent on conquest rather than extraction of tribute, Æthelred's rule collapsed. The king and his family fled to Normandy. Swein's sudden death early in 1014 gave Æthelred a second chance, though he was only allowed to resume his position as king 'if he would govern them [the English] more justly than he did before'.[18] In the dying days of his reign a power-struggle raged between Æthelred's son Edmund Ironside, Swein's son Cnut, and the senior ealdorman, Eadric Streona. Edmund and Cnut briefly split England between them in 1016 in an attempt to resolve their bloody and inconclusive warfare, and Cnut was finally left in overall control after Edmund died towards the end of that year.

The kingdom of England in the generation before 1066 was a battle-hardened entity, bled for tribute and battered by conflict with Vikings. It was also the product of highly specific circumstances which meant that it did not proceed in a straightforward way from strength to strength. There were significant setbacks along the way, above all in the years 939–54 and again in the later years of Æthelred II. These left as much of a mark on the kingdom as its many successes; the result was a regime that could be brutal and brittle as well as efficient and adaptive. A series of energetic kings from the later ninth century onwards had moulded England into a formidable military power, with a well-developed ideology of royal authority and an impressively effective administrative machine – to the point where even a king easily swayed by bad advice such as Æthelred II could enjoy a long reign. If anything, England's relative centralisation was in part its undoing, for it could endure prolonged attacks on its periphery, but knocking out the political lynchpin left the kingdom as a whole vulnerable. How England had arrived at this point requires consideration of its organisation and infrastructure.

The shape of the kingdom

The English kingdom of the 11th century was not quite identical to its modern descendant in shape, and much more diverse in its internal structure. For present purposes, four levels of authority exercised by late Anglo-Saxon rulers can be distinguished. The widest and loosest of these was hegemony over Britain as a whole: that is, over the Welsh kingdoms, Strathclyde and the kingdom of Alba (also taking shape in this period).[19] But this supremacy was invoked only periodically, and was more prominent in the tenth than the eleventh century. A second level of authority can be identified in the relationship between the English kings and the rulers of what might be called 'middle Britain', approximately corresponding to the northern part of the old kingdom of Northumbria, between Yorkshire, the Irish Sea and the Firth of Forth.[20] This region was more consistently under the overlordship of southern English kings, but operated with a high degree of autonomy and did not possess most of the institutions characteristic of the lands further south. These territories – the third level of authority – constituted the heartland of the English kingdom of the 11th century. Everywhere between the Channel, the Tees and the Welsh borders, Edward the Confessor could expect to find broadly similar legal customs, modes of political communication, local power structures and taxation. Thanks to the conquest of Viking territory, the king had also been massively enriched in lands across this area.[21] A final level of authority was confined to the southern part of that area, encompassing Wessex, London and southwest Mercia, which dominated the itinerary of the king himself.

These mechanisms resulted in an impressive degree of integration between king, court and localities. Taken as a whole, the machinery of late Anglo-Saxon government is often referred to in modern scholarship as the 'late Anglo-Saxon state', and has been represented as one of the most sophisticated polities in early medieval Europe.[22] Of course, 'sophisticated' in this context also meant 'harsh' and at times even 'savage'. The effectiveness of late Anglo-Saxon government came at a high cost, and was exploited even more zealously by William the Conqueror and his heirs.[23] But it was limited in important respects. For all that the leading figures of local communities were integrated into networks that placed them only a few steps away from the king, this still did not make those communities especially effective in enforcing laws or judgements on a case-by-case basis.[24] Moreover, on a local and individual scale the exertion of power – even 'state' power wielded by the king – was much more a matter of interpersonal relations and obligations. These percolated down to the very lowest levels: there were multiple texts generated by or for late Anglo-Saxon reeves (estate managers) which revelled in the diverse duties pertaining to different gradations of peasants; gradations which were a cause of confusion for Norman incomers after 1066.[25]

Agents, associations and institutions

At the opposite end of the social spectrum to the peasants were earls (ealdormen before the time of Cnut): royal appointees to leadership of one or more shires. Their duties included military command, support of the king and supervision of local courts; among their benefits were a share of certain fines paid within their territory and access to estates delegated to the support of whoever the local earl happened to be.[26] Although powerful, there were important restraints on earls which made them quite different from (for example) the increasingly assertive regional and local lords of tenth- and eleventh-century France or dukes in contemporary Germany. The geographical breadth of royal and high aristocratic landholding gave all parties a vested interest in maintaining a single state rather than splintering into separate territorial lordships. But the much larger wealth of the king placed him and his operations on a whole different level.[27] A separate network of personnel, such as shire-reeves (sheriffs), upheld his interests at a local level, sometimes coming into conflict with earls. One ealdorman in the time of Æthelred II, Leofsige, tried (unsuccessfully) to challenge the actions of two sheriffs, and in 1002 he was exiled for killing another 'high-reeve'.[28] Kings also had the capacity to remove and reassign earls. Harold Godwineson held East Anglia and then land in the southwest Midlands before taking on Wessex after his father's death in 1053, while Tostig was transplanted into Northumbria (not previously held by his family) in 1055, but was in turn displaced in favour of Morcar in 1065. Of course, the king could only push his hand so far: Edward's expulsion of Godwine and his sons in 1051 backfired when they returned in force the following year. Mighty earls could be dangerous enemies as well as strong allies. It was partly for this reason that kings and their administrative machinery also depended heavily on bishops. They were major magnates comparable in prestige and wealth to earls, and like them had judicial responsibility and direct access to the king. Some even led armies, like Leofgar, bishop of Hereford, killed in battle against the Welsh in 1056.

Below these high magnates was a large and highly diverse body of individuals known as thegns. Derived from an Old English word meaning 'servant', the term originally denoted direct service to the king in any form. Over the tenth century, however, thegns assumed loftier status.[29] Military service and other prestigious duties remained important, but landholding and other material trappings of wealth also came to be expected. Several late Anglo-Saxon writers tried to pin down criteria for thegnly status, which implies contention about who qualified: thegn covered an extremely broad range of conditions, from those who were barely distinguishable from peasants to men like Beorhtric son of Ælfgar who held over 600 hides (a hide being a unit of land capable of supporting one family) in southwest England in 1066 and therefore stood close to earls in terms of landed wealth.[30]

Domesday Book included reference to who owned what land at the time of Edward the Confessor's death in January 1066, and is as such a precious window onto the underlying basis of power among the late Anglo-Saxon elite: landholding. Estates were the most reliable source of substantial income; in addition, possession of landed property was closely correlated with status. On multiple levels, having lands to dispense on either a permanent or temporary basis was a vital form of patronage. King Edward was, as might be expected, the dominant landholder by a significant margin in 1066.[31] He was unique in possessing the power to bestow land in perpetuity, and had a constant stream of properties leaving his hands by this route and entering them through death and forfeiture; he also had a more stable core of large estates supplying the needs of himself and his household.[32] Major churches and aristocrats were in a similar position with regard to distribution of land for patronage, though the former were better placed to build up long-term strategies of exploitation extending across generations.[33] These networks of dependent landholding, along with other connections such as personal commendation and loose legal jurisdiction (known as *soke*), spanned the whole kingdom and were formidable in their complexity but also pivotal to harnessing the support of a rich and politically engaged local elite in favour of earls, major thegns and churches.[34] Behind such bonds lay close personal relationships forged at feasts, hunts and on the battlefield.

Early medieval statecraft and the face-to-face qualities of early medieval lordship were inseparable.[35] Meetings therefore played a critical role, and none more so than those assembled by the king himself (sometimes known in older scholarship as the *witenagemot*).[36] As well as the king, these would feature bishops, abbots, earls and thegns, plus all of their attendants. Witness lists of charters give some flavour of the top-ranking people who might be present, drawn from far and wide. Documents of this kind are the most plentiful form of evidence for such meetings, and production of royal diplomas and other charters was clearly an important part of royal gatherings, but much else went on besides, only some of it recognised in other sources (for example, hearing legal disputes and issuing law-codes). Ritual and symbolic projections of power were doubtless also important aspects of royal meetings; so too was the opportunity to hobnob with key players and advisers.

The key meetings below this level were held on a shire by shire basis. Typically they would be presided over by the local earl and bishop, and attended by important men and women of the district. Communication between king and shire was routine by the time of Edward the Confessor, and took the form of 'writs': short, formulaic letters in Old English which confirmed actions or issued commands.[37] The shires themselves are the ancestors of the ceremonial counties of modern England (see Figure 1). A total of 33 existed by 1066, varying widely in size and history. Essex, Kent, Surrey and Sussex had been distinct kingdoms in the early Anglo-Saxon period, and Norfolk and Suffolk may once have been units of the kingdom of the East Angles. The shires of Wessex go back at least to the ninth century. Those north of the Thames are more problematic. Most are only mentioned for the first time between the later tenth and early eleventh century. However, the prominence of the fortress-towns on which they were normally centred can be traced back to the earlier tenth century, when they served as key points in the campaigns against the Vikings or as mint-places under Æthelstan. An earlier date for administrative divisions based on them cannot be ruled out, though the full range of functions associated with shires probably only developed gradually. Besides the holding of meetings for the adjudication of legal disputes, these functions included the gathering of tax and tribute, and the raising of military forces.[38]

Shires were well entrenched as the key unit of local governance in England by the time of Edward the Confessor. Major landowners organised their estates by reference to which shire they lay in, and the earliest surviving English cartulary (a collection of copies of charters in a book) made at Worcester early in the 11th century is structured on shire divisions, as also is the Domesday survey.[39] Earldoms were seen as collections of shires, not units in and of themselves. Shires also provided a basis for other forms of organisation. Towns or boroughs (*byrg*, as they were known at the time) already provided numerous focal points for trade and defence in the early tenth century, and eventually had their own reeves and meetings. By 1066, England was dotted with towns large and small. The rural portion of each share was divided into smaller units known as hundreds or (in former Viking areas of eastern England) wapentakes. Hundreds had their own assemblies for the airing of disputes (which would be passed on to the shire if unresolved), and were used for assessing various burdens at a more granular level; they seem to have emerged from territories of roughly 100 hides in the course of the tenth century.[40]

Recent scholarship has stressed that although the late Anglo-Saxon 'state' was formidable, it was in a constant state of evolution. Much of the machinery outlined above can only be seen emerging gradually over the tenth and eleventh centuries. Edgar's reign saw impressive progress in consolidating earlier developments, but even this drew heavily on precedents from earlier in the tenth century (and indeed from the Carolingian Empire), and was adapted further by his heirs.[41] The coinage provides a good illustration. Towards the end of his reign Edgar enacted a currency reform which standardised the appearance,

Figure 1. Known and probable mint-places in England c.925–1066, superimposed on Domesday Book-era shire boundaries (shire map courtesy of UCL Landscapes of Governance project).

inscriptions and fineness of silver pennies minted from Yorkshire to Devon and Kent. This replaced a coinage which had given the names of king and minting official (or moneyer) but which was quite diverse in other respects, reflecting the piecemeal growth of the tenth-century kingdom and its major regional divisions.[42] The new pennies spoke loud and clear as a statement of unity and royal authority. But under Æthelred II a further innovation gradually emerged: frequent, kingdom-wide recoinages, undertaken probably in response to moral imperatives emanating from an increasingly troubled royal court.[43] In 1009 an especially severe Viking attack even led the king to incorp-orate the coinage into a national campaign of prayer and penance. An image of the holy lamb and dove briefly replaced the bust of the king and cross normally found on coins.[44] Æthelred's successors in turn maintained the principle of frequent recoinage but for other reasons, probably including the raising of revenue. Political and military crises, together with shifts in the personnel and mood at the heart of the kingdom, could thus have a dramatic effect on the development of its institutions.[45]

The same is also true of another financial innovation: the tributes and taxes raised in response to Viking raids. Two kinds of payment need to be distinguished, and were not necessarily raised in the same way. Tribute (*gafol*) was money paid, on several occasions from 991 onwards, to buy off specific Viking forces; it could be gathered from churches, aristocrats, nationally or locally. Altogether over £200,000 was raised in this way – a staggering sum, the likes of which English kings did not wield again until the later 13th century, and so large that some historians have even doubted the credibility of these payments.[46] But desperate times called for desperate measures, and greater clarity about the second, distinct kind of payment lends weight to the first: a more regular tax (*heregeld*, later *geld* or Danegeld), levied on each hide of land on a shire by shire basis, started at another crisis point in 1012 to pay a standing army of Viking mercenaries.[47]

The late Anglo-Saxon 'state' was just one dimension of power in 11th-century England. It was, however, a large and well-articulated one. At its head was the king, and it can be understood as the agglomeration of bodies and processes which served his commands. But, as such, it had to evolve with each king as he met new challenges, and by no means embraced all areas of life or exertions of power. The mechanisms of the 'state' often ran in opposition to those of local agents, and royal interests did not always come out on top.

'What was noblest in England': the nature of the kingdom

As tensions rose in the autumn of 1051, the king and Earl Godwine gathered their respective armies in the vicinity of Gloucester. Fortunately, cooler heads eventually prevailed, because (in the words of the 'D' manuscript of the Anglo-Saxon Chronicle) 'some of them thought it would be a great piece of folly if they joined battle because in the two hosts there was most of what was noblest in England, and they considered that they would be opening a way for our enemies to enter the country'. The same concern again prevented fighting the next year when Godwine's fleet and the king's met at London: 'it was hateful to almost all of them to fight against men of their own race because there was little else that was worth anything apart from Englishmen on either side, and they did not wish the country to be laid more open to foreigners through their destroying each other'.[48] Among these men there evidently existed a strong sense of common identity, framed in terms of an in-group – the English – arrayed against enemies or foreigners; a common identity strong enough to prevail over kings and earls who wished to join battle. There is no getting around the xenophobic dimension of this sentiment. It was partly grounded in the specific circumstances of Edward's reign, but there was a long history of rulers fanning a lingering distaste for outsiders among the English at times of tension. Æthelred II decreed that on 13 November 1002 all Danes in the kingdom should be killed, allegedly because they were hatching a plot against him. One charter from Oxford records how Æthelred's decree was brutally enforced on a group of Danes who were burned alive in a church, and mass graves found at Oxford and in Dorset may relate to the massacre.[49] This attack probably targeted recent incomers rather than men and women of Scandinavian descent in eastern England, who even after 1066 would often have had Old Norse names and possibly still spoken the language of the Vikings.[50]

English identity as expressed in this way was essentially a construction of the late Anglo-Saxon period, beginning in the time of Alfred the Great.[51] Political unification of the Anglo-Saxon kingdoms coincided with the vigorous development of administration and literature in the vernacular.[52] A prefatory letter ascribed to Alfred and appended to one of these Old English texts is larded with references to England, the English and 'the language that we can all understand'.[53] Widespread use of the vernacular in all manner of written contexts was one of the hallmarks of Anglo-Saxon England. Laws, poems and documents had already been set down in Old English since the seventh and eighth centuries, but the period from Alfred's reign onwards saw writing in the vernacular grow dramatically in quantity. This did in part reflect a growing sense of English identity, but also had a strong pragmatic appeal in a land where the vernacular bore so distant a relationship to Latin. Old English was used for religious literature (homilies, sermons, saint's lives and more), for history (the Anglo-Saxon Chronicle), for the Bible (in partial translation) and even for monumental inscriptions, often in a semi-standardised form that was current across the country from Yorkshire to Kent and Devon. Legislation, the interconnections of high-ranking clergy and trade as manifested through the circulation of coin all also helped consolidate a sense of common identity across the English kingdom. In this way, the implicit connection between nationhood and statehood which had started rolling in the late ninth century gathered momentum through the tenth and eleventh; it underpinned the Chroniclers' concern at Englishmen fighting Englishmen in 1051 and 1052, and contributed to the late Anglo-Saxon state's strong ideological and administrative foundations.[54]

But assertions of Englishness like those of 1002 and 1051–2 are reminders of how contested the label remained. English identity was in a state of constant evolution in the centuries before 1066, and never quite had a one-to-one correlation with the boundaries of the English kingdom. There were speakers of Old English, with as much cultural and historical claim to Englishness as anyone, who ended up outside the bounds of the late Anglo-Saxon kingdom of the 11th century, most notably the inhabitants of Lothian.[55] Conversely, the English kingdom incorporated several peoples who did not historically identify as English: Danes in eastern England (plus more recent Scandinavian incomers who had settled elsewhere under Cnut),[56] Cumbrians in the northwest, and Britons in Cornwall and the shires bordering on the Welsh kingdoms. In one sense all were English, but the separateness of these peoples, under the umbrella of English overlordship, could come to the fore in certain circumstances. A remarkable series of charters from the mid-tenth century (known as the 'alliterative charters') revelled in the multifaceted nature of the king's authority, entitling him ruler of 'the Anglo-Saxons and Northumbrians, of the pagans and the Britons'.[57] This portmanteau vision of kingship perhaps served to call attention to the recent challenges Edmund and Eadred had overcome in welding the kingdom of Æthelstan back together. In legal contexts, the distinct practices of the Danes were repeatedly highlighted, to the extent that the 'Danelaw' remained one of three regional legal divisions into the 12th century.[58] Fault-lines also existed in the traditionally 'English' portions of the kingdom. These tended to follow long-established regional divisions, most notably between Mercia and Wessex. A distinct voice giving a Mercian take on the campaigns against the Vikings in the early tenth century was preserved in two manuscripts of the Anglo-Saxon Chronicle.[59] Some ealdormen and earls were assigned to territories that roughly corresponded to earlier kingdoms, and were referred to as such: Eadric Streona, for instance, was ealdorman of the 'kingdom/ land of the Mercians'.[60] A trend which seems more threatening at first glance was for Mercian and West Saxon elites to nominate different candidates to the throne: this took place in 924, 957, 975 and 1035. For brief periods the kingdom did indeed split along the Thames (possibly in 924, more clearly in 957–9 and 1016). Yet in all these cases (save 1016) the decision was between sons of earlier kings. It surely seemed less and less likely as the tenth and eleventh centuries wore on that Mercia and Wessex would break apart on a permanent basis.

By the middle of the 11th century there is little doubt that the English had a strong sense of their own identity, some idea that this correlated roughly to a political unit, and a healthy suspicion of foreigners. But like British as opposed to English, Scottish or Welsh (or indeed 'northern' or 'Londoner' within England) identity in modern times, the late Anglo-Saxon concept of Englishness was just one layer of identity among many, and as a strategy could be downplayed or advanced for various ends. It is not difficult to peer either side of the mainstream English label and discover other ways of constructing identity in the tenth and eleventh centuries. All the peoples of Britain, Ireland and its neighbours in western Europe by this time were Christians, for example, and in the era of the Norman Conquest consciousness of the 'otherness' of heretics and Jews was gaining ground at an aggressive pace.[61] For some purposes Britain itself was a helpful frame of geographical reference, while within England several levels of collective or geographical identity, such as region (that is, Danelaw, Mercia or Wessex) and shire, were mediated through – and probably often played second fiddle to – the personal bonds of kinship and lordship. A heroic poem celebrating the last stand of Ealdorman Byrhtnoth and his men against the Vikings at Maldon in 991 highlights the way in which these loyalties dovetailed. When asked by the Vikings for tribute, the ealdorman retorts: 'tell your people a much less pleasing tale: that here stands with his company an earl of unstained reputation, who intends to defend this homeland, the kingdom of Æthelred, my lord's people and country'. For Byrhtnoth, all these allegiances combined without mentioning England as such once. Conversely, after Byrhtnoth had fallen, an aged warrior named Byrhtwold distilled why he saw it as his duty to stand and fight: 'spirit must be the firmer, the heart the bolder, courage must be the greater as our strength diminishes. Here lies our leader all cut to pieces, the great man in the dirt. He will have cause to mourn forever who thinks of turning away from this battlegame now'.[62] Loyalty to lord came first when the chips were down.

Conclusion

Another poem found in two manuscripts of the Anglo-Saxon Chronicle brings us back to the opening scene of this chapter: the death of Edward the Confessor. It was written between January 1066 and Harold II's death at Hastings on 14 October, and offers a vivid encomium of what made England and its kingship great. It portrays a king who embodied many virtues: some common to many medieval kingdoms, some grounded in centuries of English tradition. The tone is deeply archaic. Edward 'lived ... in kingly splendour, strong in counsel', master of 'all that the cold sea-waves encompass' including 'Welshmen ... Britons and Scots [as well as] Angles and Saxons'. He was a wise and pious king – wise enough, in fact, to 'entrust ... his realm to a man of high rank, to

Harold himself, a noble earl'; but he was in addition a king in the mould of *Beowulf* who was 'lavish of riches', stoic in exile and courageous in 'guarding his homeland, country and subjects'. The poet looked forward to a glorious reign for Harold, who 'had loyally followed his lord's commands with words and deeds, and neglected nothing that met the need of the people's king'.[63] This poem encapsulates what one poet considered to be the public-facing qualities of his king and kingdom: British hegemony, heroic and dutiful leaders reared in a venerable and distinctly English tradition, and a secure front against foes. All were to be transformed by events of the coming years.

3

William the Conqueror and the capture of London in 1066

Edward Impey

Introduction

> Sparsit fama volans quod habet Londonia regem/Gaudet et Anglorum qui superest populus.
>
> ('The report flew around that London had a king and the English survivors rejoiced.')[1]

These lines are from the *Carmen de Hastingae Proelio* ('Song of the Battle of Hastings', hereafter *Carmen*), in its surviving form, an 835-line poem written by Guy, bishop of Amiens, within two years of William's victory.[2] They describe the reaction of the English at large, within weeks of defeat at Hastings and the death of Harold II, to the 'election' of Edgar the Ætheling, the legitimate but as yet passed-over heir to the English throne.[3] For present purposes it is the statement that *London*, rather than England, had a king, which bears the greatest significance: the former had a king, but the latter rejoiced – the implication being that if London 'had a king', so did they. This, as the 1970s editors of the *Carmen* pointed out, indicates 'the excellence of Guy's information' regarding the longstanding and crucial role of the city in the creation of England's kings and the direction of its politics.[4] But while the general point about the city's status is unarguable, these lines do raise the question of whether its place specifically in William's plans, and the role of its capture in the success of the Norman Conquest, has to date been underplayed. Quite probably it has: while a Norman defeat at Hastings would have been the end of William and his adventure, victory in the field, and even Harold's death, could not alone have guaranteed success; there were, as events proved, both short- and longer-term obstacles to overcome, of which London was unquestionably one. This article considers why this was so, and attempts to reconcile some inconsistencies in the sources regarding his itinerary and activities on the way there. It then questions what actually happened when London was encountered, in the light of the four main near-contemporary accounts: was there a siege or a battle, as the *Carmen* and William of Jumièges's *Gesta Normannorum Ducum* (*GND*) respectively recount?

Was the handover, if not necessarily enthusiastic, at least wholly peaceful, as William of Poitiers's *Gesta Guillelmi* (*GG*) and the Anglo-Saxon Chronicle (ASC) would have us believe? Or, as is suggested here, while William's victory is not in question, can the narratives be reconciled to the extent that surrender was offered by one party in the city and resistance by another?

The importance of London

Why William's fleet sailed for the south coast and not, in particular, the Thames estuary,[5] why most of it landed at Pevensey, and how well he understood the geography of England, are only partly understood.[6] Nevertheless, he would have been aware that confronting an army in the field – whether Harold Godwineson's or Harald Hardrada's – would be an early challenge, and that victory, let alone his opponent's death, could hardly be assumed. After his success at Hastings – *pace* the *GG*, which later claims that William conquered 'all the cities of the English between the third hour and the evening'[7] – William would have been aware that this was, at best, the end of the beginning. Nevertheless, he stayed at Hastings for a fortnight after the battle, partly to rest his men,[8] but more importantly in the hope that the remaining English parties would come in to submit.[9] Once this failed, in considering his next move he presumably realised the importance of securing the ecclesiastical power base of Canterbury, and perhaps the potential to undermine the position of Archbishop Stigand, who was then in London and implicated in resistance.[10] The urgent submission of Winchester, the importance of which is acknowledged in the *GG* and implied in the *Carmen*, as the ancient capital of Wessex, seat of its treasury, Stigand's second see, and held by the Confessor's widow, must also have been an early objective.[11] In the event, William's immediate route was probably determined by the dangers of venturing too far inland, and its eastward coastwise direction by a wish to avenge the actions of the men of Romney,[12] the reports of English re-grouping at Dover,[13] and to advance in the general direction of Canterbury.[14] These objectives were met. At Romney, retribution was meted out,[15] and at Dover, where, according to the *GG*, a 'great multitude had gathered',[16] the threat was extinguished, although the sources differ as to how;[17] according to the *GG* he spent eight days there,[18] and according to the *Carmen*, a month.[19] While at the (tantalisingly) still-unidentified 'Broken Tower', the duke's first halt after Dover, he received the submission of Canterbury.[20] Winchester, meanwhile, responded favourably to the duke's demands for tribute and submission issued from Dover,[21] avoiding the need for a major military expedition to the southwest.

London, however, must have been his ultimate destination.[22] Most blatantly the *GND*, which omits most of the intervening action, states that 'Early next morning (that is, after Hastings) ... having looted the enemy and buried the corpses of his own dear men, he set out for London':[23] the *Carmen* dates the march to 'where populous London gleamed' from his first halt after Dover.[24] This must have been largely due to the threat that it posed in 'abounding', as the *GG* tells us, 'in a large population famous for their military qualities',[25] swollen by 'a crowd of warriors flocked in from elsewhere' in such numbers that 'the city, in spite of its great size could scarcely accommodate them all',[26] along with, or also meaning, 'the obdurate people who had been defeated in battle' mentioned in the *Carmen*.[27] Wace, writing in the 12th century, but as ever full of extra and enthralling detail, tells a similar tale: 'some English who escaped from the field did not stop until they reached London', adding that on the way a bridge (not named) broke under their weight and 'many were drowned.'[28] As it happened, these assessments of the Londoners' warlike spirit were soon to be confirmed by their assault on William's advance party – the first proper armed encounter between the Normans and the English after Hastings – at the gates of Southwark.[29] Meanwhile the city's wealth, in addition to the perfidy of its inhabitants, is emphasised in the *Carmen*, which describes it as 'a most spacious city, full of evil inhabitants, and richer than any-where else in the kingdom'.[30] Precedent may also have enhanced the city's importance, in particular Cnut's failure to capture it in 1015;[31] more recently, its importance would also have been underlined by its use as Harold's central rallying point on arriving in the south,[32] as the suggested venue for a pre-Hastings regrouping by Harold's brother Gyrth,[33] and as the place where, presumably, the duke's envoy met Harold in the care of the monk of Fécamp.[34] More generally speaking, William would also have recognised cities as seedbeds of revolt and resistance, as they proved to be in England, in the case of Hereford, Exeter, York, Durham, Chester and again on the continent in 1069 at Le Mans.[35] Conversely, his foundation of Caen as a place of import-ance in the late 1050s is a sign of the importance he attached to towns as agents of government and control.[36] Since William's objective was to become king of England, he and his advisers must also have had an eye on the symbolic status of Westminster, practically at the gates of London: while the Confessor had been crowned at Winchester, Harold had been crowned at the abbey,[37] and the importance of the adjacent palace as the venue for 'crown wearing', an important public assertion of kingship, was certainly known to Guy of Amiens, and, he implies, to the duke.[38]

All these factors would have pointed to London's likely role as a focus for further resistance and its subjugation as a necessary objective. Its significance on both counts was enhanced by the strength of its Roman defences,[39] apparently repaired by King Alfred after 883,[40] while a system for manning them had been in place by the 11th century,[41] and had combined to defy Cnut's amphibious assault only 50 years before.[42] The defences are also mentioned in the near-contemporary texts, most volubly in the *Carmen*, which refers to the city's protection, viewed downstream and from the west, 'on the left side (that is, inland) by walls and on the right side by the river',[43] and later mentions both 'defences' (*menia*), walls (*mures*),[44] towers (*turres*),[45] and a 'high tower' (*turris elata*);[46] the *GND* at least infers strength in noting that preparation was made for 'the utmost resistance',[47] while men 'high on the towers' are mentioned by Baudri of Bourgueil, writing in about 1100.[48] Finally, the vulnerability posed by the very length of the walled circuit – the longest in northern Europe – would presumably have been offset by the influx of 'warriors', although this would have brought its own problems of supply.

The sources are also informative, if not wholly consistent, about the potential leaders of resistance in the city, along with the multitude of refugees, in the weeks after Hastings. The 'D' manuscript of the ASC implies that Archbishop Ealdred (of York) and the earls Edwin and Morcar were among them;[49] John of Worcester, writing in the early 12th century but close to contemporary sources, states the presence of the earls as fact and adds that of Bishop Wulfstan of Worcester (in office 1062–95) and Walter the Lotharingian, bishop of Hereford (in office 1061–79).[50] The *GG* adds Stigand to the party.[51] This was a powerful combination. In Ealdred, the London assembly had a senior ecclesiastic of near unblemished record with a history of involvement in dynastic affairs, and who (although the *GG* says otherwise),[52] had crowned Harold and enjoyed a powerful role in his government.[53] With Stigand, since 1052 both archbishop of Canterbury and bishop of Winchester, this would have added up to a powerful 'church' party.[54] In Edwin and Morcar, meanwhile, respectively earl of Mercia (since 1062) and earl of Northumbria (since 1065), still theoretically in control of the north of England, supporters of Harold's regime, and possibly also at Hastings,[55] the provisional government included the most powerful laymen in the kingdom. It was also a close-knit group: Wulfstan was a protégé of Ealdred, who had had him appointed first as prior of Worcester about 1055, and arranged his election as bishop of Worcester with the support of Earl Ælfgar, Edwin and Morcar's father. Both bishops would also have known Bishop Walter.

Crucially, whatever their different positions and intentions, their ambitions united in the person of Edgar 'the Ætheling' (that is, in Anglo-Saxon, *æþeling*, person dynastically eligible for kingship), who, as a descendant of King Alfred and great-nephew of the Confessor, with the 'line of Cerdic' behind him, had, as noted even by the French sources,[56] all the attributes of legitimacy that Harold had lacked. Support was also broadly based, including not only from the 'the rulers and magnates' (*rectores atque potentes*) and defeated English soldiery, but the 'populace' (*vulgus*) of London.[57] Raising Edgar to kingship was the obvious next step: as the *Carmen* puts it, 'finally the governors and magnates in consultation thought it advisable to consecrate as king a boy (*puer*) of the royal lineage lest they remain without a ruler', although it goes on to criticise their dubious motivation, the 'puppet' nature of the appointment, and the folly of their decision: 'For the foolish mob thought that they could be protected solely by the name, not the power, of a king. The boy is elected by them to be the image of a king; and his protection produced ruin'.[58]

Not inconsistent with this, the author of ASC 'D', with whom Ealdred was closely associated, attributes the raising of Edgar to Archbishop Ealdred and the citizens (*burhwaru*) of London,[59] and adds that 'Edwin and Morcar promised him that they would fight for him';[60] John of Worcester cites the support of Ealdred, the earls, and specifically the citizens and sailors (*butsecarlis*) of London.[61] The *GG*, for good propagandist reasons, if inaccurately, attributes the initiative to Stigand, along with 'the English'.[62] Edgar's status as king was sealed, according to the *GG*, by 'election',[63] that is, acceptance by proclamation, and according to the *Carmen* to selection by the *senatus* – that is, presumably, an assembly including the figures mentioned above.[64] In using the word *sacrare* ('to consecrate'),[65] the *Carmen* also implies that some sort of rite was envisaged, and certainly there were enough senior clergy on hand to perform one. Edgar's own wishes, willingness and reaction are unknown, but that he was the crowned king of England between the reigns of Harold and William cannot be ruled out, although uncrowned status, held by many Anglo-Saxon kings until long after their accession, would not alone have weakened his position.[66] Full recognition of his standing within the city is in keeping with the single but significant indication that he was recognised as king by 'the English' outside it: the ASC 'E' version, in what is probably an insertion after its compilation began at Peterborough in 1116, records that the monks successfully sought his sanction for the election of their candidate abbot, Brand, 'because the local people expected him to become king'. Not only did the Ætheling 'happily agree',[67] but the appointment followed and, for a while, survived the change of regime.[68] As Higham puts it, in a real sense, Edgar was 'dispensing royal patronage from the centre of power in London'.[69] This was a direct challenge to William's position and intentions, making the submission of London all the more essential if he was to take and retain the throne. How, then, did he set about it?

The descent on London

The Normans' route from Kent has been much studied, although Francis Baring's Domesday-derived conclusions of 1909[70] have been queried and improved upon in recent years.[71] For present purposes, the first London-related incident appears in the *GG*, to the effect that, having left Dover, the duke 'took up a position not far from London, where he heard that they most often held their meetings.'[72] Partly as the context suggests that 'they' were the high-ranking English and that it was near London, and in keeping with the account of later events in the *Carmen*,[73] the meeting place has sometimes been identified as Westminster, but this is ruled out by the fact that the 'position' of the Normans was clearly on the southern or *right* bank of the river. This is consistent with the *GG*'s later placing of William's first Thames crossing at or near Wallingford,[74] but is confirmed by the statement that the 500 Norman knights, having confronted a sortie of Londoners, 'set fire to all the houses on this side of the river'[75] – clearly not, then, the side occupied by the city. As others have implied,[76] the sortie must have been made from the south end of London Bridge, and the 'walls' (*moenia*) behind which the English survivors retreated those of the *burh* of Southwark which guarded the bridgehead; the burnt houses, meanwhile, must have been its own extra-mural suburb, and the 'position' probably the traditional open-air 'meeting place' at *Brixges Stane*, in the (eponymous) Hundred of Brixton, about three miles to the south.[77] That the *burh* was capable of playing such a role is clear from the existence of substantial defences by 1014,[78] mentioned in two sagas,[79] which successfully challenged Cnut in 1016,[80] and have been identified through excavation.[81] The significance of the Southwark incident, given that William's knights were sent 'in advance' – and, therefore, may have provoked rather than responded to the sortie – is in suggesting that the duke's initial plan for taking London may have been to use the bridge, and thus that the menacing march beyond the city, usually credited as a long-planned tactic, was in fact 'Plan B': as David Bates has put it, 'all this must have confirmed William in the view that London was too large and well-defended to be taken by direct assault',[82] even if, in the end, this turned out to be necessary.

Both the *GND* and the *GG* agree that the duke then went to Wallingford and that this was the point of departure for the final descent on London.[83] An attraction of Wallingford, just as it had been for Swein Forkbeard in 1013, en route from London to Bath,[84] was as the site of the lowest all-year-round ford across the Thames, or at least the first one wide enough to allow the passage of an army.[85] By 1066 it may also have had a bridge, *if* that was indeed the one mentioned in the *GG*, but for which there is no other evidence before 1141.[86] If William and his officers were not already aware of these advantages, riverside dwellers and boatmen could easily have told them. But at this point the *GG* narrative presents two other challenges, in stating that William 'having crossed the river Thames by ford and bridge at the same time, came to the town of Wallingford' ('*transmeato flumine Tamesi, vado simul atque ponte ad oppidum Guarangefort pervenit*'):[87] first, as Wallingford is on the right bank of the Thames,[88] this would mean that before arriving there he had already crossed it somewhere else; second, we also need to explain a simultaneous crossing by ford and bridge. The simplest explanation on both counts is that the *GG*'s sequence was mistaken, and that the duke came to Wallingford and *then* crossed the river, as is tacitly assumed by most historians; as the surrender or capture of the strongly defended *burh* would have to have preceded a crossing by this route, this would be consistent with the recent suggestion that the thegn of Wallingford, Wigod, had some leanings towards the Normans.[89] This would also explain the dual crossing, in that some of the army could have used the putative bridge and others the ford, and if there was not yet a bridge at Wallingford itself, alternatively, he could have used the one at Shillingford, less than five miles upstream, for which there is good evidence since the mid-tenth century.[90]

Nevertheless, a crossing either upstream of the town (at Shillingford) or downstream (at Moulsford)[91] before arrival at Wallingford, consistent with a literal reading of the *GG*, would have been possible,[92] although this could not, given John of Worcester's statement that the army ravaged Kent, Sussex and Hampshire en route (that is, on the 'south' side of the river),[93] have been very far downstream. Such a manoeuvre could be explained if William's initial aim was to bypass Wallingford rather than subdue it, as crossing elsewhere and attacking the town from the left bank, across the river, would have been as risky as at Southwark: just possibly such a convoluted itinerary was the result of a change of plan thanks to unanticipated peaceable overtures from the town, triggered, for example, by the arrival and submission of Stigand;[94] the dual crossing would then have been to, not from, the town, if necessarily followed by a re-crossing to resume the march on London.

Whatever the truth of the Wallingford episode, important differences then arise in the written accounts of the duke's subsequent itinerary and in the order in which he received the submissions of his future subjects. The *GG* relates that 'As soon as William, advancing from there [Wallingford], came in sight of London, the chief men of London came out to meet him' and 'submitted themselves and the whole city to him just as the men of Canterbury had done previously';[95] the *Carmen* omits the Wallingford incident, but its involvement is not incompatible with the itinerary in the *GG*. The ASC 'D' version and John of Worcester, however, introduce an intermediate incident at (respectively), *Beorh ham stede* and *Beorhchamstede*, that is, Berkhamsted, where the duke paused before descending on London.[96] Again, this is not fundamentally incompatible with the 'French' itineraries if we accept that their authors omitted or were ignorant of the event, known to the others thanks to greater local knowledge. Assuming, then, that a place called Berkhamsted was involved, a question remains as to whether it was 'Great' Berkhamsted or 'Little', both in Hertfordshire – the former 25 miles west of the latter. Francis Baring, noting the extensive waste in Domesday Book around it, favoured Little Berkhamsted,[97] a choice most subsequent authors have followed. However, a number of factors implicate, for preference, the other: first, the route there from Wallingford to Great Berkhamsted, up the Icknield Way through the

Chilterns and then eastward along Akeman Street, was far easier and more obvious than that to Little Berkhamsted; in addition, the route from Great Berkhamsted to London, via Akeman Street and Watling Street, would have taken him straight to Westminster and thence to the city at Newgate. Great Berkhamsted was also a place of some status – a *burh*, the seat of Edmer Ator, a major landholder,[98] and soon to be the site of a great castle built by the Conqueror's half-brother, Robert of Mortain: as such, it was a likely enough place to have been chosen in advance rather than being simply where the protagonists converged.

Great Berkhamsted's inclusion in the itinerary can therefore be seen as information additional to, but not incompatible with, the *GG* or the *GND*. The ASC's account of what actually happened there – that the duke was met by 'Archbishop Ealdred and Prince Edgar, and Earl Edwin, and Earl Morcar, and all the best men from London',[99] is, however, technically speaking at odds with the *GG*: this tells us that 'As soon as William … came in sight of London, the chief men of the city came out to meet him; they submitted themselves and the whole city to him',[100] as neither of the Berkhamsteds is actually intervisible with London. That the submission of London, however, was offered to the duke as, by whatever route, he approached it, is related both by the ASC and the *GG*: the latter does not specify who the party consisted of, other than that it included bishops,[101] one of whom he presumably assumed to have been Ealdred, and the 'chief men' (*principes civitates*) – that is, laymen acting in some authoritative capacity – who 'begged William to take the crown', and who had therefore also forsaken the Ætheling; Edwin and Morcar, according to the *GG*, submitted only after the duke's coronation. Two of the main near-contemporary sources therefore describe a peaceful surrender of important men, and (the *GG*), of London, well outside the city and before William's arrival there. This, too, was the narrative believed by their 12th-century successors: William of Malmesbury's *Gesta regum Anglorum*, of the 1120s, describes only how, on the duke's arrival in London, 'the citizens … burst out in waves from every gate to welcome him',[102] Henry of Huntingdon's *Historia Anglorum* of the 1130s that the duke was 'received peacefully',[103] and Orderic that 'the Londoners … took the wise course and surrendered to the duke'.[104]

The capture of London

This version of events, while not inconsistent with an encounter of some sort at Great Berkhamsted, is, at least at first sight, incompatible with two other important sources – William of Jumièges's *GND* and the *Carmen*: while Sir Frank Stenton's reminder in 1943, 'Of what happened at the end of the march nothing is certainly *known*'[105] remains the case (author's italics), these sources would have us believe that London's submission required force: the *GND* describes a battle, or at least a bloody skirmish, while the *Carmen* graphically describes a full-scale siege.

As the former has it:

> From there [Wallingford] he [William] moved on to London, where upon entering the city some scouts, sent ahead, found many rebels determined to offer every possible resistance. Fighting followed immediately and thus London was plunged into mourning for the loss of her sons and citizens. When the Londoners finally realised they could resist no longer, they gave hostages and surrendered themselves and all they possessed to the most noble conqueror and hereditary lord.[106]

The *Carmen* tells us that, after the election of Edgar, the duke

> learnt what had been done in London contrary to justice and by fools, he ordered his troops to approach the walls of the city. And immediately, swifter than the wind, a column of soldiers arrived to take up position. He then surrounded the walls on the left side with encampments (*castra*), set close together, and ordered his men to be ready for battle.[107]

He then

> built siege-engines and made battering-rams with horns of iron as well as machines for mining. Then he thundered forth menaces and threatened punishment and war. He vowed that, given the chance, he would raze the walls, level the bastions and reduce the proud tower to rubble.[108]

These accounts, apart from ASC, are the closest to the period in question and cannot be ignored. Guy of Amiens's account was written in 1068[109] and William of Jumièges's in the years 1067–70, and although revised and extended by Orderic and Robert of Torigni, the passage cited is original.[110] The *GG*'s omission of the London incident cannot, therefore, be given greater authority than its inclusion by the other two, as this was compiled later, between 1071 and 1077,[111] and is variously considered to have relied on eyewitness accounts (to which, as one of the duke's chaplains, he would have had ready access) and even on William of Jumièges and the *Carmen*.[112] Why he might have wished to omit events at London is another question: possibly aspects of them were in some way to the duke's discredit, or they would have undermined the neat finality of the great victory at Hastings; perhaps this untidy tale would have jarred with his carefully built-up depiction of the duke's invincibility and the successive submissions made by the awestruck English. Alternatively, of course, he may simply have had good reason to believe that Guy of Amiens and William of Jumièges were wrong.

Assuming, however, that there is substance in these two accounts, why then do they differ so widely from the *GG*'s and the *Carmen*'s, and which are the most credible? The differing narratives owe something to the agendas of the authors, but that the submission of London's senior figures was not a single, one-event occasion is pretty clear: rather, in various possible permutations, they surrendered separately. This must have owed in part to the divisions in interests, opinion and leadership in the city itself as William approached, falling, it would seem, into three main parties: the churchmen, the earls Edwin and Morcar, and a London party under Ansgar the staller, all of whom had initially supported Edgar.[113] Of the churchmen Stigand appears to have been the first to defect, submitting at Wallingford:[114] perhaps, not loved by the English, and assessing the odds in favour of the duke, he was trying for a new beginning under the new regime, in which he was initially successful; Ealdred, according to ASC 'D', submitted with the earls at Berkhamsted.[115] The part played in this by the bishop of London, William the Norman (1051–75) is unknown, but his loyalties would probably have led him to flee the city as English resistance coalesced, or perhaps to have defected from the fading cause with the other clergy.[116] The defection of the earls is as, or more easily, understandable. First, while from the duke's perspective their presence in London was very significant, the ASC 'D' version hints that their commitment to the Ætheling had been lukewarm from the start: having given it, 'but always when it [that is, the consolidation of Edgar's regime] ought to have been furthered, so from day to day the later the worse it got, just as it all did in the end'.[117] Second, however high their rank, their actual military capability is likely, by then, to have been very limited: they had suffered heavy losses at the Battle of Fulford, and Edwin is unlikely to have been able to draw on the resources of distant and war-weary Northumbria, still less on those of Wessex and East Anglia,[118] problems compounded by their own need to stay at the seat of government in London. As such, they would have realised that, however well-prepared, without hope of relief a siege could only end in surrender. The puppet Ætheling, of course, had to be surrendered with them. So from whom, if we accept that these senior figures did indeed surrender in advance, could the resistance of the city noted in the *Carmen* and the *GND* have come?

The answer may relate to Ansgar,[119] not mentioned by name among those who submitted, and a man perhaps of more significance in this context than is usually acknowledged (and who had probably met William, if, as seems likely, the duke had visited England in 1051).[120] While the *Carmen* is the only near-contemporary narrative source to mention him, he was certainly a historical figure – a major landholder before the Conquest, and the grandson of the distinguished thegn Tofi the Proud.[121] His first appearance is in 1042–4, when, already *staller*, he was entrusted by the Confessor, along with Bishop Ælfweard and London's *burgthegns*, to uphold the confirmation of a grant to Westminster Abbey.[122] The office or title of *staller*, loosely speaking an official answerable to the king and sometimes with territorial responsibilities, was probably never precisely defined, but included and probably emphasised military rather than civil and fiscal authority.[123] In the case of Ansgar, military credentials are supplied by the *Carmen*'s statement that he was 'crippled by a weakness of the loins and therefore slow on his feet, because he had received some few wounds in the service of his country.'[124] Whether he was wounded at Hastings, as was assumed by Freeman and has been by others since, is not clear,[125] although if so this would have been highly significant, if, as Wace claimed, the London contingent had the special duty to defend the king and his standard.[126] Ansgar's possession of substantial authority and resources are also indicated by the king's grant of his lands to endow Geoffrey I de Mandeville, sheriff of Middlesex.[127] Meanwhile, Ansgar's authority in the city after Hastings is emphasised in the *Carmen*, which explains that in spite of his infirmities, 'he commanded all the chief men of the city, and [that] the affairs of the community (*res publica*) were conducted by his aid';[128] the fact that the duke had by then secretly sent an envoy to him, with the ambiguous and curious suggestion that Ansgar's authority would be backed by the duke (now called 'king') if Edgar was relegated to the puppet status ('let him only be *called* king'), reveals that he too understood Ansgar's position in the beleaguered city;[129] his death after the Conquest, in the king's custody, allegedly laden with chains, is in keeping with a history of resistance from a position of some strength.[130] As such, with professional responsibilities, much to lose by way of rights and property, a vested interest in London itself, and real authority, he would have had the motive and the means to lead an unreconciled faction within the city after Ealdred, Edwin and Morcar had forsaken the Ætheling and surrendered.[131]

Nevertheless, Ansgar's authority at the moment of crisis was clearly not universally acknowledged even in the city: the ASC states that the 'chief men from London' (*ealle þa betstan men of Lundene*), the *GG* that the 'chief men of the city' (the *principes civitates*), and John of Worcester that 'the more noble citizens of London' (*de Lundonia quique nobiliores*), were among those who surrendered before the duke reached the city.[132] The implication must be that 'London party' was itself divided, or split as the crisis came to a head. Who, then, were these 'chief' and 'more noble' men? What offices and authority may they have held, and who besides them may have played a part in London's fate in 1066? How London was governed on the eve of the Conquest is hard to define, but three principal types of official were involved. First, there were the *stallers*, for Ansgar was not, at least always, the only one: in the 1040s he was accompanied by another, Osgod Clapa,[133] and latterly by Leofwine, Harold's brother, briefly wielding authority in Middlesex and Hertfordshire in the 1050s and 1060s.[134] Second, there were the two classes of reeve, also royal officials – the *portreeve*, with responsibilities relating to the trading place and settlement, that is, the city; and the *shire reeve* or sheriff, with responsibilities which perhaps overlapped but which were focused on the surrounding shire, that is, Middlesex. The known occupants of the office, at least shortly before 1066, were

Wulfgar (portreeve 1042–4),[135] Leofstan (occurs 1051–66),[136] Alestan in 1066 (although possibly a corruption of Leofstan),[137] Ælfsige in 1051–66,[138] and Gosfregth/Goisfredus, the portreeve to whom William's writ to the Londoners is addressed.[139] Their responsibilities appear to have been largely civil, and in particular fiscal. In addition, it seems that there was also a class amongst the population who, while not officials or royal officers, enjoyed prestige and authority – a sort of urban aristocracy, although no doubt possessed of property outside the city too, inferred by the reference to the *burgthegns* of the 1040s[140] and John of Worcester's *nobiliores*. Finally there were the people – the *vulgus* of the *Carmen*. So while Ansgar is likely to have wielded considerable authority, not least in military terms, he retained it only over part of the population; which part is less clear, but it included officialdom and ordinary citizens.

Nevertheless, by the time Ansgar is first encountered in the narrative, the decision by others to desert the cause had been made and, as he acknowledged, the situation was desperate: according to the *Carmen* he gathered the city's elders (*natu maiores*) and pointed out their parlous position:

> You see the walls assailed by powerful assaults and encompassed by countless disasters. The siege-engine that has been erected overtops the bastions. The walls, split by the blows of its rocks, are falling down. From the many breaches ruin threatens on every side.[141]

Ansgar then recommended sending an envoy to William to buy time and 'counterfeit homage' but the envoy returned, laden with gifts, offering William's clemency, saying 'The king [*sic*] sends you a message of peace and wishes you well … Therefore, if you wish to survive, only one course is open to you: restore to him by your hands his lawful rights'.[142]

At this point resistance collapsed: 'The people (*vulgus*) and the Witan (*senatus*) allowed that it was just, and both assemblies (*coeti*) denied that the boy was king', and then set out to the king's palace (*aula regis*) – that is, to Westminster – to offer him the keys: 'With heads bowed to the ground, they proceed with the boy in an orderly procession to the royal hall, seeking to surrender the city by its keys and to appease wrath by making a gift with their hands'.[143] More difficult perhaps to reconcile are the *Carmen*'s account of a siege followed by surrender, and the fighting between the duke's forces and the 'rebels' *within* the city (*in platea urbis*, that is, 'in the street of the city'), mentioned in the *GND*: possibly it referred to a repulsed incursion on the arrival of the Norman army, or (depending on the meaning of *platea*), a sortie which met bloody defeat.[144]

Overall, however, it can be concluded that there was indeed a period after Hastings when London 'had a king', that effective resistance could have been possible, and that the outcome or at least the pace of William's adventure could have been very different. In the event,

William's relatively easy capture of the city owed to disunity within it, and it was this genuinely confusing turn of events which led to the apparent contradictions in the sources. They are not, therefore, necessarily incompatible, and it seems clear that after the surrender of the churchmen and the earls, a faction in London, high and low, briefly sustained a siege under the leadership of Ansgar. It was military action, therefore, that prompted the surrender and paved the way for the elevation of duke to king.

4

The armour and weapons of the Anglo-Saxons and Normans

Thom Richardson and Robert C. Woosnam-Savage

Armour
Thom Richardson

From the late Roman period there was a great continuity in the armour of Western Europe. Even the centres where it was made remained constant: the *fabricae* of the Rhine–Danube limes evolved, by and large, into the armour-making centres of Medieval Europe.

The principal metal body armour of Imperial Rome, in the west at least, was mail. Formed of interlocking links of iron wire closed by rivets, mail formed the ideal flexible defence for close combat. Despite the fragility of mail in most archaeological contexts, surviving examples of mail from the late Roman period do, remarkably, exist, one of the best being from the Vimose bog in Denmark, dateable to the second to third centuries AD.[1] With mail links ranging in size from 7.2 mm to 10.5 mm in diameter, of wire about 1.5 mm in diameter, its construction is half riveted: that is, of alternate rows of forge-welded and of riveted links (Figure 1). Link analysis by Wijnhoven shows that it was constructed as a poncho, joined at the side seams. Of these Danish finds the finest mail is from Hedegaard, the links of which have a diameter of around 5 mm and a wire thickness of around 0.95 mm. The same construction was common throughout the Roman Empire too, as the similar shirt from Nova in Italy shows. Because of its nature, mail survives poorly in archaeological contexts, usually concreted at best, fragmentary or entirely of iron oxide at worst. What should be a pivotal piece of Saxon mail, the Sutton Hoo shirt, remains a concreted mass.[2]

In the late Roman armies mail was used by cavalry and infantry, and by the 11th century the same applied; deep-skirted mail shirts called *byrnies* were worn by both sides, horse and foot, on the Bayeux Tapestry. The Tapestry is not alone in depicting mail in a highly stylised way. Mail is difficult to depict, and artists tended to develop conventions for it, which gave rise in turn to a complex typology of mail including chain mail, mascled mail, trellised mail and others, whose physical

Figure 1. Diagram showing the construction of the Vimose and other half-riveted mail. Martin Wijnhoven.

manifestation can be seen in William Burges's reconstructions of mail types from sculpture, preserved in the British Museum. Burges's and De Cosson's landmark exhibition in 1880, however, marked the start of the modern scientific study, still in its infancy, of mail as a type of armour.[3]

Few examples of mail contemporary with Hastings exist. Close is the fragmentary shirt from Gjermundbu, now in the Museum of Cultural History, Oslo, also of half-riveted construction. The links are 8.2 mm in diameter, with 1.2 mm wire. It is frequently suggested that the solid links are stamped from iron sheet because of their square section and faceted shape, but where such links have been analysed elsewhere they have proven to be forge-welded.[4]

Closest of all, conventionally dated to the tenth century, is the mail shirt of St Wenceslaus (I, Duke of Bohemia 921–35) preserved in the

Figure 2a. Mail shirt of St Wenceslaus, 11th century, preserved in the Cathedral Treasury of Prague. © Prague Castle Administration. Photo: Jan Gloc.

Figure 2b. Detail of the Prague mail, showing half-riveted construction. © Prague Castle Administration. Photo: Jan Gloc.

Cathedral Treasury of Prague. This has an associated later and very heterogeneous mail collar or standard associated with it, but the shirt itself is of half-riveted construction, with long sleeves and skirts (Figure 2).[5] The rivets of all this mail, from the Vimose finds onwards, are circular, in contrast to the riveted wedges found as the predominant type in high medieval European mail. Such circular rivets remained the norm in later eastern European and in Asian mail, where the half-riveted system of construction, abandoned in Europe in the middle of the 14th century, continued to the end of the practical use of mail in the 18th century.

The cut of the short-sleeved shirts shown transported on poles on the Bayeux Tapestry is also found on the Wenceslaus hauberk. Along with some later half-riveted shirts, the Wenceslaus shirt has a reinforcement in the form of a double-thickness section of mail at the neck opening, noticed for the first time by Checksfield, and, as he observed, this may be the origin of the square panels depicted at the necks of the Tapestry shirts. The external diameter of the mail links ranges from about 5 mm to 7 mm, so it is unusually fine for mail of this period. Wearing of padded garments under mail was always essential, and the way in which these linings were associated with mail garments (as adjacent layers or as permanently sewn-on linings) is poorly understood, but this may also go some way towards explaining the bordering bands on the tapestry. The extensive effort involved in making these shirts, as well as the materials involved, is reflected in the few valuations we have; a hauberk was valued at £7 in a Jumièges charter of about 1045–9.[6]

One new feature that appears on the tapestry is mail defences for the legs, called *chausses* in later literature. These became rapidly the norm in knightly armour, as shown in countless manuscript illustrations and funerary effigies and brasses, until they were replaced by plate leg harness in the later 14th century. Though none survive from the period and most of the later medieval examples are fakes, constructed to fill out armours for display purposes, recent analysis of an example in the collection of the Metropolitan Museum of Art, New York, confirms from its half-riveted construction early 14th-century dating or earlier (Figures 3 and 4).

A few of the Norman cavalry on the Tapestry have mail head defences or coifs, worn under their helmets and probably separate defences from their hauberks, though we cannot be certain of this from the Tapestry. Such mail coifs or *thena* became, like the mail *chausses*, a standard part of knightly harness from the 12th to the mid-14th century, and a few half-riveted examples, probably from the early 14th century but possibly earlier, survive. Some of the literature of the subject has suggested that what are interpreted here as mail shirts may be other forms of defence (scales or even rings sewn into a fabric coat). Certainly there is no evidence in the archaeological record for northern Europe for this period of scale armour. There is for splinted armour, however: the finds from Valsgarde 8 have been reconstructed as splinted iron forearm and leg defences rather than as the splinted cuirass of an earlier reconstruction.

Helmets, likewise, show a remarkable continuity from the Imperial Roman period. The cross-reinforced skulls of the Adamklissi *metopes* of the mid-second century show the real fighting armour

Figure 3. Mail chausse, early 14th century or before. New York, Metropolitan Museum of Art, no. 29.158.199a, Bashford Dean Memorial collection. Author's photo.

Figure 4. Detail of the New York chausse, showing half-riveted construction. Author's photo.

of the legions, far from the stylised forms of Trajan's Column. The numerous Imperial Gallic helmets include the same feature. By the period of the Late Empire, simple band helms with two-piece skulls – such as the Intercisa group from the Hungarian National Museum, Budapest, probably the latest infantry helmets, and the magnificent jewelled cavalry helmets of the late Empire, such as the Berkasovo and Duerne helmets – represent the beginning of a long tradition which would extend into the tenth century. The crested helmet construction of these pieces was continued in the northern European tradition after the fall of Rome.

The Spangenhelm group, which are also brought in from Asia, appear also in the fourth century with the Deir el-Medina helmet from Egypt, and came to dominate southern European production in the post-Roman period with the Ravenna group, but were not the type most popular in northwest Europe.

The crested helmet type includes the few surviving Anglo-Saxon helmets, the earliest of which is Benty Grange, with its boar crest and horn panels; contemporary with the Spangenhelm group, the crested group are all north European, and include Sutton Hoo, Coppergate and Pioneer. Coppergate, like several of the Scandinavian helmets, has a mail aventail attached by a wire round its lower edge. The mail is of the same half-riveted type seen on contemporary hauberks. Much richer is the Scandinavian group of crested helmets, including Valsgarde 5 with its pendant lappets and binocular mask, Vendel 14 with its nasal and hinged cheekpiece like Coppergate and Pioneer, and Valsgarde 8 with its mail aventail and binocular mask. Another group of helmets, the segment helms formed of four riveted triangular plates without an internal cross-framework, appears around the tenth century, centred around northeast Europe.[7]

A new type appeared in the tenth century, forged from a solid piece of iron. Closest to Hastings in date is the helmet associated with St Wenceslaus in Prague, still accepted as tenth-century, and the eleventh-century helmet from Moravia in the Hof Jägd und Rüstkammer of the Kunsthistorisches Museum in Vienna (Figures 5 and 6). The latter is the earliest accepted helmet of what has come to be called the 'Norman' type, after the Tapestry. Unfortunately, the proliferation of helmets of this type during the last three decades, simple to make and of high commercial value, some of which at least have been demonstrated by scientific analysis to be fakes, has led to a deep suspicion about purported finds of helmets of this type in recent years.

The Germanicisation of the Imperial Roman army led to the abandonment of the traditional rectangular legionary *scutum* and the adoption of circular shields for both cavalry and infantry in the late Empire. Their use continued for a millennium, illustrated at intervals by manuscripts such as the Golden Psalter of St Gallen, dated to the ninth century. The Sutton Hoo shield illustrates the construction, a circular board formed usually of planks covered in glued leather, with either a circular central hole for the hand and a separated applied grip or a theta-shaped hole, covered on the outside with a shield boss which had both a defensive and an offensive function. Numerous finds of shields from Scandinavia illustrate the same form, such as the group from Thorsburg Moor in Schleswig Holstein (Figure 7). The commonly held idea of the cross-ply construction of these shields is not born out by the actual finds, such

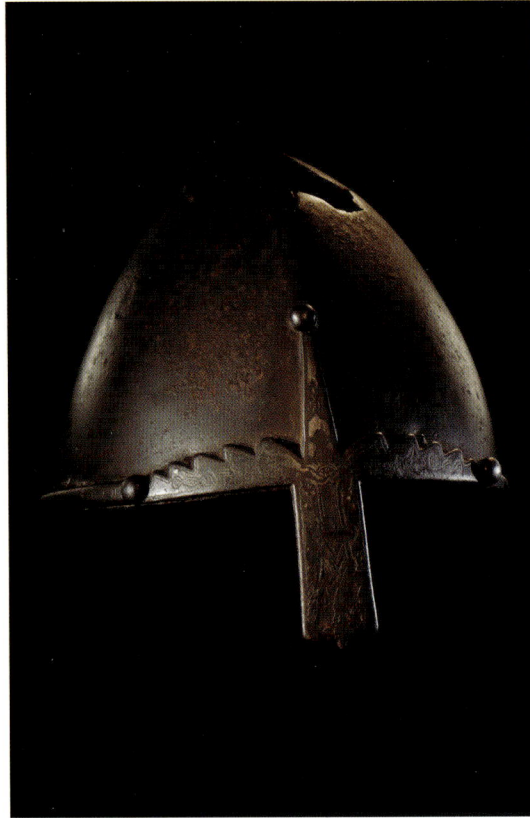

as the tenth-century shield excavated at Trelleborg, Denmark, in 2008 (Figure 8).

During the first half of the 11th century a transition took place in northwest Europe from the round shield to the long, pointed or kite-shaped shield. This transition is illustrated in the British Library Harley Psalter, where both types are in use simultaneously by both cavalry and infantry (Figure 9).[8] The same transition occurred in the Byzantine world: the 12th-century Madrid Skylitzes shows both types in use, the 'new' kite-shaped shields generally by the *Romaioi* (Figure 10). Though both sides on the tapestry use the new kite-shaped shields, some traditionalists among the Saxons retain round shields. No securely dated kite-shaped shields are known to survive: the earliest of the later heater or flat-iron shaped shields, from the Church of St Elizabeth in Marburg, that were associated with Konrad von Thüringen (1206–40), grand master of the Teutonic Knights, can be dated stylistically to the late 13th century.

Such is the appeal of the armour of the 11th century, however, and the relative ease of manufacture, that scarcely a sale goes by without a Norman helmet and a kite-shaped shield. A group of nasal helmets

Figure 6. Nasal helmet, 11th century, from Moravia, in the Hof Jägd und Rüstkammer of the Kunsthistorisches Museum, Vienna, no. A41.

Figure 7. Shield from Thorsberg moor, Archaeological State Museum, Schloss Gottorf, Schleswig-Holstein, about AD 300. Source: Wikimedia Commons, CC-BY-SA 3.0.

which appeared from eastern Europe in the early 1990s was subject to an analysis which revealed them to be made of iron which had undergone a modern electric crucible process, but it is rare for such scientific testing to be carried out on them. Though some pieces have a serious

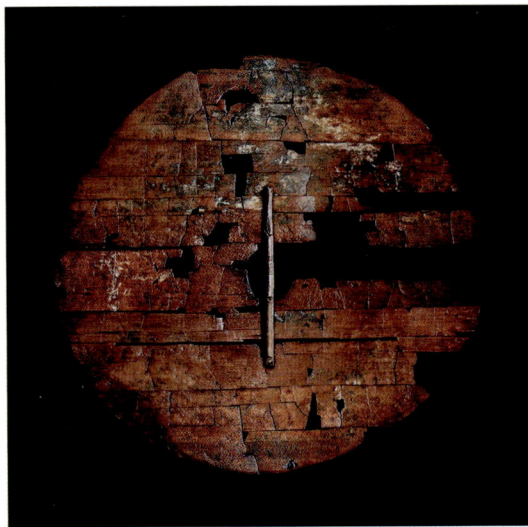

Figure 8. Interior of the shield from Trelleborg near Slagelse, Denmark, excavated in 2008, probably tenth century, showing single-layer pine board construction, central hole and grip. © National Museum of Denmark.

Figure 9. Round and kite-shaped in use simultaneously, both by cavalry and infantry. British Library, MS Harley 603, fo. 69r.

Figure 10. Battle between Byzantines and Bulgars, Madrid Skylitzes. Madrid, Biblioteca Nacional, MS Graecus 26-2, fo. 107v.

claim to authenticity, most of these objects can be easily dismissed. The group of 'helmet rims' recently 'excavated' from the alternative site of Hastings turned out on analysis to be relatively modern barrel bands. Others are much tougher; no doubt some of the claimants will be authenticated, but at present this is a poorly populated field, which in turn makes identification more difficult.

Weapons
Robert C. Woosnam-Savage

Introduction

This summary describes the basic types of weapons that would have been used during the Battle of Hastings and the Norman Conquest by both the Anglo-Saxon and the Norman participants, and their probable effects. It also brings up to date thoughts regarding this equipment, as the most often-cited reference regarding this material was written some 30 years ago.[9] From archaeological evidence it would appear that there was very little difference between the weapons carried by the Normans and the Anglo-Saxons,[10] and so the summary, apart from a couple of exceptions, looks at them by type rather than by which particular group used what. Those hoping to find a discussion regarding the 'agency ... of ... medieval things' or the Norman sword 'as a phallic symbol' will be disappointed; these topics are left to others better versed in such matters.[11]

Unfortunately, despite the claims of some (such as those with a sword to sell[12]) and the hopes of others, no confirmed weapons, or even parts, have ever been found at the generally accepted site of the battle of Hastings.[13] Even alleged finds from other suggested sites, such as the claims of remains of a crossbow, are fraught with enormous difficulties.[14] Neither have any of the remains of the dead, singly or in mass graves, yet been identified, despite the initial excitement in 2014 engendered by a skeleton bearing the trauma of many sword blows, which was claimed to be possibly from the battle.[15]

Surviving examples of medieval arms of the period of the Conquest are rare, as such weapons were used to destruction, re-used, or have simply rotted and rusted away.[16] Those few surviving examples of weapons of the period show us some, but not all, of the types of weapons used. Information about the range of weapons used can be gleaned, however, from the various chronicle accounts of the battle and from contemporary or near-contemporary artworks, including, obviously, the Bayeux Tapestry, which itself depicts 201 armed warriors, both mounted and on foot (Figure 11).[17] The author is, of course, aware of the reliability, or otherwise, of the Tapestry; however, it cannot be ignored and, indeed, it would be perverse to do so as the Tapestry provides illustrations of almost every type of weapon that could conceivably have been used

Figure 11. A detail from the Bayeux tapestry showing the loading of material onto William's ships, including swords and spears. Note that one of the swords is depicted as slung by its wrist loop from a carrying pole.

at Hastings.[18] Quite simply, the main source of information regarding Norman and Saxon arms at Hastings *is* the Bayeux Tapestry, which depicts the Norman invasion of England in 1066. If used judiciously, it provides a dynamic picture of such arms in action.[19]

Swords

The Anglo-Saxon warrior classes were defined by their ability to bear arms, as ownership of both sword and spear was a prerogative of freemen; slaves were forbidden to bear arms. Key among these weapons was the sword. Swords used during the Conquest, on both the Anglo-Saxon and the Norman side, would have been largely interchangeable and were little altered from their earlier Viking antecedents, the blade forms being basically the same, although some were slightly longer. Swords, together with shields, were used by both cavalry and infantry. A sword usually had a long, straight, double-edged iron blade with parallel edges and a rounded tip. A ground hollow, the 'fuller', ran down most of the length of the blade, making the blade lighter but not diminishing its strength.[20] These swords were made primarily for cutting with the edge, although the point could be used to deliver a thrust when required. They were about 86–100 cm (34–40 in) long, but some were considerably shorter, and generally weighed only between 0.9 kg and 1.4 kg (2–3 lb). A suitable pommel, which acted as a counterweight to the blade and locked the blade and hilt components together, made the sword feel light and responsive in the hand. Around the tang of the blade a bound wooden grip allowed the sword to be held, and a simple straight or slightly curved cross-guard, usually of square cross-section, protected the hand from blows. This form of sword had appeared during the Migration Period (300–700) and, after developing a longer blade, became the template for most sword types of the Conquest period.

Figure 12. Sword, with 'tea-cosy' or 'beehive' pommel, European, about 1100 (Royal Armouries IX.1081).

Figure 13. Sword, with 'lobated' pommel and pattern-welded blade, Anglo-Saxon, ninth century (Royal Armouries AL.201 28).

Between the ninth and eleventh centuries a number of different pommel forms were used and some, such as the descriptively named 'lobated' (that is, possibly BT 70), 'tea-cosy'/'recumbent D' and disc pommels are depicted in the Bayeux Tapestry (that is, BT 22 and 23).[21] The most common form of pommel at the time of Conquest was probably the so-called 'brazil-nut', which, although not obviously depicted in the Tapestry, had appeared in about the mid-tenth century.[22] Some swords had a form of wrist loop, as one sword is clearly depicted with something akin to this in the Bayeux Tapestry (BT 38), to prevent the sword being lost when wielding it (Figure 11).[23]

Originally most blades were made from small pieces of iron forge-welded into a single blade (Figure 12). But by the seventh century many of these sword blades were manufactured using the more complex 'pattern-welding' process. Several wrought iron and mild steel bars were twisted into rods and hammer-welded together to create the body of the blade. Steel cutting edges were forge-welded on either side of the bar. Blades were tempered by being heated, then quenched (cooled rapidly in oil or water), then heated again to a lower temperature. This gave the blade both hardness and toughness. After grinding and polishing, acid was used to etch the surface of the blade and reveal the complex twisted patterns within. Letters forming inscriptions, and patterns, could be created by hot-hammering iron wire or pattern-welded rods into chisel cuts in the blade (Figure 13).[24]

It has been calculated that a basic pattern-welded sword blade might take 43 hours or more to make, the hilt and scabbard adding additional time and costs,[25] and a fine sword might take upwards of 200 hours to produce. Such swords were extremely expensive and the mounted warrior, the wealthy knight, came to be identified by these swords, as a symbol of power and nobility as well as a first-class fighting weapon. And indeed swords of state are also seen in the Bayeux Tapestry worn by, or alongside, those in positions of power when enthroned, such as in the Coronation of Harold scene (BT 31).

Figure 14. Sword detail with disc pommel, European, found at Newbury, Berkshire, probably 11th century (Royal Armouries IX.12).

Figure 15. Two swords, possibly 'Viking', both north European, the first 10–11th century (Royal Armouries IX.859), the second, with a large 'tea-cosy' pommel, about 900–1150 (Royal Armouries AL.23 4).

From about the tenth century many blades were of simpler 'homogeneous and laminated'[26] construction and by the eleventh century swords were being mass-produced in continental European centres like Lorraine, Cologne and Solingen. By 1066 Milan already had a *Via del Spada*, the 'Street of the Swordsmiths', and swords from these centres were exported throughout Europe.

Frankish swords were highly regarded and many bore the name of their makers, or more probably their workshops, such as those of the ninth to the eleventh century marked 'Vlfberht', which, although presently unidentified, appears to have been active in the present-day region of Solingen in Germany and connected with an ecclesiastical or monastic institution,[27] and from the tenth century, those marked 'Ingelri'.

The excellence of such swords had long been noted. When the 'Kings of the Northmen' sent their own swords as a sign of loyalty to a grandson of Charlemagne, Louis the German (about 804–76):

> ordered the swords … be passed to him … so that he could test them himself … Lewis took one of them by the hilt and tried to bend it from its tip to its handle. His hands were stronger than the sword, and the blade snapped. Then one of the envoys drew his own sword from its sheath and handed it to Lewis … so that he might test that. 'My Lord,' said he. 'I think that you will find this sword … flexible and strong.' The Emperor took the sword … He bent the sword like a vine-twig, from the extreme tip back to the hilt, and then let it gradually straighten out again.[28]

The accompanying envoys were suitably impressed by Louis's strength, but equally remarkable was the quality of the second sword.[29] The bending of sword blades remained a manufacturing test of quality until well into the 20th century, so there is no reason to think that similar tests were not being applied to swords at the time of the Conquest (Figure 15).

It is known that valued Viking swords, like other material including spears and shields, acquired names, such as 'Fierce', 'Pruner', 'Serpent of the Wound' and 'Battle-snake', and some swords of the Conquest probably also bore names.[30] The slashing blade was effective, as a later

Figure 16. A detail from the Bayeux Tapestry showing some of the Norman cavalry with swords held aloft.

account describes: 'Thorbjorn [Clerk] swung at him, but Asolf parried the stroke with his hand, which was sliced off'.[31] And, unsurprisingly, warriors' legs were prone to targeted attack: 'Then Egil ran at him and struck at him. He dealt such a blow that that Ljolt stumbled and dropped his shield. Egil struck Ljolt above the knee, chopping off his leg. Ljolt dropped dead on the spot.'[32] In this regard one calls to mind the names of Bolli the Gracious' sword 'Fótbitr' ('Foot-Biter') and Magnus Barefoot's sword 'Leggbitr' ('Leg-Biter') (Figure 16).[33]

Wace describes how a number of horses were brought before William and 'Each one had a good sword hanging in front from its saddle-bows'.[34] Weapons were commonly later suspended from the saddle bow, and might include a second sword for close work, but it is not clear whether this is what Wace is describing (and one should, of course, obviously be aware of the later date of Wace, about 1170, and any contemporary glosses he has added). Incidentally, this method of suspension is not illustrated in the Bayeux Tapestry. William himself is described as fighting with a sword as 'With his angry blade he tirelessly pierced shields, helmets, and hauberks'[35] and his mounted warriors are known to have 'challenged the event with their swords' after the initial attack by Norman archers.[36] William is also noted as having attacked the killer of one his horses: 'With a hard thrust of his right hand and his weapon's sharp point, he pierced his groin and spilt his entrails on the ground'.[37]

Figure 17. A detail from the Bayeux Tapestry showing the gathering up of swords after battle.

The singular act of a Norman using a second sword may also be depicted (BT 70) but it seems far more likely that the Norman has successfully disarmed his Anglo-Saxon opponent and is using the latter's sword against him, while his own sword still remains sheathed at his side. Otherwise it is difficult to explain the depiction of an apparently unarmed Anglo-Saxon in the midst of battle.[38] Another suggestion, that this might 'indicate that reserve weapons were worn',[39] could tie in with Wace's comments regarding the sword on the saddle-bow, mentioned above.

The value of swords, like much other material, is shown by the lone figure in the lower border of the Bayeux Tapestry who, towards the closing of the battle, is shown collecting swords from the battlefield (BT 71) (Figure 17).[40]

Swords were worn in scabbards which protected both the edge of the sword and the wielder from unnecessary damage. Scabbards for swords were often made from two thin laths of wood covered in leather, the interior lined with fleece, the lanolin in the wool helping to protect the blade from rust. The scabbard often bore a metal chape to protect the tip of the blade (Figure 18).

The scabbard was suspended either from a waist-belt or a diagonal belt, or baldric, over the shoulder.[41] It may also have been secured to, and suspended from, the belt by a cross-strap or lacing, as seemingly depicted on a fragment of a frieze of about 1000–1050 from the Old Minster, Winchester, which shows a sword-bearing warrior.[42] Some forms of the belt appear to have been attached directly to the scabbard itself in some manner, if some depictions in the Tapestry are accurate (BT 9) (Figure 19).[43]

The Bayeux Tapestry indicates that both Norman and Anglo-Saxon warriors fought with the sword worn not only at their side (BT 55 and 69), but also beneath their mail hauberks. The sword-hilt protruded out of what appears to have been a small slit at the left hip and, sometimes, the lower half of the scabbard emerged from what seems to have been another slit in the hauberk (BT 23), or from beneath its hem-line. Harold

Figure 18. Sword with 'brazil-nut' pommel, for a boy, retaining traces of its scabbard, north European, 11th–mid-12th century (Royal Armouries IX.5610).

is depicted specifically with this latter suspension method when he is bestowed with arms by William (BT 24). Whether this is of particular significance is unknown and how this actually worked is speculation, although it has been suggested that it was worn under the hauberk 'presumably to prevent it from being cut' (Figure 20).[44]

Daggers and knives

Although there appears to be no references to daggers or knives being used at the battle of Hastings, it is likely that they were commonly used by both the nobility and common soldiers on both sides. Many soldiers' knives also served as a tool or utensil as well as a weapon.

Certainly the Anglo-Saxons would have had the short knife-like *seax*, but this was a secondary weapon, one probably used for the hunt or status and a weapon of last resort.[45] The longer *seax* used by the Anglo-Saxons and others, although also not a primary weapon, was, in effect, a single-edged sword which could be over 80 cm (31.5 in) long (Figure 21). It often bore a hardened steel edge and may well have been suitable for battle: 'Then again the king himself … drew a slaughter-seax, bitter and battle-sharp'.[46] *Seax* may be the weapons used by the two soldiers who are depicted apprehending Harold (BT 6–7) and by a lower-border figure being attacked by animals (BT 20).

Staff weapons share the common feature of being mounted on long wooden hafts.[47] Wace mentions that some Anglo-Saxon peasants bore what they could find: 'cudgels, and great pikes, iron forks and clubs'.[48]

Spears

The spear was an infantry weapon carried by all ranks, from king and earl to freeman, with a large closed-socketed iron head, of triangular or leaf-shape and often of flattened diamond cross-section. It was probably, in all its forms, the primary – and most common – arm of the Anglo-Saxon warrior, and some were no doubt symbols of status.[49] The head was mounted on a long wooden haft of between about 1.6 and 2.8 m (5 ft 3 in to 9 ft 3 in) in length and often of ash, hence the contemporary synonym '*Æsc*' ('ash').[50] Different forms of spear seem to have existed, with differing types of spear-heads,

Figure 19. A detail from the Bayeux Tapestry showing how swords were worn at the waist-belt.

ranging from long thrusting spears to light ones for throwing; javelins or 'darts'[51] (Figure 22 and Figure 23).

The spear was primarily designed for thrusting at the enemy and was gripped underarm, with the arm at full stretch, enabling the full reach of the spear to be used, or held overarm, enabling thrusts at the opponent's upper body and head. It could be used with two hands if required. 'Shield walls' (the *scyldburgh*, literally 'shield-fort') consisted of lines of spear- and shield-bearing foot-soldiers who fought in close formation. Spears could overcome the comparatively effective protection mail offered: '[Thorolf] drove his spear through the earl's coat of mail, into his chest and through his body, so that it came out between his shoulder blades, lifted him up on it above his own head and thrust the end into the ground ... the earl expired on the spear.'[52]

Some spear-heads, according to the Bayeux Tapestry and other contemporary sources, bore short lugs or wings on their sockets, an earlier feature seen in those used by Charlemagne's army, which had similar flat triangular wings.[53] As the archaeology of the period has refused to give up any similar heads, in England at least, it has been suggested that the later representations, including those in the Tapestry, hark back to earlier artistic influences or that the lugs are in fact protruding rivet heads.[54] This is not necessarily so, as a few rare 11th-century winged spear-heads do exist.[55] It has also been suggested that winged spears were used only for hunting, but this ignores the fact that specialist

Figure 20. A detail from the Bayeux Tapestry showing Harold being bestowed with arms, wearing a sword using an apparently different suspension method.

hunting weapons arguably did not really appear until the 15th century. A winged spear-head could perform a number of important functions; it could be used as a parrying device, prevent over penetration of a beast – or human opponent (which could then run up the haft of the spear and injure or slay its wielder) – and also ease withdrawing it from an impaled victim.[56] Some of the Anglo-Saxon spearmen bear spears with pennons (BT 61 and 62). The haft of one (BT 62) is depicted in a manner that apparently implies it is thicker than most, though why this is so is unclear (see also lances below regarding similar apparent thickening), and a mailed defender uses a pennoned lance or spear to hand over the keys of Dinan (BT 23) (Figure 24).

Figure 21. Two short Seax knife blades, both north European, tenth–eleventh century (Royal Armouries X.1603 and X.1602), together with a long Seax blade, also north European, eighth–ninth century (Royal Armouries IX.1105).

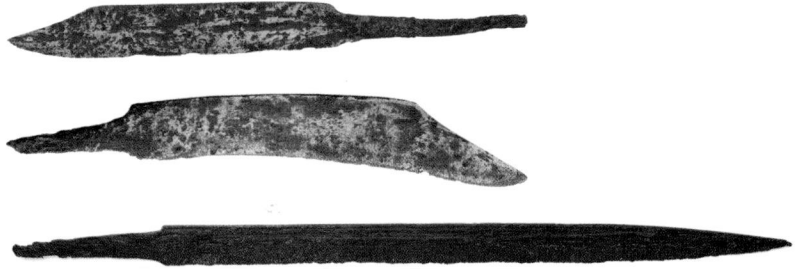

Figure 22. Two spear-heads, the first Anglo-Saxon, tenth–eleventh century (Royal Armouries AL.201 31; British Museum 1862, 0803.3), the second with a long, thin blade, Viking, eighth–tenth century (Royal Armouries VII.3014).

Some light forms of spear, such as the javelin, with a smaller leaf-shaped head, were designed to be thrown as missile weapons.[57] According to the Bayeux Tapestry, and other illustrations, it would appear that they were carried by some spearmen at least, in sheaves or bundles (BT 62), ready to cast. With the spears/javelins used as a primary weapon, the spearman would resort to his secondary weapon, the sword or axe, once the supply was exhausted. It was noted that the Anglo-Saxons 'threw javelins' at the Normans, who were the target of this 'death-dealing mass' and that the Normans also used 'javelins'.[58] Two of William's horses are described as having being taken down by Anglo-Saxon javelin strikes.[59]

The barbed heads depicted in the Bayeux Tapestry are not borne out by archaeology apart from the heads of earlier throwing spears, like the *angon*, which were long and barbed.[60] Used throughout Europe, and by earlier Saxons, the *angon* worked on the principle that if it didn't incapacitate an opponent with a direct hit it would lodge in their shield, the barbs keeping it firmly attached to the shield. This made it difficult for an opponent to remove, and weighed the shield down so much as to compromise defences, such as the shield wall, leading to its break-up and possible eventual defeat.[61]

Lances

The mailed cavalry had become the core of the Norman army, partly through the use of the stirrup, together with the high-cantled saddle, which provided a secure mobile fighting platform for the Norman knight. Standing in the stirrups, firmly held in the saddle, he could now not only deliver stronger blows with the sword but also use the

Figure 23. A detail from the Bayeux Tapestry showing the 'shield-wall' in action and also Anglo-Saxon warriors holding bundles of spears. Also note the lone Saxon archer and the warrior apparently about to hurl his small throwing axe.

Figure 24. Three more spear-heads, the first with a diamond-shaped blade, north European, seventh–eleventh century (Royal Armouries VII.3541), the second with lugs or wings, north European, eighth–ninth century (Royal Armouries VII.2950) and the third of 'Angon' type, with a barbed blade, possibly Anglo-Saxon, fifth–seventh century (Royal Armouries AL.201 1).

lance more effectively (Figure 25). The lance was a cavalry spear with a leaf-shaped iron spear-head and a wooden haft between 2.7 m and 3.5 m (9–11 ft) in length, often of ash or applewood.[62] It appears that it could be thrown overarm (BT 61) or used – probably more commonly – overarm to thrust down and jab at infantry from horseback (BT 62).[63] More importantly, however, seemingly after about 1050 when the rider charged with the lance 'couched' under his right arm, the weight and speed of horse and rider combined at the moment of impact to help break an enemy's line.[64] The Norman knights are described as bearing 'lances in their hands'[65] and the Bayeux Tapestry shows the Normans running through Anglo-Saxon opponents with 'couched' lance, but on only three occasions, (BT 6, 64, 67).[66] It should also be noted that there does appear to be one horseman shown in the Bayeux Tapestry whose lance *may* be crossed over the neck of his horse in the accepted manner of charging with a 'fully couched' lance (enabling the lance to be more balanced and meaning that charging opponents approach each other shield-side to shield-side). This is the

Figure 25. A detail from the Bayeux Tapestry showing Norman cavalry with lances.

lance held by one of the riders attacking Dinan (BT 20).[67] This could be a misunderstanding on the part of the Tapestry designer, artistic licence, or it could be that at Hastings the Norman cavalry was not facing other similarly mounted and armed forces but infantry and so simply did not need to cross the lance.[68] Maybe the Tapestry is actually capturing the fact a 'new' tactic 'was being developed' and is confused as to how to depict it.[69] The nearside-to-nearside form of mounted combat ascribed to the Normans at Hastings does not appear to have become common, however until the mid-late 12th century, possibly connected to the First Crusade or development of aspects of the tournament, so indeed it would be 'remarkable to see it at this early date' (Pierce, 1988, 245).[70]

Interestingly, whether artistic licence or not, a few of the lances depicted in the Bayeux Tapestry (BT 44, 46, 50 and 53–4) appear to be thicker than others, perhaps an indication of lances for couching and charging with as opposed to just throwing or lunging with.[71] Some also have pennons attached (BT 18, 21, 23, 24, 39, 44, 49, 50, 53, 55, 57, 58, 59, 61), which again indicate that they are not intended to be thrown (Figure 26).

At the opening of the battle the mummer Taillefer is said to have 'pierced the Englishman's shield with his keen lance',[72] and William himself is described at the end of the battle as 'armed … with only the stump of his lance'.[73] A later account of the battle of Hastings describes the effect of 'mounted shock combat':

> A mercenary from France … spurred his horse … raised his shield … and struck one of the Englishmen cleanly with the lance he was holding, beneath the chin, on the chest; the iron passed right through his spine.[74]

And it must not be forgotten that the war-horse itself, a stallion in Western Europe, was a weapon in its own right, bred and trained to flail with its hooves and trample enemies. The charge of heavy cavalry will have had a psychological impact on those opposing it, as well as

AD PRELIVM: CONTRA: HAROL DVM:REGE: HIC

a physical one.[75] It was noted that William's 'charger strikes many a corpse'[76] and another Norman 'using his horse's chest he sent many tumbling that day'.[77] A French mercenary 'on the fine horse turned around ... but encountered an Englishman and shoved him so hard with his horse that he very soon knocked him down and trampled him under foot'.[78]

Figure 26. A detail from the Bayeux Tapestry showing the Norman cavalry with lances that are depicted as being thicker than some of the other lances shown, and two with pennons attached.

Axes

Axes were favoured by the better-armed infantry and are mentioned by chroniclers as a major weapon, with particular reference to the English and the members of the professional royal household known as *huscarls*. Although without doubt predominantly used by the Anglo-Saxons, the axe was also possibly used by some Normans as well (BT 10, 38).[79] The two-handed battle-axe appeared as an important weapon in Scandinavia in about the eighth–ninth century in the form of the 'bearded' axe (*skeggøx* in Norse[80]) used by Vikings and others, which had a curved cutting edge drooping towards the haft, like a beard (Figure 27).

By the tenth century the form had modified slightly and had developed into the broad (*breidøx*) 'Danish' axe (the *hache norresche* of Wace[81]) which was used alongside the bearded axe during the 11th century. The broad axe had a 30 cm (1 ft) broad convex blade with a honed steel-edged cutting edge mounted on a 122–183 cm (4–6 ft) long wooden haft (Figure 28). These distinct edges are possibly depicted in the Bayeux Tapestry where some of these axes have a different-coloured edge (BT 28, 31, 62, 65, 66, 70, 71 and 72).[82] Certainly earlier axes bore descriptive names such as 'Death', 'Ogress of War' and 'The Fiend of the Shield' (which would appear to make reference to its use and effectiveness against the shield, either when used in a group 'shield-wall' or for personal defence).

Figure 27. Two axes, both possibly Viking, 10th–11th century (Royal Armouries AL.10 2 and 1).

Figure 28. Axe-head, possibly Viking, north European, 10th–11th century (Royal Armouries VIII.124). The hardened edge has been welded onto the body of the blade.

Axes were used by Anglo-Saxons at the battle of Hastings to inflict noteworthy and devastating injuries: 'an Englishman with a long-handled axe struck … [a Norman who, ironically, was trying to grab a 'coveted' axe] in the middle of the back, shattering all his bones; one could see all his entrails, his lungs and his innards'.[83] William himself was apparently struck as 'a man … with an axe … charged up with great power and struck the duke on the head, damaging his helmet severely; but he did not wound him greatly'.[84]

Another incident saw 'an Englishman … equipped with … a very fine Norwegian axe, its blade more than a full foot in length … came straight up to a Norman who was armed and on horseback. He intended to strike him on the helmet with his axe of steel, but the blow slipped right past him. The axe, which was very sharp, skidded on the front of the saddle-bows and sliced crossways through the horse's neck, so that the blade of the axe, which was heavy, went right into the ground; the horse fell forward onto the ground along with its master … Normans who saw the blow gasped in amazement.'[85] This illustrates the idea

Figure 29. A detail from the Bayeux Tapestry showing Anglo-Saxon axes in action. Note an axe-head being cut off from the haft.

that the long-hafted axe was used, at least in part, as an anti-cavalry weapon.[86]

However, this fearsome weapon did have a weak point: the haft of an axe is shown in the Bayeux Tapestry being cut through by a sword and the axe-head flying off uselessly (BT 65). It is also interesting to note the expression on the face of the warrior who has just lost his axe-head, as the blow seems to be carrying through to his neck (Figure 29). Such blows would be countered in later centuries by either winding a strip of metal around the haft (as seen on Norwegian 'walking axes' of the 17th century) or by langets (two long metal strips running down the haft from the head) which prevented the head from being cut off. There is no evidence of anything similar being used at this time, although a few axe-heads of the tenth and eleventh centuries do bear decorated metal sockets which may partially have been designed to protect the haft from such blows.[87] However using such a weapon created problems for its wielder, for it was observed that 'a man who intends to strike with an axe cannot give his mind to protecting himself, as he has to hold it in both hands if he wishes to strike with great vigour'[88] and it is legitimate to consider whether axe-men fought as part of small combat groups, supported by fellow warriors.[89]

The long-hafted axe also appears to have been used as a symbol of authority for ceremony and is also associated with rank and status (BT 28). Such axes are depicted three times in the Bayeux Tapestry. Guy of Ponthieu is depicted with such an axe, with a possibly reinforced edge, at one point (BT 10), as is Harold himself (BT 31).[90]

Single-handed axes were also used, and sometimes used as a missile-weapon, as is apparently depicted in the Bayeux Tapestry (BT 62), where an axe, with its head held away from the direction it is to be thrown, appears about to be released (Figure 23).[91] Stylistically this is very similar to the plain hand-axes or hatchets axes used by woodsmen, and this type of axe may also have been used as a form of sidearm, as they were in later centuries. It is probably axes of this sort that were thrown rather than the particular type of throwing axe, developed between 400–500, the *francisca*, so-called because of its use by the Franks. This form of axe was used widely throughout Europe, particularly by Germanic warriors, and may just have remained in use by Anglo-Saxons and others into the 11th century. This is disputed,[92] but even if it did remain in use, it is unlikely to have been common.[93] In any case, William of Poitiers describes how the English at Hastings 'threw … murderous axes',[94] so it seems that axes of one form or another were still being used as a missile weapon at the time of the Conquest.

Clubs and maces

The *mace* was a form of wooden hafted club with a lobated metal (copper alloy or iron) head and appears to have been less common than the sword[95] (Figure 30). The mace was simple and effective; it could be

Figure 30. A detail from the Bayeux Tapestry showing a tri-lobate mace being borne by William.

used to smash and break mail armour, as well as to damage unarmoured flesh and bone: 'the French mercenary seized the bludgeon [mace] that hung on his right arm and struck the other Englishman an upwards blow, shattering and breaking his head'.[96]

They could also be used as missile weapons, as is depicted in the Bayeux Tapestry, where one is shown being thrown through the air, apparently by one of Harold's army (BT 61) (Figure 31). Following the account which states that the Anglo-Saxons 'threw … murderous … stones tied to sticks',[97] one might wonder if this mace-head was actually made of bound stones, but there is no evidence to suggest that true maces had anything but metal heads.

It has been suggested, and is a common misconception, that Bishop Odo used a mace to avoid the shedding of blood.[98] It was, and is, claimed that fighting clerics and bishops only used maces, rather than swords, to allegedly escape the denunciation that 'all they that take the sword shall perish with the sword' (The Bible, Matthew 26:52). As has been pointed out, 'there exists not a single shred of evidence for this charming fabrication'.[99] Sir Walter Scott is sometimes, but incorrectly, blamed for giving rise to this myth and it has also been suggested that the source for this idea was Edward Freeman in his *The History of the Norman Conquest of England* of 1870–9.[100] However the concept was

Figure 31. A detail from the Bayeux Tapestry showing a mace being used as a missile weapon by being thrown against the Normans by an Anglo-Saxon warrior.

widespread well before then: by 1807 it had been noted that 'Otho [Odo] is represented with a mace in his hand … that when he despatched his antagonist, he might not spill blood, but only break his bones'.[101] The right of clergy to bear arms was a complex issue and the church had indeed threatened excommunication for those bearing arms from 1034, but how effective and extensive this ban was is not clear. Odo himself appears to have had no problem with instilling a 'martial reputation'. A now-lost seal, known only from a 17th-century drawing, depicts him in full armour and armed with sword and shield.[102] It would seem that at lower levels, such as diocese, local exigent circumstances dictated when clergy fought, and various bishops and abbots were obviously excluded from any ban. Despite clergy being expressly forbidden to bear arms some 12 times between 1049 and 1079,[103] several, including the Bishop of Cassano (1059), fought without any penalty.[104] In 1069 Bishop Geoffrey of Coutances, who had also been at Hastings, 'marched against [the West Saxons], killed some, captured and mutilated others, and put the rest to flight'.[105] This was a time of belligerent and war-like prelates.

The myth probably does partially derive from the scene in the Bayeux Tapestry (BT 67) in which Odo is depicted (and described) holding a wooden club (particularly described as 'baculu[m]' – 'rod', 'staff' or 'mace'), but it is clearly of a different form to the mace flying through the air and maces depicted elsewhere on the Tapestry. It appears to be a roughly shaped wooden club, still bearing knots or stumps of twigs, and Odo appears to be using it at a moment when some young warriors need encouraging – in other words, as a symbol of leadership and power.[106] Interestingly, William of Poitiers states that Odo, in fact, bore no arms, and this is indeed perhaps what the Bayeux Tapestry shows (Figure 32). William, aside from his half-brother Odo, is the only other person depicted with a similar object (unless it is Robert, William's other half-brother, who is also depicted on the Bayeux Tapestry (BT 54), although the mace borne here appears to have a true tri-lobate head, probably of metal) – and neither of them are using it as a weapon to deliver a blow. William bears such a knobbly wooden club while on campaign; when approaching Mont-St-Michel (BT 18); when questioning Vital (BT 54); with a smooth version again before the battle (BT 57); and during battle, when raising his helmet to be recognised (BT 68).[107] So it is probably not so much a weapon but, again, a signifier of rank, authority or status; more akin to a commander's baton.[108] Certainly by the late Middle Ages maces were indeed a signifier of rank, as well as being weapons, as is shown by an incised slab of a sergeant-at-arms, who bears a mace, of about 1400 at the abbey of Saint-Denis, Paris.[109]

It is also uncertain what three of the retreating unarmoured men at the present end of the Tapestry are holding (BT 73). The mace-heads appear identical in profile to that of the mace seen being thrown through

the air, mentioned above. It is not known if these are just arms or if they signify a form of 'herald' on the way to London to tell of the battle.

Projectile weapons

Bows were commonly used throughout Europe, but were not regarded as an aristocratic weapon in Anglo-Saxon England and so were, perhaps, not seen as an important weapon for the army.[110] William and the Normans, on the other hand, did use the archers who were deployed in the first line of troops.[111] The Bayeux Tapestry shows both Norman and Anglo-Saxon archers at Hastings (Figure 33), 29 in total, though the Anglo-Saxons, who were obviously aware of the bow,[112] seemingly with much fewer; hence there being only one, quiverless, Anglo-Saxon archer depicted in the Bayeux Tapestry (BT 62).[113]

These were self bows, made from a single rounded stave of wood, and this type was used by both Normans and Anglo-Saxons.[114] Yew was often chosen because, uniquely, the 'back' (the side of the bow away from the archer) can be made of the softer sapwood and the 'belly' (the inner side) of heartwood. The more elastic sapwood works under tension, the resilient heartwood under compression, creating a natural spring. When the bow is drawn, both come into play as the bow stores this energy, which is transferred to the arrow as kinetic energy upon release. Arrows with apparently barbed heads are depicted on the Tapestry (BT 60, 62, 68, 69, 70), but this is in seeming contradiction to the surviving archaeology which implies that leaf-shaped heads were used at this time, although barbed heads might have existed and were certainly in use by the late 11th century.[115] The Norman archers at Hastings are all shown with quivers, worn over their shoulders or at the waist (BT 60, 68, 69, 70), which carried their immediate supplies of arrows.[116]

Figure 32. A detail from the Bayeux Tapestry showing William with a 'knobbly' club before Mont-Saint-Michel, with a smooth wooden club or staff when questioning Vital and again with a 'knobbly' club during battle.

Figure 33. Two details from the Bayeux Tapestry showing Norman and Anglo-Saxon archers.

Whether 'longbows' or 'shortbows' were used at Hastings is a debate decades long, and despite the apparent short draw shown in the Tapestry (BT 60, 62, 68, 69, 70) the most recent, definitive, thinking has it that the idea of the 'shortbow' being used at Hastings is nothing more than a 'myth'.[117]

Archaeology would appear to confirm this, too, as although no traces of shortbows have been discovered, longbows have, such as the tenth-century Hedeby bow, which is 192 cm (6 ft) long and made of D-section yew; a longbow by any other name. The difference in proportions to the archers shooting with them is all down to a matter of artistic style and interpretation.[118] It is perhaps also worth noting that one Norman archer is shown, spurred, mounted, pursuing the fleeing Anglo-Saxons (BT 72–3) and another Norman archer is shown armoured, perhaps signifying rank (BT 60).

It is said that William 'placed foot-soldiers in front, armed with arrows and cross-bows'.[119] The battle seemingly opened with a one-sided archery duel: 'First the [Norman] infantry units, furnished with quivers, attack and from afar transfix their bodies with their darts'.[120] Wace goes further, describing how the archers shot and their effectiveness: 'The archers adopted this plan, and shot high above the English. When the arrows came back down they fell onto their heads, piercing their heads and their faces, and putting out the eyes of many of them;

they did not dare open their eyes or reveal their faces. Arrows flew more densely than raindrops in the wind; they flew very thickly and the English called them mosquitoes [*wibetes*].'[121]

The crossbow had been known in the west since at least the first century AD and, although recorded at sieges such as Senlis (947), it appears to have been little used on the battlefield until Verdun (985).[122] The Normans were using crossbows before 1060, when a 'Fulcher the crossbower' is mentioned.[123] The lath of the bow would have been made of wood, and the bowstring of early crossbows was drawn back until caught and held by a notch cut into the upper surface of the 'tiller' until pushed out by a peg attached to a simple trigger. They shot a short, thick, iron-headed wooden arrow; a 'bolt' or 'quarrel' which was no doubt capable of piercing mail armour. Although there are no references to the Anglo-Saxons using crossbows it is clear that the Normans used them during the Hastings campaign, for at least two sources mention their use, despite them not being depicted in the Bayeux Tapestry: 'He [William] placed foot-soldiers in front, armed with ... cross-bows',[124] and 'He put in front the infantry to attack with arrows, and set crossbowmen in their midst so that their flying weapons should hit the enemy in the face ... Against quarrels shields are not secure' and 'Crossbowmen, with a shower of blows like a storm of hail, strike and destroy shields'.[125] The *Carmen*, in particular, also states that the crossbows shot square-headed bolts.[126] It is quite apparent that the role of the Norman archers at Hastings was as important as any other section of the Norman army, such as the cavalry, if not more so.

Slings were known for hunting, and although the Saxons may not have used them in battle,[127] the Normans possibly did.[128] They probably had a range of over 80 m (87 yards), and their Anglo-Saxon name *liðere* may indicate that they were made from leather.[129]

Fire could, of course, be – and was – used as both a weapon of 'mass destruction', as in the besieging of a military wooden motte and bailey castle (such as Dinan, BT 23), and also as an indiscriminate 'terror' weapon when burning down domestic dwellings, such as houses, and the driving out of civilians (BT 50). This use of fire ('hIC DOMVS INCENDITVR') is also noted when William, having 'invaded the land, wastes it and sets it on fire',[130] which has been seen as an act of provocation.[131]

One cannot leave the Battle of Hastings and the weapons used during the Conquest without making a passing reference to the death of King Harold. Whether by arrow, lance or sword, or a combination, his death was no doubt bloody.[132] One account, which to a degree matches the death of Harold as depicted on the Bayeux Tapestry (BT 71), has a group of four Norman knights, including William, kill him:

> The first of the four, piercing the king's shield and chest with his lance, drenched the ground with a gushing stream of blood; the

second with his sword cut off his head below the protection of his helm. The third liquefied his entrails with his spear [lance]. And the fourth cut off his thigh and carried it some distance away.[133]

This has been described as being too detailed and, therefore, in effect, an 'embroidered' fictional account. But it is not impossible; the thigh cutting is quite possibly a euphemism for cutting off Harold's genitals.[134] Mutilation of the dead on the medieval battlefield has been observed on some of the dead of Towton (1461) and on the skeleton of Richard III from Bosworth (1485), so this should not be regarded as fanciful. We simply do not know for certain, however, how Harold was slain, and we probably never will – unless the skeleton of Harold is found – though the 'arrow in the eye' tradition has become increasingly less convincing.[135] Until then the discussions over how he died will continue.

There can be no doubt that medieval weapons resulted in bloody and violent deaths and perhaps in the future some of the mass graves of the Normans may give up the grim evidence of the effectiveness of the weapons of the Conquest.

5

Myths and mysteries of the Bayeux Tapestry

Michael Lewis

The Bayeux Tapestry is among the most important sources for understanding the events leading to the Norman Conquest of England in 1066. It also provides insights into 11th-century material culture, and is undoubtedly one of the most significant monuments of medieval art, rightly celebrated for its craftsmanship, inventive storytelling and aesthetic appeal.[1] William Stukeley, onetime secretary of the Society of Antiquaries of London, was surely correct in his assertion that the Bayeux Tapestry is 'indubitably the noblest monument of English antiquity abroad': the question of its origin will be discussed in due course.[2]

The imagery of the Bayeux Tapestry is instantly recognisable to most. Its key scenes, such as the oath Harold made before Duke William (Scene 23), and its depictions of the Anglo-Saxon shield-wall during the Battle of Hastings (52), as well as King Harold's brutal death (57), are memorable. Other parts, such as its illustrations of the Breton campaign (16–22), William's harrying of Harold's lands in Sussex (40–1), and some of the border imagery, are less well known. Even those who have studied the Tapestry in detail notice new things every time they see it. Indeed, while the work appears to be a relatively simple creation, its imagery is actually pretty complex.

Besides being an important tourist attraction (about 400,000 people go Bayeux every year to see the Tapestry), this medieval masterpiece is also extensively marketed beyond France, having a special appeal to the English and many in the English-speaking world. There is no lack of imagination in those who use the Tapestry's imagery to sell objects of all kinds, including mobile phone covers, mugs, pens, clothing (including very tight leggings, reminiscent of the Tapestry's trousered garments), and books! In short, the Tapestry offers the town of Bayeux, and numerous other enterprises, massive commercial benefits and popular exposure.

Not only has the Bayeux Tapestry been exploited as a source of revenue, but it has also offered an opportunity for those seeking political benefit. In 1803, Napoleon Bonaparte had the Tapestry moved to the Musée Napoléon, Paris, for public display, to rouse popular support in advance of his planned invasion of England.[3] Following the fall of Normandy (during World War II), the occupying forces became intrigued by the Tapestry, not least because of its perceived links to Germanic culture;[4] Rollo, the first duke of Normandy (c.918), was a Viking. Although this interest seems perverse today, the research team that studied the Tapestry from 1941 was of high academic calibre, though the results of its study are still largely unknown. More recently, the Tapestry has been used, predominately as a visual tool, to comment on Britain's relationship with Europe, particularly the French. It is part of the English consciousness that Anglo-Saxon England was (somehow) more egalitarian than under the 'French' rule that followed. This rebellious spirit, harking back to 1066, was evoked by chief Brexiteers during the 2016 referendum of Britain's membership of the European Union: Nigel Farage (then UK Independence Party leader) occasionally sported a Bayeux Tapestry tie, and Boris Johnson (formerly Mayor of London, latterly British Foreign Secretary) said, of then Prime Minister David Cameron's attempts to coax business to openly praise the success of his negotiations with EU leaders to get a 'better deal for Britain', that it was 'the biggest stitch-up since the Bayeux Tapestry'.[5] Ironically, this excitement over '1066 and all that' is not widely shared by the French, who generally see the Norman Conquest of England as a historical sideshow, relevant only to the history of provincial Normandy.

'The biggest-stitch up' in the tale of the Bayeux Tapestry is in fact that it is not a tapestry at all, but embroidery-work. Almost every scholar who has written on the subject has highlighted the absurdity of this error, but accepted that to call it by any other name now would be pedantic.[6] The object was created by sewing woollen thread onto linen, using two main stitches: an 'outline stitch' for creating the outline of the figures, animals and objects, and 'laid-and-couch work' for filling in spaces with colour, a stitch (the 'Bayeux stitch') which appears to be unique to the Bayeux Tapestry.[7]

There is an additional problem with the embroidery's name, for the work is unlikely to have been made in Bayeux. This is not to deny the town of Bayeux a special role in the Tapestry's story, or indeed the history of the Bayeux Tapestry itself. Bayeux (spelt *Bagias*) is mentioned once in the textile (Figure 1), when Duke William is shown leading Earl Harold, under custody, back to his palace, probably at Rouen (14): in 1064 Harold had come to Normandy, by apparent accident ending up on the shores of territory controlled by Count Guy of Ponthieu, a vassal of Duke William of Normandy, who subsequently handed Harold over to his lord. It is also known that the Tapestry was displayed in Bayeux cathedral by 1476, where it is listed in an inventory of its treasures. Here it is described as 'a very long and very narrow strip of linen,

Figure 1. Bayeux, as shown in the Bayeux Tapestry.

embroidered with figures and inscriptions representing the Conquest of England, which is hung around the nave of the church on the Feast of Relics and throughout the Octave'.[8] It is not known when this tradition began or ended, but it was in Bayeux that the Tapestry was rediscovered in the early 18th century. Bernard de Montfaucon, a Benedictine monk, traced it down following antiquarian interest in a drawing of part of the Tapestry, albeit no one knew what the drawing showed, exactly, or even that it was an embroidery.[9] It is likely, therefore, that the embroidery had come to Bayeux in the Middle Ages and never left the place until the modern era.

The question of who made the Bayeux Tapestry has troubled historians most. Truthfully, we can only surmise who lay behind the inception of the embroidery, based on rather scant evidence and deductions influenced by a modern view of the medieval world. Originally it was believed that the Tapestry was made by William's queen, Matilda, and her ladies-in-waiting (Figure 2).[10] There is nothing much to support this theory, apart from it being known that Matilda gave gifts to her husband – including the Mora, his flag-ship for the Conquest (see below) – and that it is known that some embroiderers were royal women: for example, the *Vita Ædwardi Regis* records that Queen Edith, wife to Edward the Confessor, embroidered garments for her husband.[11] Until quite recently, signs in Bayeux guided visitors to *La Tapisserie de la Reine Mathilde*, showing this tradition to be firmly established, at least in the public consciousness. Matilda's name stuck, even when some historians questioned an 11th-century date for the Tapestry's manufacture; in 1769, Lord Lyttleton proposed that the Tapestry was made upon the orders of the Empress Matilda (1102–67),[12] a view still being supported some 40 years later.[13]

Figure 2. Queen Matilda
embroidering the Bayeux
Tapestry. Alfred Guillard,
La Reine Mathilde
travaillant à la 'Telle du
Conquest', coll. MAHB.

Nowadays most historians agree that the Bayeux Tapestry was
commissioned by Duke William's maternal half-brother, Bishop Odo of
Bayeux. It is a theory first proposed by Honoré François Delauney in
1824,[14] though mostly sustained by circumstantial evidence.

Odo was born in about 1032/3, the child of the marriage of Herluin
de Conteville and Herleva, mistress to Duke Robert I of Normandy,
Duke William's father. When Odo was about 18 years old, William
bestowed the bishopric of Bayeux on him, and subsequently the
earldom of Kent.[15] These two positions afforded Odo great wealth,[16]
also helping to sustain the belief that the Bayeux Tapestry was produced
for the consecration of Bayeux cathedral in 1077.[17]

It has been argued that the Tapestry has an 'Odonian view of the
Conquest'.[18] It is certainly the case that Odo has a central role in the
embroidery, unlike that in any other surviving account of the Conquest.
Although he first appears quite late in the story, Odo's impact on the

narrative is unmistakable: he advises William to build his fleet (Scene 35), says grace at the banquet after the landing (43), dominates the subsequent council of war (44), and in a critical moment of battle rallies deserters (54). Also shown in the Tapestry are three named individuals believed to be Odo's men: Turold (10), Wadard (41) and Vital (49).[19] Their occurrence advocates the hypothesis that Odo, or someone close to him, was fundamental to the Tapestry's inception.

One of the most important scenes in the Bayeux Tapestry is the moment 'where Harold made an oath [upon holy relics] to Duke William' (Scene 23). The embroidery says nothing about the circumstances of this oath, but it is clear this event became 'the crux of the Norman claim to the English throne'.[20] Harold, whether under duress or not, agreed to help William succeed Edward the Confessor as king of the English; an oath he subsequently broke. It is significant that the Tapestry places this oath at Bayeux, whereas other sources suggest Bonneville or Rouen.[21] Given Bayeux was Odo's episcopal seat, this is surely no coincidence, though it is intriguing that Odo himself is not present in the Tapestry's illustration of this event.[22]

Not all agree that Odo was the patron of the Bayeux Tapestry. Most recently it has been proposed that the embroidery was created by the community of monks at St Augustine's Abbey, Canterbury, as a commemorative piece.[23] This theory also helps explain why the Tapestry names individuals from Kent, associated with Odo, and also the profound impact late Anglo-Saxon Canterbury illumination has upon the work (to be discussed shortly). Another submission is that Edward's queen, Edith, commissioned the Tapestry while at the nunnery of Wilton.[24] She is an interesting hypothesis as it is known that Edith successfully attempted to immortalise the memory of her husband, and blood kin, in the *Vita Ædwardi Regis*. Others have put forward the case that Eustace of Boulogne,[25] or even Archbishop Stigand,[26] initiated the Tapestry, though these suggestions have received little scholarly support. The fact remains that for many Odo is the prime candidate responsible for the Tapestry's inception.

Alluded to above, and impossible to dislocate from the question of who commissioned the Bayeux Tapestry, is where the embroidery was made. At the time of the Norman Conquest the English were renowned for their textile work; William of Poitiers recognised this skill, recording that 'the women of the English people are very skilled in needlework and weaving gold thread'.[27] There is an assumption, therefore, that a product such as the Bayeux Tapestry is likely to have been made by the Anglo-Saxons, but there are a variety of textiles from across Europe with which it can be broadly likened in design and style. Examples regularly cited include examples from Baldishol, Oseberg, Rolvsøy and Røn (all Norway), albeit most are later in date than the Bayeux textile.[28] Also noted is a poem of Baudri, abbot of Bourgueil, which refers to an embroidery, seemingly much like the Bayeux Tapestry but worked

Figure 3. The feast scene in the Bayeux Tapestry (Scene 42). Copyright of Cambridge Corpus Christi College.

with gold thread and encrusted with jewels.[29] Its existence suggests that such hangings showing historic events were once relatively common, to which could be added the embroidery commemorating the death of Earl Byrhtnoth at the Battle of Maldon (991), gifted to Ely Cathedral.[30] Extant examples of Anglo-Saxon textile work are rare, however, but most famous (besides the Bayeux Tapestry) is the stole, girdle and man-iple worked upon the orders of Queen Ælfflæd, wife of Edward the Elder, for Bishop Frithestan of Winchester, later deposited in the tomb of St Cuthbert at Durham.[31]

Central to the belief that the Bayeux Tapestry was made in England is the similarities it has, in terms of both design and style, with Anglo-Saxon art, particularly manuscript illuminations associated with Canterbury.[32] By the 11th century it was common for artists to copy one another and borrow motifs from other art forms; the example *par excellence* is the *Harley 603 Psalter* and its derivatives, which was a copy of the Carolingian *Utrecht Psalter*.[33] In very general terms the Tapestry evokes 'the spirit' of late Anglo-Saxon art, especially in terms of the vigour and expressiveness of the human form.[34] More signifi-cant, some of the embroidery's imagery seems to be directly borrowed from manuscripts likely to be in Canterbury at the time the Tapestry was produced. Preeminent in this respect is the *Old English Hexateuch*, which shares with the Bayeux embroidery a depiction of bird-scaring (Scene 10) and an escape scene (18), besides other images that are more superficially alike.[35] Also significant is the depiction of the Last Supper in the *St Augustine's Gospels* (a late sixth-century Italian manuscript, owned by St Augustine's Abbey, Canterbury, at the time of the Norman Conquest), which parallels to an extraordinary degree the Norman feast scene in the Tapestry (43) (Figure 3).[36] Important in placing the

production of the Tapestry at Canterbury is an otherwise inconspicuous drawing of a 'labourer' carrying a 'coil' in a late tenth-century copy of *Prudentius' Psychomachia*, owned by Christ Church, Canterbury, a motif which is then replicated in the Bayeux Tapestry (41); other, earlier, manuscripts of the *Psychomachia* appear to show the figure carrying a boulder, suggesting that the Tapestry designer copied an error first produced in the Canterbury manuscript.[37]

Besides these exact parallels, it is evident that the Tapestry's images have commonality with many drawings in Anglo-Saxon manuscripts of the late tenth and early eleventh centuries. In addition to the *Old English Hexateuch* might be highlighted *Junius 11*, which also has an extensive illustrated narrative sequence.[38] Such illuminations are not as common as might be expected. This is an important consideration, as many more manuscripts with rich picture cycles are likely to have been in circulation during the late Anglo-Saxon period than exist today, and therefore our deductions using only those that survive nowadays might be misleading.

Although it is the Tapestry's imagery which captivates the viewer, a crucial component of the work is its Latin inscription. This was almost certainly produced at the same time as the visual narrative: it was not an afterthought, though it has (partly) been restored, sometimes imprecisely. The brevity of the inscription is frustrating, adding little detail to the Tapestry's story, and its Latin is by no means perfect, inconsistent in both spellings and grammar. The Tapestry's inscriptions add credence to the view it is an Anglo-Saxon work. Old English letter forms include Ð, Æ and the Tironian 'et'. It is also generally agreed that proper names are mostly spelt in an English way,[39] though some Norman forms also occur. Such a coexistence of English and French features is perhaps to be expected in a work of the Anglo-Norman period.[40] Indeed, while multi-coloured script, such as that found in the latter part of the Tapestry, is more pronounced in Norman manuscripts, the use of inscriptions with pictorial matter is better represented in English art.[41]

Although the evidence strongly suggests that the Bayeux Tapestry was made in England, probably at Canterbury, some scholars have argued otherwise. Noted are the Tapestry's stylistic similarities to 'French' art, especially illuminations created at Mont-Saint-Michel and Saint-Vaast.[42] This has led to the hypothesis that the embroidery was manufactured in Normandy, or even further afield, such as at the abbey of Saint-Florent of Saumur in the Loire Valley.[43] There is no doubt that the Bayeux embroidery should be studied much more within the wider sphere of European art than has hitherto been the case. Complicating factors are, however, that Anglo-Saxon art was to have a profound impact abroad, and that the potential influence of 'French' art upon the Bayeux Tapestry has not been as closely considered as those from Anglo-Saxon England, particularly Canterbury. It is also known there was much movement of people and books between religious communities across Europe.

Probably influential in the context of the production of the Bayeux Tapestry was the arrival at St Augustine's, Canterbury, in about 1072, of Abbot Scotland, previously a monk of Mont-Saint-Michel.[44] The circular nature of this argument (whether the Bayeux Tapestry was made in England because it can be likened to Anglo-Saxon art, or that it was made in France on the basis of the influence of Anglo-Saxon art abroad) has been expounded recently, specifically in the context of an inherent bias in the survival of illuminated manuscripts from Canterbury over other scriptoria.[45]

It is likely that the Bayeux Tapestry was made soon after the events it depicts, almost certainly before the death of Bishop Odo of Bayeux (in 1097), and quite possibly before his imprisonment in 1082, when – for reasons which are unclear, but which may have been linked with his attempts to intervene in papal politics – he fell out of favour with his half-brother; this argument assumes Odo's involvement with the Tapestry's production. If it is also the case that Abbot Scotland helped facilitate the Bayeux Tapestry's production, then it is likely to have been produced after about 1072, perhaps in time for the consecration of Bayeux cathedral five years later: although several scholars have questioned whether the Tapestry's imagery made it suitable for display in a religious context – suggesting instead that it might better suit a secular setting, like a great hall in a castle[46] – it is known that by the 15th century this was not an issue (it was on display in Bayeux Cathedral).

It is commonly believed that the Tapestry was produced as a political tool, essentially being pro-Norman – 'little more than a mendacious propaganda "strip-cartoon" designed to justify William's unjustifiable invasion of England'.[47] This view is clearly an oversimplification, which fails to fully appreciate nuances within the work itself, or consider the Tapestry's narrative alongside other contemporary accounts of the Conquest.[48] Still, the embroidery leaves no doubt that Duke William was the victor of Hastings, and (as highlighted above) also shows Bishop Odo of Bayeux in a favourable light. It might be presumed that that Harold is the Tapestry's anti-hero, but he is perhaps better seen as an unfortunate victim of circumstances he could not fully control.

It is not known exactly why Harold went to Normandy in about 1064, or why he landed in the county of Count Guy of Ponthieu, but it is obvious his arrival was not expected. Almost as soon as he lands, the Tapestry (Scene 7) shows him being seized by Guy's men; Harold's futile attempt to defend himself with a small knife highlights his impossible situation (Figure 4). The English Earl then becomes a pawn in a political game, not only within the context of the succession crisis of 1066, but also within the political sphere of Normandy and its continental neighbours. When 'Harold and Guy talk' (9), presumably at Beaurain, the swords of the two men serve to highlight their relative predicament: Guy's sword points upwards, showing him to have the upper hand over his illustrious prisoner, whereas Harold holds his sword before him, pointing

Figure 4. Harold being arrested by Count Guy of Ponthieu's men (Scene 7).

downwards, sheathed and still attached to the sword-belt, its effect-iveness as a weapon muted. Be that as it may, Guy is required to hand over his prize to William (12–3), and for Harold his situation becomes even more ominous. Although Harold is later knighted by William in recognition of his deeds during the Breton campaign, the scene (21) only serves to highlight that he is William's man. This position of apparent vassalage is cemented when Harold swears upon holy relics at Bayeux (23), presumably offering to help William succeed to the English throne upon King Edward's death, though whether that is the case is uncertain. Although Harold's predicament is often stark, the Tapestry designer is nonetheless sensitive to Harold's status. For example, even when the English Earl is escorted as a prisoner (Scene 13) he is shown riding a horse and holding a hawk, signifiers of his rank.[49] Likewise, Harold's piety is not questioned. At Bosham (3), Harold and a companion are shown entering the church to pray before his crossing to Normandy; though it does not seem his prayers, presumably for a safe voyage, were granted. Harold also undertakes great feats of bravery, such as on campaign against the Bretons (17), when he rescues at least two Normans from drowning in the waters of the Couesnon, the river that divides Normandy from Brittany.

Unlike the 'Norman sources', notably William of Poitiers and William of Jumièges, the Bayeux Tapestry recognises that Harold was a legit-imate king.[50] He appears to be nominated by Edward as his successor (Scene 27), following the account in the *Vita Ædwardi Regis*.[51] He is then shown being chosen by the Witan to rule (29) and is then crowned king (30), albeit by an archbishop (Stigand) whose eligibility to officiate has been questioned:[52] it is intriguing that Archbishop Ealdred of York is not shown. With the benefit of hindsight, the Tapestry also foretells

Figure 5. Women and child flee a burning house in the Bayeux Tapestry (Scene 47).

Harold's impending doom. A fiery star (known to us as Halley's Comet) is seen in the sky (32), interpreted by contemporaries as a portent of bad fortune, with a ghostly fleet below: scholars normally interpret these ships as a premonition of the Norman invasion fleet, but they might also be understood as part of the Anglo-Saxon defence fleet, stationed off the Isle of Wight.[53] Often overlooked is the fact that the Tapestry shows Harold dying a hero's death (57). Like in other Anglo-Saxon epics, such as *Beowulf* and *The Battle of Maldon*, Harold stands his ground with his men, joining them in death.

The historical accuracy of the Bayeux Tapestry has been questioned,[54] perhaps unfairly, since perceptions of 'truth' and 'accuracy' in the modern sense are likely to have been very different in the past: take, for example, the tradition of medieval saints' hagiographies, where deeds described seem incredulous to us today.

The Tapestry, nonetheless, does not hold back in its account of the brutality of war; both men and animals are hacked apart, and innocent suffering is depicted, epitomised by a women and child fleeing a burning house (Scene 47) (Figure 5). It also shows key moments in the battle collaborated by other sources, including rumours of William's death (55), the 'malfosse incident' (53) – where Normans pursuing the fleeing English became mired in boggy ground – and the brutality of Harold's death (57). The Tapestry supports our understanding of the tactics used by both sides, including how the Anglo-Saxons defended themselves within a shield-wall on higher ground (52–3), that the Normans deployed archers (55–6) and cavalry (48–58), and that they also attempted 'feigned flight' (54) to encourage the English to break ranks.[55] The bloody aftermath of battle is recorded, especially the pursuing of the defeated (58) and the looting of the dead (56–7).

Some key events in the Bayeux Tapestry, nonetheless, remain ambiguous. As noted before, the Tapestry is silent on the reasons for Harold's journey to Normandy in 1064. Its opening scene (1) shows King Edward, enthroned, speaking to two men, one of whom – though smaller than the other – is (presumably) Harold. All the Tapestry's inscription tells us is that Harold 'and his soldiers' ride to Bosham, and then (after visiting the church and feasting) they 'sailed the sea … to the land of Count Guy'. No other reasons for the voyage are given. Similar is the scene (15) showing Ælfgyva, within an arch, being touched on the face by a cleric. Although many scholars have tried to interpret the

Figure 6. William tilts back his helmet to show he is alive in the Bayeux Tapestry (Scene 55).

scene,[56] it remains an enigma, though is likely to relate to a well-known sexual scandal of the time; mimicking the priest's pose is a naked individual in the lower border.

Occasionally the Bayeux Tapestry recounts events in a way that suggests they were directly borrowed from other contemporary sources. William of Poitiers describes how, during the Battle of Hastings, Duke William uncovers his head to show that he is alive amid rumours of his death: 'having uncovered his head and taken off his helmet, [William] shouted "Look at me! I am alive, and will be the victor, with God's help!"'.[57] This scene (55) is clearly shown in the Tapestry, where William tilts back his helmet to reveal his face (Figure 6). Earlier, when the Norman fleet crosses the Channel to England, the embroidery illustrates a ship with a cross-shaped motif at its mast, and a figure (or figure-head) at its stern blowing a horn (38). Because the ship stands out from the others it has been identified as the *Mora*, given to William by his wife, Matilda.[58] Again, William of Poitiers seems to describe what we see in the Tapestry: 'the Duke issued verbal orders … that the ships were to be at anchor close to him … until they should see a lantern lit at the masthead, and then at the sound of a trumpet at once set course'.[59] It is not altogether clear, however, whether the masthead motif is a lantern; it was once suggested that this is the papal banner given by Pope Alexander II in support of William's expedition.[60]

At other times, the Bayeux Tapestry seems to illustrate events as told in the English sources. Of particular note is the scene (25) where Edward appears to admonish Harold on his return to England from Normandy.[61] The Tapestry's inscription only says that Harold 'came to King Edward', but its imagery shows Harold stooping apologetically and Edward pointing at him.[62] It parallels the story told by Eadmer's *Historia Novorum*, where he makes it clear that Edward was not impressed that Harold had agreed to help William become king: Edward saying to him, '"Did I not tell you that I knew William, and that you going [to Normandy] might bring calamity upon this kingdom!"'.[63]

One of the most remarkable occasions where the Bayeux Tapestry parallels another contemporary source is in its account of King Edward's death bequest. The embroidery shows Edward's demise in two parts of the same building (Scenes 27–8), with its imagery reflecting conventions found in some late Anglo-Saxon illustrated narrative sequences.[64] The upper scene (27) shows Edward terminally ill in bed, with a figure helping the king to sit, an ecclesiastic performing the last rights, Harold touching hands with Edward, and a female figure, presumed to be Harold's sister (Edward's queen) Edith, weeping at the foot of the bed. The same scene appears to be described in the *Vita Ædwardi Regis*, which it is believed was commissioned by Edith herself: 'He [Edward] addressed his last words to the queen [Edith] ... and stretching forth his hand to his governor, her brother, Harold, he said, "I commend this woman and all the kingdom to your protection"'.[65] It is these words that support the view held by many that even if Edward had promised William the kingdom previously, his death bed wish was that Harold was to rule instead.[66]

There are times when the Bayeux Tapestry's account is at odds with events as described in other contemporary sources. A particularly intriguing anomaly is its account of the Breton campaign, of which an extraordinary ten per cent of the embroidery is dedicated to this apparent sideshow of Anglo-Norman history (Scenes 16–21).[67] In the Tapestry, Harold joins William on campaign to root out the Breton rebel Conan, driving him from place to place across Brittany until he surrenders at Dinan: Conan is shown handing over the keys of the town to Duke William (20) (Figure 7). The only other account of this campaign is offered by William of Poitiers, who records a less comprehensive victory for the Norman Duke.[68] According to Poitiers, Duke William decided to not pursue the fleeing rebel, but instead ended his campaign at Dol; the Tapestry shows a wonderful scene (18) of Conan escaping from Dol, almost certainly inspired by a drawing in the *Old English Hexatuech* (discussed above). In support of his view that the Tapestry was made at Saint-Florent of Saumur, George Beech has argued that its 'artist presents a more complete and more accurate story of what happened than did William of Poitiers', but this view has gained little scholarly support.[69]

Given that the Breton campaign receives significant attention in the Bayeux Tapestry, it is surprising that some important events from the English perspective are excluded. Nothing is said of the Norwegian invasion of northern England by Harald Hardrada, supported by Harold's

Figure 7. Conan surrenders Dinan to Duke William, in the Bayeux Tapestry (Scene 20).

brother, Tostig Godwineson. Tostig had been Earl of Northumbria (1055–65), but had been banished by King Edward following rebellion against his rule over the Northumbrians.[70] Blaming Harold for his demise (Harold's negotiations with the rebels, on Edward's behalf, had led to Tostig being ousted), Tostig had gone to Flanders (perhaps also to Normandy), then Scotland, to seek support for a forceful return to England, before joining forces with King Harald, one of the most notable warriors of his age. The Norwegian invasion of Northumbria had gone well, with defeat of the northern earls Edwin of Mercia and Morcar of Northumbria at Fulford Gate (20 September 1066) before taking the city of York. Moving to Stamford Bridge and setting up camp there, the invaders were surprised five days later by King Harold (Godwinson), whose army decimated the Norwegians; both Harald and Tostig were killed along with so many men that only 24 ships were needed to take the survivors home.

Neither does the Tapestry recount the plans King Harold made to defend the south coast of England from potential Norman invasion, perhaps only represented by the Tapestry's ghostly fleet, noted earlier. It is known that he had a naval fleet stationed off the Isle of Wight for many months during the summer, but then disbanded it when provisions became short and it was deemed unlikely that an invading army would cross the Channel.[71] It was in fact the case that it had proved a disaster for William moving ships from Dives to Saint-Valéry-sur-Somme. Some of the fleet was lost and news of the fatalities had to be suppressed.[72]

The richness of the Tapestry's visual narrative, and the fact that it is a primary source in its own right, has been used to develop accounts not fully apparent in historical sources. The most famous example is its interpretation of Harold's death – by an arrow in the eye (Scene 57). The Tapestry's inscription records 'here King Harold was killed' and below him is shown two men: the first, below (and dividing) the word *Harold*, apparently clasping an arrow that has struck his face; and to the right, beneath *interfectus est*, a man with an axe falling backwards beneath a mounted knight. It is generally thought that both men are Harold, shown sequentially, as in a modern-day cartoon.[73] It is apparent, however, that over time the Tapestry has been successively restored,[74] and antiquarian drawings of this scene (such as Montfaucon 1730 and Lancelot 1733) indicate that the figure with an arrow in his eye might have once held a spear; this seems to be corroborated by the reverse of the embroidery, which clearly shows stitching holes of a longer object. By 1812 Charles Stothard's facsimile drawings of the Tapestry illustrate the lance as an arrow, and this (it seems) was the inspiration of those who repaired this scene, probably during the late 19th century; Stothard probably reconstructed this scene based on the tradition of Harold's death rather than on any other evidence. Martin Foys examined sources describing Harold's death by an arrow, suggesting the tradition dates to about the 12th century.[75] It seems, therefore, that Harold did not die from an arrow to an eye, but was hacked to death as described in the earliest accounts of his death. It might still be that both figures in the Tapestry are Harold, but only the latter shows his destruction.

Occasionally considered by scholars of the Bayeux Tapestry is the role of art in its narrative. Although the Tapestry appears cartoon-like, its narrative techniques are greatly influenced by those used in early medieval art, especially manuscript illuminations. Mostly the embroidery reads from left to right, as might be expected, but occasionally scenes are reversed for special effect; a well-known example is the reversal of the scenes (26–8) showing the death and burial of Edward the Confessor, so that there is a clearer visual link between the scene of the King's death and the Witan choosing Harold as his successor (29). It is also the case that trees, and sometimes buildings, are used to divide scenes from one another, ensuring the narrative is compartmentalised and easier to understand.[76]

Nothing is known about the relationship between the Tapestry's patron and designer, nor between the designer and the embroiderers, nor even about the design process itself. Although we do not know the terms of the commission, it might be supposed that the designer would have worked to a basic, even detailed, design concept, which was written or verbal. It seems probable that this reflected instructions from the patron, though if this was Bishop Odo it appears it was not as strong as it could have been: take, for example, his lack of presence during the oath scene (see above). The designer, it seems, had 'a fair degree of freedom to select and mould the material according to the canons of his own art and style':[77] while he was clearly influenced by contemporary art, particularly late Anglo-Saxon illuminations, he also shows ingenuity and inventive.

It is well known that the Tapestry designer used certain 'cultural' attributes to distinguish between the Anglo-Saxons and Normans,[78] particularly in the early part of the embroidery. It can be seen, for example, that many Anglo-Saxons have moustaches, while the Normans have a shaved-back hairstyle. Intriguingly, these motifs are phased out, with the design becoming simplified, perhaps in order to save time or money.[79] The scene-numbering that was added to the backing cloth (perhaps in the 1840s) functions as an index to this; most of the individual scenes occur in the first three (of its nine) sections of the Tapestry, accounting for 60 per cent of its scenes in about 40 per cent of its length.[80] Similarly, the designer also uses certain artefact types to distinguish between the Anglo-Saxons and Normans, especially in scenes of confused battle.[81] Typically identified with the English are axes and round-shields, whereas the Normans are only mounted in battle scenes, and it is they who are mostly armed with the bow. These 'rules' are not always followed, but they certainly enable the viewer to distinguish between the two sides, especially given that otherwise Anglo-Saxons and Normans wear similar dress and armour.

Certain attributes are also used to identify individuals of status.[82] For example, the horse is used to highlight the Anglo-Saxon elite; this is not the case for Normans, who are shown using the horse in war. Persons of rank are also portrayed wearing cloaks, pinned by brooches, which in reality must have been worn by a greater social strata.[83] As might be expected, the elite are often shown taller than those around them, and their garments sometimes are embellished, mimicking embroidery.[84] Some of these conventions also appear in late Anglo-Saxon art, but it is apparent that the Tapestry designer uses a greater variety of attributes, and with a larger degree of inventiveness, than his contemporaries.[85]

Significant embroidery errors in the Bayeux Tapestry, such as the failed rendering of the sail of a ship in Scene 5,[86] provide evidence that the designer was not much involved during the embroidery stage, else surely such errors would have been corrected. The embroidery was almost certainly undertaken by Anglo-Saxon women, whereas the design was undoubtedly the work of a man. He could have been English or Norman, though the former is probably more likely.[87] The close relationship between the Tapestry and late Anglo-Saxon illuminations strongly suggests that the designer, probably a cleric, visited various religious libraries to copy drawings from manuscripts, probably compiling them in a model-book. The designer would have then marked his design (even if rudimentary) onto the Tapestry's linen for the embroiderers to follow, perhaps using charcoal; to this day there are outline drawings on the embroidery,[88] though these are antiquarian, probably to inform restoration.

It is not known where the Bayeux Tapestry was made, but it must have been in a workshop accustomed to embroidery work. The fact that it was constructed of nine individual lengths of linen (which have been joined together), and that some artefacts, attributes and motifs appear to be particular to certain lengths, has given rise to the theory that individual parts were made in distinct workshops.[89] The design has a completeness and continuity in style, however, which indicates otherwise. It seems likely that the Tapestry was made by a single embroidery team, working systematically from left to right. Some embroiderers would even have worked on the design upside down,[90] giving rise to errors.[91] The use of one team would have had time implications, suggested by the fact that the design becomes simplified.

An aspect of the Tapestry's design that divides scholarly opinion is the relationship between its main frieze and borders.[92] Several commentators have contended that the borders provided additional gloss or commentary on events in the main frieze,[93] whilst others considered them primarily decorative.[94] For the most part, the borders show paired beasts, both animals and birds, but also fantastic creatures, either facing or looking away from each another. At times, a beast or pairing is less usual, suggesting that the placing is purposeful; a good example is where two peacocks are illustrated (above, 14) where William and Harold first meet, and is hence analogous of their discussions.[95] Even the paired beasts in the borders do not relate directly to events in the main frieze, though the fact that they bite and fight one another certainly fits in well with the violent nature of the Tapestry's narrative. Several sequences in the borders appear to be adaptations of Aesop's fables.[96] Even if these were added principally for decoration, their significance as stories of cunning and betrayal should not be underestimated, even if it is often unclear which fables are represented. Shown also are scenes of agricultural life (10), such as ploughing and sowing, almost certainly borrowed from manuscript calendar illustrations,[97] but why they were chosen is not altogether clear.[98] Some scenes, such as that of Ælfgyva and a cleric (15), demonstrate that, at times, the borders directly reflect upon events in the main frieze. Other naked individuals are shown (13, 48), but it is not known how they might relate to the main frieze.[99] Later in the Tapestry, particularly from its seventh length (52), the border becomes extra space for the designer to spill events from the main frieze. Even earlier on, the church of Mont-Saint-Michel (16) towers into the upper border, extenuating the topographical nature of the place; this also serves as a space to picture a man seated on a stool, recently proposed to be Scotland of Mont-Saint-Michel, future abbot of St Augustine's, Canterbury.[100] During the scenes of the Battle of Hastings a whole line of Norman archers is shown in the borders (55–6), as are the fallen dead, mutilated and being looted (52–8). An important consideration is whether these border depictions were conceived by the designer or added after the main frieze was created, perhaps left to the imagination of the embroiderers.[101] If this was the case, it is not to say that they are a subtle, or even subversive, commentary on the events in the main frieze as has been suggested in the past;[102] indeed, anything obviously rebellious would surely have also been understood by the Tapestry's Norman patron.[103]

The Bayeux Tapestry survives today incomplete. Its current end is significantly damaged,[104] probably due to the fact that it was once coiled around a winding machine, described as much 'like that which lets down buckets to a well'.[105] It must be a consideration that the Tapestry was never finished, though most commentators assume it once ended with the depiction of William's coronation in Westminster Abbey,[106] as reconstructed by Jan Messent.[107] We are, of course, unlikely to ever know, but that is only part of the enigma of the Bayeux Tapestry.

6

William the Conqueror and London's early castles

Edward Impey

Introduction

Once William had captured London he had to hold it: 'he saw that it was of the first importance to constrain the Londoners most strictly', and took immediate and longer term measures to do so.[1] At his disposal he had the persuasive power of several thousand men, although the demands for their housing and provision – presumably imposed on the city – would not have made this task any easier. He also had the powers of propaganda and diplomacy, exercised through the assurances at his coronation,[2] the 'good works'[3] and 'many wise, just and merciful provisions' that followed,[4] to which the famous writ, issued before March 1067, confirming the Londoners' rights as in King Edward's day, gave real substance.[5] He also, however, had the means and the know-how to create fixed fortifications with which to mark his permanent presence, to provide a secure refuge, and quite probably to help house, control and protect his troops. This he did, and it has long been recognised that one of the products was the Tower of London (as it was called by 1097), which went on to become one of the largest, most sophisticated and politically significant castles in northern Europe.[6] It has also been assumed since at least the late 16th century that Baynard's castle, at the west end of the city, dated from William's reign, and since the 1930s that its initial creation was a royal initiative.[7]

This chapter reconsiders when, within the recorded but confusing sequence of events in the first few months after the city's capture, the castles may have been established. This includes, in particular, an attempt to understand the real meaning of William of Poitiers' *Gesta Guillelmi*'s assertion (henceforth *GG*) that, prior to his coronation, William required a fortress (*munitio*) to be built in the city, and that afterwards, having retired to *Bercing*, he ordered the addition of further fortifications (*firmamenta*): were there, as this narrative implies, separate orders before and after the coronation, and what should we make of the *Bercing* incident? It then turns to examine the siting of the early castles and the reasons for the choice, and then the extent, layout and the form of their defences. Finally, it touches on the specific roles of the castles and the identity of their associated officials.

The origin and siting of London's castles

It should be said immediately that understanding the establishment of London's castles as an initiative of 1066 and the earliest part of 1067 depends almost wholly on the *GG*; Orderic tells the same story, but in an uncritical paraphrase of the earlier text.[8] Nevertheless, creating strongholds within the newly captured city would have been a natural first act in consolidating his position, and one William had already used, if under rather different circumstances, before reaching London: the *GG* tells us that on landing the Normans 'occupied Pevensey with their first fortification',[9] and the *Gesta Normannorum Ducum* (henceforth *GND*) that William 'at once built a strongly entrenched fortification',[10] implying that the Roman fort, then occupied by a *burh*,[11] was both occupied and reinforced.[12] The same sentence in *GG* mentions the stronghold (*munitio*) swiftly created afterwards at Hastings,[13] as does the Bayeux Tapestry.[14] At Dover, according to the *GG*, William reinforced an existing *castellum*,[15] probably the *burh* within its Iron Age ramparts.[16] He may conceivably have established the castle at Wallingford,[17] while before his departure for Normandy in 1067 he 'built a fortress (*munitio*) within the walls' of Winchester.[18]

While it makes sense to accept the *GG*'s assertion that the main function of the London castles was 'as a defence against the inconstancy of the numerous and hostile inhabitants, for he saw that it was of the first importance to constrain the Londoners strictly',[19] as their new lord he also needed to protect his subjects from external attack – in particular, in the 1060s, from the Danes. As importantly, he also had a duty to protect his soldiers, strangers in the new country, dependent on the king for sustenance and surrounded by a resentful population – a consideration which may have had a bearing on the form of these early fortresses (below, 106). All three factors were probably important.[20] If he was already planning to return to Normandy in the spring, the creation of this infrastructure, in addition to making strings of important appointments, would have been all the more important.

The *GG* records, on the face of it, two fortress-building initiatives in the early months of the Conquest. The first was his order 'to build a fortification (*munitio*) in the city', following the submission of the Londoners but preceding, and accompanied by, the preparations for William's coronation.[21] The second is implied by the *GG*'s statement that, after his coronation, the king 'retired to Barking while certain defensive positions (*firmamenta*) were being completed in the city'. The second passage has two implications – one, that in addition to the initial *munitio*, one or more other fortresses were subsequently required, and another relating to the new king's itinerary. In addressing the first point, some care is needed as to what the author meant by *firmamentum*. The word is used three other times in the *GG* with a broader meaning than the more usual and specific *castrum*, *castellum* and *munitio*: in the context of William's three-year siege of Brionne (begun in 1047), it is used in the plural to describe parts of a castle rather than the whole thing,[22] as it is of Arques, where William seized the *firmamentum* of the 'lofty refuge' (*editius*), that is, parts of, or the defences of, the castle.[23] But the fact that at Le Mans in 1063 William is described as having captured '*urbis firmamentum*', unambiguously its castle,[24] shows that the use of the word in London to mean independent strongholds in their entirety, by the same author, is perfectly plausible.

The question of the king's itinerary, meanwhile, is important in this context as it infers that one was begun, if not completed, before the other. However, this nicety of precedence, and the hint that the Conqueror improved upon his initial fortress-building plans after his coronation, only arises if we believe in the *GG*'s '*Bercing*' episode. The place in question has usually been taken to mean Barking in Essex,[25] and has been accommodated, to reconcile *GG* and the Anglo-Saxon Chronicle, by most historians.[26] There are reasons to question this, however. First, why would the king have wished to move from the comforts and convenience of the established royal palace at Westminster,[27] supplemented probably by the abbey's new conventual buildings, to a place eleven miles distant and nine miles east of the city? And what could have been the particular appeal of Barking? The usual explanation for the latter, that the king stayed at the nunnery of St Mary, of seventh-century origin and a place of some wealth in Domesday Book,[28] and better ones suggested by Paul Dalton, are still not wholly compelling.[29] The answer probably remains that William never went there at all: is it not more likely that the similarities between the names of the two places led William of Poitiers to identify Berkhamsted, the existence of which he was unaware of, and rendered in the ASC as *Beorh ham stede*, but equally frequently at the time as *Beorcham*,[30] as Barking – better known and closer to London? If so, it would help explain why William of Poitiers, understanding the duke to have approached London from Wallingford (that is, from the southwest) had to place this incident – apparently in what would then have been unconquered hinterland – *after* the submission and capture of the city. It would also explain why he has to place the submission of Edwin and Morcar, which the ASC places at Berkhamsted, after the coronation – an inherently unlikely sequence of events given the dangers that would have been posed had the unreconciled earls been still at large.[31] The conclusion must surely be, as suggested by G. T. Turner in 1912 and hinted at by David Douglas in 1964,[32] that the 'Barking' sojourn was invented by William of Poitiers, that the new king remained at Westminster, and that both London's castles originated in a single command made between the submission of the city and his coronation.

With regard to siting of the castles, William would have had a free hand – and, as is clear from his actions in other towns, the will – to site castles as he saw fit; the overall scheme for implanting fortresses in the city was probably his own. This was the case, for example, in siting the castle at Saint-James de Beuvron (Manche) in 1064,[33] and was to be again in 1068 at Exeter where he 'chose a spot within the walls where a castle was to be built', and presumably again at York in 1069.[34] Placing of fortresses at its extreme ends held London in a pincer-like grip, but also allowed independent access to the surrounding country,[35] while their riverside position made for easy supply and added to the impressive aspect of the city from the water (Figure 1). Both also had their innermost defences up against or in the corner of the Roman walls, an arrangement with encouraging precedent in the ducal castles in Avranches,[36] Bayeux[37] and Rouen,[38] but also offered obvious advantages of speed in respect of their construction. William was also to use this device elsewhere in England: the site of the castle at Winchester, begun through the agency of William fitz Osbern between Christmas 1066 and February 1067, was in the southwest corner of the Roman circuit,[39] and the one he chose at Exeter in 1068 was in the northern corner of the circuit, its highest point.[40] William himself may have had a hand

Figure 1. The position and suggested extent of London's castles in c.1080, overlaid on a modern street plan.

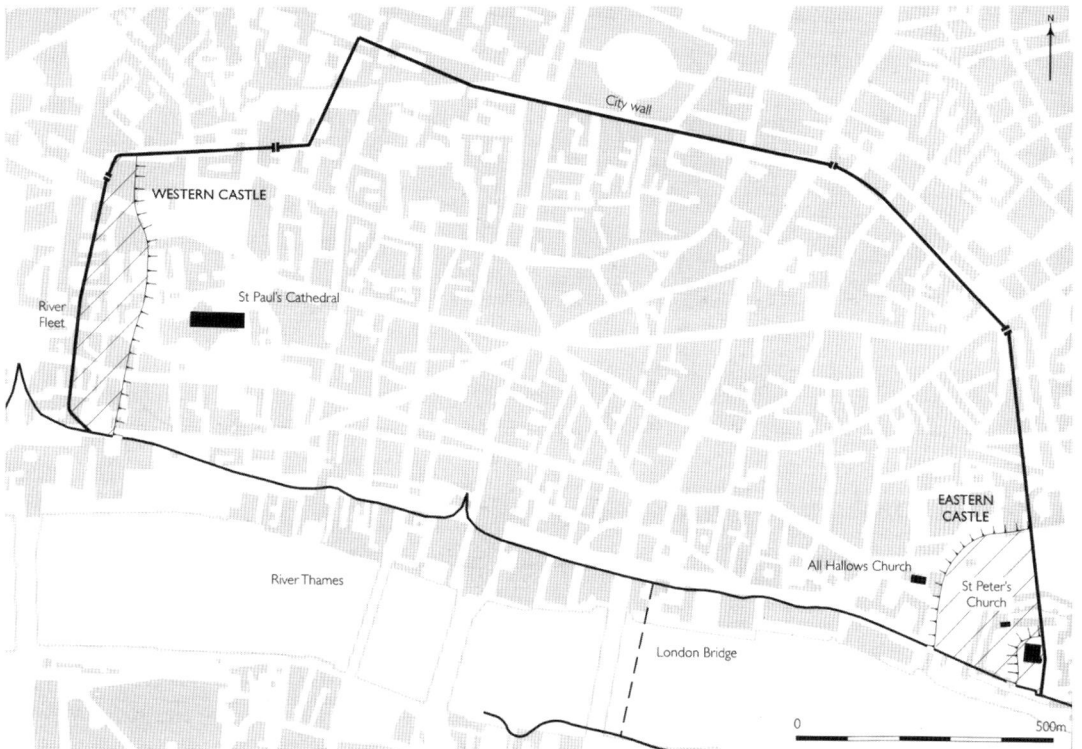

not just in creating but in siting other castles in analogous positions at Cardiff, Gloucester,[41] Lincoln,[42] Wallingford (within the pre-Conquest defences),[43] and at Worcester.[44]

The eastern castle: form and extent

The townscape into which the eastern castle was planted is poorly understood,[45] and all that can be said with confidence is that All Hallows Barking, to the northwest of the Tower in its present form, had been established in or by the early 11th century, and the churches of the Holy Cross and St Mary Magdalen, as well as St Peter ad Vincula, by or soon after 1050.[46] The churches at least loosely suggest a local population, and thus that a clearance of houses to build the castle, of the kind recorded in Domesday Book (for example) at Lincoln, Shrewsbury, York and Wallingford,[47] or known from archaeology (as at Oxford, Northampton and Winchester),[48] may have been necessary.

Most of what is known of the early castle's form was recovered by excavation in 1963–4, although this is frustratingly fragmented and remains to be fully published. The crucial discovery, as the excavator described it, was:

> a ditch, 8 metres wide by 3.5 metres deep, running from northeast to south-west across the Parade Ground [i.e. between the White Tower and the Waterloo Block] at this point, finally turning south to run toward the river. The ditch had later been deliberately refilled, masons' debris tipped in from the outer edge ... the pottery from the lowest level of silting in the ditch was apparently of eleventh-century date.

He concluded: 'We have thus an enclosure some 100 metres long by 50 metres wide, defended on the east side by the old City Wall of Roman London ... on the south side by the river, and on the north and west sides by a new ditch and presumably also a rampart'.[49] This has been the basis of our understanding of the early castle ever since, and neatly tallied with assumptions already made about the early castle by Harold Sands, William Page, Alfred Clapham and Howard Colvin.[50] Davison's discoveries were supplemented by that in 1974–5 of another stretch of ditch, to the north of the Wakefield Tower, outside of, but roughly parallel to, the surviving 13th-century western wall of the Inmost Ward (Figure 2).[51] This has been interpreted as the southern continuation of, and coeval with, Davison's southward-turning ditch, although they are on slightly different alignments – the kink perhaps having accommodated a re-entrant gate, or having been designed to avoid Roman foundations. As such, as illustrated in a number of models and reconstructions since the 1960s, this modest enclosure (about 1.25 acres; 0.5 hectares) would essentially have conformed to the second most numerous type of Conquest-period castles, that is, the 'ringwork',

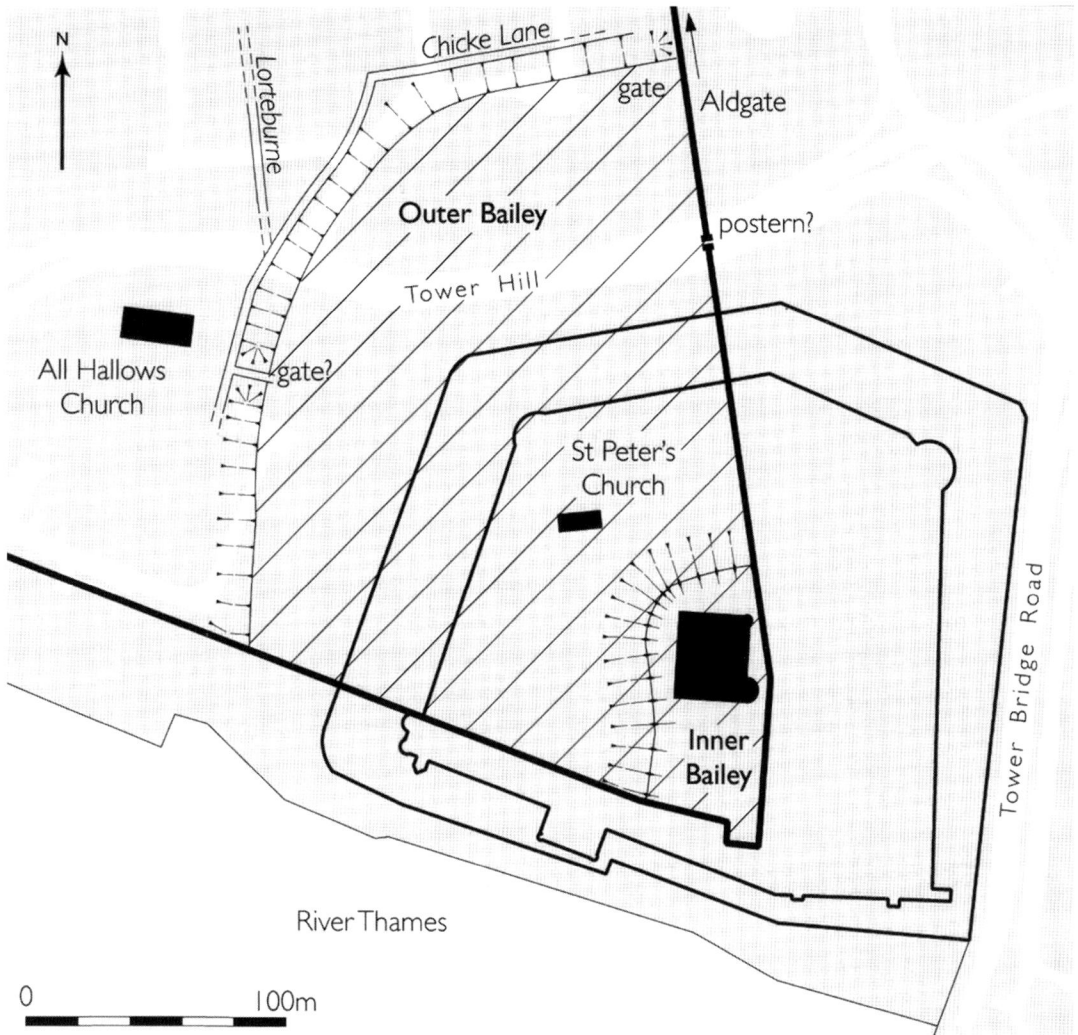

Figure 2. The defences of the early castle on the Tower site and related topographical details as they may have existed in c.1080. The inner bailey and its defences are known or inferred from archaeological evidence and assumed to be those of 1066. Documentary evidence suggests that an outer bailey was created at the same time or soon after, and that it covered an area roughly co-extensive with the intramural area of the later Tower Liberties. Note that the courses of the Lorteburn (at least to the north of All Hallows), of Chicke Lane and of the streets to the north and west are those they are understood to have followed in c.1270, and that the plans of All Hallows and St Peter's are indicative only. The outer edge of the Tower's late-13th-century defences and the outer edge of the existing moat and the river's edge are shown for scale and orientation.

a strong enclosure without a motte,[52] of which 190 have been counted, and probably the most common form of pre-c.1070 urban castle,[53] those at Exeter (1068) and Winchester (1067) being among them.[54] Some of these later acquired mottes – as perhaps at Winchester – and those at Canterbury, York and Wareham may also have been added to ringworks. However, although one could have been added at the Tower, this seems unlikely, not least as the building of the White Tower, which would have required the motte's removal, may have been envisaged by William from the first.

There is, however, evidence that the 'ringwork' was accompanied from the start, or very soon after, by a much larger but short-lived outer bailey extending over much of the intramural area of (what was later defined as) the Tower Liberties. This is largely associated with the history and location of the church of St Peter ad Vincula, usually assumed to have been included within the castle only in the 13th century under Henry III. This first appears by implication in a reference of 1128–34 to Dermanus, who is named in a slightly later document as 'the priest of St Peter's', as 'priest of the Tower' (*sacerdos de Turre*).[55] This suggests that his church was within the castle, but, more importantly, in 1157 the same church is called 'St Peter of the Bailey' (*Sancti Petri de Balli[v]o*),[56] and in similar terms (that is, *in balli*o) in 1237 (twice),[57] in 1239,[58] and twice again in 1240.[59] *Ballium* has a number of meanings, including that of jurisdictional area in the sense of 'bailiwick', rather than as an enclosure or 'bailey' in the castellological sense, and this has perhaps been assumed to apply in this case.[60] In fact, while it no doubt was such an area – and as such lived on after the Middle Ages as the Liberties – the physical sense is more plausible, and is supported by the meaning of *in ballio* applied to other churches in the Middle Ages. Among these are the churches of St Paul's, St Clement's and All Saints within the area of the Roman upper city at Lincoln, all bestowed by 1200 with the suffix 'in the bail'.[61] Similarly, at Norwich, at least in the 16th century, the church of St Martin, included within the castle in the 11th century, was known as St Martin *in Balliva*;[62] St Peter-*ad Castrum* in Oxford, on its original site, and attested and so called as early as 1122 and later called 'Le Bailey',[63] may also owe its name to former inclusion within a large outermost bailey to the west of the castle. Both Lincoln and Norwich also provide important parallels for the existence of other vast, early, but short-lived outer baileys, in the case of the former covering the whole area of the Roman upper city.[64] In the case of Norwich, the core of the castle of 1067–70 was adjoined to the northeast by an enclosure of about 7.6 acres.[65] Similar arrangements appear to have existed at Nottingham,[66] Rochester,[67] probably Chester,[68] and, incidentally, at Le Puiset (19 acres) in France (Eure-et-Loir).[69] As in London, none of these outlived the Middle Ages: at Lincoln the castle had contracted to the strongly fortified nucleus in the southwest corner of the upper city by the mid-12th century,[70] and at Norwich the redundant enclosure was ceded to the citizens in 1344;[71] Nottingham and Rochester had gone the same way respectively by the 1270s and the early 1480s.[72]

In the case of the Tower it is worth adding that the presence of an early outer bailey may also help to explain an aspect of its earliest history that has puzzled historians since the 1890s: this is the reference to the 'small castle that was Ravengar's' (*parvo castello quod fuit Ravengeri*), granted by the Empress Matilda to Geoffrey II de Mandeville, along with the custody of the Tower of London (*turris*) in 1141:[73] the fact that *castellum* is used in numerous 12th-century contexts, including at Arques, Caen, Colchester, Gloucester, Hereford, Torigni and Worcester,[74] to mean the bailey associated with a great tower (as opposed to the whole complex), and that in this context *turris* must refer to the White Tower, implies that Ravengar was holding the bailey at its foot: the comparative *parva*, meanwhile, implies the existence at that stage of a larger (outer) bailey from which it needed to be distinguished.

It remains to consider the extent, boundaries, date and longevity of the early outer bailey. The essence of the first two are to be found, remarkably, in a single document – a description of the boundary of the Soke of Aldgate, purporting to be that confirmed by Queen Matilda, but while of 15th-century date, preserving earlier passages.[75] According to this, the boundary ran

> from the gate of Aldgate [i.e. a gate in the city wall] down to the gate of the bailey of the Tower which is called *Cungate*, and along the whole length of the lane called Chicke Lane towards Barking church as far as the cemetery[76]

before threading its way northwards back to the gate. Since the *Cungate* led into the bailey, and was the point at which the boundary turned westwards across the north end of (what became) Tower Hill before running south towards the cemetery, the bailey must have been almost precisely coextensive with the intramural area of the Liberties, loosely defined in writing as early as 1382, and clearly delineated by the Haiward and Gascoyne plan of 1597.[77] This interpretation is at least consistent with the probable course of the Lorteburn, a stream that joined the Thames at the point marked by Tower Dock and which could therefore have served effectively as a defensive ditch on the outside of the bailey's western rampart. The *Cungate*, meanwhile, must have been a gate or postern hard against the Roman wall, presumably spanning what had been an intramural street, standing approximately where the post-medieval Liberty boundary met the wall, and therefore in or to the south of the yard behind numbers 8–10 and 42–3 Coopers Row, where a stretch of Roman wall in fact survives.[78] In total, the early castle would therefore have covered about four hectares (9.8 acres) – large, but well within the range of the early castles to which it has already been compared: Chester covering 3.7 hectares (9 acres), Lincoln 15 hectares (37 acres), Nottingham 4.5 hectares (11.1 acres) and Norwich 5 hectares (12.3 acres), or with William's own foundation of the early 1060s at Caen, which covered more than 5 hectares (12.3 acres).[79] How and how strongly the perimeter was fortified is unclear, other than the probable use of the *Lorteburn* (above), but its length and short life both suggest that they were, compared to those of the inner 'ringwork', relatively light – which has implications for the purpose of the enclosure and others like it, discussed briefly below (106).

The date of the outer bailey is unknown. It could perhaps have been the *weall* that the Anglo-Saxon Chronicle tells us was built at such grievous cost of the 'wall that they built about the Tower' in 1097,[80] but it is most likely to have followed on very swiftly from, or even accompanied, the creation of the inner 'ringwork': reasons include the early date of the parallels given above, but more particularly that its creation after William's issue of his writ to the Londoners would surely have been in blatant contradiction of its terms. Precisely how long it survived is unknown: while the naming of St Peter's *in ballio* in 1237 might suggest that it then still existed; the fact that in the following year Henry III's new works needed the protection of a palisade[81] suggests otherwise. Possibly it had ceased to exist in its original form even before the 1120s, the *in ballio* suffix by then merely perpetuating the name after its topographical sense had been lost. However, the approximate definition of its boundaries and jurisdictional dependence on the Tower lived on in the form of the Tower Liberties, a development that neatly mirrors those at Norwich, Chester and elsewhere.

The western castle

That there was a castle – and, subsequently, castles – at the west of the city in the 12th century is not in doubt, as they are attested in 1111,[82] and FitzStephen, writing in the 1170s, famously mentions not only the 'palatine citadel' in the east but what were by his time 'two strongly fortified castles on the west side'.[83] These castles were respectively known, by 1111 and 1137,[84] as Baynard's Castle and Mountfichet's castle, and the former still commemorated by the name of Castle Baynard Street (EC4). However, as will be seen, the first fortifications formed a single royal stronghold.

The key evidence for the extent of the primary fortress is archaeological, consisting of a north–south ditch, of natural origin but artificially enlarged, running approximately parallel to the city wall and between 100 m and 150 m to its east.[85] This was encountered in 1907 on the Greyfriars site in Newgate Street, in the early 1960s in Paternoster Square, and in the mid-1980s on the south side of St Paul's churchyard, at the bottom of Addle Hill (immediately to the east of St Andrew by the Wardrobe), and at the medieval riverbank.[86] This would have carved out of the city an intramural area of more than 6 hectares (14.8 acres), making it the second-largest urban castle known in England. Its total area may have been larger still, if this can be inferred, once again, from the use of the word *ballium*: in particular it has been suggested that its use by the 1160s, in 1190, and in the 1240s for what later became 'Old Bailey', and the suffix of 'in the Bailey' attached to St Sepulchre's church by 1243, indicate that it extended beyond the city wall (Figure 3).[87] It is also conceivable that the substantial stone building discovered in the

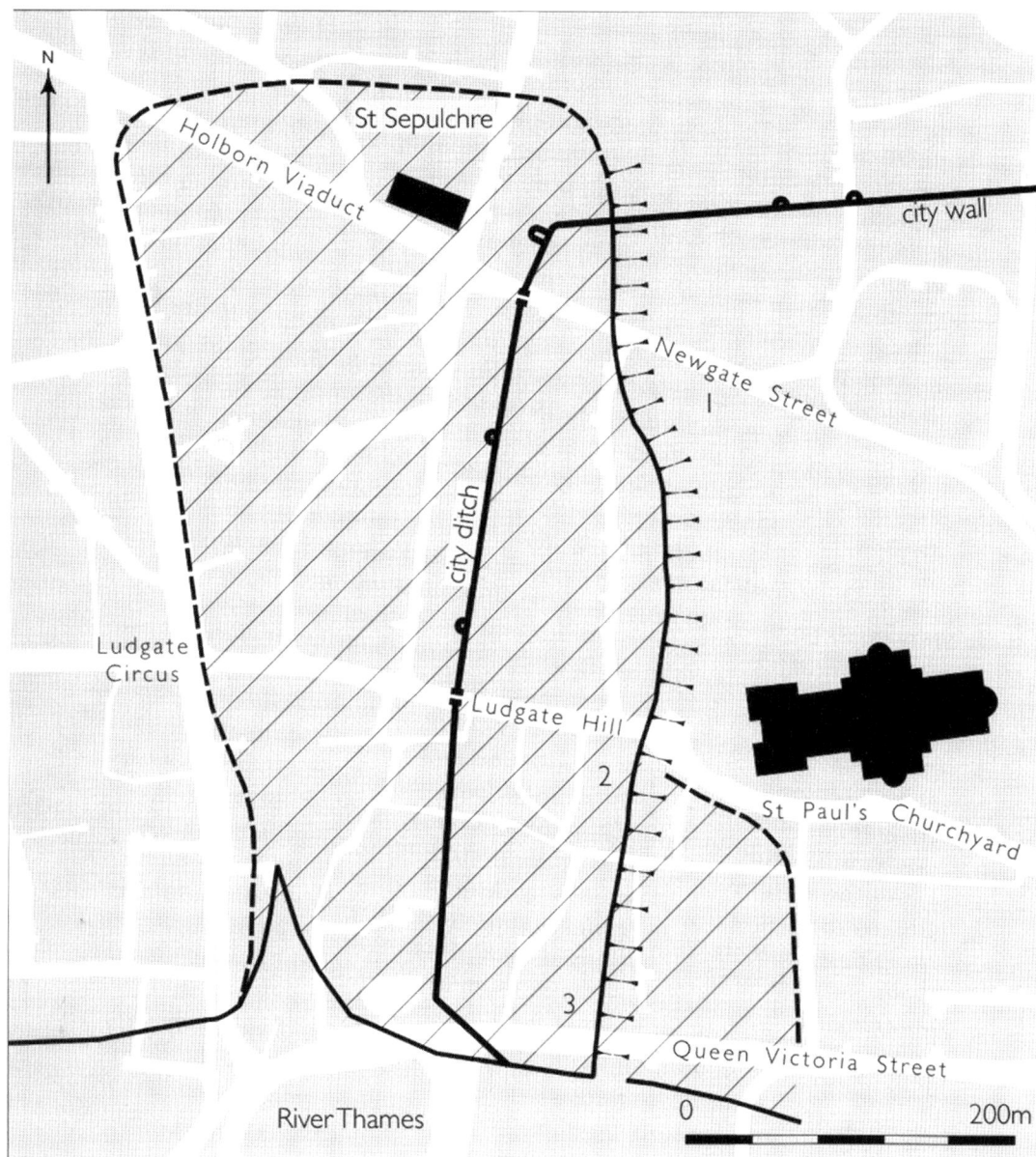

Figure 3. The likely extent and boundaries of the western fortification, which, it is suggested, was created in 1066–7 and administered as a royal castle until c.1087. Numbers indicate the points at which the part-natural, part-artificial watercourse that is taken to have been its eastern ditch has been identified archaeologically. Marked in a dotted line to the west are the possible limits of a second fortified area, later known as the 'old bailey', which in the early years may have been considered as part of the same complex. To the east, a second additional area may have lain between the main ditch and the approximate line of modern Godliman Street. Indications of the modern street pattern and the position of the 17th-century cathedral are given for orientation.

1990s on the site of the Fleet Prison (with dimensions of 12.5 m by 10.5 m and with what appear to be turret bases at its corners)[88] formed part of its defences, while the east bank of the Fleet river would have made an obvious course for the associated rampart.[89] In addition, the extent of the Soke of the Lord of Baynard's castle, as it existed in the 14th century, suggests that the defences may also have taken in, at the south end, an additional intramural area to the east of the ditch, extending eastwards to modern Godliman Street.[90] This castle may have taken on the name of 'Baynard's castle' as early as 1100, when William Baignard was a king's minister,[91] or even from the time of Ralph Baignard, William's uncle, a very substantial landholder in Domesday Book, and sheriff of Essex and London sometime between 1072–1080/6;[92] certainly the castle was in his possession and named after William Baignard by 1111, when he forfeited the *Castrum Baynardi* for rebellion.[93]

The break-up of the vast royal castle and the origins of its successors probably followed the great fire of 1087, which, according to the Anglo-Saxon Chronicle, destroyed St Paul's and 'the finest part' of the city, leading to a major re-ordering of the quarter.[94] Since the London *castellum* for which the king required services in the years 1094–7 must have been the Tower, this too suggests that the western castle had lost its significance as a royal stronghold by that period.[95] This was certainly the case by 1111, when, after Baynard's forfeiture, Henry I granted the Bishop of London substantial parts of the 'ditch of my castle (*castellum*)' to build a precinct wall and create a roadway outside it, with the clear implication that its usefulness as a fortress, at least to him, had ceased.[96] The later history of the site is largely beyond the scope of this chapter, but, in short, it was then granted to Robert fitz Richard of Clare, and so became a baronial seat, retaining the name of Baynard's Castle. Mountfichet's castle came into existence sometime after fitz Richard's niece married William Mountfichet in the 1120s or the 1130s,[97] and appears as the '*castellum de Munfichet*' in the early 13th century (Figure 4).[98]

In castellological terms, the early fortresses in London, along with others sharing early, usually short-lived, but 'outsize' outer baileys, form an interesting group. The inner defences of both London's early castles no doubt differed little from those of any other, but the baileys imply a rather different or additional purpose, in keeping with a general point made by David King: many early castles, he wrote, 'were extremely large in area, and have been reduced in size', citing the urban castle of Norwich (above) as an example, and the rural one built by Odo of Bayeux at Deddington (Oxfordshire).[99] The reason may be that, in the early months and to a lesser extent in the first few years, the needs of the Normans were rather different to those of more settled times later on. In London, as in the other urban examples, and the rural one of Deddington, the baileys can be better seen as clearly defined enclaves or cantonments, providing William's army or its detachments,

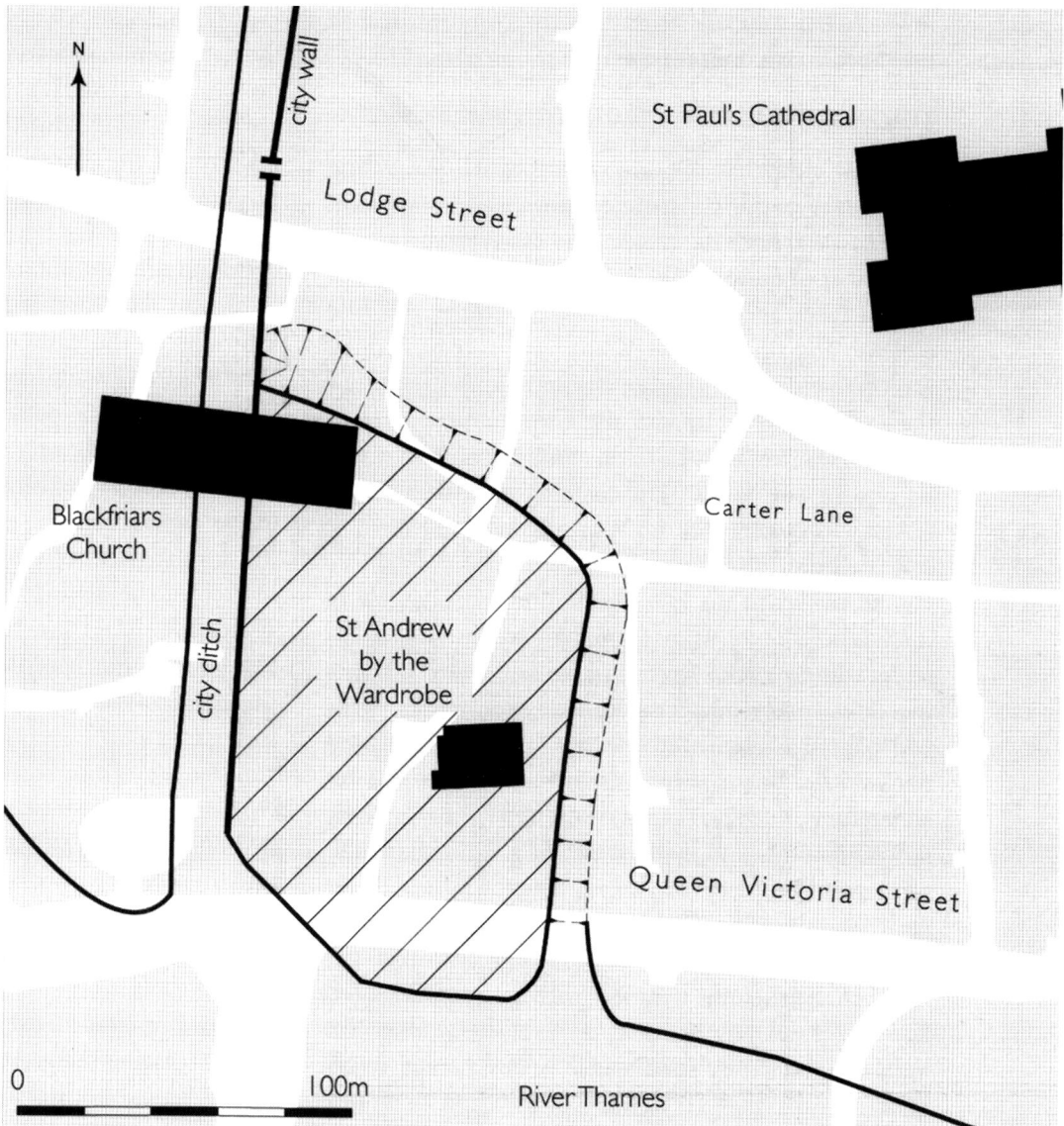

Figure 4. The suggested extent of the combined area of Baynard's Castle and Mountfichet's Tower, successors to the much large royal castle, as they may have existed by the mid-12th century. Baynard's Castle is known from 1111, originating probably as the inner part of the royal castle. Mountfichet's Tower, in existence as a separate stronghold by 1137, seems to have originated as a subdivision of Baynard's, although the course of the boundary between them is unknown.

and as importantly their horses, with secure quarters immediately pre-dating the Norman settlement of the surrounding country.

As with any fixed defences, William's new fortresses would have been useless without an accompanying administrative structure, men available to man them and someone in charge: to this end he had, for example, placed Humphrey of Tilleul in charge of the hastily built 'campaign' castle at Hastings,[100] and, if not quite so swiftly, handed Winchester to William fitz Osbern[101] and Dover to his half-brother, Odo of Bayeux, although both would necessarily have appointed deputies.[102] Given their importance, it is only to be expected that William would have made similar arrangements in his London castles. In the case of the eastern one, it is generally and reasonably assumed that Geoffrey I de Mandeville was made its guardian or castellan before March 1067,[103] and, it seems, endowed with Ansgar's former property to support him.[104] As Geoffrey I was also, from 1067, sheriff of Middlesex, and at various times of Essex, London and Hertfordshire, the castle was also the base for important aspects of government both locally and further afield.[105] We should also not forget Ravengar, a former tenant in five Essex manors but dead or dispossessed by 1086,[106] and who is likely to have a role at the Tower subordinate to or in parallel with de Mandeville's; his appointment may have been in some way related to their common landed interests in Essex, including 12 acres at West Tilbury held of de Mandeville himself.[107]

The management and administrative functions of the western castle, meanwhile, appear to have mirrored those of its eastern counterpart as neatly as its siting: it seems both in itself and for other reasons more than likely that Ralph Baignard and Geoffrey (probably his son) were castellans or constables of the castle that took their name, while Ralph, like de Mandeville, was sheriff – in this case of Essex – in the 1070s and 1080s. They may also have already been endowed with some of the London-specific military functions held by the 'Lords of Baynard's castle' in the 1130s.[108] Both families can be expected to have used their respective castles as their 'seats', that is, to have had a residence or living quarters within them, perhaps also fit for occasional use by the king: in the case of the eastern castle, the White Tower, soon to be built within it, may have contained suites of rooms both for the king and his castellan.[109] The fact that, important though London was, neither appointee had the standing of fitz Osbern or Odo can be explained by the exceptional strategic importance of Winchester and Dover and by the vast military and governmental responsibilities given to both of them in 1068.[110] Nevertheless, the presence of these officials and the nature of their duties endowed their castles with the joint residential, defensive and administrative functions which typified such institutions for the next four centuries – and in the case of the Tower, into modern times.

7

1066 and warfare: the context and place (Senlac) of the Battle of Hastings*

John Gillingham

1066 is a year like no other in English history. During its course both York and London surrendered to an invader. Within a few weeks in the autumn there were three major engagements (Fulford on 20 September, Stamford Bridge on 25 September and Hastings on 14 October). Two kings were killed in battle.[1] War is at the heart of the story, and although we know virtually nothing about the campaigns in the North of England – unless, rashly, we choose to believe what the Icelander, Snorri Sturlason, writing 150 years later, wrote about them – the Norman Conquest was such an astonishing event that on this subject we have, by contrast with the meagre descriptions of western European warfare in the previous six centuries, a remarkably rich evidence base.[2] On Duke William's invasion, there are no less than three substantial contemporary narratives.[3] They are an untitled Latin poem of more than 800 lines, now known as the *Carmen de Hastingae Proelio* by Guy of Amiens; a very long (36 pages) Latin prose account in William of Poitiers' sycophantic account of the conqueror, now known as *Gesta Guillelmi*; and 25 scenes (34 to 58) in the embroidery now known as the Bayeux Tapestry.[4]

How should we approach the stories they tell? Traditionally the history of warfare has been a product of military academies, staff colleges and retired officers, who have analysed battles and sieges and the campaigns leading up to them, often in the hope of discovering principles of strategic conduct, lessons that might be applied in present and future wars.[5] This school has achieved important results by testing the assertions made by medieval authors 'against the known realities of human physiology, physical topography and technological capacity at a given time and place'.[6] In the last generation a more explicitly cultural approach to war has won adherents. This, while acknowledging

* My thanks to Matthew Bennett for preliminary skirmishing, to Matthew Strickland who, at the shortest of notices, found time to read and improve it all, and to Brigadier Hugh Willing, who has often walked the field with a modern soldier's eye and who, on the question of location, has come to substantially the same conclusion.

that the constraints of material reality mattered greatly, also investigates the cultural considerations and constraints that in all ages and places have fundamentally shaped warfare.[7] In practice, most historians have – consciously or not – combined the two approaches. Nonetheless, the emphases of the two are different. The traditionalists have paid (and often continue to pay) virtually no attention to what happened (or might happen) after the battle had been won. 'Mission accomplished', as George W. Bush proclaimed on 1 May 2003. In contrast, proponents of the cultural approach have discovered that by asking questions about what happened after the fighting was over, about, for example, the treatment meted out to the defeated, combatants and, importantly, non-combatants alike, they have been able shed new light on both the purposes and methods of warfare. In this essay, I shall first be extremely traditional by focusing on the Battle of Hastings (or, better, Senlac) and then turn briefly to what happened afterwards.

Battle

Guy of Amiens, the Bayeux Tapestry and William of Poitiers all told a story of Norman triumph, and none included a narrative of the events in the north – events which, if included, might have diminished the magnitude of William's achievement.[8] All three represented William in a positive, indeed a heroic, light, but each had their own variation on the theme. William of Poitiers (henceforth WP), as a ducal chaplain and a former soldier, was more knowledgeable than the others; this does not mean that he was any more objective than them. He portrayed the duke as noticeably more merciful – to the extent of concealing the manner of Harold's death – than Guy of Amiens did, while the Bayeux Tapestry (henceforth BT) represented Harold more sympathetically than the other two. Although the Tapestry's design created a lower margin that could be used to show men of lower status, the primary focus of all three was on the deeds of the horse-riding aristocrats. More than any other source the Bayeux Tapestry's vivid snapshots of the battle created the impression that medieval warfare was dominated by the figure of the knight on horseback.[9] It has become increasingly evident in recent decades that this is mistaken.[10]

Few images are more misleading than that scene (51) (Figure 25 on p. 68) showing Norman cavalry attacking the English shield-wall. By appearing to show a 'level playing field', the designer omitted the most important dimension of all, one insisted upon by both Guy of Amiens and WP – the slope up which the Normans had to ride.[11] There is nothing to suggest that any of the three ever visited the battlefield, and by the early 12th century the Tapestry was plainly much better known than the site of the battle. Only those narratives composed by monks of Battle knew that the English took their stand on a ridge. The historians of the 12th-century mainstream – William of Malmesbury,

Henry of Huntingdon and, in the vernacular, Wace – were all influenced by the work of this artist, not by the topography of East Sussex.[12] It was indeed the Tapestry that led to the battle acquiring its all too familiar name. Although modern historians have tended to accept the name on the good authority of Domesday Book (1086–7), that is not a place to which anyone in the late 11th or 12th century who wanted to know where the great battle had occurred would ever have turned.[13] The Battle of Hastings it is because that is how William of Malmesbury referred to it.[14] Almost certainly he called it that because that is how BT represented the event. Hastings is the only place name that appears three times in the Tapestry – no other place is mentioned more than once – and Hastings is the last place name to appear in the Tapestry: *Hic milites exierunt de Hestenga et venerunt ad prelium.*

For an author as determined as WP was to show off his familiarity with classical Latin literature, the temptation to compare the Norman invasion with Caesar's was irresistible. Over two chapters he showed that Duke William had faced greater difficulties and achieved greater success, concluding that:

> If you look closely at the deeds of that Roman and those of our leader, you will rightly say that the Roman took risks and trusted too much to luck, whereas William always acted with foresight and succeeded more by good planning than by chance.[15]

Shrewdly, during these two chapters WP made no mention of Harald Hardrada's invasion of the north in September. By forcing Harold to turn his attention away from the south, this was plainly a huge slice of luck for William. According to the 'C' Chronicle, Harold 'went northwards by day and night as quickly as he could assemble his force', and succeeded in taking his enemies by surprise on 25 September.[16] Unfortunately, although matters such as speed of march and consumption of food can both be calculated at a theoretical level, we have no information on them for 1066. It is often said, for example, that when Harold's army went north they rode the 180 miles from London to York in four days, a phenomenal speed. But since we do not know what triggered Harold's response (was it news of the initial Norwegian landing on the Tyne, or of Hardrada's meeting with Tostig, or of their joint forces sailing up the Ouse?), we do not know how fast he in fact travelled.

After that, we have no further secure date for Harold until the night of 13 October, by which time he was already in Sussex and close to William's invasion force based in and around Hastings. Too close. Presumably, as the Norman sources all say, he had hoped to take them, too, by surprise, but William's alertness put paid to that. According to the 'D' Chronicle, 'William came against him by surprise before his troops were marshalled'. He was at least able to occupy a strong position, though with no time to add to its natural defences.[17] In retrospect, it would have been better had Harold followed the usual Vegetian defensive strategy as described, for instance, by William of Malmesbury: getting close enough to inhibit ravaging and foraging –but not so close as to be unable to avoid battle.[18] In September Harold, knowing that William was poised to invade in the south, could not afford to be tied to the north by a defensive strategy. But by October, having eliminated one army, he could afford to take his time. He did not need a battle, whereas William did. Indeed, William must have come to England seeking battle. His awareness of this probably added to the intensity with which he ravaged an area in which many of Harold's estates lay. Harold may have placed too much confidence in the strategy of speed and surprise that had been so successful at Stamford Bridge; he may have underestimated William, whom he had witnessed conducting a cautious campaign in Brittany in 1064. But if WP's account of Duke William's earlier military career is anything to go by, then Harold ought not to have expected to take the Normans by surprise. This account represented the duke as a commander who, had always placed an unusually high priority on acquiring accurate information and responding rapidly. As the Tapestry suggests, there can be little doubt that both commanders sent out scouts.[19] Duke William differed, wrote WP, from both the great Roman generals of Antiquity *and* (my italics) from the other commanders of his own day because he not only sent out reconnaissance patrols, but often led them himself.[20]

We do not know how big any of the armies of 1066 were. Apart from the statement made by an Irish monk living in Germany that well over a thousand English (both laymen and clergy) were killed at York, there is no contemporary evidence for the numbers involved in the battles in the north.[21] The evidence for Hastings, though plentiful, contains few numbers. William of Poitiers put the figure of 60,000 Normans into the duke's mouth, and strongly implied that Harold had many more.[22] Certainly, had Harold in October 1066 been able to put every available man into the field, he would have had an overwhelming superiority in number, but politically he could not and logistically it would have been a nightmare. Logistical considerations alone mean that WP's 60,000 was impossible. A few figures look more plausible than others, but modern historians have preferred to turn to intelligent guesswork, usually arriving at a figure of 7,000–8,000 on each side, based upon the assumptions that Harold's troops occupied the crest of the south-facing ridge on which Battle Abbey would be built, and that William must have had at least as many.[23] But these assumptions are just that.[24] The only near certainty 'is that William would not have embarked without knowing that he had an army large enough to match the force that it was probably going to have to fight'.[25]

We are equally ignorant of the relative numbers of cavalry and infantry (including archers and crossbowmen) on both sides.[26] It has been argued that the Normans had the advantage of a greater number of missilemen, and perhaps also, since the crossbow seems to have been unknown in England before 1066, an 'edge in technology'.[27] This could well be so, although not until over 60 years later did an author – Henry of Huntingdon (c.1129) – suggest this when he put into Duke William's mouth the assertion that the English lacked arrows.[28] Against this is the fact that neither Guy nor William accorded the archers a decisive role.[29] Their aristocratic bias has to be kept in mind, of course, and unquestionably the BT's lower margin indicates a clear Norman superiority in archers, especially prominent towards the end. It is almost certainly on this image that Henry based his idea that at a late stage in the battle William ordered his archers not to fire directly at their enemy but to loft their arrows instead – itself another indication that Henry was unaware of the English possession of the higher ground.[30] The idea that Harold was hit in the head by an arrow has been a natural interpretation of the way the Tapestry represented his death from very early on, and was adopted by the two most influential early 12th-century historians, William of Malmesbury and Henry of Huntingdon.[31] But the earliest written accounts know nothing of this. Neither William of Jumièges nor William of Poitiers said anything about how Harold was killed; Guy of Amiens credited the swords and lances of four nobles, William first among them, with the deed.[32] There's no doubt that missile weapons were particularly useful against an enemy who chose, as the English very sensibly did once they had lost the element of surprise, to stand and fight on foot in a strong position. If, as seems likely, William had expected them to adopt this tactic, then he might well have made a special effort to recruit archers and crossbowmen. On the other hand, although the BT vividly suggests that William's army had been well supplied with arms, if the English had lacked equivalent numbers of bowmen – some of whose arrows could have been re-used by the Normans – then the invaders would have had to husband their arrows carefully if they were not to run out of 'ammunition' during the course of a very long battle.

That it was an unusually long battle all the French sources agree. According to William of Jumièges, after a Norman advance from camp at first light (in mid-October about five-thirty a.m.; sun above the horizon, six-thirty a.m.), the fighting started at the third hour (about nine a.m.), and continued until nightfall (sunset about five p.m., dark by six-thirty p.m.).[33] Plainly a battle that lasted about nine hours must have consisted mostly of pauses between the fighting. Both Guy and WP were emphatic that it was a close-run thing, that at one stage the Normans appeared to have lost – partly because they feared that the duke himself had been killed – and that in the end what won it was the Norman soldiers' greater experience of war and their guile, the feigned flights that lured the English into making premature attacks. Otherwise the strong English position on the ridge and their defensive battle tactics would have made them unbeatable. All three main sources place Harold's death near the end of the fighting, and imply that resistance collapsed when they realised he was dead. William of Jumièges made this explicit: 'when the English learned that their king had met his death, they feared for their own lives and, with night approaching, they turned in flight'.[34]

Despite recent attempts to site the battle elsewhere, the evidence that Harold was killed where the ruins of Battle Abbey now stand is strong.[35] In the words of the 'E' Chronicler, William 'set up a famous monastery in the same place where God permitted him to conquer England'.[36] Although this otherwise exceptionally well-informed chronicler may not have been familiar with the district, his statement is confirmed by the *Brevis Relatio*, composed by a monk of Battle writing during the abbacy (1107–24) of Ralph, formerly one of William I's chaplains.[37] It is, of course, unlikely that the slab that marks Harold's tomb is in the 'very spot' that Harold's standard fell, but the ruins of the abbey church, situated on the higher (over 85 m; 250 ft) parts of an approximately kilometre-long ridge running roughly east–west, may well sit roughly where the final stages of the battle had taken place.

On the basis of topography, all scholars have long been agreed that William must have approached this place along, or very close to, the line of the modern road from Hastings. The road now, and presumably the track then, runs along what Freeman described as 'a sort of isthmus of somewhat higher and firmer ground' standing more than 65 metres above sea level.[38] In consequence, it was from this direction, east-southeast, that the slope up to Harold's army was gentlest. As J. N. Hare, the archaeologist of Battle Abbey, observed, the site on which it was built 'was restricted by the road to the north, fell gradually to the east and west, and very sharply and quickly to the south'. Despite this it has for a very long time been assumed that the main Norman attack on the English position came from the south. So powerful has this assumption been that Hare himself, in analysing alterations to the ground level just south of the abbey church, noted that 'the present slope bears little relation to the much steeper one up which the Norman cavalry would have had to charge'.[39] Based on this assumption, nearly all maps purporting to show the positions of the two armies just before battle was joined place William's centre south of the abbey – where the slope was steepest! – with his left wing about three-quarters of a kilometre further west, where the slope up to the abbey is once again relatively gentle, and the end of his right wing on and to the right of the Hastings road. Correspondingly they show the English drawn up along the greater part of the ridge, including much ground well to the west of the abbey, and facing south (Figures 1 and 2).[40]

But all these maps are surely misleading. The main Norman attacks must have come along roughly the same line as the saddle, Freeman's 'isthmus'. Even if in 1066 the track ran directly up to the top of the hill, rather than – as now – skirts around it on the eastern and northern sides,

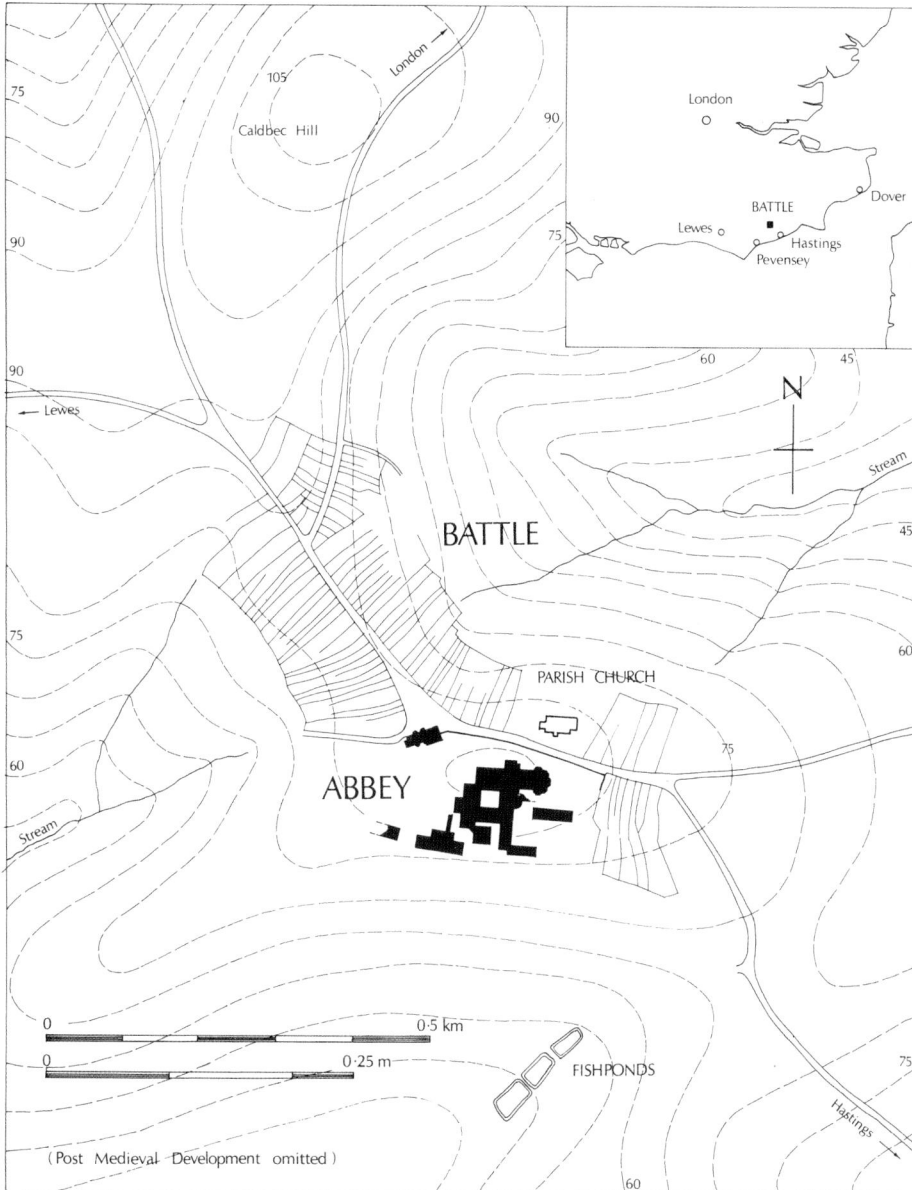

BATTLE ABBEY · LOCATION

Figure 1. Battle of Hastings contour map. Source: Hare, J., 1985, *Battle Abbey. The Eastern Range and the Excavations of 1978–80*, London: Historic Buildings and Monuments, 10.

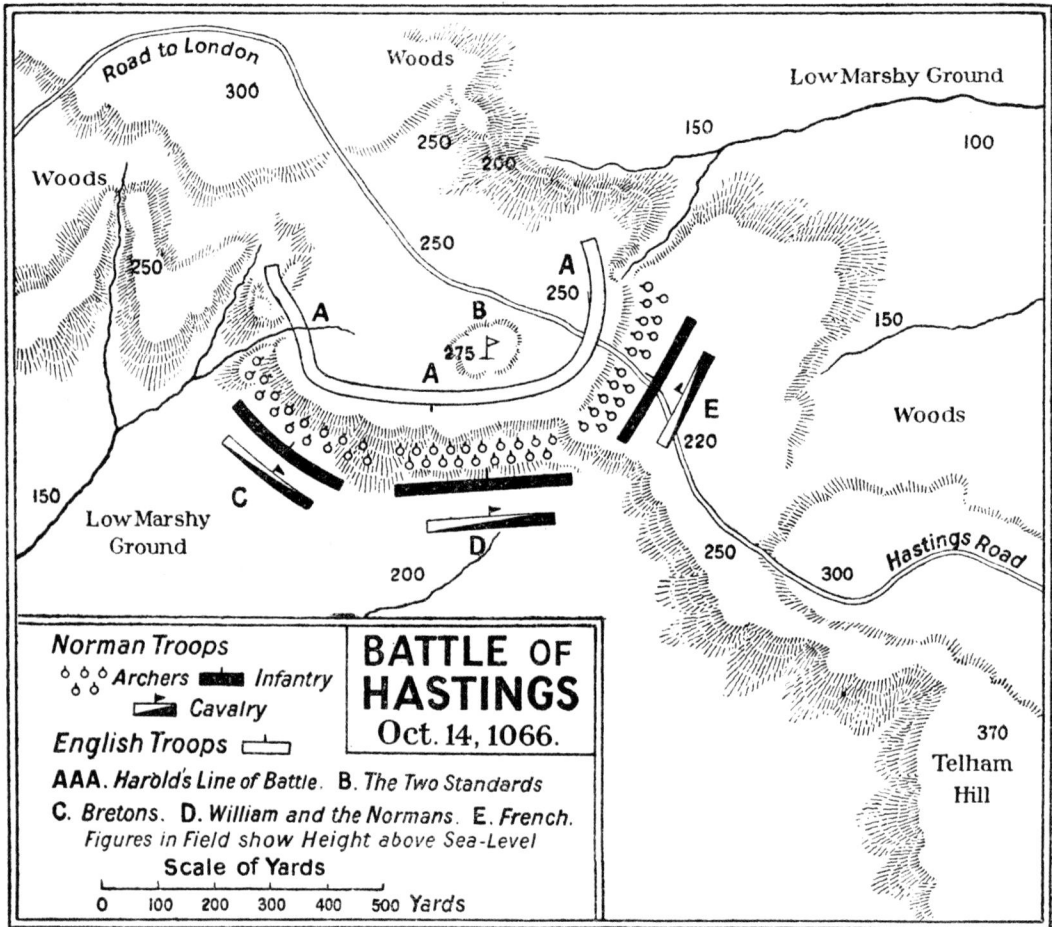

Figure 2. Traditional disposition of armies before battle was joined. Source: Oman, C., 1991, *A History of the Art of War in the Middle Ages: 378–1278*, London, Greenhill Books.

the Normans would still have preferred the relatively gentle route to the top that took them through what are now the back gardens of houses lying to the east of the abbey precinct.[41] It was this front, stretching east-wards from the abbey, that Harold must have been most concerned to protect, and where his best troops would have been stationed. If the end of his left wing had been placed on or just beyond the Hastings road, where many modern maps put it, he would have made it unnecessarily easy for the Normans to outflank him since the slope there, roughly where the modern Sedlescombe road (now Marley Lane) runs, is much gentler than the south-facing slope.[42] As for William's tactics, Colonel Lemmon, working on the assumption that William's army was 8,000 strong – his average of 11 modern estimates – reckoned it would have taken an hour or so to complete the deployment, and would have 'necessitated a flank march by most of the troops within 200 yards of the enemy line, a dangerous manoeuvre'. Why, Lemmon wondered, did

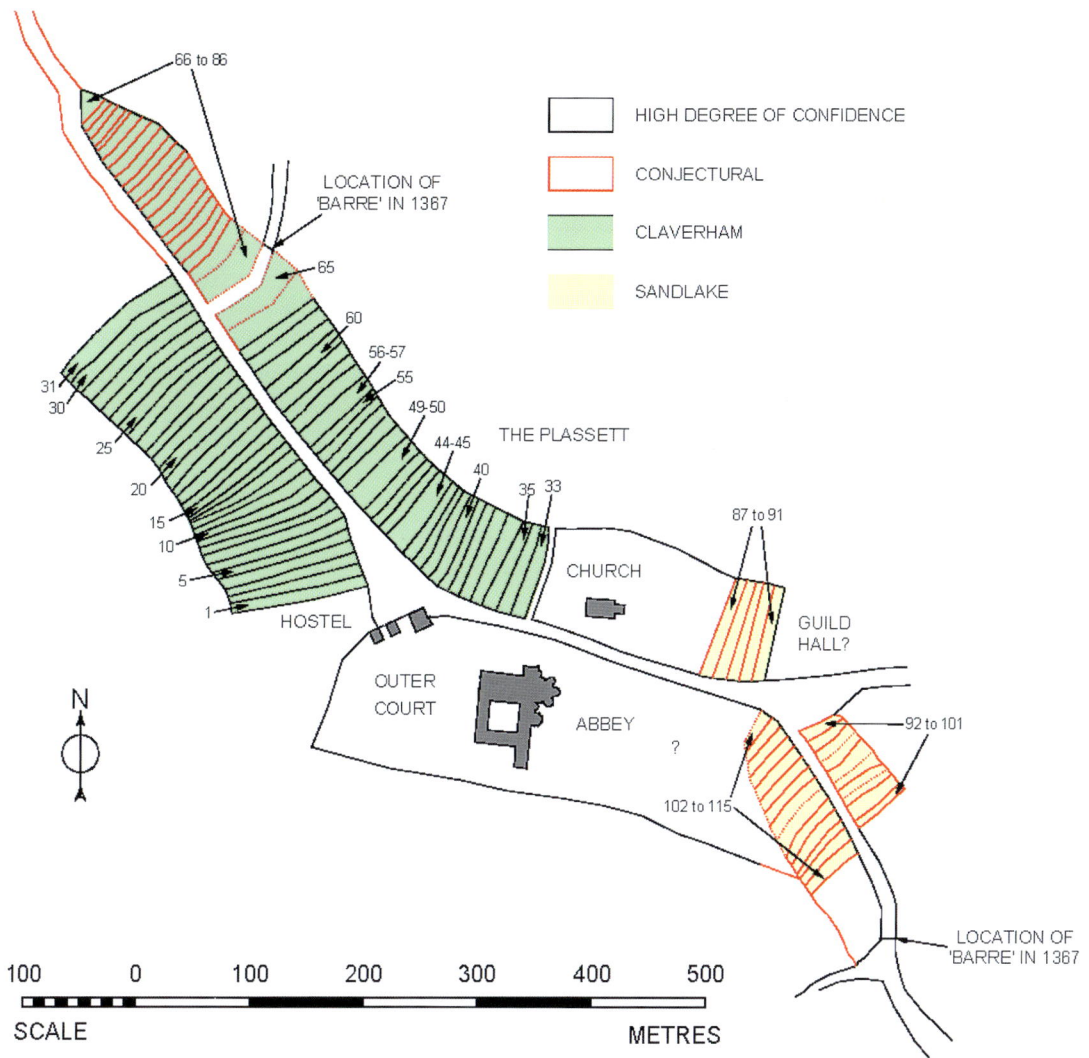

Legend:
- HIGH DEGREE OF CONFIDENCE
- CONJECTURAL
- CLAVERHAM
- SANDLAKE

Map labels: 66 to 86, LOCATION OF 'BARRE' IN 1367, 65, 60, 56-57, 55, 49-50, 44-45, 40, 35, 33, 31, 30, 25, 20, 15, 10, 5, 1, THE PLASSETT, HOSTEL, OUTER COURT, CHURCH, ABBEY, 87 to 91, GUILD HALL?, 92 to 101, 102 to 115, LOCATION OF 'BARRE' IN 1367, N

SCALE 100 0 100 200 300 400 500 METRES

the English not seize the opportunity to attack? His only solution to the problem he had created was to suggest that 'a custom of the age forbade such action until the battle had been formally joined'.[43] Either very wisely, or simply assuming that he and his readers 'knew' that medieval warfare was quaintly chivalrous, he offered no evidence for the existence of any such custom.[44]

An alternative scenario that does away with such poor generalship on both sides is to minimise the spatial extent of the deployment. Harold's main concern must surely have been to hold the hilltop and the road, if – as seems most likely – it ran along or close to the line of the modern road, but not necessarily so much of the ridge to the west. William's aim would have been to break through where the slope made this most feasible, that is, on the east. No doubt he would have wanted,

Figure 3. The early development of Battle town. Source: Martin, D., Martin, B. and Whittick, C., 2016, *Child of Conquest. Building Battle Town. An Architectural History, 1066–1750*, Burgess Hill: domtom publishing.

and very probably tried, to outflank the English on the west, but since they enjoyed the double advantage of higher ground and interior lines, it should not have been easy. If the duke's centre was on the road and his left wing faced the steepest slope, it will hardly come as a surprise if it was, as WP claimed, the Bretons and auxiliaries on his left who were the first of the attackers to turn in flight.[45] There are other indications that the confrontation took place, exactly as David Bates has written, 'on a relatively narrow front'.[46] In the early 12th century John of Worcester, with a now-lost version of the 'D' Chronicle to hand, said of the English that 'many slipped away because they were drawn up in a narrow place.'[47] According to WP, the English 'all lined up on foot in a dense formation', and on several occasions in his subsequent battle account he commented on how tightly packed they were.[48] Guy of Amiens referred to the English as being 'a serried mass' or 'in the closest order', and as 'a dense forest'.[49] The Battle *Brevis Relatio* imagined the Normans seeing Harold's standard in 'a very dense formation on the top of the hill'.[50] None of this sits easily with the idea that the English were drawn up along the length of the Battle ridge.[51] While allowing for skirmishing both to the left and right, it makes better sense to locate the bulk of the fighting on a relatively restricted front to the east of the abbey and either side of the Hastings road (Figure 2).

As it happens, when the new town grew up to supply the needs of the new and generously endowed abbey, the area to the east of the abbey became known as the 'borough' of Sandlake. By about 1105, the date of the earliest survey, this borough was already big enough to contain 24 house plots on both sides of the Hastings road – in other words, where the modern roads 'Upper Lake' and 'Lower Lake' stand.[52] It can hardly come as a surprise then that Orderic, writing some 20 years on, should several times refer to what we call 'the battle of Hastings' as 'the battle of Senlac', locating it 'on the field of Senlac'.[53] Neither of the Battle Abbey chronicles gave the battlefield a name; they were, after all, writing for an audience who knew its location perfectly well already. Orderic's history, so well-known today, circulated hardly at all in his own day, and although William of Malmesbury very probably knew of the monk of Saint-Évroult's existence and ambitions, there is no sign that either he or any of the other historians who 'made' English history ever saw Orderic's account of the Norman invasion. In consequence, no one else – until Freeman – called it the battle of Senlac. How, then, did Orderic come by the name? A Shropshire lad placed in the Norman abbey of Saint-Évroult as a boy, he subsequently visited several Benedictine houses in England (Worcester, Crowland and probably Thorney). Since his own account of the battle, derived from William of Jumièges and WP, gives not the slightest hint that he had visited the place or was aware of its ridge-top location, it seems likely that he picked up this name not at Battle itself, but indirectly via a Benedictine network.[54] If Senlac was the battle's local name, and it is hard to see what else it can be, then that adds weight to the proposition that it was on and around the road from Hastings that the struggle was at its most memorable.

This, of course, is to place it on land that for centuries has been buried under road, houses and gardens. This is ground that has few attractions for anyone wishing to show visitors the site of England's most famous battle, let alone for re-enactors. Luckily the history of the building of Battle, both town and abbey, have ensured that the area to the south of the abbey remained part of the abbey's park, a fairly open expanse over which it is relatively easy to imagine men fighting and horses charging. Not surprisingly, most modern accounts and maps of the battle give the impression that this is where England's fate was decided.

What decided the issue? The Normans may have won because they significantly outnumbered the English, or because – more plausibly – they outnumbered them in missilemen. If so, it's not what the winners said. Guy's and WP's accounts do contain some plausible points. The Normans, they both wrote, had more experience of war than the English. Both in effect illustrated this by describing the Norman capacity to feign flight and to regroup when things were going badly – hazardous manoeuvres in which experienced cavalrymen were vital.[55] Given the frequency of warfare in northern France and the relative infrequency of war in England (except on the Welsh border), these are plausible points. Both claim that William took an active part in the fighting and had either two or three horses killed under him.[56] Since both saw the fate of the army commanders as crucial turning points in the battle, highlighted by Norman panic when it was believed that their duke had been killed, it follows that both implicitly acknowledged that on the day William had been luckier than Harold. Not only than Harold; also luckier than his brothers Gyrth and Leofwine. In Matthew Strickland's words, 'Anglo-Saxon England suffered ultimate defeat not because of any technological inferiority or the absence of crossbows, cavalry or castles, but because of an unusually decisive victory which annihilated effective dynastic members, paralysed the remaining leadership and resulted in a rapid and widespread political submission'.[57]

The aftermath

According to William of Jumièges, the battle ended at about nightfall when the English fled. 'The most valiant duke, after slaughtering the enemy, returned to the field of battle at about midnight.'[58] The battle had turned into a slaughter. There are no reports of any prisoners being taken. 'Far and wide the earth was covered with the flower of the English nobility and youth, drenched in blood', wrote William of Poitiers.[59] If we look at battles in England before Hastings, there appears to be nothing exceptional here. As Matthew Strickland showed in a key article published in 1992, at Hastings William fought a battle in traditional Anglo-Scandinavian fashion.[60] According to Orderic Vitalis, so great had the bloodshed been at Stamford Bridge that 'travellers cannot fail to recognize the field, for a great mountain of dead men's bones still lies there and bears witness to the terrible slaughter on both sides'.[61] According to the Anglo-Saxon Chronicle, when Cnut won the battle against Edmund Ironside at Ashingdon in 1016 'there were killed all the chief men of the English people'.[62] A similar pattern can be detected in the other battles against the Danes, at Ringmere (1010), at Thetford (1004), and indeed against an alliance of Scandinavians and Scots at Brunanburh in 937.[63] But it appears that it wasn't just in the wars between the English and foreigners that in England battles involved very high death rates among the leaders of the defeated. What little we know about wars between Anglo-Saxon kingdoms shows that the concepts of ransom and of immunity to be afforded to those of noble birth were almost wholly absent. Given this conduct between warrior elites, it is not surprising that equal ruthlessness was shown to non-combatants. When a victorious army rampaged around the country one of their sources of profit was slaving, especially seizing and enslaving women and children. Although the capture and enslavement of women and children has entered European consciousness as pagan Viking behaviour, in fact in Britain, too, war as slave raid was standard Christian practice. 'The Saxons, Welsh, Strathclyde Britons, Irish and Vikings shared the same general attitude to the enslavement of prisoners of war. Males stood a greater chance of being slain outright, while women and children were destined for the slave markets'.[64]

On the continent, however, warfare was becoming noticeably more chivalrous. By the 11th century, except on Europe's far eastern frontier, slaving and slavery had died out. In continental warfare the death rate among combatants – at any rate, among those of higher rank – was falling; for the first time a writer expressed surprise at how few men were killed in a battle.[65] It appears that more were being captured and ransomed.[66] Thus, whereas there is no sense of shock in the English ('D' and 'E') Chronicles' reports of casualties at Senlac, authors writing on the continent took a different view. According to an annalist at Angers, William won the kingdom of the English *in bello publico* with great and heartrending cruel slaughter (*magna ac miserabili cede cruento*).[67] Adam of Bremen, writing in about 1080, regarded the conquest as so important as to justify a digression in his History of the Archbishops of Bremen. It begins, not as in the English translation with the words 'that memorable battle', but with 'that memorable slaughter' (*illa clades memorabilis*). He reckoned that almost 100,000 died.[68] In one 11th-century work a distinction was made between the actions of peasants who killed their prisoners and those of the 'men of honour' who looked after their prisoners. Treating rich prisoners well was a sign of nobility. Nobles at least had the resources and contacts that enabled them to organise the collection of a ransom; as the BT illustrates, ordinary soldiers were better off killing and stripping their prisoners. By these

standards the Normans at Hastings behaved like peasants.[69] By analysing Frankish and Norman war on the continent, Strickland showed
just how atypical the conduct of the Normans had been in 1066.[70]

That in October 1066 William was prepared to fight in the old style
was partly a measure of his ruthlessness – a ruthlessness which clearly
dismayed his panegyrist, his chaplain, William of Poitiers, who espoused
more chivalrous values. It may also have been easier for him because
many continentals regarded the English as cruel and savage barbarians,
and may have felt that, when fighting them, it was not necessary to act
according to your own civilised standards.[71] But WP argued that after
the battle William treated the defeated English mercifully, and up to a
point his case is a good one.[72] Under the rule of William the Bastard and
his sons, slave-taking and slavery died out in England. The changes in
political values consequent upon the Norman Conquest meant that for
200 years Hastings was the last old-style battle to be fought on English
soil. Very few men of high status were to be killed in the battles of the
Standard in 1138, Lincoln in 1141, Alnwick in 1174 and Lincoln in
1217. This new pattern lasted for 200 years, until broken at Evesham
in 1265.[73]

For William, Senlac was atypical in another sense. Throughout his
earlier career, his 20 years of military experience, he had taken to heart
Vegetius' injunction to avoid battle and instead use devastation as an
essential element in campaign strategy, just as it was when he ravaged
Harold's estates.[74] In this kind of warfare, destruction of property was
routinely combined with both foraging and looting. Soldiers who were
either not paid at all or paid only poorly expected to be able to take and
keep booty. William, no doubt, was fighting to win the kingdom he truly
believed was rightfully his. It has indeed been plausibly argued that only
the duke's certainty that his cause was just can explain his commitment
to an enterprise that involved both the dangers of a seaborne invasion
and the risks of battle.[75] But what were the thousands of 'ordinary'
French soldiers fighting for? This was not a question that traditional
military historians paid much attention to, and it has been argued that
'most men who participated in offensive wars, whether large or small,
did so because of their legal obligation to serve, not because of the lure
of booty'.[76] This was plainly not the case with the many non-Normans
who joined William's army. According to WP, moreover, William
answered those Normans who doubted the feasibility of the enterprise
by claiming that victory would go to the man who was prepared to
be generous with his enemy's possessions.[77] For those defending their
land, a sense of obligation, both moral and legally enforceable, was
strong. But even those defending their homeland, if they defeated an
invader, might expect a share of the winnings. According to William of
Malmesbury, after his victory at Stamford Bridge Harold failed to share
out the plunder, and in consequence many of his men slipped away,
abandoning him as he headed towards the south. Whatever Harold did

or did not do in September 1066, this observation tells us much about the culture of war.[78]

The brutal art of ravaging could also be taken to extremes, as William showed when he carried through the 'harrying of the North'. 'In his anger he commanded that all crops and herds, chattels and all kinds of foodstuffs, should be collected up and burned, so that the whole region north of the Humber might be stripped bare. So terrible a famine resulted that more than 100,000, men and women, old and young, perished of hunger.' This kind of brutality – collateral damage – may not have troubled William as much as it troubled Orderic (and no doubt also his reluctant soldiers as they watched some of their profit go up in smoke).[79] But the atypical savagery at Hastings may have troubled him. He allowed, probably in 1067, a papal legate and Norman bishops to promulgate a penitential chiefly to address the sins committed by those who fought 'in the great battle'.[80] And he founded Battle Abbey on the spot.

8

1066 and the English

Ann Williams

The major impact of the Norman Conquest on English society was the replacement of a native aristocracy by a foreign-born baronage.[1] By 1086, only four men of English origin held 'estates of baronial dimensions': Edward of Salisbury, sheriff of Wiltshire (lands assessed at 312½ hides); the Yorkshire magnate Gospatric Arnkell's son (145½ carucates); Thorkell of Warwick (132 hides); and Colswein of Lincoln (101 carucates).[2] Smaller estates were held by two surviving members of the West Saxon royal line, the Confessor's great-nephew Edgar Ætheling (two manors in Hertfordshire assessed at just over eight hides), and his sister Christina (land in Warwickshire and Oxfordshire assessed at 57½ hides). Both had probably received their estates from King William after the fall of Earl Edwin of Mercia in 1071. Their cousin Harold fitz Ralph held the remnant of the estate which had belonged to his father, King Edward's nephew (36 hides in Gloucestershire, Worcestershire and Warwickshire).[3] Other English landholders include William Leofric (just over 62½ hides in Gloucestershire, Berkshire and Essex, all once held by his putative father, Asgot of Hailes), and a woman called Eadgifu or Ealdgifu (a manor at Chaddesley Corbett, Worcestershire, assessed at 25 hides).[4]

Of the four 'baronial' holders, three were (or had been) in the king's service; Edward was sheriff of Wiltshire, Thorkell had probably been sheriff of Warwick, and Colswein may have had some official role in Lincoln.[5] Five other English landholders fall into this category. Godric *dapifer* (the steward, about 20 carucates of land in East Anglia) was administering some of the estates forfeited by Earl Ralph Guader in 1075, and Kolgrimr (land assessed at some 22 carucates in Lincolnshire) may have been reeve of Grantham.[6] Two minor Buckinghamshire landholders, Alric the cook (*coquus*) and Alsige (20 and 10 hides respectively), seem to have been in the service of Queen Edith, and Alfred Wigod's nephew (two manors in Oxfordshire assessed at eight hides) was connected with another ministerial family, that of Wigod of Wallingford.[7] All five are unusual in being assigned individual entries;

most Englishmen who held land of the king in 1086 are lumped together in composite entries as 'king's thegns' (*taini regis*).

The English survivors of 1086 have aptly been described as 'the flotsam and jetsam of an aristocracy wrecked in the storms of the Conquest'.[8] Those who held of the king were a tiny minority; most were holding fragments of their former estates as tenants of the incoming continental magnates. It is usual at this point to adduce the case of one Ailric (OE Æthelric, Ægelric) who, as Domesday Book tells us, continued to hold his land at Marsh Gibbon (Buckinghamshire) but as a tenant of William fitz Ansculf, 'heavily and wretchedly (*grauiter et miserabiliter*)'.[9] Before we shed too many tears for Ailric, we should remember that anyone mentioned by name in Domesday counts as 'upper class'. To put Ailric's dilemma in modern terms, he had probably had to sell the Porsche and his wife's Renault and rely on the four-wheel drive, but I doubt he was actually on the breadline. Ailric's predicament, as the Domesday entry makes clear, arose because he was holding Marsh Gibbon 'at farm' (*modo tenet ad firmam de Willelmo*), that is to say he paid a fixed yearly sum which he hoped to recoup from the profits of the estate. Many such arrangements are recorded in Domesday Book, often accompanied by complaints that the sum was set too high.[10] For this reason, farming land was very unpopular among both incomers and indigenes, and the Anglo-Saxon Chronicle has some bitter words on King William's abuse of the system:

> The king sold his land on very hard terms – as hard as he could. Then came somebody else, and offered more than the other had given, and the king let it go to the man who offered him more. Then came the third, and offered still more, and the king gave it all into the hands of the man who offered him most of all, and did not care how sinfully the reeves got it from poor men, nor how many unlawful things they did.[11]

Once beyond the great divide of 'slave' and 'free', Old English society knew only two ranks, 'free men' (*ceorlas*) and 'aristocrats' (*þegnas*)', and as a thegn, Ailric would have been entitled to the same wergild (the compensation due to his kin if he was killed) as Earl Harold Godwineson.[12] But though both ranked as thegns, they were not 'equals'. Earls stood at the summit of pre-Conquest society, alongside bishops and archbishops. Their rank, conferred by the king, was personal, not heritable, although in practice sons were often appointed to the offices held by their fathers, or were given other earldoms as soon as they were fully adult.[13] By the mid-11th century, the office of earl was more or less restricted to the families of Earl Godwine, Earl Leofric, Earl Siward and the lords of Bamburgh beyond the Tees, all of whom were not only politically powerful but also rich; indeed, Earl Harold was richer than any layman except the king.[14] Below them were a hundred or so families whose landed endowment (on the Domesday assessments) entitled them to the description of *optimates* ('best men') or *proceres* ('leading men'); 'magnates' is a reasonable translation. The cut-off point between them and the lesser thegns (the 'better' as opposed to 'best' men) seems to have been possession of land assessed at 40 hides or more.[15] Not that it was wealth alone which conferred status. The word 'thegn' means 'servant', and a thegn's social standing depended in part on the rank of the lord whom he served. The Secular Code of Cnut divides the lay aristocracy into earls, king's thegns, and *medumne* (median or middling thegns).[16] The magnates were probably all king's thegns, but not all king's thegns were personally wealthy; they might be men of quite modest means, whose status depended upon their position as royal servants and officials. Conversely, median thegns, many of them in the service of lords other than the king (earls, magnates, bishops, abbots), might have as much land as some king's thegns – or more.

When the axe of the Norman Conquest fell on this complex structure, it was the head which suffered the most damage. The families of all the great earls and many of the magnates were effectively destroyed, and their lands re-distributed among the incoming Normans and Frenchmen. The most thorough dispossession took place in the immediate aftermath of the Battle of Hastings, when the property of all those who had stood against Duke William's army was confiscated. Those most affected were the thegns of the southeastern shires and the West Saxon heartlands. Further dispossessions occurred in the wake of the English rebellion of 1069–70, but were not as wholesale, so that 'most of the great families of which the English descent is beyond question … belong to Northumbria or to the northern parts of Mercia'.[17]

The effects of the Conquest upon the lower ranks of the Old English aristocracy were rather different. In central Wessex, the shires from Hampshire to Somerset which clustered around the main seat of royal government at Winchester, there were in 1086 many Englishmen styled *taini regis* with small amounts of land, whose status rested on the service they rendered to the king. The day-to-day management of the king's household had always depended on such service, and the *taini regis* had much to offer in the way of experience and skill to the new regime.[18] In a similar way the new landlords who succeeded to the confiscated estates of earls and magnates drew upon the expertise of their predecessors' men to run them. A few examples will illuminate the situation.

We may begin with an Englishman who had actually prospered after the Conquest. In 1086, Robert Latimer was holding seven manors in Kent from the bishop of Bayeux, and some smaller tenements from Christ Church Canterbury and St Augustine's, Canterbury, none of which had belonged to him (or to his father) before 1066. Indeed, Robert's name, which was common in northern Francia but not in pre-Conquest England, might suggest that he himself was a newcomer, but he was in fact an Englishman; his father Æthelric had been priest of Chatham and a canon of Rochester, and his mother was Æthelric's wife Godgifu.[19] Both parents bear impeccably Old English names, as does Robert's brother, Ælfwine, reeve of Chatham. Robert's 'original' name may have been Leofgeat, if he was (as seems likely) the Robert *Livegit* who held half a knight's fee of the archbishop of Canterbury in 1096.[20] He would not have been the only survivor to signal a change of allegiance by adopting a continental name; William Leofric had done the same, as had Eadsige Gerald, another Kentishman, whose grave-stone was found at St Augustine's, Canterbury.[21] Robert and his brother Ælfwine survived because they were officers of the sheriff (*ministri vicecomitis*), and therefore useful to the new regime.[22] Robert's byname indicates the kind of service he could offer, for 'Latimer' is derived from *latinarius*, 'interpreter', and his duties presumably included interpreting between the French-speaking sheriff of Kent and the largely English-speaking members of the local community.[23] The king's service could be very lucrative, and Robert was comfortably off, since he could afford to pay £114 per annum for the estates which he held of Odo of Bayeux. He had clearly managed his affairs better than the unfortunate Ailric of Marsh Gibbon.

Robert was a royal administrator, useful to the new king and the sheriff of Kent. Others might survive by becoming the men of the incoming continental lords. This seems to have happened at Badlesmere (Kent), which in 1086 was held by Ansfrid of the bishop of Bayeux, but claimed by the abbot of St Augustine's, Canterbury. When the case came to court, the jurors of the shire and of Faversham Hundred (in which Badlesmere lay) supported the abbot, but the son of the pre-Conquest holder, Godric *wisce*, testified that although the land owed customary dues to the abbot, his father could choose whomever he wished as his lord.[24] Though Domesday Book does not say so, it seems that after the Conquest either Godric *wisce* or his son had chosen Ansfrid as his lord, and the son was holding Badlesmere of him in 1086.[25] The dispute illustrates the tension between personal lordship (commenda-tion) and lordship over land (soke); it was soke which conferred title (as the abbot of St Augustine's rightly asserted), but even before the Conquest, lords were not above appropriating the lands of those over whom they had only commendation. This, it seems, is what Ansfrid had done at Badlesmere. His success in holding the tenement in defiance of the abbot's claim is not a complete surprise, for Ansfrid himself was the man of Odo of Bayeux, who was William the Conqueror's half-brother and earl of Kent and thus president of the Kentish shire-court. Nothing really changes.

The Badlesmere dispute is important in another respect, for it reveals a third level of tenure not obvious in the Domesday entry for the estate: Odo of Bayeux held Badlesmere of the king, Ansfrid held it of Odo, and Godric's son held it of Ansfrid. Domesday Book nor-mally records only the names of those who held land directly of the king ('tenants-in-chief'), and their immediate tenants ('mesne-tenants').[26]

Lower levels of tenure usually come to light only when the entries in Domesday Book can be compared with other sources produced in the course of the great survey of 1086. It is Exon Domesday, the source of Domesday Book's account of the southwestern shires, which reveals that the nine thegns who held land at Rollington (Dorset) in King Edward's time continued to hold it in 1086 as tenants of Roger de Tilly, who himself held of Roger Arundel, who in turn held of the king.[27] Likewise the near-contemporary Geld Rolls for the southwestern shires record that Harding, the pre-Conquest tenant of land at Bredy (also Dorset), was still holding land in Godderthorn Hundred (in which Bredy lay) at farm of Berengar Giffard in 1086.[28] Harding had been a member of Queen Edith's household before the conquest, and his survival, like that of Robert Latimer, was probably due to his administrative expertise.[29]

Such scattered references to Englishmen and women whose tenure in 1086 is omitted by the Domesday scribe may not seem very important, but if this were a regular practice, it would be a different matter. The *Inquisitio Comitatus Cantebrigiensis*, the main source for Domesday Book's account of the shire, was produced during the survey of 1086, and records the names of the jurors who swore to the veracity of its account.[30] For each hundred, eight men are named, four French, four English, none of them of baronial rank.[31] Most are not named in Domesday Book itself, though in order to be selected as jurors they must have held land in 1086. One of the jurors of Wetherley Hundred, Thorbert of Orwell, appears in Domesday Book's account of Orwell only as its pre-Conquest holder, but he clearly continued to hold his land there in 1086 as a subtenant of Picot the sheriff, who himself held Orwell of Count Alan, who held of the king.[32] Other jurors come from the ministerial category; Ælfric, a juror in Longstow Hundred, was a reeve of Eudo fitzHerbert, himself a household official of King William.[33] One particularly interesting addition is Robert the Englishman (*anglicus*) of Fordham, a juror in Staploe Hundred, who was holding land at Fordham of Wymarc, himself a tenant of Count Alan. In Robert of Fordham, we have another Englishman who, like Robert Latimer, had adopted a continental name.[34] In all, the Cambridgeshire Inquest adds some 60 English names to the 17 recorded among the mesne-tenants in the Domesday record of the shire. If such a dramatic under-recording of English survivors is typical of Domesday Book, then the traditional picture of the fate of the English needs drastic revision. As Galbraith remarked long ago, 'behind many Norman subtenants ... there may have been a great many unrecorded Saxons who continued actually to farm the land', in which case 'we can easily exaggerate the severity of the tenurial upheaval'.[35]

Galbraith's conclusion is supported by the Domesday account of Shropshire, whose tenurial structure was unusual both before and after 1066. The major landowner in King Edward's day, eclipsing even the king, was Earl Edwin. It was Edwin's death in 1071 which opened up the West Midlands to continental settlers, but as early as 1068 the king had appointed Roger de Montgommery as earl of Shrewsbury. As earl, Roger received not only the royal lands in the shire but also the comital holdings (attached to the earl's office), and after Edwin was killed his personal estate too passed to Roger.[36] This accounts for the unusual layout of the Domesday folios for Shropshire, which divide Roger's huge fief into numbered sections for each of his major tenants and, since their tenants are named in turn, the 'third layer' of tenure, concealed elsewhere, is fully revealed.[37]

The names of many third-layer tenants are of continental origin, but there is a high proportion of English names. It is not easy to determine how many individuals are represented, but they include Eadric the Wild and Siward, Æthelgar's son, who had been among the richer and more powerful men of the shire in King Edward's day. They were also kinsmen. Eadric's father Ælfric was nephew to Eadric *streona*, ealdorman of Mercia (1007–17), who married Eadgyth, King Æthelred's daughter, while Siward was Eadric and Eadgyth's grandson, and thus a great-nephew of Edward the Confessor.[38] Eadric the Wild, whose lands were assessed at 100 hides, seems not to have participated in the Battle of Hastings, and probably submitted to King William with the rest of the Mercian hierarchy in January 1067.[39] By the summer of the same year, however, he was involved in a violent dispute with the Norman castellan of Hereford, and he also took part in the English revolt of 1069. In 1070 he was pardoned and reconciled with the king, and in 1072 he accompanied a royal expedition to Scotland.[40] In 1086 he was holding land of Much Wenlock Priory, and as Eadric of Wenlock, he attests a charter of the bishop of Hereford in 1085.[41] In addition to this, three of the manors which he had held in King Edward's day, at Eudon, Walton and Overton, are later found in the possession of one William le Sauvage, whose name (OFr. *salvage, sauvage*) is a translation of Eadric's English byname 'the Wild' (Latin, *silvaticus*). If William le Sauvage was a descendant of Eadric the Wild, it may be that Eadric was still holding the manors, as a sub-tenant, in 1086.[42]

Siward son of Æthelgar, who held 80 hides of land before the Conquest, had done even better.[43] In the 1080s he could still be described as 'a rich man of Shropshire' (*dives homo de Scropscyre*), and in 1086 he continued to hold manors at Cheyney Longueville, Frodesley and Overs as Earl Roger's tenant.[44] In addition, he and his brother Ealdred held some of their former lands as tenants of Osbern fitzRichard and Roger de Lacy.[45] Siward had been a patron of St Peter's minster at Shrewsbury, where the historian Orderic Vitalis, born at Atcham (Shropshire), had received his early schooling, and Orderic records the family's history in some detail.[46] Shrewsbury Abbey, which replaced St Peter's, also remembered Siward son of Æthelgar's gift of the manor of Cheyney Longueville, disputed by his son Ealdred, to whom the abbey paid compensation early in the 12th century.[47] It is possible that some of the later Shropshire families who bore the surnames 'Seward' or 'fitzSeward' were descendants of this family, but one of Siward's sons, Edward, sought his fortune in Scotland. By 1130 he had become constable to King David, perhaps helped by the fact that he could claim kinship with Scottish as well as English royalty.[48]

The careers of Eadric the Wild and his kinsman Siward suggest that some English thegns were not so much dispossessed by the settlement as depressed in status. They were no longer courtiers who had the king's ear, but local worthies, important only in their shire communities. It should be remembered, however, that the great Norman and French barons, who held the biggest estates and formed the king's court, were themselves a small and tightly knit group which, in numerical terms, formed only a minority of the landholders in post-Conquest England. Much more numerous were the less wealthy landholders, especially those who lived as dependent tenants on the estates of largely absentee landlords. Not all of the latter were of aristocratic status. Domesday's record of such dependants includes numerous anonymous knights (*milites*), men (*homines*) and Frenchmen (*francigenae*), whose status differs little, if at all, from that of their English counterparts, the equally anonymous thegns (*taini*), 'free men' (*liberi homines*), sokemen and riding-men (*radmen, radcnihtas*). Free but not noble, they form what Hugh Thomas has aptly characterised as 'the middling sort'.[49] Their 12th-century successors were holders of fractional knight-fees and free tenants (franklins), who not only owed customary services to their lords but also participated in the public business of the shire and hundred communities.[50] They were the rural counterparts of the merchants and tradesmen from the continent who settled among the indigenous burgesses of the English towns and urban centres.

It is at this level that intermarriage between French incomers and English residents was most likely to occur; indeed, Orderic Vitalis, himself the child of a French father and an English mother, claims that such marriages were common in English towns and cities.[51] There are few examples in the Domesday corpus, though Little Domesday records that one of Earl Ralph Guader's men fell in love with (*amavit*) a woman at South Pickenham, Norfolk, and married her; the story is the more poignant in that the names of the parties are not recorded.[52] Unlike high-status marriages (like that of Earl Waltheof to King William's niece, Judith, for all the good that it did him), unions of individuals below the highest ranks are rarely mentioned.[53] The monastic *libri vitae*, which record the names of benefactors for whom prayers should be offered, are useful in this context, because the names of the laity often occur in family groups.[54] Though personal names are not a straightforward indication of ethnic origin, couples with one continental and one insular name are a likely indicator of intermarriage. The *Liber Vitae* of the New Minster, Winchester, for instance, commemorates Walter Scot and his wife Leofyve (OE Leofgifu), and Teotselin *laicus* with his wife Ealdgida (OE Ealdgyth). The names of the husbands, which suggest an origin in north Francia and the Rhineland respectively, reappear among the witnesses to an agreement made in the 1080s by Rhiwallon, abbot of the New Minster.[55] Teotselin (Tesselin) indeed is recorded in Domesday Book, holding of Hugh de Port, sheriff of Hampshire.[56] Another 'mixed' couple from the New Minster *Liber Vitae* are the Englishman Edwin the huntsman (*venator*) and his wife Odelina, whose name indicates a continental origin; like Teotselin, Edwin appears in Domesday Book, holding two hides in Kingsclere Hundred as a *tainus regis*.[57] Husbands with insular names and wives with continental names are found less often than men with continental and women with insular names, but Godric the steward's wife bore the continental name Ingreda.[58]

Intermarriage presumably played a role in the change in English naming practices, in which the insular name-stock – Ælfric, Eadric, Tovi, Thorkell – was replaced by names of continental origin – Robert, Roger, Hugh, William.[59] From the earliest surviving records we find instances of parents with insular names giving their sons names of continental type; for example, the survey of Winchester (c.1110) includes Herbert fitzEdwin, Ralph Holinsone, Robert fitzNunne and Ruald fitzFaderlin among the city's residents.[60] Charters in the archives of Bury St Edmunds reveal that Adam of Cockfield, a tenant of the abbey in the time of Abbot Anselm (1121–48), was the son of Lemmer (OE Leofmaer) and the grandson of Wulfric of Groton, both insular names.[61] The first named mayor of London was Henry fitzAilwin (OE Æthelwine, Ægelwine), whose grandfather Leofstan may have been a brother of the wealthy moneyer Deormann, holder of land in Middlesex, Hertfordshire and Essex in 1086.[62]

By the time of the second survey of Winchester in 1148, the proportion of insular to continental names in the city had shrunk from a third to a quarter, and a similar transformation can be seen in the rentals for property in Canterbury between about 1166 and about 1200.[63] Rural as well as urban communities were affected; a survey made for Shaftesbury Abbey, Dorset, in the mid-1120s shows that 90 per cent of the tenants bore names of insular stock, shrinking to 25 per cent in the second survey of about 1170, and the same trend is seen among the tenants of Bury St Edmunds, on the other side of the country.[64] Presumably fashion was at work in this process, just as it was in the 11th century, when English men and women gave their children names of Scandinavian origin, but Scandinavian names never displaced the insular stock.[65] By contrast, the 12th-century switch in naming patterns left only a handful of insular names in common use, though the fact that English women continued to be given insular names long after their brothers regularly received continental ones suggests a wish to commemorate both branches of a mixed ancestry.[66] It is also the case that many OE personal names survived as patronymic by-names and (eventually) the family names which emerge in the later Middle Ages.[67]

By 1086, English landholders were few in number, though greater than a cursory reading of Domesday Book suggests. They were not the earls and magnates whose estates spread over several shires, but local notables, or middling thegns, some personally or tenurially dependent on the vanished Old English magnates. There is a marked geographical variation in that the more affluent survivors are found in the shires of Mercia and Northumbria (it is a nice irony that English thegns survived best in the areas where they resisted longest).[68] By 1086 most of them had been reduced in wealth and in tenurial status and survived by attaching themselves to Frenchmen or undertaking administrative duties. A hundred years after the Norman settlement, their position was rationalised by Richard fitzNigel, Henry II's treasurer, in his treatise on government, the *Dialogue of the Exchequer* (my italics):

> There was a general complaint by the native English, which came to the king's ears, that since they were hated by everyone, and robbed by everyone, *they would be forced to take service abroad.* At last, after discussion in council, it was decreed that they should be given an inviolable title to whatever they had acquired from their lords by their own deserts and by a lawful bargain. But they did not succeed in establishing a title to pre-Conquest property.[69]

Of course this is not history, but the perceived link between tenure and service is of interest, and Richard fitzNigel's opinion may have some basis in fact.

Those English landholders who survived into the post-Conquest world, whether as lesser aristocrats or as prosperous free men, townsfolk or countrymen, had to adapt to changed circumstances. The fall of the pre-Conquest earls and magnates constituted an unprecedented social upheaval, and their replacement by a continental hierarchy meant that, when the English survivors took service with the new masters, they had to accept new customs, the most far-reaching of which was the formalisation of the links between landholding and lordship. Yet the survival of English families, even in reduced circumstances, ensured the survival of English custom and tradition. Such families, resident (unlike their lords) in the neighbourhoods where they held land, joined their continental peers among the local knights and free men as suitors of the shire and hundred courts, on which the administration of royal power depended. It was the interaction between incoming and indigenous families at this level which was crucial in the formation of a new 'English' nation, though it must not be forgotten that there were other elements in the process, including the desire of the incoming monarchs to be accepted as legitimate 'kings of the English'.[70] How long it took before the incomers began to think of themselves as 'English' is a matter of opinion; the crucial period is agreed to be the 12th century, but whether early or late is still disputed.[71]

The disasters of 1066 and the years that followed saw the foundering of many once-powerful kindreds, whose downfall has been seen as a paradigm of the fate of the English nation. The common picture of post-Conquest England is still of a small number of foreign magnates ruling over a society of enserfed English peasants, exemplified in fiction by works like Sir Walter Scott's *Ivanhoe* (a great read, but terrible history). How such a society managed to mutate into the English-speaking community of the Later Middle Ages, self-defined as 'English', has been left vague. I hope I have demonstrated that the traditional picture is flawed because it ignores the 'middle ground', the local strata of knights, free men and townsmen, who stood between the Norman and French aristocrats and the English peasantry. On this group, Richard fitzNigel, writing in the 1170s, has some more words worth quoting:

> nowadays, when English and Normans live close together, and marry, and give in marriage to each other, the nations are so mixed that it can scarcely be decided (I mean in the case of the free men) who is of English birth and who of Norman.[72]

Close reading of Domesday Book and its associated texts reveals that this amalgamation was already in progress when King William sent his commissioners 'over all England' to discover 'how the land was peopled and with what sort of men'.[73]

9

1066 and government

Stephen Baxter

Introduction

Perceptions of 11th-century English government changed profoundly during the 20th. A century ago, the prevailing view was that the Norman conquest demonstrated the weakness of the late Anglo-Saxon state. Sir Frank Stenton's biography of William the Conqueror, published in 1908, epitomises this position. 'It is the complete decentralisation of the Old English commonwealth which first occurs to our minds when we wish to explain the double conquest which the land sustained in the eleventh century'. 'In 1066 England was found with an obsolete army, a financial system out of all relation to the facts on which it was nominally based, a social order lacking the prerequisites of stability and consistency'. It was also 'found utterly lacking in all qualities which make a state strong and keep it efficient'; indeed, 'the Old English state' was 'trembling to its fall' before the Normans so much as landed on English soil.[1]

By the end of the 20th century, historians were making precisely the opposite case: that the government of late Anglo-Saxon England was powerful and sophisticated. Several scholars contributed to this historiographical revolution. Stenton himself took a more positive view of the capabilities of the 'Old English State' when he published a more considered treatment of the subject in his great survey of Anglo-Saxon England.[2] Michael Dolley, Michael Metcalf and other numismatists subsequently demonstrated that late Anglo-Saxon kings possessed one of the most elaborate and effective monetary systems in the medieval west.[3] David Hill and others drew out the significance of the text known as the 'Burghal Hidage' which, when taken in conjunction with landscape and archaeological evidence, reveals that a network of fortified towns was planned, constructed and maintained in the late ninth and early tenth centuries, mobilising manpower on a major scale, using systems of administration based on the hide.[4] Warren Hollister showed that similar fiscal structures were used to mobilise and finance military resources on the eve of the Norman conquest.[5] A debate between Ken Lawson and John Gillingham on the 'Danegeld and heregeld' contested the absolute levels of the sums raised to pay tribute to the Danes during the reign of King Æthelred II, and to finance a fleet of warships equipped with professional warriors between 1012 and 1051; but this debate left no room for doubting the basic fact that a land tax was regularly levied on a considerable scale, again using complex and flexible assessment systems, throughout the early 11th century.[6] Simon Keynes made a strong case for postulating the existence of a central agency for the production of royal charters,[7] and was among those who stressed the extent to which English government was mediated through written documents, presupposing significant levels of literacy within elite society.[8] John Maddicott showed that the origins of the English parliament can be traced to pre-Conquest royal assemblies.[9] Patrick Wormald argued that many of the foundations of English law were laid by 1066: he showed that most of the kings of Wessex and England between Alfred and Cnut issued legislation, at a time when few rulers in the medieval west did so; and argued that, although that the relationship between lawmaking, written law and legal practice was complex, late Anglo-Saxon government was responsible for a major shift in legal culture. Among its achievements was the construction of a new machinery of justice, consisting of a network of local courts and surety groups (shires, hundreds and tithings), which enabled the state to intervene more actively and directly in the administration of justice, most notably in the pursuit and punishment of crime: the bloodfeud was not eradicated in late Anglo-Saxon England, but judicial self-help was significantly constrained.[10] Wormald was also among a group of scholars who placed emphasis on the political and administrative unity of the late Anglo-Saxon polity, and argued that its government drew upon and facilitated a strong sense of national identity.[11] Sally Harvey showed that Domesday Book could not have been made without the structures and written records of Anglo-Saxon government.[12] James Campbell drew many of these strands together to formulate a 'maximum view' of the late Anglo-Saxon state. In doing so, he observed that late Anglo-Saxon government shared many elements in common with that of Carolingian Francia, including frequent, well-attended royal assemblies; the regular production and dissemination of legislation; networks of local courts administered by royal officials; loyalty oaths; the use of assessment systems to mobilise, feed and finance armies; the production of surveys and inventories used for the administration of royal and aristocratic property; and the use of coins and toll to tap the growth of towns and trade. Campbell concluded that, although the channels of influence are far from clear and difficult to date, late 11th-century English government shared much in common with Carolingian Francia, not because England was conquered by Frenchmen in 1066, but rather because it had evolved along Carolingian lines for at least two centuries before that date.[13] Finally and most recently, George Molyneaux has refined understanding of the formation of the kingdom of the English, not least by identifying regional and chronological variation in its development: the intensity English royal authority varied within different zones of lowland Britain, and increased markedly (except in the far north) during the last three decades of the tenth century and the first two decades of the eleventh, when, for example, the shire network, the reformed coinage and a national land tax make their earliest impression on the historical record.[14]

Few of these scholars explicitly connect their findings with the events of 1066, but the clear implication of their work is that the Norman Conquest was not a function of the weakness of English government. On the contrary, its structures were sufficiently robust to withstand two conquests in the 11th century substantially intact: continuity demonstrated its strength. Needless to say, the 'maximum view' of the late Anglo-Saxon state has not gone uncontested, but those who have emphasised its shortcomings have tended to focus on dynastic and political instability, not institutions of government.[15] What follows shares elements in common with both the proponents and critics of and the maximum view, but nevertheless develops a different case: that the very strengths of late Anglo-Saxon government made a causal contribution to 1066 and its aftermath and that although most of the structures of English survived the conquest, none were left unchanged.

Late Anglo-Saxon government

The strengths of late Anglo-Saxon government contributed to its demise in three main ways. First, the fact that England was both wealthy and effectively governed made it an attractive target. Peter Sawyer made precisely this point 50 years ago.[16] Subsequent studies of Domesday, coins, towns, trade and the rural economy have tended to endorse his basic premise, that by the mid 11th century, the English economy was not so much developing as highly developed.[17] Domesday Book suggests that by 1066, the population exceeded two million, and demonstrates that the rural landscape was exploited with sufficient intensity not only to feed that population but also to generate considerable surpluses for peasant farmers and their lords.[18] A recent study has identified a series of momentous changes in farming practice in later Anglo-Saxon England – including a major expansion of arable farming, associated with a contraction of open grazing, a marked shift towards free-threshing cereals, the growing importance of the heavy mouldboard plough and increasing use of oxen for plough traction – and concludes that all this 'added up to a revolution in farming ... comparable to the those of the eighteenth or twentieth centuries'.[19] The rural economy was monetised to the extent that peasants routinely paid rent in coin,[20] and the silver currency also made it possible to collect the land tax regularly and efficiently. Manorial surpluses and taxation enabled kings and lords to fund lavish lifestyles,[21] displaying their status by investing conspicuously in precious objects,[22] religious patronage,[23] and an increasingly sophisticated built environment.[24] Landed society's demand for conspicuous consumption also encouraged economic complexity, manifest in urban growth, large-scale specialised production and long-distance trade.[25] That trade with the near continent and Scandinavia was an important element in the late Anglo-Saxon economy is strongly suggested by the pattern of coins found singly, which has a marked concentration in the south and east of England;[26] and by the fact that the English silver coinage remained abundant and high quality even though major quantities of bullion flowed out of the kingdom in tribute and heregeld payments – a point which strongly suggests that exports, probably of wool among other goods, were sufficient to draw silver back into the economy on a major scale.[27] However, the wealth of England attracted invaders like bees to nectar, and the coinage and taxation systems made it relatively easy for conquerors to capture. It is no coincidence that kings Cnut and William both levied heavy gelds in the immediate aftermaths of their conquests in 1016 and 1066.[28]

Second, late Anglo-Saxon political structures proved vulnerable because they were effective. As Tim Reuter and Chris Wickham have shown in seminal papers, the English kingdom formed during an age of assembly politics when kings and princes could only govern effectively provided they were able to attract the leading members of their nobilities to their courts and assemblies on a regular basis;[29] English kings did so throughout the tenth and eleventh centuries, whereas their neighbours in Francia did not, and the result was political unification in England and disintegration in France.[30] It is, therefore, significant that the witness lists of royal diplomas prove that English aristocrats were assiduous in attending royal assemblies. Consider, for example, a royal diploma which was issued in 1044 and survives in its original single-sheet form (Figure 1).[31] This records a grant by King Edward of seven hides at Dawlish in Devon to Leofric, his chaplain, and bears the subscriptions of King Edward *rex totius anglice gentis*, plus two archbishops, five bishops, five abbots, four earls and thirty-five thegns, written in columns and organised in groups, each with their own hierarchy. There are excellent reasons for thinking that the people named in such witness lists were physically present at the royal assemblies, where the diplomas themselves were usually (though not invariably) drafted before being ceremonially bestowed upon the beneficiary.[32] The witness lists of 42 of King Edward's diplomas remain extant, and when these are analysed in sequence, it is possible to obtain vivid, if fleeting, impressions of the dynamics of assembly politics.[33] For instance, we can observe laymen rising up the ranks of the king's thegns, in some cases attaining promotion to the rank of earl. We can also see factional groups forming: in this case, the prominence of Earl Godwine and his sons Earl Swein and thegns Harold, Tostig and Leofwine (all of whom subsequently became earls) is unmistakable; and we may legitimately wonder if this was a cause for concern for thegns such as Odda of Deerhurst, Ordgar and

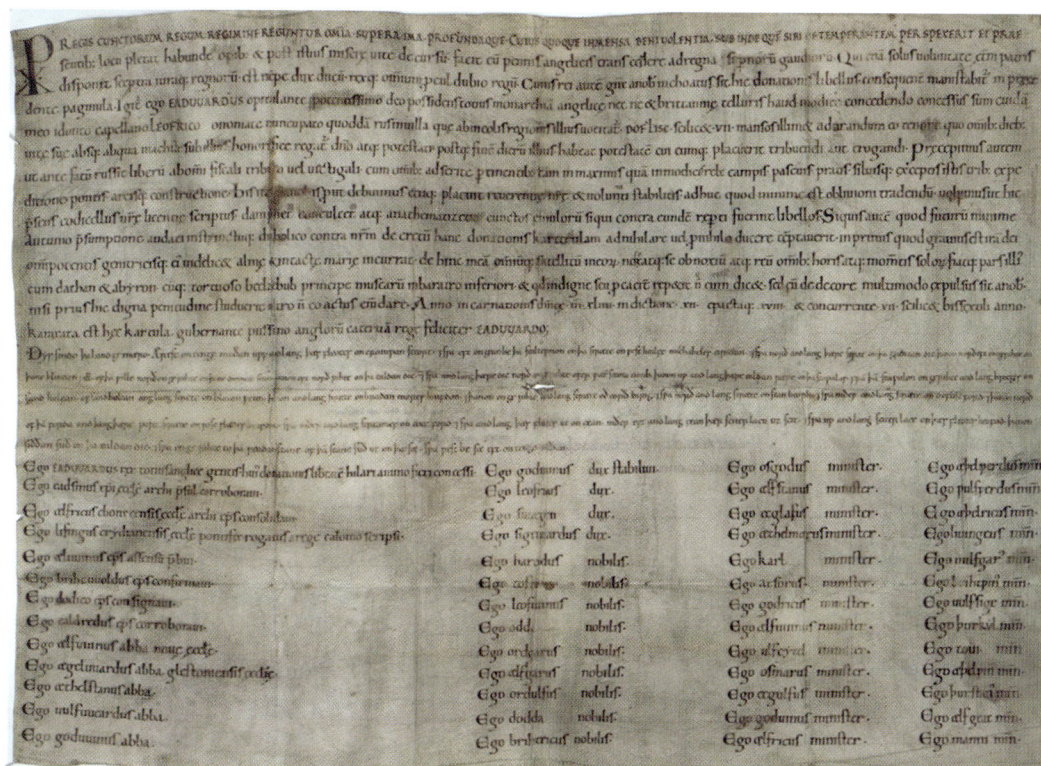

Figure 1. Exeter Cathedral Library, MS 2526 (S 1003). A diploma dated 1044 recording a grant by King Edward the Confessor to Leofric, his chaplain, of seven hides at Dawlish in Devon. Reproduced with permission. © Exeter Cathedral, Dean and Chapter.

his brother Ælfgar, and Osgot Clapa, all of whom had hitherto enjoyed a pre-eminent position among the king's thegns; and for Leofric and Siward, earls of Mercia and Northumbria respectively, who tended to oppose Godwine's faction.

Why did so many members of England's landed elite travel long distances to meetings of royal assemblies? One answer is that it gave them access to power, for the range of business transacted at late Anglo-Saxon royal assemblies was considerable: kings were made and crowned; their sacrality was ritually recreated at subsequent crown-wearings, performed during the principal religious festivals; law was made, legislation was issued, state trials were heard; consensus was achieved and decisions made concerning war, peace, taxation and the governance of the Church.[34] Another answer is that it gave them access to wealth: aristocrats went to royal assemblies to compete for royal patronage. Land was the principal source of wealth and power, and English kings had plenty of it. The essence of Chris Wickham's explanation for the contrasting political trajectories of England and west Francia in the tenth century is that, whereas the Frankish royal demesne contracted to a relatively small core near Paris during the tenth century, the English royal demesne grew rapidly by conquering the Danish-controlled parts of lowland Britain at much the same time. English kings, therefore, had more to give away; and this helps to explain the powerful gravitational pull they exercised over the English nobility. Domesday Book demonstrates that this argument holds good for the eleventh century as well as the tenth. It proves that the royal demesne remained extensive: King Edward was an order of magnitude richer than any other lord, and his estates were widely scattered across the kingdom (Figure 2, where demesne estates are shown in blue, estates loaned to tenants in red, and estates held by commended men in green). It also proves that the king enjoyed extensive powers of patronage, not just because he was rich himself, but also because he retained a significant degree of control over the wealth of the leading nobles, for many of the richest estates held by earls and other leading office-holders were held on a temporary, *ex-officio* basis.[35] Like the rulers of Carolingian Francia, late Anglo-Saxon kings distinguished between family property, which was heritable, and property which came with office, which was not; and they were able to ensure that the latter remained more valuable than the former. Put in modern terms, King Edward the Confessor could make someone the equivalent of a multi-millionaire by granting him or her a large estate of bookland – that is, land vested by royal diploma – which was in theory irrevocable and conferred full property rights upon the beneficiary; but he could also create billionaires by loaning on a more temporary and revocable basis the vast landed endowments that came with the office of earl. That does much to explain why aristocrats attended royal assemblies regularly. Indeed, many aristocrats organised their property with such journeys in mind. Although Winchester was a significant focal point, there was no fixed centre of government in this period, and royal assemblies were convened in a variety of places, most often within an egg-shaped zone between Westminster, Winchester and Gloucester; and a recent study of the distribution of pre-Conquest landholdings in Domesday Book has revealed that their manors often formed stepping stones towards this zone (Figure 3).[36]

This helps to explain one of the most striking features of English politics in the early English kingdom: endemic and often explosive factional rivalry. Factions formed to enable interest groups to compete for royal patronage at royal assemblies, and to protect their gains from rivals in the localities. The rivalry between the families of Earl Godwine of Wessex and Earl Leofric of Mercia during the mid-11th century, which the *Vita Ædwardi Regis* describes as an *odia vetera*,[37] is particularly well documented, partly because it shaped the production of contemporary narratives. For example, the Anglo-Saxon Chronicle for the mid-11th century consists of three distinct, politically-inflected texts, including one (the E-text) which was written at St Augustine's, Canterbury and is partisan in favour of the house of Godwine, and another (the C-text) which was written in the Midlands and is notably hostile to the house of Godwine and favourable to Leofric's faction.[38] The matter was

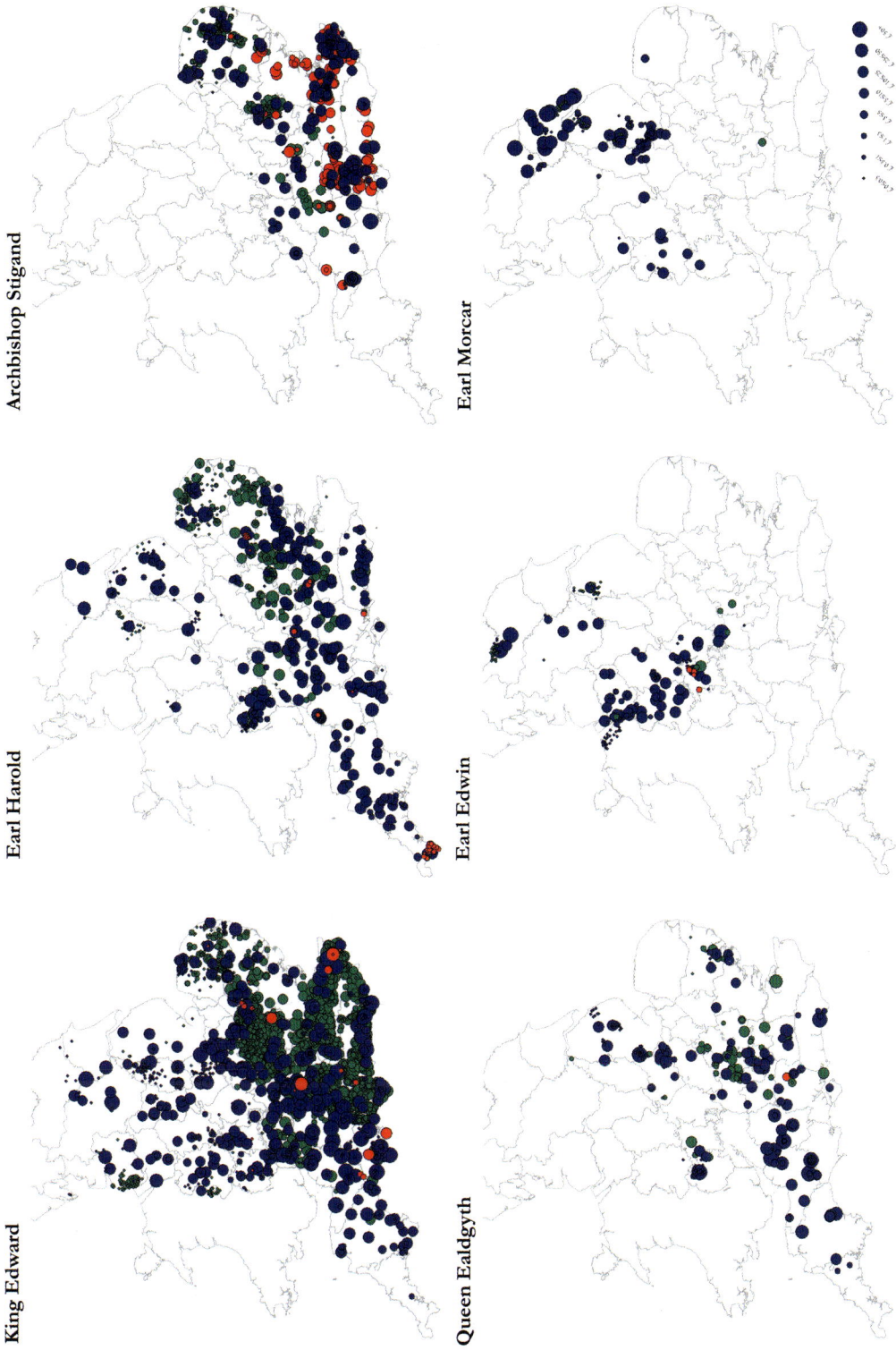

Figure 2. Maps of the estates and lordships attributed to King Edward, Queen Ealdgyth, and selected earls in Domesday Book.

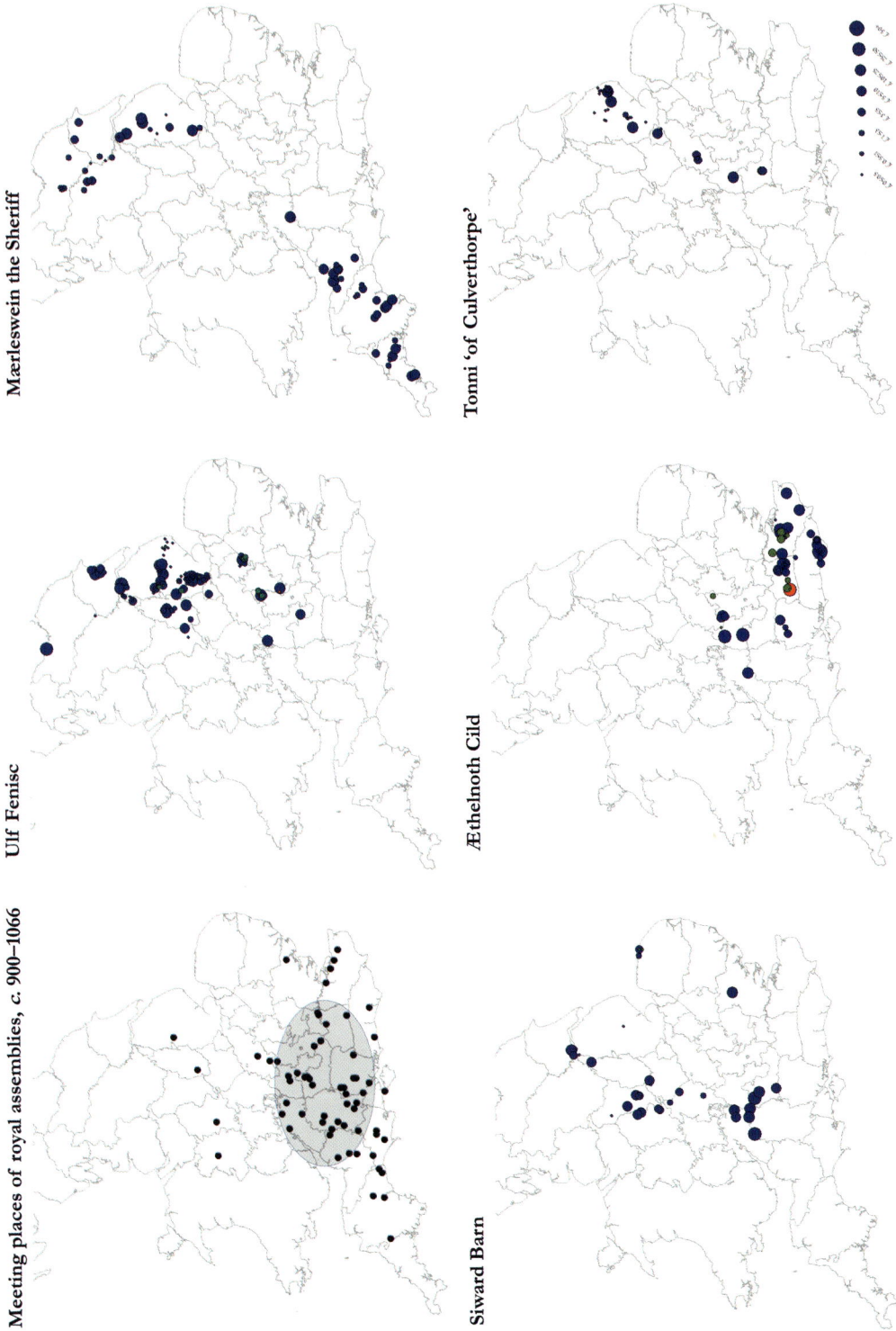

Figure 3. Maps of the meeting places of royal assemblies, c.900–1066 (top left), and of the estates attributed to selected laymen in Domesday Book.

complicated by the fact that rivalries also existed within Godwine's family: indeed, the disastrous consequences of intra-familial strife is a leitmotif of the *Vita Ædwardi*, which was commissioned by Godwine's daughter, Queen Edith. These rivalries caused much political turbulence. Members of the families of Godwine and Leofric rebelled, were exiled, and attempted to recover their earldoms using violence where necessary in 1047, 1049, 1051–2, 1055, 1058 and 1065–6. There were plainly deep divisions within the English nobility, and deep anxieties about its effects, for near-contemporary writers repeatedly expressed their fear that political conflict in England threated to make the kingdom more vulnerable to invasion: for example, the D-text of the chronicle observes that civil war was averted in 1051 because wise men argued that this would open 'a way for our enemies to enter the country and to cause great ruin among ourselves';[39] the same text says in its annal for 1052 that peace was made between Godwine and King Edward because 'they did not wish the country to be laid open to foreigners through destroying each other';[40] and *Vita Ædwardi* states that a peaceful resolution to the crisis of 1065 was temporarily achieved because the people were horrified by the prospect of civil war.[41]

In the end, such fears were realised. In the late summer of 1065, a faction rebelled against Earl Tostig's rule in Northumbria and demanded that he be replaced by Leofric's grandson, Morcar, brother of Eadwine, then earl of Mercia. The rebellion succeeded, in part because Tostig's brother Harold refused to support him, and Tostig was forced into exile. In the summer of 1066, Tostig returned to England with an army, and eventually threw in his lot with Harald Hardrada's invasion force, fighting against Morcar and Eadwine at Fulford Gate, and against King Harold at Stamford Bridge. In Tostig's absence, Harold had tried to form a marriage alliance with Eadwine and Morcar by marrying their sister Ealdgyth, but this proved fragile as soon as it was put to the test, for although they survived Fulford Gate, Eadwine and Morcar did not fight alongside Harold at Stamford Bridge or at Hastings.[42] The English were unable to offer a united resistance to invasion in 1066 in part because its political structures fostered rivalry and division.

Early Norman government

The third way in which the power of the late Anglo-Saxon state contributed to its demise is that, precisely because its institutions were centralised and effective, they were easily taken over. That, at least, is the prevailing orthodoxy, and up to a point it works, for it is demonstrable that much of the machinery of English government remained functional during the early Norman period. This is not surprising, for the Normans were pragmatic opportunists, adept at taking over and working with whatever institutional structures they found. They had done so in Normandy in the tenth century, and did so in the eleventh when they conquered southern Italy and Sicily.[43] However, when specific features of the government of conquered England are considered more closely, it becomes apparent that all of them were affected to some degree (some considerably).

The monetary system is a good example, for it represents one of the most promising cases for continuity. There can be no doubt that its main characteristics were preserved. This is brought out by Figure 4, which illustrates three silver pennies struck in the names of kings Edward the Confessor, Harold II and William I immediately before, during and after 1066: all three bear the king's name and a crowned figure in profile on the obverse, and the name of the moneyer Anderboda of Winchester on the reverse, so they were struck by the same moneyer in the same mint. It will be apparent that all three share the same fundamental characteristics. These coins are compared in the same figure with two Norman derniers, representing the coinage current in Normandy c. 1050 × 1075. The former bears an unintelligible inscription on the obverse and a building on the reverse, which represents a devolved version of the Temple type that occurs on many Carolingian coins; the latter names the city of Rouen (ROTOMAGVS) on the obverse, and the reverse has a devolved version of the Carolus monogram of Charlemagne, which also occurs on many Carolingian coins. The difference in quality between the two coinages is immediately apparent in these images, and reflects a gulf in the power and sophistication of English and Norman government at the time of the conquest. It should occasion no surprise, therefore, that the Normans chose to preserve the main features of the English coinage system and made no attempt to import their own coinage to conquered England. William's coinage in England shared the following features in common with those of Edward the Confessor and Harold II: it was voluminous, struck in large quantities, sustaining a currency of considerable scale such that a significant proportion of the economy was monetised; it was uniform, produced to a single, standardised design, and possessed a consistently high silver content; it constituted a royal monopoly, for no other lords other than the king were authorised to issue coins in their own names (though a few shared the profits and prestige of minting), and foreign coin did not circulate in England in significant quantities; its designs constituted an important expression of royal authority and medium for symbolic communication; the system was both centralised and flexibly devolved, for royal officials controlled the design, production and distribution of the dies, and the fact that coins bore the names of moneyers and the place of minting served as a check against the production of fraudulent and low-quality coin; the network of mints places was extensive and geographically widespread such that it would have been rare to be more than a day's ride from a mint anywhere in England south of York; and this network helped to facilitate a system of *renovatio monetae*, which involved frequent, if not necessarily regular, recoinages.[44] In addition, the designs of William's coins were broadly

Obverse (a)   (b)   (c)

Reverse (a)   (b)   (c)

Figure 4. Three English pennies of Edward the Confessor, Harold II, and William the Conqueror, all struck by the moneyer Anderboda of Winchester: (a) Edward the Confessor Pyramids type (BM 1851, 3–13, 19); (b) Harold II PAX type (BM 1851, 3–13, 92); William I Profile or Cross fleury type (BMC William I, no. 53). Reproduced with permission. © The British Museum.

Obverse   (a)   (b)

Reverse   (a)   (b)

Figure 5. Two Norman derniers, representing the coinage current in Normandy c. 1050 × 1075, from the Fitzwilliam Museum Cambridge collection: (a) CM.PG.2500–2006; (b) CM.PG.2490–2006. Reproduced with permission. © The Fitzwilliam Museum, Cambridge.

conservative, drawing on a similar repertoire of styles and motifs: for example, William's first issue preserved the broad design of Harold's bust, though for all the obvious reasons the word PAX (peace) was removed from the reverse of his first issue, which reverted to a more traditional cruciform design (Figure 4). Foreign coin did not circulate in significant volumes in England, or for that matter in Normandy – there was no attempt to establish a currency union in William's reign, or at any point before 1204.[45] A large proportion of moneyers remained in office, and the overwhelming majority of moneyers remained English. Fifty years ago, Dolley estimated that about 100 of the 140 moneyers who struck the coins of Harold II also struck coin for William I and William II, and that 375 of the 400 moneyers who struck coin for William bore indigenous names.[46] Studies of more recent datasets have refined this picture without transforming it. It now looks as if there may have been a short-term disruption to mint organisation in the immediate aftermath of the Conquest, for the rate of continuity of moneyers and mints between Harold's coinage and William's first issue is slightly lower than is typical between reigns. All the same, between half and two-thirds of the moneyers who struck the first two issues of William's coins had also struck coins for Edward the Confessor or Harold II; the mint network soon recovered to the extent that, with the single exception of Droitwich, all of the mints that struck coin for Harold struck coin also for William; and the overwhelming preponderance of William's English coins were struck by moneyers bearing English and Anglo-Scandinavian names.[47]

Even so, the impact of conquest remains visible in the numismatic record. King William increased his share of the profits of coinage, introducing a new and more onerous way of taxing moneyers.[48] The geographical spread of minting began to expand in the mid to late 1080s with the introduction of mints at Durham, Rhuddlan and two or three places in south Wales (St David's, Cardiff and just possibly Abergavenny).[49] In addition, recent estimates of the size of the currency have produced suggestive evidence of a further significant shift. The best available index for the size of the currency is the average number of coins found singly per year of issue, and the average for the period between 1066 and 1100 is roughly half that of the period between 1042 and 1066.[50] It is therefore probable that there was a sharp reduction in the size of the currency between 1066 and 1100. The extent to which this was caused by the Norman Conquest or wider economic developments remains unclear, for England, like much of western Europe, was affected by a precipitous decline in the supply of silver from mines in Germany in the late 11th century.[51] All the same, there remain grounds for suspecting that large-scale exports of coin to Normandy was a contributory factor. In a vivid passage, William of Malmesbury described a pair of conjoined twins – one laughing, eating and talking, the other crying, fasting, and silent – and compared this unfortunate prodigy to the Anglo-Norman economy: 'Normandy, dead and nearly sucked dry, is supported by the financial strength of England'.[52] Numismatic evidence lends this horrific image historical credence.[53]

The English coinage system was not the only form of government affected by conquest. Royal priests, among them Regenbald 'the chancellor', continued to serve the king in England by drafting writs and royal diplomas cast in similar diplomatic form, but from the early 1070s, writs were usually issued in Latin, not the vernacular as was the norm before 1066.[54] The shire remained the most important unit of local government, and the sheriff remained responsible for administering it, but the Conqueror's sheriffs tended to be much wealthier and more powerful than the Confessor's, many of whom had been relatively modest landholders.[55] The growth of the power of sheriffs coincided with a decline in that of earls. The Conqueror made comital appointments sparingly; he also dismantled earldoms, reducing the number of shires assigned to each such that the remaining earldoms tended to be concentrated power blocs in frontier zones.[56] The Anglo-Saxon Chronicle, the Northamptonshire geld account, and the geld accounts in Exon Domesday confirm that the Conqueror's regime continued to levy the geld. However, the Exon geld accounts reveal a new system of geld exemption in operation. The demesne portion of barons' demesne was exempted: in other words, the burden of the geld fell principally upon subtenants and the dependent peasantry, and not on tenants-in-chief (landholders who held directly from the king). Pre-Conquest kings are known to have reduced the geld liabilities of particular manors as a way of exercising patronage, but this systematic method of exemption was unprecedented.[57]

William revived the practice of issuing legislation, which had been in abeyance since the reign of Cnut, and some of the Conqueror's legislation, including his prescriptions on loyalty oaths and frankpledge, forms an integral part of a sequence of legislation concerned with the pursuit of crime which began in the late ninth century.[58] However, much of the Conqueror's legislation explicitly discriminates between the *Franci*, defined as Frenchmen who followed William to England in and after 1066, and the *Angli*, defined as those who were in England before the conquest regardless of their ethnicity. William I's legislation on exculpation made it easier for *Franci* than for *Angli* to clear themselves of blame for an alleged crime: in certain circumstances, the former could clear themselves by swearing oaths, whereas the latter had to undergo the ordeal. Similarly, the Conqueror's *murdum* fine prescribed specific, heavy penalties for lords and hundredal communities in the event that *Franci*, not *Angli*, were murdered in any given locality. Although there were pre-Conquest precedents for elements of this law, the *murdrum* fine brought them together for a new purpose; namely, the protection of Frenchmen in newly-conquered hostile territory.[59] This was novel, ethnically discriminatory justice: in effect, apartheid justice.

The Conquest also caused profound changes to England's political structures. There was, admittedly, much continuity in the form and function of royal assemblies: they dealt with similar business, and were often convened at Gloucester, Winchester and Westminster, perpetuating a rhythm established during the Confessor's reign.[60] But there was a dramatic shift in the royal itinerary, because the king was in Normandy more often than England: indeed, the best available evidence suggests that he was in Normandy for roughly 75 per cent of the time between 1072 and 1087.[61] There was also a drastic change in personnel. The witness lists of two diplomas issued in May 1068 suggest that William then intended to govern through an Anglo-Norman elite just as Cnut had done 50 years earlier, for both contain vernacular and Latin text, and more significantly both contain exactly equal numbers of *Franci* and *Angli* (Table 1).

The rebellions between 1068 and 1071 caused William to change this policy abruptly. There followed a purge of the secular and religious hierarchies, and from the mid-1070s onwards, royal assemblies were dominated by Frenchmen.[62] The exercise of royal patronage also changed beyond recognition. Domesday Book records the most sudden and dramatic change to the propertied classes in Britain's recorded history. William redistributed the lands of about 38,000 Englishmen to fewer than 1,200 tenants-in-chief, who in turn enfeoffed about one-third of their landed wealth to each other and about 6,000 other subtenants. The royal demesne doubled, and there was sharp concentration of wealth such that 90 per cent of the kingdom's wealth was controlled by about 150 people. Only a handful of these lords were English, and considerably less than ten per cent of the kingdom's manorial surpluses remained in English hands. By 1086, all landholders were considered to be the king's tenants, for all land was held immediately or mediately from the king: as one entry in Domesday remarks, it was not permissible for anyone to possess land 'except by grant of the king' (*nisi regis concessu*).[63] King Edward was rich and enjoyed extensive powers of patronage, but not on this scale or in this way.[64] These tenurial changes may well have resulted in a significant shift in the kingdom's political structure, for a powerful case has been made for thinking that assembly politics became more closely tied to tenure shortly after the Conquest, such that tenants-in-chief were summoned to royal councils by virtue of their fiefs, and in the expectation that they should provide their royal lord *consilium* in respect of them.[65] It is hard to think of an institution of royal government which did not survive the Conquest, but it is also hard to think of one that survived unchanged and many were changed profoundly.

Domesday Book

The Domesday survey was one of the most awesome feats of medieval government, hence its very name. It successfully recorded information relating to about 29,000 pieces of property in 13,000 places south of

	Regesta, ed. Bates, no. 286		Regesta, ed. Bates, no. 181	
	Franci	Angli	Franci	Angli
1	King William	[Giso, bishop of Wells]*	King William	[Ingelric, the king's priest]
2	Queen Matilda	Stigand, archbishop (of Canterbury)	Queen Matilda	Stigand, archbishop (of Canterbury)
3	Odo, bishop (of Bayeux)	Ealdred, archbishop (of York)	Richard, the king's son	Ealdred, archbishop (of York)
4	Hugh, bishop (of Lisieux)	Hereman, bishop (of Ramsbury)*	Odo, bishop (of Bayeux)	William, bishop (of London)*
5	Geoffrey, bishop (of Coutances)	Leofric, bishop (of Exeter)	Hugh, bishop (of Lisieux)	Hereman, bishop (of Ramsbury)*
6	Remigius, bishop (of Dorchester)	Æthelmaer, bishop (of Elmham)	Geoffrey, bishop (of Coutances)	Leofric, bishop (of Exeter)
7	Earl William	William, bishop (of London)*	Earl William fitzOsbern	Giso, bishop (of Wells)*
8	Robert, the king's brother	Æthelric, bishop (of Selsey)	Robert, the king's brother	Eadwine, abbot (of Westminster)
9	Roger princeps	Walter, bishop (of Hereford)	Robert, comesᵃ	Wulfwold, abbot (of Bath)
10	Walter Giffard	Wulfsig, bishopᵇ	Earl Roger	Baldwin, abbot (of Bury St Edmunds)*
11	Hugh de Montfort	Æthelnoth, abbot (of Glastonbury)	Richard fitzGilbert	Æthelsige, abbotᶜ
12	William de Courseulles	Leofweard, abbot (of Muchelney)	William Malet	Thurstan, abbot (of Ely)
13	Serlo de Burcy	Wulfwold, abbot (of Bath)	Herfast, the king's chancellor	Brand, abbot (of Peterborough)
14	Roger Derundel	Wulfgeat, abbot (of Athelney)	Michael, chaplain	Ælfwine, abbot (of Ramsey)
15	Richard, the king's son	Earl Waltheof	Gilbert, chaplain	Æthelwig, abbot (of Evesham)
16	Walter the Fleming	Earl Eadwine	William, chaplain	Sihtric, abbot (St Benet of Hulme)
17	Rambriht the Fleming	Tofi minister	Thomas, chaplain	Earl Eadwine
18	Thurstan	Ælfgar of Thornfalcon	Bernard, chaplain	Earl Morcar
19	Baldwin de Wartenbeke	Bondig the staller	Walter, chaplain	Earl Waltheof
20	Othelheard	Robert the staller*	Robert, chaplain	Osbern, chaplain*
21	Heimericus	Wulfweard		
22	Dinni	Hearding		
23	William de Vauville	Adzor		
24	Robert d'Oilly	Brixi		
25	Roger pincerna	Brihtric		

Table 1. The composition of the witness lists of two royal diplomas issued in May 1068ᵈ

a Robert de Commines?

b Probably a scribal error for Wulfstan, bishop of Worcester.

c Of St Augustine's, Canterbury?

d In this table, asterisks indicate Angli (men of continental origin present in England before 1066) and square brackets indicate the beneficiary of the diploma, not named in the witness list.

the Tees in a matter of months. This astonishing exercise reveals much about the resources and priorities of early Norman government, so it is worth pausing to ask: how and why was it done?[66]

The survey was launched in late 1085 in an atmosphere of crisis. Earlier that year, King William was in Normandy when the news broke that King Cnut IV of Denmark and Count Robert of Flanders were planning to invade England. William crossed the Channel with a great army and set about strengthening the kingdom's defences. Then, in mid-winter, he convened a royal assembly at Gloucester and, after much thought and deep discussion with his counsellors, launched the Domesday survey.[67] The survey's terms of reference were issued, the kingdom was divided into seven circuits consisting of several contiguous shires, and groups of commissioners were made responsible for surveying each circuit. There followed an intensive phase of fieldwork, during which royal officials assembled information relating to the geld, pre-Conquest landholding and lordship arrangements, drawing extensively on existing geld lists, and tenants-in-chief collected further details relating to each of their manors. The commissioners then made appointments to meet, inter- view and 'inbrief' each tenant-in-chief behind closed doors. During these meetings, the commissioners' scribes produced a first draft of the survey by splicing together the information collected by royal and bar- onial officials. At this stage, the text was organised geographically, by hundred, vill and manor in that order, and the output consisted of a series of booklets, each containing information relating to manors in a specific hundred. We know this principally because we have *Inquisitio Comitatus Cantebrigiensis*, a fragmentary 12th-century copy of a text produced in Cambridgeshire, which was written at this stage of the survey and is organised by hundred and vill; and because there is a pronounced hundredal grouping of manors throughout the remainder of the Domesday corpus. The first phase of the inquest thus generated cadastral documents: material organised geographically in the same way that the geld was administered and collected. The logistics were tight, but it is demonstrable that, provided each group of commissioners employed several scribes and kept them occupied with a steady flow of work, there was enough time to complete this stage of the survey before Easter (5 April) 1086, when a royal assembly was convened at Winchester.

After Easter, the cadastral documents were checked in public sessions. These consisted of extraordinary meetings of shire courts, presided over by commissioners who were neutral to the extent that they did not hold land in the regions they surveyed, and attended by tenants-in-chief, their entourages, and by jurors representing each hundred and vill. The cadastral documents were read out, and the jurors were placed on oath and asked to verify or contest their content. The principal focus at this stage was on questions relating to title: 'who held in the time of King Edward, and who holds it now?' and 'has anything been added to or taken away from the estate'? The answers to these questions recorded in the cadastral documents were scrutinised, and the commissioners took special note of disputes between the king and tenants-in-chief and between the tenants-in-chief themselves. When disputes arose, the commissioners recorded the relevant details, but did not usually attempt to resolve them. The cadastral documents were thus augmented with judicial material, which was recorded and subsequently transmitted in various ways in different circuits: some circuits produced separate lists of disputes, which survive as the *clamores* of circuit VI in Great Domesday Book, the *invasiones super regem* of Little Domesday, and the *terrae occupatae* of Exon; other circuits found different ways to integrate judicial matter into the cadastral text. The volume of disputed material was considerable, between five and ten per cent of manorial entries were challenged. Nevertheless, provided the commissioners maintained good order and a high tempo, it was logistically feasible for them to complete this checking phase between Easter and Whitsun (24 May 1086), when a royal assembly was convened at Westminster.

Then, between Whitsun and Lammas (1 August), the material was reconstituted into a feudal order, grouped by tenant-in-chief. Exon Domesday is the only surviving manuscript witness to this stage of the survey. It covers five southwestern shires (Dorset, Wiltshire, Somerset, Devon and Cornwall), and reveals a group of about two dozen scribes working under considerable pressure, and therefore collaborating in ways that maximised their productivity.[68] Their task was to extract all of the information relating to particular tenants-in-chief from the hundredally organised texts and to record this information in fresh booklets, each representing the fief of a particular tenant-in-chief. They arrived at an ingenious way of doing this without getting in each other's way. The hundredal booklets were laid out in sequence, forming a production line, and the scribes worked down this line extracting information from each booklet in sequence; when they encountered a gap in the sequence caused by the fact that the next booklet was being used by another scribe, they simply put the fief they had been working on in a pending tray next to this gap to indicate how far it had progressed down the production line and started again from the beginning with a new fief; once the missing hundredal booklet was returned to its former position, another scribe could resume work on the fief in the pending tray. This process resulted in one of the most distinctive features of Exon Domesday: namely the fact that different hands are often visible at work on the same page (Figure 6). The transitions from one scribe to another invariably occur at hundredal boundaries because the availability of hundredal booklets determined their work flow. Finally, a summary of each fief was made, which calculated the total amount of land held by each tenant-in-chief in the southwestern shires. At that point, Exon Domesday was bound to make it suitable for presentation to King William. The other six circuit returns perhaps received the same treatment: the Anglo-Saxon Chronicle certainly records that

& ii· bordarios· &· ii· seruos· &· iiii· agros nemoris· & viii· agros pti· & xxv·

agros pascue· hęc uales· vii· sol· &· vi· den· & qu comes recep ualebat· xii· den·

hanc tenrã comes cu honore Edmeratoru·

Comes he i ma q uocat· Doneuoldehama· q ten Ademar ei die q

E· rex· f· ii· &m· & ista tra e coniuncta tre Ermaratoli· Er redd gild

p̃· v· uirga· &· i· fortino· has poss arar· iii· carr· Eo Aluered ten ea de Comite·

Inde he· A· in dnio· i· fertd· & uill· i· uirga· &· iii· carr· Ibi he· A· vi· bord

&· i· seruu· &· v· ag nemoir· & iiii· ag pti· & uat p ann· x· sol· & q dor

nat· v· sol· Comes he· i· manu q uocat· Scę Marię Cherche· q ten Or

dolf² ea die q rex· E· f· ii· &· cn· &⁷ redd gildu p· i· hida· hanc poss arar

·iiii· carr· hanc ten· Ricard² fili² Torolui de Comite· Inde he· R· in dnio

·ii· uirg· &· ii· carr· &⁷ uill· ii· uirg· &· i· carr· & dim· Ibi he· R· v· uill·

⁊ viii· bord· &· iii· seruos· &· i· rucin· &· iiii· aalia· &· v· porc· & c· x·

oues· &· i· ag pti· & uat p ann· xl· sol· & qn Recep comes· xx· sol·

Comes he· i· ma q uocat bonetona q ten Elmerus ea die q rex·

E· f· ii· &· cn· & redd gildu p· v· hid· has poss arare· & xviii·

in dnio· ii· hid·
carr· hac teni· Droeus de C· hnhe· & uill· iii· hid· & xvi· carr· Ibi te

A· xx· iiii· uill· &· vi· bord· &· iii· serui· &· ii· anull· & iiii·

poras· &· c· oues· xxiiii· &· l· agros nemoris· &· xviii· agros

pti· &· i· leug inlong⁊ pascue &· v· quadrag in latitud· & i·

all the 'records' (*gewrita*) were brought to the king.[69] It also says that all the landholders of any account met at a royal assembly convened at Old Sarum on 1 August 1086, and there performed homage to the king.[70] In a famous paper, Sir James Holt asked (reasonably enough) what they performed homage for and answered (persuasively) that they did so for in return for their land, now recorded in writing.[71]

Shortly afterwards, King William travelled to the Isle of Wight before making what turned out to be his last Channel crossing, but work on Domesday continued in his absence. Some of the circuit returns needed to be tidied up before further progress could be made with them: Little Domesday Book appears to be a fair copy of the circuit return for Essex, Norfolk and Suffolk, and was probably written at this stage. Meanwhile, the task of turning the circuit returns into a single volume, Great Domesday Book, was assigned to a single, exceptionally talented scribe, supported by at least one other scribe who helped him with corrections. The main Great Domesday scribe abbreviated the text by about 40 per cent by using snappier formulae and by omitting certain categories of data, including livestock. He also reorganised the material, presenting it first by shire, within shire by fief, and within fief by manor; and he added tables of contents at the beginning of each shire sections, together with headings and rubrics throughout the text. This made the text much easier to navigate, and made it for readers possible to identify the holdings of tenants-in-chief in each shire very efficiently. Precisely when this was done remains uncertain, but the balance of evidence strongly suggests that the writing of Great Domesday commenced immediately after the survey, in the autumn of 1086. It is also probable that all but one of the circuit returns had been written when news of the king's death (in Normandy on 9 September 1087) arrived, and that a decision was then made not to abbreviate the one remaining circuit, but instead to add a table of contents and colophon to Little Domesday to make it resemble Great Domesday. If so, the two volumes of Domesday Book would have been complete prior to the coronation of King William II.

Why was all this done? Throughout the 19th and early 20th centuries, the prevailing orthodoxy was that the Domesday survey was principally concerned with the administration of the geld.[72] In the mid-20th century, Vivian Galbraith advanced a radically new interpretation, arguing that Domesday Book was intended to strengthen the king in the exercise of his feudal rights over tenants-in-chief.[73] Sir James Holt concurred, reasoning that Domesday Book was carefully structured to inform the administration of the profits of royal lordship by sheriffs and treasury officials, but he also observed that the survey could not have been undertaken without the cooperation of the barons, and suggested that this was because the survey also gave them something they desperately wanted: a record of their property rights which would give them greater security of title.[74] Subsequent scholarship has posited further motives for the survey: for instance, it has been suggested that it was a response to the threat of Danish invasion and the logistical and financial problems this posed.[75] It has even been suggested that the Domesday survey and the making of Domesday Book itself were quite separate initiatives, and that the latter was commissioned by King William II with different objectives to those of his father.[76]

The interpretation advanced here is that the Domesday survey was intended from the inception to generate several different outputs, including Domesday Book itself, and that each was designed to serve a different purpose, yielding a range of benefits to various parties. The king wanted to maximise his income, of course, but he also wanted to be strengthened in his rights as the source of all tenure, and to reassert his authority. The survey provided for all this. A vital point to register here is that the king generated income and did so from a range of different sources, and that to manage them efficiently, royal officials needed information structured in different ways. The best way to get a sense of how Anglo-Norman kings generated income is to consider the Pipe Roll of King Henry I for 1129–30.[77] This reveals that Henry's income was derived from four main sources: 'county farms' (that is, income from royal demesne), the geld, and the profits of government, justice and royal lordship (Figure 7). The specific accounting processes revealed in this pipe roll doubtless evolved between 1086 and 1129, but a treasury (*thesaurius*) unquestionably existed at Winchester in 1086, for it is first documented in Exon Domesday, and it is demonstrable that money flowed into the Conqueror's treasury from broadly similar sources. It is also clear that the Domesday survey created different kinds of document, each structured to facilitate the administration of specific income streams. Thus, the first stage of the survey generated cadastral documents, which were arranged in the same way that the geld was administered, presumably because they intended to make the administration of the geld more efficient. The second stage of the survey resulted in long lists of property disputes, which gave the king abundant scope to generate profits from justice by offering disputants 'help with judicial matters' as the Pipe Roll puts it. The third stage of the survey reconstituted all this into feudal order, so that the king possessed lists of the manors held by each tenant-in-chief, together with summaries. This was done on the presumption that, sooner or later, the honours of all tenants-in-chief, whether secular or lay, would fall into royal con-trol: some only briefly and notionally, until the king determined how much its successor should pay for the right to succeed to the honour, and some for much longer periods. The Domesday fief summaries were designed to enable royal officials to establish the total size and value of each honour quickly and efficiently, since that information would strengthen the king's hand when it came to negotiating feudal incidents. In addition, the detailed descriptions of fiefs in the circuit returns were carefully designed to enable royal officials to administer honours more efficiently, for each entry revealed how much income manors currently

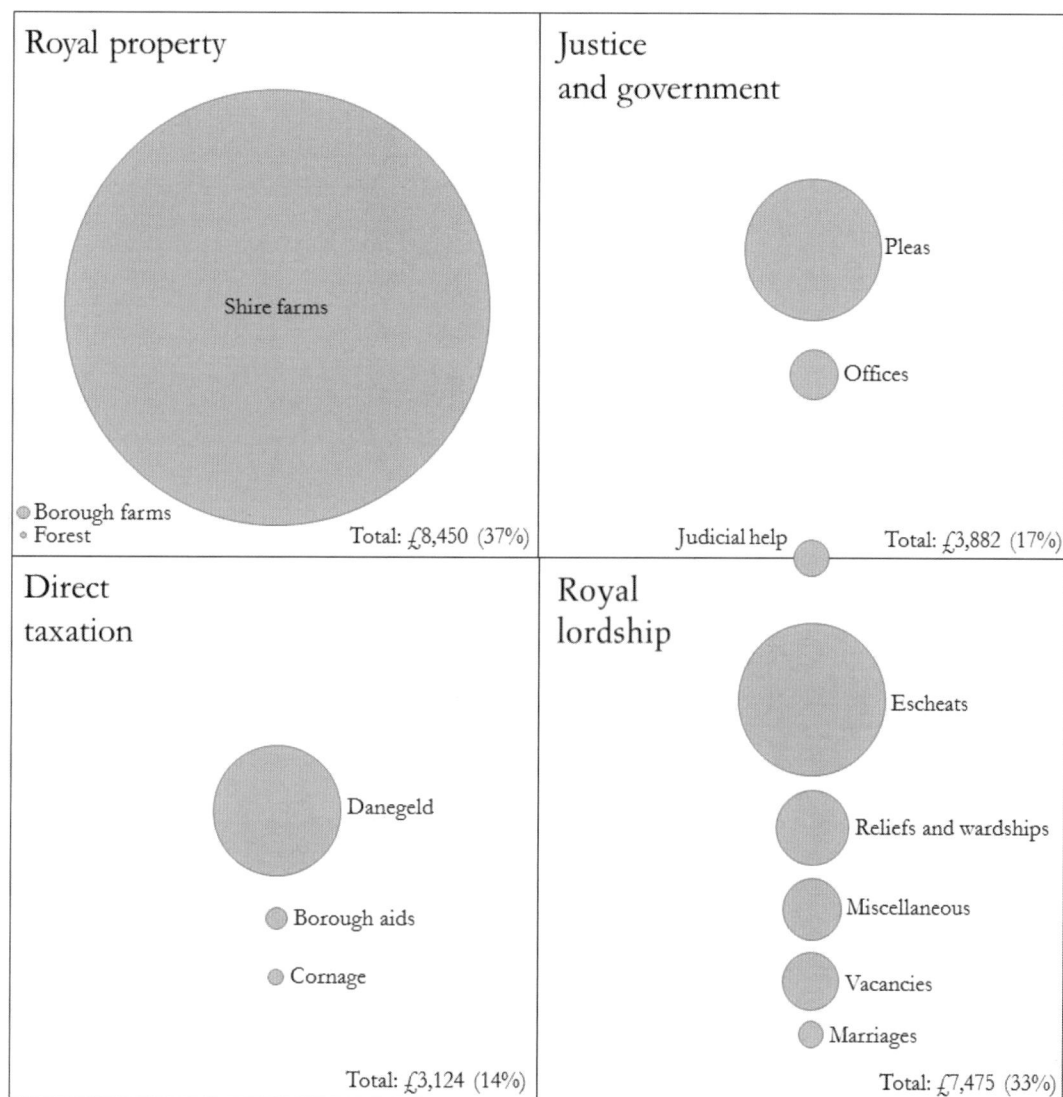

Royal property

Shire farms

Borough farms
Forest

Total: £8,450 (37%)

Justice
and government

Pleas

Offices

Judicial help   Total: £3,882 (17%)

Direct
taxation

Danegeld

Borough aids

Cornage

Total: £3,124 (14%)

Royal
lordship

Escheats

Reliefs and wardships

Miscellaneous

Vacancies

Marriages

Total: £7,475 (33%)

generated, and whether there was potential to squeeze more out of them: they thus answered the last question in the survey's terms of reference, which asked if more could be taken than was currently taken from each manor. Finally, Domesday Book itself rearranged this information by shire and compressed it to make it more user-friendly for the treasury officials and sheriffs who administered these income streams. In addition, the feudal arrangement of the circuit returns and Domesday Book itself constituted a comprehensive survey of the royal demesne, which was also administered by sheriffs. Nor was this all. The Domesday survey was an extraordinary, carefully choreographed assertion of royal

Figure 7. Analysis of the Pipe Roll of King Henry I for 1129–30 illustrating amounts paid into the treasury during that financial year.

might, designed to make the king's authority manifest in every household in the kingdom: it was an act of symbolic communication on an
unprecedented scale.

Why did the barons participate? Holt was right to ask this question,
and right to answer as he did: the barons fell over themselves to give the
king what he wanted because they got something precious in return. The
Domesday survey embodied virtually all the ritual and documentary
elements customarily associated with land conveyance.[78] The first stage
of the survey grew out of geld lists, and was integrated with the collection
of the king's geld; English law privileged the rights of those anyone who,
in Domesday parlance, 'defended' their land to the geld. The second
stage of the survey ensured that property rights were witnessed in public
courts. It also drew upon sworn testimony, and so, like the anathema
clauses of charters, invoked the sanction of divine retribution. The third
stage of the survey reconstituted this matter into feudally-arranged lists,
which were analogous in form to Carolingian estate surveys,[79] and comparable in function to pancartes – comprehensive confirmation charters
which became much sought after in Normandy during the Conqueror's
reign.[80] The whole exercise culminated in the performance of homage
at a royal assembly. This amounted to just about the most comprehensive package of security that was conceivable within the framework
of dependence that the survey enshrined. Christmas 1085 was an
unusually opportune moment to launch the survey because most of the
leading barons were then in England. The survey was not a response to
the threat of invasion, but was made possible by it.

The survey's benefits also flowed further down the social hierarchy.
The subtenants of tenants-in-chief obtained greater security for their
holdings for much the same reasons as their lords. Indeed, the annal
for 1086 specifically states that the oath of Salisbury encompassed all
landholders of any account, no matter whose men they were.[81] The
survey also afforded subtenants greater protection when their lords'
honours escheated to the king or descended to heirs, for if subtenants
were dispossessed in the process the survey would provide them with
evidence in support of claims of the kind later known as novel disseisin.
There was perhaps even something in the survey for lesser landholders.
The news from Denmark allowed the regime to position the survey as a
response a threat to the *res publica*, as William of Malmesbury put it.[82]
The survey perhaps gave the English a sense of closure, and its public
sessions were doubtless a spectacle that few would have wanted to miss.
There were undoubtedly consensual and communal elements in the
Domesday survey: since it mobilised thousands of minor landholders
as well as the entire landholding elite, that could scarcely be otherwise.
On the other hand, we must recall that the author of the annal for 1085
in the E-text of the chronicle was shocked by the survey's intrusiveness;
that landholders were required to attend the survey on pain of forfeiture,
and that jurors did so on pain of fine; and that most of the Englishman

who attended the survey would have been compelled to witness and confirm, on oath, both the loss of their patrimony and the diminution of their social status. When Æthelric of Marsh Gibbon told the Domesday commissioners that he held four hides there freely in 1066, but now held them 'at farm' from William fitzAnsculf *grauiter et miserabiliter*, he captured something of the essence of the survey's mood.[83] Domesday acquired an awful reputation and name for good reasons. It was one act of domination that recorded the effects of another.

Conclusion

English government was complex and powerful before 1066. Paradoxically, this helps to explain why it was conquered: the efficiency with which England's surplus wealth was extracted by its kings and lords made it an attractive target; the nature and scale of royal patronage made assembly politics viable, but also engendered political division and therefore diminished the kingdom's capacity to resist invasion; and the fact that the machinery of royal government was robust meant that it was relatively easy to take over as a going concern. However, none of that machinery survived the Norman Conquest entirely unchanged. The Domesday survey was in this respect characteristic. It could not have been completed without the institutions bequeathed to the Normans by the English: the fact that it peters out in the un-shired north makes that point eloquently. However, those institutions had never been deployed on quite this scale or for anything like these purposes. Nor were they the survey's only models, for it also drew inspiration from continental technologies and practices. The production of cadastral records to establish landed society's taxable capacity recalls a central feature of late Roman government;[84] the closest parallels to Domesday are Carolingian estate surveys and Norman pancartes; the language and working methods of the scribes who wrote Exon Domesday suggests that they were trained in northern France. Domesday, therefore, has a deep contextual hinterland, but nothing quite like it was achieved by any other medieval polity. The survey was brilliantly conceived, executed with astonishing efficiency, and driven by the limitless energy of William the Conqueror. It also reveals a different mode of government in action, serving new masters with novel priorities that were a function of the tenurial transformation that it records.

10

1066 and the Church

Tom Licence and T. A. Heslop

The usual narrative concerning the English Church in 1066 is that it was lax, worldly and in need of reform. Practices condemned by the Gregorian party of the papacy, including pluralism, nepotism and clerical marriage, were sanctioned by its leaders, and of the two archbishops, Stigand was a usurper who held his pallium from an antipope, while Ealdred had narrowly avoided deposition for moving from one see to another without papal permission. The arrival of William's army brandishing – if we believe the ducal apologist William of Poitiers – a papal banner sounded the death knell not only for King Harold, who had perjured himself on holy relics, but also for a national Church which could be regarded as a rotten tree, ripe for the bonfire. Contemporaries who accepted the idea that the Conquest was God's punishment of the English for their sins embraced the circular logic of their premise, that the English Church was corrupt. The author of the Life of Edward the Confessor, writing in about 1067, claimed that Edward had declared on his deathbed that the earls, bishops and abbots and all those in holy orders were not what they seemed to be, but, on the contrary, were servants of the devil.[1] A few years later, in 1070, senior prelates who had survived to that point, including Stigand, the archbishop of Canterbury, were deposed on papal authority, and leadership of the English Church passed into Norman hands. Abuses were then stamped out, we are told; relations with the Papacy were restored; the arch-see of Canterbury was occupied by scrupulous and learned men – Lanfranc in the first instance and then Anselm, both Benedictine monks. Libraries were stocked with patristic texts of unimpeachable authority; new monasteries were founded, and dingy Anglo-Saxon churches were replaced with grand specimens of Romanesque architecture which signalled both modernity and reverence for early Christian commitment in their grand scale and stylistic integrity.

Though initially there was scepticism about the sanctity of some 'English' saints, especially the recent ones such as St Ælfheah (an archbishop of Canterbury killed by the Danes), some of the newcomers realised local cults were a major asset, devotionally and economically.[2] For Susan Ridyard, the Conquest was 'one of the better things ever to happen to the saints of the Anglo-Saxons',[3] and the general drift in the primary and secondary literature is that 1066 was a 'Good Thing' for the Church.

Criticism of the late Anglo-Saxon Church established a narrative in which both the victors and the vanquished colluded. The English had learned long ago from Archbishop Wulfstan II of York (and other Jeremiahs such as Alcuin) to see defeat as a form of divine chastisement for their sins. 'God's dues have dwindled too long in every district within this nation, and the laws of the people have deteriorated all too much, and sanctuaries are violated far and wide, and the houses of God are entirely despoiled of ancient privileges and stripped inside of all that is seemly … And therefore we all through God's anger are frequently disgraced.'[4] Perhaps ironically, this trope started with the British historian Gildas, who saw the Angles and Saxons as the pagan agents of God's vengeance.[5] Later, the Anglo-Saxons regarded the Vikings as God's pagan scourge for their sins, and now – in 1066 – they saw the Normans in the same light. In espousing the 'fact' that worldliness was the cause of their downfall, the English establishment was accepting the rhetoric that had justified their own conquest of Britain. Battle Abbey was planted on the site of ultimately victorious bloodshed because it suited the Normans to expiate their violence cloaked in the white mantle of divine approval.

In the years after the Norman invasion of England, it also transpired that the zealots in Rome won out over the moderates. The latter had been more receptive to the idea of clerics holding multiple benefices, marrying and strengthening church unity through bonds of kinship – that is, by advancing their relatives in the Church. In the reign of Edward the Confessor it was far from clear which of these competing factions (representing – to put it crudely – idealism and pragmatism) would ultimately prevail. Nor was it clear which was more in the right. Such was the drift towards zealotry by the late 1070s under Pope Gregory VII that even King William and Lanfranc baulked at his commands.

There is a further reason the last century of the Anglo-Saxon Church is thought of as a phase of spiritual decline. Edgar's reign (959–75) witnessed a revival of Benedictine monasticism, which was remarkable for its amalgamation of visionary leadership, its reproductive vigour – displayed in the proliferation of new and reformed monasteries – its independence, coherent purpose and dedication to learning.[6] Another monastic revival of sorts occurred in the first two generations after the Conquest under Lanfranc and Anselm. Monasteries multiplied once more, abbots acquired reputations as strenuous pastors of their flocks, and Latin learning put forth green shoots and branched into new forms of historical writing. The most influential Church historians then and in the 20th century – one thinks of David Knowles – were monks themselves and admirers of monasticism.[7] For that reason, they tended to regard the 970s and the decades after 1070 as high points of religion with a vast trough between. In the words of Antonia Gransden: 'Historians have seen the tenth-century monastic revival and the Anglo-Norman reformation as two peaks of monastic excellence, each rising steeply from a plain of decadence'.[8] To Frank Barlow and H. R. Loyn (who borrowed his words) the entire English Church in our era 'existed in a period of slack water between two tides of reform'.[9]

The problem with this viewpoint is that monks were not the Church, though they sometimes liked to give the impression that monasticism was the measure of its spiritual health. Monks, nuns and hermits were committed to a life of prayer and ascetic practice which was believed to benefit their own souls and the souls of the limited number of people who sponsored them. It was also believed that their prayers protected the king and the realm from harm by warding off evils of various sorts and keeping the devil in check. The other category of religious men comprised the 'secular' clergy, who vastly outnumbered monks. Minster priests, mass-priests and parish priests were, almost without exception, 'seculars', meaning clergy who had not taken monastic vows and did not live inside monasteries but in the community tending to the souls of the laity. Many bishops were seculars, too, though the number of monk–bishops had grown since Edgar's time, and the number of cathedrals staffed by monks rather than secular clergy had been increasing too, as part of the ongoing 'monasticising' of the Church. Unlike monks, who did much of the writing, these seculars left very few narrative sources to balance our perspective. Yet they were the shepherds who looked after the great bulk of God's flock.

The Church is an institution – historians often envisage it in this way – but it is also and more meaningfully the congregation of the faithful abiding on earth, preparing for heaven. The Church in 1066 was not just the bishops, the monasteries, the buildings, though these were its dominant components. What we mean when we refer to 'the Church' then and today is the community of Christians under the leadership of pastors whose task was to guide them on the path to eternal life. In this respect – leaving aside ups and downs in monasticism and circular arguments about conquest being a punishment for sins – there is little reason to discredit the pastoral leadership that was in place in 1066. As in any historical endeavour seeking to avoid anachronism, we must assess the late Anglo-Saxon Church on its own terms, which means assessing it not by the standards of monks, or of the Normans who benefited from undermining its reputation, nor even by the standards of those English who reckoned it must have been corrupt, but by its own salvific aspirations; by the extent, that is, to which it bound together the faithful in devotion and guided them to Christ. For that is the only sense in which the Church in any age can properly be judged. We must ask, therefore, was the English Church achieving these things on the eve of the Conquest, and what effect did the Conquest have on its spiritual mission?

There are many kinds of sources that can help us grasp the levels of institutional Christian commitment among the English population between about 1000 and the Norman invasion. Two, however, stand out. One is the liturgical calendars which recorded devotion to saints whose cults were celebrated on certain days of the year. Although most extant texts are monastic in origin, there is no reason to doubt that from around the millennium the English increasingly acknowledged the powers of saints, both local and exotic, as potent guardians of the wellbeing of their bodies and souls. Before about 1000 calendars were sparsely populated with holy days, but by the 1060s up to half the days in the year were 'named' for a given saint.[10]

How far the process of labelling days reached into the awareness of the population at large is harder to assess. One way of attempting to gauge how far daily life revolved around feasts of the Church is by noting when charters or chronicles record an event as happening on St So-and-So's day, which would be a fair indication of the currency of the celebration. The other is to examine early records of church dedications. For churchgoing generally we can turn to Domesday Book – the second source that helps us grasp levels of Christian commitment. It provides various details about church ownership and endowments that indicate the extent to which the population was investing in places of worship. There are six mentioned in Derby, two belonging to the king and four to citizens.[11] Given the population size, that equals roughly 40 burgess families per church. The five churches in Shrewsbury, for a similar number of people, held over five hides of land (notionally about 600 acres) between them.[12] In towns, it appears to have been primarily individual citizens or groups of them who took responsibility. In Ipswich, for example, with 538 burgesses before the Conquest, eleven churches are named, three of which are owned by priests, the remainder by laymen.[13] Similar proportions appear to have applied in pre-Conquest Norwich, with 1320 burgesses in King Edward's time and 26 churches by 1086. Four of the churches were associated with former bishops of East Anglia and two with priests, but another eighteen at least with laymen. Of these, 15 had endowments totalling 181 acres – an average of 12 acres per church. In addition to the endowed churches there were 43 chapels in Norwich, which by implication were privately funded rather than holding lands or rent income.[14] In the countryside the initiative was largely that of the manorial lords, those people of thegnly rank or with substantial local landholdings. A thegn in Norfolk called Fathir held land in Wilby, Bircham, Banham and Lexham. The last two had churches with thirty acres of land, and that in Wilby had ten acres.[15] This can be taken as prima facie evidence that Fathir had founded and endowed them. On this kind of showing it would be hard to argue that the population was lacklustre in its commitment to Christianity in the years before the Battle of Hastings. As Ann Williams has demonstrated by cataloguing all sorts of cases, thegns in Edward the Confessor's reign invested in the Church.[16]

One process at work from the 960s, if not earlier, was the subdivision of 'minster' parishes into smaller units. In the century before the Conquest, the old system of parochial care, which saw the clergy ministering from large collegiate churches called minsters, gradually gave way to a more localised arrangement with landowners of thegnly status planting churches on their estates. These landowners were able to plant their churches not only because of the wealth now flowing around England – the same wealth the Vikings were often keen to plunder – but also because of legal concessions which allowed them to divert a portion of their tithes to churches on their own estates.[17] Before Edgar's reign, those tithes were owed to the minster, but Edgar's law code of the early 960s decreed that if churches with graveyards are founded within the territory of an existing minster the mother church is still to retain two-thirds of the tithing.[18] In effect, this was a concession allowing a third to be spent on a private foundation. By diverting tithes into their own church-founding projects, the landed elite brought pastoral care closer to their homes and more under their control. In effect they were claiming back tithe-payers' money. As they laid out villages for their tenants, they planted churches, setting down foundations for the networks of parishes that underpin the Church even today. By 1086, this process was very far advanced, with over 700 churches in the diocese of East Anglia – comprising Norfolk and Suffolk – alone.[19]

A good many of those churches were standing in 1066, though the records seldom identify which. Sometimes Domesday Book provides clues by illuminating the parental relationship between a minster and the daughter churches within its 'parrochia'. In Thetford, it records, 'there is one church of St Mary ... Always attached to this church have been the four churches of St Peter, St John, St Martin and St Margaret'.[20] Though 'always' must be taken as an exaggeration, the relationship was clearly well established, so we can infer that all five churches predated the Conquest. In Norwich north of the River Wensum, the church of St Clement had similar priority over later foundations, such as St Martin at Oak and St Augustine's.[21] This arrangement transcended the Conquest, as St Martin's was probably built well before 1066, whereas St Augustine's almost certainly dates from the first half of the 12th century. As this example shows, there is no doubt that more 'parish' churches were being founded in the countryside and in towns after 1066. There are, however, no real statistics for England as a whole. Where details are available, the scale of additions was not extensive but merely filled in gaps as new rural communities and suburbs were established on the margins. The Normans, evidently, were witnessing the tail end of a process begun long before.

Very few churches built before 1066 survive in anything like their original form. For standing buildings, almost all we have to go on is the material evidence of a corpus of stone buildings that, on conventional dating by style, becomes considerably richer during the second half of the 11th century. There are two problems with this: deciding which buildings or parts of them are pre-1066 and which post-, and how far those that might be from the last third of the century are perpetuating Anglo-Saxon techniques and aesthetic preferences.[22] A separate issue is the status of the churches: are they monastic, parochial or private? In some cases where the fabric is pre-Conquest the answer seems clear: at Sherborne (Dorset) there are some elements of the substantial monastic cathedral which allow a fair reconstruction including a western block, nave with aisles, a central tower and transepts.[23] Much simpler in form, but still on an impressive scale, is the church at Worth in Sussex with a nave floor area of 1,500 square feet, on an estate held by Helgi from Edward the Confessor. By comparison, Odda's chapel at Deerhurst (Gloucestershire) was a mere 400 square feet, perhaps primarily for family use.[24] None of these buildings is likely to have been typical, if by that is meant the kind of minster or parish church that most of the population would have attended for regular worship. The 11th-century wooden church of St Andrew at Greensted in Essex is more what we would expect a pre-Conquest parish church to look like.[25]

The limited survival of pre-Conquest fabric is partly due to the fact that so many of the smaller churches would have been constructed of wood. What can be gleaned about their layout usually relies on careful excavation of post holes or lines of foundation timbers still discernible even after the wood has rotted.[26] Their elevations are a matter of conjecture and thus, too, the relationship of their articulation to those of extant stone churches. Were the sizes and proportions similar, were the door and window openings of similar character, and what about the surface finish? Below-ground archaeology has revealed the groundplans of major churches on the eve of the Conquest, including Canterbury and Winchester cathedrals and the abbey of St Augustine's, Canterbury.[27] All these buildings were composites, with accretions of various dates to extend them or join existing smaller compartments together. The very different plans that resulted from this additive approach suggest that there was no well-established format being followed. At foundation level the effect is rather messy, but no doubt efforts were made to create more spatial harmony above. One author implied that the interior of Winchester was disorientating, like a labyrinth.[28] This, however, might have been thought to add to its spiritual appeal, just as the knotty interlaced patterns in Anglo-Saxon artwork guided the mind to deeper truths.

The premise of this additive approach of incorporating existing structures was the reverence that was felt for sacred buildings, associated as they were with the saints and the worship of former generations, and a desire to incorporate them into the new. Norman ideas about how to organise church buildings as spaces for worship were more coherent and consistent, but necessitated building churches anew to a set template. In the process, as Wulfstan – the last English bishop – complained, the depth and resonance of centuries-old spiritual activity was lost.[29] Imagine a higgledy-piggledy inn, enlarged over several centuries, where guests have come and gone and left something of their bustle behind in the atmosphere of the building. Now imagine ripping it down and replacing it with a chain hotel, with an open lobby and orderly suites, and you will have an idea of what the Normans did with the principal Anglo-Saxon churches – only we need to magnify this, for inns lack the emotive and spiritual associations of a treasured place of worship.

The age, mystery and labyrinthine qualities of some of those old churches were key to the atmosphere their custodians wished to create. As important to the English as the fabric of a church was its adornment with imagery and precious materials. Stephen Baxter has shown that for the thegns who were now free to spend their tithes investing in them, adorning the inside of churches was 'a way for noblemen to propitiate their Lord with the full vigour of their culture and the most valuable of their possessions'.[30] Just as they demonstrated their wealth by flaunting their silks and riding gear, they showed their love of God by lavishing riches on church interiors.[31] The spiritual advantages of doing so had long been recognised.[32] Bede's exegetical treatise on the construction of Solomon's Temple noted that images of Christ on the Cross or performing miracles would elicit compunction in the beholders and bring Christ's story to life in the minds of the illiterate.[33] In 11th-century England the principle still operated to powerful effect, for the interiors of churches, like the liturgy and private prayers, focused worshipers' minds upon the presence of Christ and his saints and upon the splendours of the heavens.[34] What Caroline Walker Bynum has termed 'Christian materiality' – an investment in the notion that material objects such as statues and shrine-jewellery make the divine immanent on earth – had its roots very firmly in our period.[35]

During the second quarter of the 11th century, a fashion was developing for adorning church interiors with life-sized crucifixes, crucifixion groups (that is, statues of Christ on the Cross, Mary and John) and large statues of saints, which would heighten the perception of their immediate personal presence. Waltham minster in Essex possessed a life-sized crucifix carved from black rock, which its lay patron Tofi the Proud had adorned with a sword and girdle. In Edward's reign, large crucifixes or crucifixion groups were installed at Winchester, Bury St Edmunds, Ely, Evesham and Durham.[36] The abbot of St Augustine's commissioned statues of the sixth-century saints Queen Bertha and Bishop Liudhard, which were set above their tombs. About the same time, in the 1040s or 1050s, statues of the bishop St Swithun were erected at Winchester and Sherborne by Bishops Ealdred of Worcester and Ælfwold of Sherborne.[37]

In the days of King Edward, the established minsters were sumptuously adorned with gold and silver: with hangings and altar cloths of silk or silk-shot taffeta, often woven with gold thread or encrusted with gems, and with precious vessels for Mass, precious metal candelabra to bear the candles that betokened Christ's light, and exquisite vestments that had been woven to beautify communal worship.[38] Heavenly aromas from incense mingled with the scent of flowers strewn about the altars. The total effect was the creation of an environment in which it was possible to encounter the divine. This sort of imagery influenced the most prolific hagiographer of the late 11th century, Goscelin of Saint-Bertin, who settled in England no later than the 1060s.[39] Most of the churches he visited were native Anglo-Saxon edifices, not yet turned into 'chain hotels'. When Goscelin wished to evoke the splendour of the heavenly kingdom, virtues of the saints or the beauty of spiritual truths, he employed the imagery of glittering pearls, sparkling gems, precious metals, flowers and fragrances. Most of these features the Normans retained in their Romanesque churches, but in broader, lighter spaces where the effect could not have been the same. The native church interiors were so familiar to Goscelin that he used the richness of their material display to evoke the mystery of heavenly ascent. Their intensity was meant to be a stimulus to the pious imagination, ensuring that the life-sized statues, wall paintings and gem-studded panels would linger in the mind's eye through the dark stretches of the night when worshipers kept vigil or dreamed.

Heavenly communications would not have seemed out of place in these mysterious settings, and the many reports of visions or significant dreams suggest that churches acted as portals to the world beyond. Some years before she died, Abbess Ælfgifu of Wilton (c.1065–7) told her sister – who later told Goscelin – that the holy virgins Agatha, Cecilia and Lucy had appeared to her, promising that she would join them in heaven. When Ælfgifu lay dying, one of the nuns heard a voice in her sleep saying that holy Mary and a host of virgins waited unseen in the highest tower of the church to receive the abbess's soul.[40] Christ, too, like His mother, was not averse to appearing. We see His manifestations in the Old English account of the visions of Earl Leofric, written not long after his death in 1057.[41] Leofric's visions are mysterious, even opaque in ways that imply an attempt to report real experiences. One is a vision of Paradise. Leofric crosses a bridge into a sweet-smelling field, where heavenly beings await him. In a second vision, the earl witnesses unearthly lights and sounds when passing a night at prayer in Canterbury cathedral. In another vision the earl is attending mass at St Clement's church, Sandwich, when he sees what appears to be the hand of Christ raised in blessing above a cross. King Edward is present in the vision, attending mass, and there is an unspoken sense in which the hand of God is with him. What is striking about these visions is their imaginative engagement with a mystical world evoked in the context of late Old English devotion. It was a world capable of drawing abbesses and earls alike into mystical communion with heaven.

Gradually we begin to see how spiritual yearnings, expressed in dark church interiors amid the glittering gold, candles and statuary, yielded to mystical experiences and inspired creative impulses. Tofi, who founded Waltham Holy Cross in Essex, felt sufficient connexion to the life-sized crucified Christ carved in black rock which was its centrepiece to fasten his sword around the effigy's waist. Gytha, his wife, found the statue so compelling that she placed on its head a golden crown, studded with precious stones for thorns. She also placed a pure gold circlet round his leg and established a support under its feet. Both were likewise of gold and precious stones.[42] Lady Godiva, Earl Leofric's wife, gave a statue of Mary to Evesham Abbey, which was dedicated to the Virgin, and hung her own necklace of gems around the Virgin's neck.[43] No doubt some were moved to tears simply on seeing these statues, just as a Brazilian Catholic friend was moved to tears in 2016 on seeing a statue in a monastery we entered in Rio de Janeiro. Tears were regarded as evidence that God had touched a human heart. In a sinner they were a symbol of compunction. Prelates such as Stigand who paid to install statues in churches were not doing so merely as 'patrons of the arts' (as historians have put it), but because they understood that statues and images could prepare human hearts for heaven. Godiva was remembered for her devotion to Mary, King Edward for his devotion to St Peter. The vibrancy of Peter's cult in the 1050s can be seen in the wealth built up by the abbey of Peterborough – 'Goldenborough' as it was then known – and in Edward's re-foundation of Westminster Abbey in honour of the Prince of the Apostles.[44]

Earl Harold's great minster at Waltham, consecrated in 1062 on the site of the earlier church built by Tofi and Gytha, was dedicated to the cult of the Holy Cross and furnished with a collection of relics gathered on his travels through the Rhineland to Rome. Edward added a further collection of relics on Waltham's dedication in 1060.[45] As in the collection Edward's mother Emma left to the New Minster at Winchester, relics of Christ were the principal items in the collection, and all were deposited beneath his life-sized effigy on the Cross.[46] Prominent Anglo-Saxon saints were included in the mix, but foreign ones outnumbered them, and the effect of the relic list – which was compiled in hexameters by Waltham's master Adelard of Utrecht – was to place all these relics on an equal footing as repositories of Christ's power, mediated through his saints. At Waltham, the life-sized crucifix remained the centrepiece, and like the crucifixion groups at Winchester, Ely and Bury St Edmunds, it drew attention to Christ's redemptive sacrifice. Where the context did not justify the provision of gold and jewels to enhance the worshippers' encounter with the Crucifixion, large-scale carved stone or painted

Figure 1. Stone crucifix at Langford (Oxfordshire), c.1060, based on the Volto santo of Lucca. Author's photograph.

representations were provided instead. Impressive examples survive at Langford (Oxfordshire), a manor belonging to Harold (Figures 1–2), where one of two stone crucifixes appears to be based on the famous *volto Sancto* at Lucca, and on the royal demesne at Breamore (Hants), which, though it has been defaced, is still a powerful composition.

On a much smaller scale is a class of carvings of the Crucifixion on plaques of walrus ivory, never more than 70 mm across.[47] Patterns of wear suggest that these were personal icons either regularly handled or rubbing against people's clothes (Figure 3). All known examples of this genre (about ten survive) are of southern English origin or style and suggest that this was a significant type of object, albeit one that would have been affordable only by the wealthier in the community. There is nothing comparable on the continent, and little evidence of a post-Conquest market – which reinforces the point about the focus on them by the English elite before 1066.

Stigand's gift of great crucifixes to prominent churches and their positioning over the high altar diverted worship away from the native

Figure 2. Stone crucifixion group at Langford (Oxfordshire), c.1060, digitally altered to show original composition. Author's photograph; adapted by Dr Nick Warr.

saints enshrined at those monasteries (namely Swithun, Æthelwold, Æthelthryth and Edmund) and towards Christ, the foundation of the Catholic faith. When Stigand's Norman successor Lanfranc moved the relics of Dunstan and Ælfheah from the high altar at Christ Church into the north transept, installing a crucifix framed by cherubim over the altar, his purpose was similar. In Margaret Gibson's words, he was refocusing attention on the universal Christian doctrines of the Incarnation, the Redemption and the Eucharist.[48] It has not been observed that he was furthering the initiative of his discredited predecessor.

Stigand, as a pluralist who had accumulated great personal wealth and aided Harold in his coup, was an obvious target for censure. So it is

Figure 3. Anglo-Saxon walrus ivory Crucifixion plaque, mid-11th century. British Museum 1986, 0401.1.

easy to miss the fact that the Church he presided over had its eyes firmly fixed on Christ's Cross. Perhaps that is why 'Christ's Cross' supposedly became the English battle-cry at Hastings – for it might be thought that the Normans had their eyes fixed elsewhere. A prayer used in England in Stigand's time says: 'Hail to you, life-giving cross, that carried the cost of the world and has borne the banner of the eternal king. On you Christ won the victory, and through you I, your servant N., a wretch and sinner, [have triumphed too].'[49] A mid-11th-century tract entitled 'Four reasons to revere the Cross' assured the widest of audiences that whoever revered seven crosses, or revered one cross seven times a day, should find the seven gates of hell closed to him and the seven of paradise opened; any demons that happened to be near the man that venerated the Cross would not be able to harm him, and that man would receive the gift of Christ's sacrifice and be freed from sin. The tract was read at Winchester and may have been written in England, where the Cross was inspiring artistic and literary creativity.[50]

A mid-11th-century reliquary cross of walrus ivory addresses these desires by depicting an *Agnus dei*, symbolic of Christ's sacrifice, and an eagle seizing a monster, to signify His triumph over Sin and Death.[51] The imagery of the Cross itself expanded in various ways in the mid-century. The picture of the Crucifixion in the so-called Winchcombe Psalter is inscribed *lignum vite*. As though to make the point visually, the Cambridge Homilies shows volutes of foliage emerging from the terminals of the cross-arm, as if it were coming back to life.[52] But perhaps the most potent image of the period represents Countess Judith of Flanders, wife of Earl Tostig, cleaving to the lower shaft (Figure 4). Her act of devotion is heightened by the close-lopped branches of the rood, emphasising the sharp agony of Christ's sacrifice so eloquently depicted in his arching body and deeply bowed head. Although some commentators have seen the figure at the foot of the Cross as Mary of Magdala, her reduced scale and lack of a halo make that identification highly unlikely. More probably, the much later pictures of Mary in this position derive from initiatives instigated by the likes of Judith, who must specifically have asked to be shown in this way.[53]

During the 1030s five new prayers to the Cross were added to a Psalter at Christ Church, Canterbury, and by about 1050 a vernacular 'Legend of the Cross' was in circulation, along with accompanying homilies.[54] In these texts, interest in the Cross focused on its power to liberate souls in bondage, like the eagle seizing the monster on the reliquary cross. One prayer to the Cross elicits compunction by lamenting the inadequacy of human efforts to adore it.[55] The belief that normal devotions were inadequate in view of what the Cross represented, and the related urge to tap its power, contributed to the creative drive.

A prayer to the Cross from Canterbury, like others from Bury St Edmunds, comprises seven short petitions addressed to the crucified Christ.[56] Each petition invokes him in a new role while begging his presence in a spatial sense that accords with the role envisaged. Thus the suppliant implores Christ: 'be *with* me to *defend* me … *inside* me to *restore* me … *around* me to *protect* me … *before* me to *guide* me … *behind* me to *direct* me … *above* me to *bless* me … [and] *in* me, to *lead me to your kingdom*'.[57] What is striking about this prayer is how it evokes Christ's presence as a hermetic vehicle for the soul's safe transport. Christ is asked to indwell and to surround the petitioner, sealing him off from harm. Other prayers also utilise seven-fold formulas to protect against temptation or demonic attack. A prayer to the Cross from that collection asks Christ to put a guard on every bodily member,

Figure 4. Countess Judith of Flanders, wife of Earl Tostig, cleaving to the Cross, c.1050–60. Judith of Flanders Gospels, Pierpont Morgan Library MS M 709 fo. 1v.

and specifies seven: head, eyes, lips, ears, hands, knees and feet.[58] Prayers to the Cross in a contemporary prayer-book from Winchester were supposed to be said in front of a crucifix and addressed to the seven parts of Christ's body: His right and left foot, right and left hand, mouth, breast and ears.[59] People who sought spiritual protection were supposed to cross themselves seven times each day.[60] In mystical thinking, the number seven represented the universe – the source of its magical power. Its use in connection with the Cross served doubly as an apotropaic device (like the sign of the Cross itself) and a totem to invoke Christ's presence in the world.[61]

Such formulaic devotions not only calmed anxieties; they also allowed clerics and laypeople daily access to Christ's redemptive power. They echo what would have been everyday requests on the part of the faithful, seeking protection from demons, remission of sins, deliverance from hellfire and entry into heaven. We could interpret some of the visions mentioned earlier as responses to the desires articulated in these prayers and formulaic actions – desires for safe passage in death and for Christ's protection.

As well as the increased emphasis laid on the centrality of Christ and on the Cross in the reign of Edward the Confessor, there was a turn away from monasticism to clergy who were not quite 'seculars', in that they abided by a rule, but were better placed than monks to minister to the laity. This shift did not come from Edward, who was a traditional patron of monks like his grandfather Edgar, but from bishops he appointed, including Lotharingians. The template these bishops began to impose on the communities of clerics at their cathedrals and minsters was a revised version of the rule of St Chrodegang of Metz.[62] It was favoured by the reformist party of the papacy from the time of Leo IX (1048–54), who had followed the rule himself as a canon of Toul before becoming pope. The advantage of Chrodegang's rule was that it incorporated elements of monastic discipline such as common dormitories and a common refectory without imposing the rigorous regime that tied monks to the cloister. By imposing such a rule, bishops could improve the discipline and therefore the quality of their clergy – almost to a level with monks – while still allowing them to minister to the laity.

The initiative to introduce the revised rule of Chrodegang began in the 1040s when Edward promoted his chaplain Leofric to the bishopric of Crediton. Leofric, who had been trained in Lotharingia, obtained Leo IX's consent (and Edward's) in 1050 to combine the small sees of Devon and Cornwall and move the seat of the combined bishopric to Exeter, and secondly to dissolve or phase out the congregation of monks at St Peter's, Exeter, and install canons in their place.[63] This was a direct departure from the trend since Edgar's reign of monasticising cathedral clergy. Herman, another Lotharingian chaplain, appointed by Edward to Ramsbury, the Wiltshire see, in 1045 tried to establish himself in Malmesbury Abbey – perhaps with similar intentions – but he met with opposition and withdrew.[64]

The turn towards these canons nevertheless became a trend. What few records we have reveal that the creation of communities of canons was sometimes a joint initiative on the part of the diocesan bishop and lay nobles. When Earl Leofric and Lady Godiva established canons at Stow in Lincolnshire in the 1050s they secured Bishop Wulfwig of

Dorchester's consent that the canons would adhere to the form of service that was used at St Paul's.[65] About the same time, Ælfric, son of Wihtgar, a powerful lord in East Anglia, founded a house of canons at Clare in Suffolk.[66] In the mid-1050s, Bishop Ealdred of Worcester spent about a year with Archbishop Hereman of Cologne, in which he learned about 'ecclesiastical discipline and good observance' – a reference to the revised incarnation of Chrodegang's regime. In 1061, he was appointed archbishop of York and took the opportunity to establish that rule in the minsters of the northern archdiocese.[67] By the early 1060s there were canons, or efforts to introduce canonical regimes, at York, Southwell and Beverley; at Exeter and Wells, and, possibly, Hereford; at St Paul's in London and Waltham Holy Cross in Essex.[68] These are the just the churches we know about, but there must have been similar drives at others which have left no records.

At a superficial level the canons can be seen as one of several innovations lately inspired by the German Empire, such as the fashion for imperial portraiture on the coins, for novel styles of architecture pioneered in the Empire, and the promotion of Lotharingian clergy.[69] At another level they reflect the willingness of native bishops to adopt the recommendations of the reformist papacy by establishing clerical communities that adhered to vows and a rule. Yet the purpose of these communities was to perform pastoral duties, and the need for them was structural, stemming from the very trends described earlier. For the fragmentation of the older communities of minster clergy, coupled with a surge in church foundation by the laity and a corresponding appetite for pastoral care, left fewer clergy to assist the bishops in what were often very large dioceses. As noted above, there were over 700 churches in East Anglia by 1086; but before 1070 – as far as we can tell – there were no archdeacons and no diocesan synods by which the bishop might regulate his clergy. The picture, rather, is one of highly local, de-centralised religion, where individual thegns and clerics were lords on their own turf. It is easy to see why bishops wanted to introduce canons to help with their pastoral and practical administration. The 12 golden apostles, crafted to front the altar of Harold's foundation at Waltham, may have signified the founder's intention for the community to embrace that pastoral mission, going in the footsteps of the apostles themselves.[70]

In some cases, monks were already shouldering part of the burden. When he was prior of Worcester before 1062, Wulfstan earned a foreign monk's disapproval by preaching to the people gathered in the church on Sundays and major feasts. The foreign monk complained that preaching was a bishop's office and that monks should cultivate silence in the cloister.[71] That was the ideal, but the bishop was no doubt busy elsewhere – since it was Ealdred, he may have been in Cologne learning the advantages of having regular canons. For Wulfstan, contemplation and action were not incompatible, provided each was allowed its own sphere. As well as preaching, Wulfstan found time for reading, solitary prayer, and venerating each of Worcester's eighteen altars seven times a day.[72] In these devotions, he could have used a seven-part formula for venerating the Holy Cross like the one described earlier. It should be stressed also that there was a tradition of English monks preaching to the laity, which can be traced back to Ælfric of Cerne in the 990s and onwards to the 1090s, when Herman, a senior monk, preached to the people at Bury St Edmunds.[73] Rubrics to vernacular sermons in monastic books hint that other monks did so too. Tiberius A iii contains ten sermons for lay audiences: 'To eallum folke' or 'To eallen folke', and two for mass-priests.[74] As if to affirm the idea that action and contemplation should co-exist in monastic life, the book includes a treatise on sign language.[75] Its vernacular confessional prayers and directives point as much to the needs of lay penitents as to penance inside the monastery.[76] At Worcester or nearby in Wulfstan's time, guidance and texts for handling lay confession were compiled in another book, which survives as Oxford, Bodleian Library, MS Laud Miscellaneous 482 (s. xi[med]).[77]

This leads us to another way in which the Church under Stigand was opening its doors to a wider constituency – by communicating religious truths in the vernacular, and not solely in Latin, which only superseded Old English as the preferred language for spiritual writing at some point after the Conquest. Although church services were conducted almost entirely in Latin, as one would expect, by 1066 there was a considerable body of religious literature available in English. This comprised on the one hand translations of books of the Bible, such as the Psalms and parts of the Pentateuch, or patristic classics such as St Gregory the Great's Pastoral Care, and on the other original compositions in the vernacular, particularly sermons and homilies, but also hagiography. Wilton nunnery provides a good example. In the time of Abbess Brihtgyfa, miracles that were reported and attributed to the abbey's resident saint, Edith, were written down in the vernacular.[78] Twenty years later, Goscelin wrote them up in Latin. If the vernacular versions were kept, they have been lost, but Goscelin's restyling of English texts into Latin exemplifies the shift away from the vernacular after 1066.

Although an unknown quantity of Latin hagiography from this period may have suffered a similar fate to Old English materials, having gone up in smoke at the Reformation or been lost at some point earlier, it is important to note that no extant piece of Latin hagiography from England can safely be dated to the period 1040–65, whereas a large quantity survives from Flanders and the Empire.[79] Old English hagiography, conversely, is abundant for the first three-quarters of the 11th century and may have been preferred to the Latin variety because it could provide a basis for vernacular sermons to the laity – a function it is often seen to perform in sermons of that period.[80] It is a point easily missed, that if we assess the significance of extant manuscripts solely by weight of numbers, the large number of Old English homilies that have survived the accidents and vicissitudes of intervening centuries (which were mostly insensible to their contents) suggests that reaching out to the laity was central to the strategy of the late Old English Church. N. R. Ker's catalogue lists more than 20 such manuscripts from the generation before 1066 that attest the copying or the collection of Old English sermons.[81] We can add to them didactic tracts and pastoral texts such as confessors' manuals, examples of which were mentioned earlier.

Renewed interest in pastoral care for the laity suggests that the Church was returning to the path set by Alfred the Great. Under Edgar it had lurched towards Latinate monasticism, but demand from the growing constituency of wealthy laypeople eager to invest in salvation was causing it to redress the balance in their favour. Monasteries, however, did not lose their popularity. One kind of monastery or another were founded at Rumburgh in Suffolk at a date between 1047 and 1064, and at Horton in Dorset in about 1060, and on Andersey Island in the Thames near Abingdon, where the wealthy priest Blæcman built an impressive church and cloisters covered with sculpture and paintings inside and out in honour of St Andrew.[82] Had these monasteries had the chance to grow into important houses like the several monasteries planted north of the Humber in the 1070s, historians might have praised Edward's reign for its flourishing monasticism.[83] As it happened, the Conquest swept away their English patrons before those houses were fully established. Only Edward's Westminster and a couple of others survived.

A few laypeople were investing in what would later be called chantries. In the time of Abbot Leofstan of Bury (1044–65), a couple named Osulf and Leofrun made provisions for priests to sing masses for their souls. Two priests were paid to sing twelve masses for Osulf each week at a church in Dickleburgh, and another two were supposed to sing for Leofrun. In this case, the husband and wife gave charge of the business not to the bishop, but to Leofstan, the abbot. He received their gift of land, which was intended to provide a rent to pay for the chantry; with it, he obtained control over the priests' income and maintenance.[84] It was about that time that a noblewoman named Ælfwen wished to devote her life to prayer in a tiny oratory. So she retired to live as an anchorite in the precincts of St Benet's at Holme in Norfolk, granting the abbey her land at Ormesby to pay a rent for her upkeep.[85] These two cases reveal how richer laypeople in East Anglia made provision for their souls, but it is enough to observe generally that the Church before 1066 was operating a mixed economy. A broad-minded efflorescence of Christianity, it seemed at last to have struck the right balance between the dynamic forces of ascetic withdrawal and pastoral engagement.

The impact of 1066, complex as it was, undermined the resonant vernacular faith which was the legacy of that mature, evolved dialectic. Indeed, it could not have done otherwise. The wholesale purging of the English episcopate in the years and decades after the Conquest erected cultural and linguistic barriers between the shepherds and the sheep; it also disrupted the accumulated initiatives which over the previous two centuries had blended to create a Church attuned to the needs of the faithful. The tenth century had been the age of monastic foundation; the eleventh had seen the rise of estate churches – the predecessors of many later parish churches – and the fragmentation of the old minster blocs in the pastoral landscape. The dialectic between active and contemplative religion was achieving a fruitful synthesis out of all the elements that had gone into the unique mix of English Christianity. After 1066 the Normans' attitude to the subtleties of this inheritance found its clearest – or at least its most visible – manifestation in their architectural policy of complete rebuilding, which involved the demolition of almost every major Anglo-Saxon church. They were resonant of the past, brimming with memories of the saints and the founders who had built them, and echoing with the accumulated prayers of generations.[86] The Anglo-Saxon way had been to build upon tradition while preserving and incorporating the past: in this respect, the buildings were an external metaphor for what was going on in the Church itself.

After 1066, the narratives of the faith, including written legends of the English saints, were overtaken – like so much else in the Church – by a foreign, clerical elite and were subject to manipulation. In their desire to honour God with Latinate grandeur, the Normans bypassed the language in which, for so many of the conquered, devotion had found natural expression and reverted to the language of the higher clergy. Saints' Lives were rewritten in Latin. Except in a few monastic centres where English influence remained strong, spiritual texts in the vernacular came to be regarded as rustic and uncivilised, while the desire to reach out to the laity – a largely English laity – waned with the whittling away of the native clergy. At parish level in the countryside and many towns this process sometimes took two or three generations, but by that time local priests had generally accepted the primacy of Latin.

Under the Normans, monks once again began to dominate the episcopal bench. Monasticism, with its impulse to withdraw from the world, revived, shifting the devotional dialogue once more towards elitism and exclusivity. The reformed houses of canons that had been central to the pastoral mission of the Edwardian Church suffered through their associations and kinship ties with the vanquished nobility. Even if offset here and there by the actions of newcomers more sympathetic to English traditions, these were all structural impacts of the Conquest, which affected the very character and orientation of the Church. Opinions on these effects were mixed, with some 12th-century historians praising the Norman achievement and others looking back in nostalgia at the dislocated Anglo-Saxon inheritance. Some did both. Modern historians must also factor in the increasing intervention of the papacy and shifting currents of spirituality in western Christendom, which dilute the importance of the Conquest as an agent of change, for nothing that came after it in the history of the English Church was a consequence solely of that upheaval. Myriad spiritual and political influences shaped every subsequent development. What is clear is that the Normans came with violence and imposed their will, that the experience of conquest brought much spiritual searching, and that Christ and the saints – once so close at hand – must to the English have seemed further away.

176

11

Women and fear in 1066

Elisabeth van Houts

Much of what we know about the women of 1066, as reported in contemporary sources, can be summed up in one word: 'fear'.[1] Whether English or Norman, the mothers, wives, daughters and sisters of the soldiers were terrified as a result of the unprecedented events that took place in their lives. The conquest of England was on a scale and a suddenness not seen before in the history of the country. In this chapter I will set out the some issues that faced the women who lived through the Norman Conquest of England on both sides of the conflict. Before I do so, however, I would like to stress that I am by no means the first historian to preoccupy myself with this subject. In the 19th century Agnes Strickland sketched the lives of the queens of England but only started with William's wife Matilda.[2] In the course of the 20th century as a result of the rise of social and economic history there was a burgeoning period of work on Anglo-Saxon women, not only the aristocratic but peasants and slaves. Although Eileen Power, one of the pioneers of women's history, was mostly writing about later medieval England, she put her stamp on the Early Middle Ages too.[3] Later came women historians such as Cecily Clark, Christine Fell, Eleanor Searle and more recently Pauline Stafford and Judith Green.[4] They were all struck by the lack of attention paid to women in the most famous event in European history of the year 1066.

Fear is one of the prime human emotions alongside love and affection, anger and hatred. It is an instinctive part of our being and controls much of our actions. It is also historically and culturally determined. By this I mean that although throughout the past human emotions have remained virtually unchanged, the way they are perceived and experienced has varied considerably.[5] The history of medieval fear still needs to be written. Men, and in particular the aristocratic men who made up the warrior elite, were not supposed to show fear and let themselves be cowered by it.[6] Women's fear is a much more accepted emotional state. In what follows I will discuss three aspects of women's fear: first, the fear of English women, who owned land and who had been left widowed after their husbands lost their life in battle or subsequent expeditions. Second, the fear of the conquerors' women back on the continent, who had to wait months to know about their men's fate and what the future would hold in store for them. Third, I will round off my article with a consideration of how women's fear in wartime in the here and now spilled over into their thinking about their afterlife.

Women's fear for foreign soldiers at times of conquest and warfare was grounded in reality. In any war zone, violence to women is an act of intimidation and a tool of conquerors to force the indigenous population into submission. In 1066 England the situation was no different. Significantly, the evidence for what we would now call war crimes against civilians comes from Norman contemporary sources, which were based on the premise that whereas use of force in warfare, whether as raiding, sieges or battles, was justified, use of violence against women was not. Such fear was well recognised. Shortly after the battle of Hastings, probably in early 1067, the Norman bishops issued a penitential ordinance, ratified by the papal legate Bishop Ermenfrid of Syon.[7] This was a list of categories of sins for which penance was required. Seemingly applying to all men, clause 10 states that 'those who committed adulteries or rapes or fornications shall do penance as though they had thus sinned in their own country'.[8] Note, incidentally, that penance for such wrongdoing in England was expected to be imposed according to French customs. Already at the time there was anxiety that such blanket rule would apply to men of all rank. According to the Conqueror's own biographer William of Poitiers, the ruler had warned his noblemen to restrain themselves towards their victims because they were all fellow Christians and should not be provoked into rebellions. But his warning about sexual violence was aimed specifically at 'soldiers of middling rank and common ones' against whom, so William of Poitiers maintains, 'women were safe from the violence which passionate men often inflict'.[9] Orderic Vitalis, however, disagreed when 50 years later he revised William of Poitiers' version when he complained how 'noble maidens were exposed to the insults of low-born soldiers and lamented their dishonouring by the scum of the earth.'[10] Orderic accused the Norman lieutenants Odo of Bayeux and William fitz Osbern of having condoned 'excessive plunder and dirty rape' by their men whose actions they forcefully defended.[11] Nevertheless, both chroniclers are in agreement by implying that English women had less to fear from high ranking French nobles than from their followers. If William of Poitiers is right in reporting that in the aftermath of 1066 foreign soldiers were even forbidden consensual sex with (English) prostitutes, it is perhaps no surprise that English women lived in fear and, in their own way, fought back.[12]

Aristocratic women had the option of flight, explicitly 'out of fear of the French', into monasteries and nunneries that offered a safe haven for women within their walls. Women's entry in nunneries for reasons of safety rather than religion was a problem, as is revealed by episcopal letters and hagiography. Take Archbishop Lanfranc's letter 53 to Bishop Gundulf of Rochester, written about ten years after the conquest. Responding to Gundulf's query about what to do with various categories of nuns who were not living according to monastic rules, Lanfranc replied:

> But those who have been neither confessed nor presented at the altar are to be sent away at once without change of status, until their desire to remain in religion is examined more carefully. As to those who as you tell me fled to a monastery not for love of the religious life but *for fear of the French*, if they can prove that his was so by the unambiguous witness of nuns better than they, let them be granted unrestricted leave to depart. This is the king's policy and our own.[13] [my emphasis]

We know of two such women by name, Seitha and Edith/Matilda. The first, Seitha, was an Anglo-Saxon woman of noble stock, whose story comes from Bury St Edmunds. There the *Miracles of St Edmunds*, written by Hermann and revised by Goscelin of St Bertin, report that her parents had wanted her to be married to a noble man, whose ethnicity we do not know.[14] She refused his hand and then escaped. No nunnery accepted her but Abbot Baldwin of Bury St Edmunds (1065–97) allowed her to live with her female servant Edith as a recluse in the grounds of this male monastery. She features prominently in the *Miracles* as a woman very interested in the cult of St Edmund who talked extensively with the monks, including the two authors. Therefore, our knowledge about her arrival at Bury comes from her own mouth and is – in an indirect way – autobiographical. Similarly indirect are the details about the second woman, Edith-Matilda, daughter of King Malcolm IV of Scotland, who through her mother Queen Margaret was a direct descendant of the Wessex royal family. In the autumn of 1100, about to be married to William the Conqueror's son King Henry I, Edith-Matilda recalled her time at Wilton, where her aunt Christina was abbess:

> For, when I was quite a young girl and went in fear of the rod of my aunt Christina, whom you knew quite well, she – to preserve me from the lust of the Normans which was rampant and at that time ready to assault any woman's honour – used to put a little black hood on my head and, when I threw it off she would often make me smart with a good slapping and most horrible scolding, as well as treating me as being in disgrace.[15]

It seems, therefore, that on various occasions male visitors, some as suitors, came to the nunnery, where Abbess Christina then took the precaution of pretending that the girl was a nun. Thus, fear of being physically attacked was one aspect of English women's fear, and retreat into a nunnery or monastery was one way of escaping foreigners. Escape into a monastic setting might also provide protection against forced marriage, another aspect of conquest, to which I now turn.

Fear of forced marriage during times of conquest was another realistic fear, particularly for women. At aristocratic level and among landed families arranged marriages were common.[16] Parents would choose a husband for their daughters and negotiate the deal with the parents of the spouse. Young men and women were accustomed to such arrangements and unless they wished to prefer a life as a monk or nun they normally accepted their parents' wish. In Anglo-Saxon England and in Normandy arranged marriages did not normally involve unions with foreigners with different language or customs, except occasionally at the very high level such as royalty. In times of conquest, however, marriage to a foreigner became part and parcel of the negotiations between conquered and conqueror, and thus in 1066 William the Conqueror negotiated marriage alliances with the English.[17] Although the number of cases of intermarriage is nowhere near as large as has sometimes been thought, there were a sufficient number to be commented on at home and abroad. For example, a German monk in Bavaria, Frutolf of Michelsberg, writing within two decades of the Norman conquest, noted that William the Conqueror had forced English widows to accept Norman husbands. As others before me have written, especially Cecily Clark and Eleanor Searle, such a marital arrangement would have provided an extra layer of legitimisation for the Norman male to hold English land apart from conquest. Thus the Anglo-Saxon guardian of Wallingford, the crucial Thames crossing near Oxford, agreed to marry off his daughter to the Norman Robert d'Ouilly. The Conqueror's kinsman Alan the Red, earl of Richmond, received King Harold's daughter, Gunhild, while the middle-ranking Walter of Douai married Hemming's widow Eadgifu/ Eadgytha. All these were arranged, and potentially forced, marriages, where the men and women involved had little choice. Only rarely do we find evidence of affection being involved. Domesday Book, compiled in 1086, records one such story. In Norfolk, the lower-born follower of Wihenoc, a Breton soldier, 'fell in love with a girl in [South] Pickenham,' whose small plot he subsequently held.[18] Talking about land brings me to another reason for English women's fear, namely fear about losing land.

For English women during the conquest period their vulnerability increased, and with it their fear in the absence of their male protector in captivity or after death. The wholesale redistribution of land from English to Continental tenants left English widows particularly vulnerable, especially if they remained single.[19] As Pauline Stafford has suggested, in Domesday Book we find short lists of women holding tiny portions of land.[20] These women may well be the widows of royal servants or thegns who had been able to hold on to just enough to survive. Evidence from the estates of Bury St Edmunds gives us the names of women who held land among the more than 700 free peasants in 1066. Twenty years later the number of free landholders had been reduced by

30 per cent. Forty-eight of the 700 names belong to women, many with children.[21] Their possessions range from a meagre half acre to more than one hundred acres: Lefgiva two acres, but Aelget fifteen and Alveva eight. It is, therefore, important to remember that despite the revolution in landholding, a small percentage of families, headed by women, managed somehow to hold on their possessions. Their success may have depended on Baldwin, Abbot of Bury, the protector of the recluse Seitha to whom I referred a little earlier. Baldwin, a monk from Paris, had been appointed as abbot of Bury by King Edward the Confessor.[22] A foreigner himself, he may have guaranteed the Bury landholding women his protection on behalf of the new king. It was a good medieval custom that kings were supposed to recognise the rights of widows as part of their role as protector of those who could not protect themselves (widows, orphans and monks). Nevertheless, not all abbots were so lenient. The fear of the mothers, wives and daughters of the English who suffered defeat in 1066 is thus well documented. However, very little attention has thus far been paid to the fear and anxiety of the French women of the soldiers who conquered England to which we now turn.

Medieval mothers, wives and daughters of these continental warriors were not fearful *of* their sons, husbands and brothers, but they were fearful *for* their wellbeing and survival. We have to make a distinction between the relatively short-term anxiety and fear they felt on the eve of the invasion and the growing unease, although coupled with pride, they felt after the Norman success in battle during the years that the Conqueror kept his followers in England. Well before the conquest, William the Conqueror's wife Matilda had supported him. We may surmise that she had helped to persuade her father Baldwin V of Flanders to give her husband military and financial support, hence the many Flemish soldiers who took part in the conquest.[23] Matilda herself had financed the building of William's flagship 'the Mora' in which he sailed to England.[24] But Matilda was pregnant at the time of the preparations, as we can work out because her daughter Adela (later countess of Blois and Chartres) was born in early 1067.[25] Matilda shared her husband's religious fears about the potential danger of the crossing and Conquest and between them they decided to offer their young daughter Cecilia to God. They promised her as an oblate, a child nun, to the nunnery of Holy Trinity in Caen, at the dedication ceremony of the nuns' church in June 1066.[26] The date is significant because at that time the Conqueror's large fleet and army were already congregating for the planned invasion. Cecilia was still too young to enter the nunnery and stayed at home for another nine years before she formally entered in 1075.[27]

From 1066 onwards for the next 16 years William's and Matilda's marriage was often a commuter one, with Matilda acting on behalf of William on whichever side he was not.[28] All transport in the Middle

Ages was dangerous, but sea crossings were among the most perilous ones, so the Conquest resulted in a lifestyle of being en route that now incorporated many journeys by boat.[29] Of course, Matilda was not alone; there were numerous couples who saw their lives being changed as a result of the cross-Channel landholdings that had been created. Aristocratic women as well as their servant women criss-crossed the sea with a frequency that they would not have dreamed of before 1066. They became part of the maritime 'networks of empire', to use David Bates' phrase.[30]

Fear for their fathers, husbands and sons did not mean that women were not supportive in their men's ventures. Not only were they used to see their husbands off on expeditions, but these were often in the interest of both partners.[31] One crucially important way women were actively involved, certainly at aristocratic level, was in the management of the lands while the men were away. Royal and aristocratic women were accustomed to be left alone at home to look after their husbands' estates. Similarly, lower down the social scale the women of men who had to perform military service knew that their husbands had to follow their lords. But we should not underestimate the fear of the Flemish, Breton and Norman women faced with the departure of their husbands and sons on an unprecedented expedition across the sea. Admittedly, 50 years earlier King Cnut of Denmark had conquered England building on a Viking heritage of maritime crossings and coastal attacks, but even he did not engage with the English in one decisive battle. Apart from anything else, the distance and unpredictability of success made the Norman conquest of England exceptionally dangerous. Once the battle had been fought and William had received the submission of the English he needed his continental troops in England to keep control of them. And this is what the soldiers' families at home on the Continent feared most. In the early 12th century, quoting perhaps from the now-lost portion of William of Poitiers' biography of the Conqueror, Orderic Vitalis reported on the emotions felt by Norman wives.[32] On the one hand, Orderic cited sexual love experienced by some women who threatened to take new husbands if their men would not return to Normandy to look after them and their children:

> At this time certain Norman women, consumed by fierce lust, sent message after message to their husbands urging them to return at once, and adding that unless they did so with all speed they would take other husbands for themselves.

Orderic might here be acknowledging that marriage is a sexual bond which according to the Apostle Paul meant that both spouses owed each other sex and for this reason demanded that spouses needed each other's agreement for any period of absence.[33] On the other hand, he qualified the sexually inspired emotions by saying that in fact the women feared coming to England for two reasons, fear of the journey and fear of living among bloodshed:

> For they dared not join their men themselves, being unaccustomed to the sea-crossing and afraid of seeking them out in England, where they were engaging in armed forays every day and blood flowed freely on both sides.[34]

This may be rhetoric but nevertheless Orderic (and potentially his source William of Poitiers) voiced women's mixed feelings of (sexual) love of their husbands and fear for their own lives if they joined their husbands in England. Life across the sea was far beyond their normal world and as married women, it seems that they thought to have had a choice.

But choice was not an option for the Norman women who were used as political pawns by William the Conqueror. In terms of intermarriage and forced marriage the new king used his own female relatives from Normandy to marry them off to English noblemen in an attempt to buy their collaboration. And we can only speculate as to what this meant for the women's state of mind. Already in 1064 William had promised his daughter Adeliza to Harold on a visit to the duchy.[35] This engagement almost immediately fell through when on his return to England Harold married the daughter of the earl of Mercia.[36] After the conquest, King William then promised Adeliza to Edwin, earl of Mercia himself.[37] That marriage, too, fell through because William withdrew his offer, and shortly afterwards Edwin was betrayed and killed by some of his followers in 1071, an event that was surely a product of the all-pervasive fear that was an element in the history of these times. For reasons we do not know Adeliza entered a nunnery in Normandy where she spent the rest of her life.[38] William also married off his niece Judith to Earl Waltheof, who lost his life in 1076. But not before he had conceived two daughters by Judith. According to Orderic Vitalis, the marriage was an unhappy one, with Judith having allegedly betrayed her husband to her uncle, King William, who had him executed on account of the treachery alleged by his wife.[39] The case of Judith and Waltheof illustrates the very mixed feelings Norman women must have had in sharing the spoils of conquest. Feelings of fear and guilt engendered by conquest inevitably spilt over in fears about the afterlife, and women were no exception.

In due course, many French wives would join their husbands in England or begin a commuting life on both sides of the Channel, and the issue of where to be buried became a difficult one. Should one be buried at home? Or in one's newly acquired land? Did people have a choice?[40] For women the question was more complicated, as women had already left their birth family's home to join their husband's and after the conquest a third home was added. Take the case of Gundrada of Warenne. She was of Flemish stock, born from a noble family in the north of Flanders, and she was probably related to Matilda of Flanders.[41] Her father was the advocate, lay protector of the famous monastery of St

Bertin at St Omer. Sometime before the Norman conquest Gundrada came to the attention of William of Warenne, a distant cousin and one of the closest advisers of William the Conqueror, who then married her. This marriage forms an important case study of a Norman and a Fleming who married (like William and Matilda) and then set up life in England, where William was one of the 12 richest men. The couple founded the priory of St Pancras at Lewes (Sussex), itself a daughter house of Cluny in Burgundy, as part of a penitential strategy involving Gundrada's Flemish kin, and furthermore built castles at Castle Acre and Lewes. Our knowledge about Gundrada derives in part from her tombstone, the oldest of a woman in England, which miraculously has survived.

Gundrada died in the early 1080s and was buried at St Pancras, Lewes, in a lavish grave covered with a large black Tournai marble stone with her epitaph engraved on it.[42] After the dissolution on the monasteries in the 16th century her tombstone was recycled for the burial of one of Queen Elizabeth I's courtiers. The slab was turned upside down and the blank side inscribed for him. During the building of the Brighton–Lewes railway line in the mid-19th century the tombstone was rediscovered, together with the leaden burial caskets of Gundrada and her husband William. They are now kept in the church of Southover, near Brighton, and can be visited in a small side chapel. Incidentally, Gundrada's tombstone is very similar to that of Matilda of Flanders, who was buried at Ste Trinité at Caen, the nunnery she founded and where, as I have explained, her daughter Cecilia had become a nun. Thus, whereas Gundrada was buried in England, Matilda found her final resting place in Normandy; neither woman returned to their homeland, Flanders. What is important to note is that both women were buried in the monasteries founded for deeply-felt penitential reasons, and this leads me to the final section of this chapter on women's fear for salvation in the afterlife.[43]

Whether French or English, both conquerors and conquered were Christians, and, as sharers of the same Christian fate, deeply concerned about the fate of the soul after death and committed to religious patronage as one way to alleviate their sins and achieve salvation of their souls after death.[44] I have already referred to several occasions where we have seen that the French were encouraged to pay their debt for victory over the English by penitential acts. That was the main tenure of Bishop Ermenfrid of Syon's Penitential Ordo which I mentioned earlier. The Penitential Ordo offered penance to fighters by founding a church or bestowing perpetual alms on a church.[45] As is well known, at the top end of the elite William the Conqueror himself founded Battle Abbey at the site of victory near Hastings, and his followers were encouraged to do the same. Interestingly, we do not know to what extent William's wife Matilda was involved in the decision-making process for this foundation. The shadowy role of a priest's wife in Shrewsbury in the penitential foundation inspired by her widower and effected by his lord throws intriguing light on thinking about the afterlife and making provisions in the here and now for any sins.

At Shrewsbury, Earl Roger was inspired and encouraged by his priest Odelerius, whose son the 12th-century historian Orderic Vitalis tells us about the foundation.[46] Orderic Vitalis is unusual in that he gives quite a lot of autobiographical information even though it exclusively centres on his father Odelerius. Odelerius was a French clerk and priest from Orléans, who after the conquest came to England in the following of Earl Roger of Montgomery. Odelerius settled in Shrewsbury, where his sons were born: Orderic in 1075, Benedict in 1078 and Everard in the early 1080s. There clearly was a local Shrewsbury woman with whom Odelerius had these sons – priestly marriage was very common at the time – though Orderic is completely silent about her identity, only noting that he was *Angligena*, 'born from an English mother'. She probably died around the time of the birth of Everard, when Orderic, aged five, was placed in the household of a local priest who taught him reading and writing. Two years later, in about 1082, Odelerius persuaded Earl Roger to turn St Peter, one of the seven Shrewsbury minsters, into a monastery to which he promised himself and his son Benedict as monks, and his son Everard as a lay tenant. On that occasion, too, he had already promised his eldest son, Orderic, to the Norman monastery of St Evroult. Thus, as in the case of William's daughter Cecilia, young children were promised as oblates at a far earlier stage than they actually entered the monastic life. Orderic was allowed to stay in Shrewsbury for another three years before he said farewell as a ten-year-old boy to cross the sea to Normandy. Twice in his *Ecclesiastical History* Orderic tells this autobiographical story, from the perspective of his father and in his epilogue from his own.[47] He recorded his traumatic farewell from Shrewsbury with his father and other relatives and himself in tears. Crucially, on neither occasion is there a mention of his mother, whom I suggest was by then dead.

The penitential behaviour by Orderic's father Odelerius was by any measure an extreme one. He sacrificed himself and two of his sons to the monastic life, giving the colossal sum of £200 to the newly founded monastery of St Peter's, and donating his third and youngest son with his land as a lay tenant. Where did all that wealth come from? The answer is not straightforward. Most likely, Odelerius was party to the plunder of the seven Shrewsbury churches which lost all their land and income. For one reason or another Odelerius felt extremely guilty and handed back to an English institution, St Peter's at Shrewsbury, all that he had gained in his life, and this is where we may return to his English wife. Some of this land and money may well have come from her family, as it was common in 11th-century England for churches to be handed down the generations in the families of the priests responsible for them, and priests who had no sons would on occasion offer their daughter with their church to a new priest.[48] We do not know. The wife of Odelerius, who was the mother of Orderic, is an enigma that cannot be solved unless new evidence comes to light. However, the silence about her does not prevent us from speculating on what she would have made of the foreign priest who became her husband and gave her three sons. Did she willingly join him? Was she forced to become his partner and had she made plans with her husband what to do with the children if she died? Given his penitential actions, there can be no doubt about Odelerius' fear for his destiny in the afterlife. We might speculate that his English wife did not only share but almost certainly prompted this fear.

As for aristocratic women, we have already encountered countess Judith, William the Conqueror's niece, who allegedly betrayed her English husband Earl Waltheof to her uncle. He was executed at Winchester on 31 May 1076 as the only high status Anglo-Saxon nobleman to have been killed for treason. A fortnight later Countess Judith arranged for his burial and, with the permission of her uncle the king Abbot Ulfketel of Crowland, buried him at his monastery.[49] There are traces of a local cult throughout the 12th and early 13th centuries, but he never acquired an England-wide cult-like status as an English martyr.[50] Within a decade after Waltheof's death Judith founded the nunnery of Elstow (Bedfordshire), the very first to be founded after the Conquest by a Norman female patron – an act of penance, it has been suggested, for her own action of betrayal.[51]

Let me conclude. Although we know far less about the English and Norman/French women of 1066 than we know about their menfolk, we cannot doubt that fear inspired many of their actions. For the English female victims of the Norman Conquest, fear for the safety of their bodies seems to have been the primary reason for their escape into monasteries and nunneries, a flight that was only possible for the very wealthy. Fear of the French and for their land and other possessions can be shown to have inspired English female landholders to take action to safeguard their belongings. As for the women of the French conquerors, they too feared for the future. In their case, left behind on the Continent they missed their husbands but feared the bloodshed in England enough not to wish to join them in the aftermath of the Conquest. There were high aristocratic women for whom staying put in Normandy was not an option as a few were married off by the Conqueror to English noblemen to improve post-Conquest political relationships. In the case of Earl Waltheof's wife Judith, she felt greater affinity, it seems, with her uncle the king than with her husband whom she allegedly betrayed. For all women in the post-Conquest period, whether on the side of the conquerors or the victims, religious fear for divine retribution was a constant worry. For English women there was the fear that their sins had inspired divine wrath in the form of the Conquest, while for the French women they feared divine retribution for the violence and murder perpetrated by their men. We should not underestimate the role of fear in the lives of all women who lived through the Norman Conquest and its significance in the history that followed William the Conqueror's victory at the Battle of Hastings in 1066.

12

1066 and ecclesiastical architecture

Eric Fernie

The effects of the Conquest have been widely debated, leading to conclusions ranging from the dramatic and extreme to there being no effect at all.[1] It may therefore be sensible to begin with the following statement: the effects of the Conquest varied between different groups of people and different areas of activity. That may be rather anodyne but at least few people are likely to disagree with it. It does, nonetheless, have the consequence of requiring me to divide my subject in two, separating the churches of the powerful on the one hand from those of lower status on the other; that is, on the whole, the larger from the smaller.

With the majority of the smaller buildings there was (as one might expect for reasons of economics if nothing else) a degree of continuity, whereas with the larger ones the effect was, in my view, profound. I am going to concentrate on supporting the claim of great change in the buildings of the major institutions, and to do so I have arranged the evidence in four categories: the treatment of the Anglo-Saxon cathedrals, design methods, length, and finally William the Conqueror.[2] I shall then examine the arguments in favour of continuity.

I. The case for change

a. The Anglo-Saxon cathedrals

Following the Conquest the Normans replaced every Anglo-Saxon cathedral (Table 1). They did this in two ways: by demolishing the Anglo-Saxon building and erecting a new Norman one in its place, or by deciding that the location of the Anglo-Saxon bishopric was not important enough, selecting a different town or city and building a new cathedral there. While it is impossible to prove an absence, I do not know of a single piece of standing masonry of undisputed Anglo-Saxon date surviving in any of the Norman cathedrals which were built on the sites of the earlier cathedrals. The process was extremely thorough. The cumulative effect of all this must have been devastating from an

Anglo-Saxon	Norman	
Canterbury	Canterbury	1070
Dorchester	to Lincoln	1072–5
Sherborne	to Old Sarum	1075
York	York	1075 +
Rochester	Rochester	1077 +
Winchester	Winchester	1079
Selsey	to Chichester	c.1080
Worcester	Worcester	1084
London	London	1087
Durham	Durham	1093
North Elmham	to Norwich	1096
Wells	to Bath	c.1100
Lichfield	to Chester	unclear
Hereford	Hereford	1107 +
Exeter	Exeter	1112–14

Table 1. Anglo-Saxon and Norman Cathedrals, in the order of the start of construction of the Norman buildings.

Anglo-Saxon point of view, given the central position of the Church in the Middle Ages and the importance of the episcopate in the Church, and it is difficult to avoid the conclusion that the effect was intended.

I know of three arguments that have been made against this proposition.[3] First, concerning the absence of Anglo-Saxon masonry, it has been pointed out that there is standing Anglo-Saxon masonry in the Anglo-Saxon cathedrals of Dorchester-on-Thames, Wells and Sherborne. These, however, are instances where the see was moved, to Lincoln, Bath and Old Sarum respectively, so that the presence of Anglo-Saxon masonry in these buildings does not in any way disprove the claim. Second, the Anglo-Saxon churches were considered too small. This is almost certainly correct, as there are recorded increases in the number of monks, but it is not clear that there was this practical reason in each case, rather than a wish for demolition and an increase in grandeur. Third, there is the argument that the demolition of a church should not be seen as a destructive act, but rather as a matter of bringing it up to date. This is also correct, but it describes demolitions of churches at various dates, whereas the claim proposed here involves the demolition after 1066 of *all* the Anglo-Saxon cathedrals which were not moved to a new site.

One cautionary question does nonetheless need to be asked: how concentrated was this change? As Allen Brown reminded us, it is easy to compress the passage of time in the distant past, and the time from the first start, at Canterbury in 1070, to the last, at Exeter in 1112–14, is 43 or 45 years, or almost half a century. Could this be seen as a rather leisurely process? I think that would be misleading, for two reasons. First, the last four starts, those from 1100 to 1112/14, are all in the western half of the country. There are Old Sarum and Worcester of the 1070s and 1080s respectively, but that the last four are in the west is not surprising, as that part of the country was poorer and therefore less likely to lead developments.[4] Second, the idea of a concentrated early group is supported by the two buildings of the 1090s, Norwich and Durham (Table 1), as they were begun later than expected. Norwich was begun in 1096, but right from the start, in 1071, the bishops of East Anglia had their eye on Bury St Edmunds as the site for their cathedral. Even after they had clearly lost, in the early 1080s, they went on hoping and trying until eventually they gave up and settled on Norwich. Had they succeeded in their initial gambit, there is little doubt they would have been building the new cathedral of East Anglia at Bury in the 1070s. Durham, begun in 1093, must have been affected by the state of the north following the Conquest, with its rebellion, vicious repression and lawlessness, epitomised by the murder of the bishop in 1080. Even so, the project was begun in the 1080s with the monastic buildings, which indicates that the new cathedral was already planned then.[5]

These considerations mean that there was indeed an intense period of building in the 1070s and 1080s, with the start of the replacement of seven of the nine cathedrals where the site was not moved. Nor did the buildings begun in those two decades have long periods of construction ahead: contrary to a widespread belief, medieval cathedrals did not take centuries to build. Within 15 or 20 years of their commencement most were at least half completed, and in one case, Canterbury, an eyewitness claimed it was finished in seven years (though he may have been thinking too much about Solomon and it could have taken a few years longer).[6] Add to this the rebuilding of many of the major abbey churches in the same two decades and I think the statistic makes the point about profound change on its own.

b. Design methods

Turning to matters of design, the most obvious element is the extensive change of vocabulary between Anglo-Saxon and Norman churches. This is notable in, for example, the very limited use of shafts in Saxon buildings contrasting with the half-shafts and pilasters which divide the elevations of the great majority of Norman buildings into bays. I want, however, to look less at the vocabulary and more at the process of designing, and the contrast between the Saxon and Norman approaches to it.

The crossing offers a particularly good example of how one common kind of Anglo-Saxon design (Figures 1 and 2) differs from the standard Norman formula (Figure 3). The two Anglo-Saxon buildings,

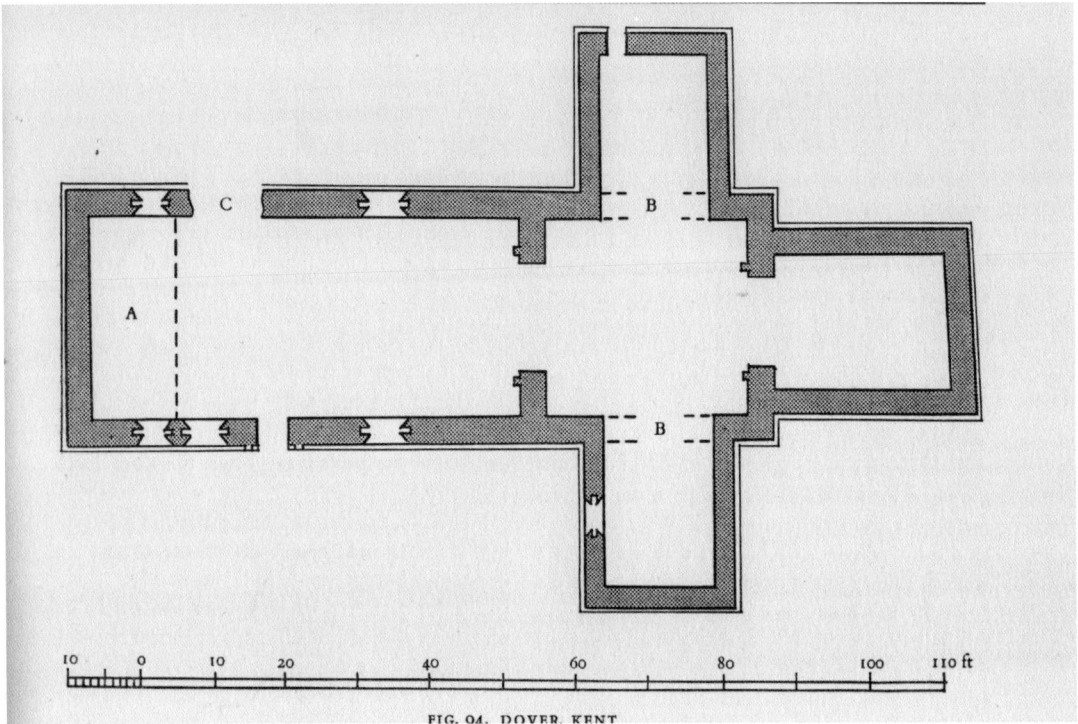

FIG. 94. DOVER. KENT

Figure 1. Dover, St Mary-in-Castro, c.1000 (Taylor, H. and Taylor, J., 1965, *Anglo-Saxon Architecture,* vol. 1, 215).

St Mary-in-Castro in Dover of about 1000, and St Mary at Stow in Lincolnshire of about 1050, are not village churches. St Mary-in-Castro was built so that the Roman pharos on the site stood in alignment at its west end, and St Mary at Stow was begun by the bishop of Dorchester-on-Thames and had as patrons Earl Leofric and Lady Godiva.[7] These were, therefore, buildings of definite status.

Designing plans of this type, with what is called a salient crossing, takes five separate steps (ignoring the lengths of the arms). The first step is to draw the central square. The second is to draw the east arm with its axis on the centre of the side of the square, determined by what will be the axial position of the altar, but with the width up to the designer. The third step is the nave. As with the east arm it has to be on axis, while the width is again the designer's choice: the full width of the central square as at Dover, or narrower as at Stow. Fourth come the north and south arms, which are of equal width for symmetry. Fifth and finally, the north and south arms do not have to be on the axis of the central square: they are at Stow, but at Dover they are nearer the eastern side of the crossing. The Anglo-Saxon sequence stands in sharp contrast to the equivalent Norman design (Figure 3), where only *one* step is needed, namely determining the side of the crossing square. Once that is decided, all the other aspects, the positions and widths of all four arms, follow automatically.

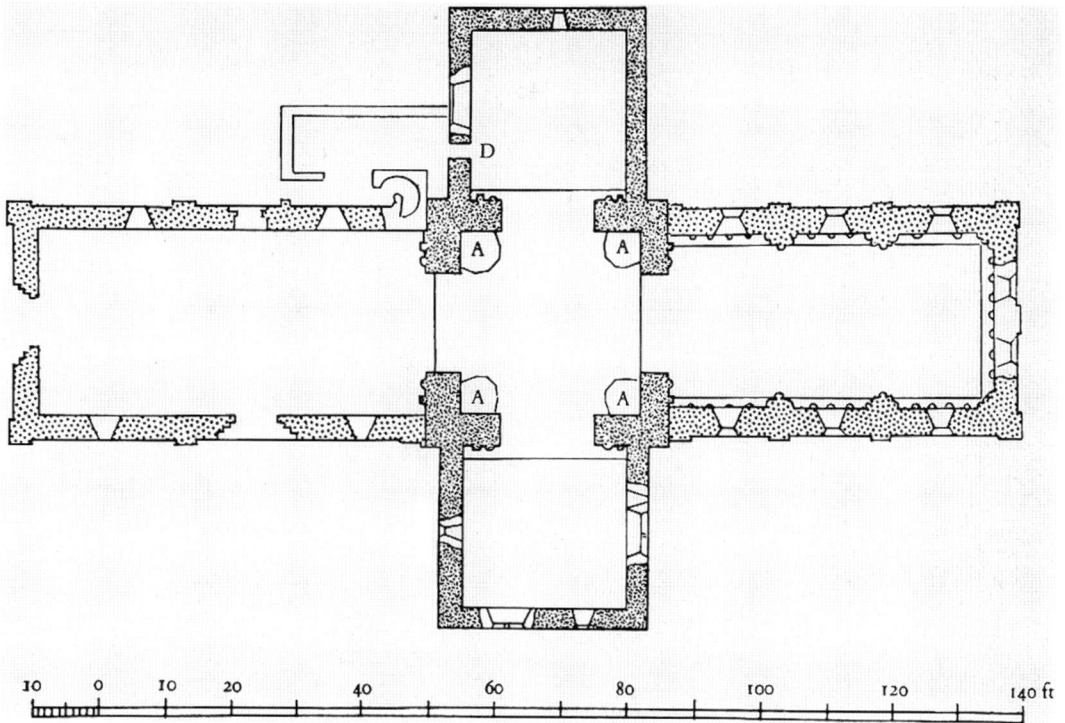

Figure 2. Stow, St Mary, c.1050 (Taylor, H. and Taylor, J., 1965, *Anglo-Saxon Architecture*, vol. 2, 584).

Looking for a label for the Anglo-Saxon mode of design I think a good word is 'additive'. The Norman one is more difficult, though perhaps 'integrated' will do, but whatever it is called it is certainly not additive.

This, of course, does not get us very far in a search for overall attitudes, as we have not yet left the architect's office. The crucial consideration is that the same approach applied once the buildings were built, as in, for example, the churches of Winchester, Glastonbury and Canterbury. Taking Winchester, the plan (Figure 4) shows the seventh-century cathedral and what was done to it in three separate stages in the tenth century: first a block was built to the west, then a structure joining it to the façade, and then there was an extension to the east.[8] This is *publicly* additive architecture, and what is perhaps most significant is that, even after all these changes, the original seventh-century church remained at the core. In this the Anglo-Saxons were very different from patrons and architects in Normandy, which is to say France, who preferred on the whole to keep churches as being of a single period and not adding or rebuilding major parts of them. This is not a rule, but it is a definite tendency.

The majority of the large churches built by and for the Normans in England in the century following the Conquest follow the preference for a single period. Then the Anglo-Saxon approach reasserted itself,

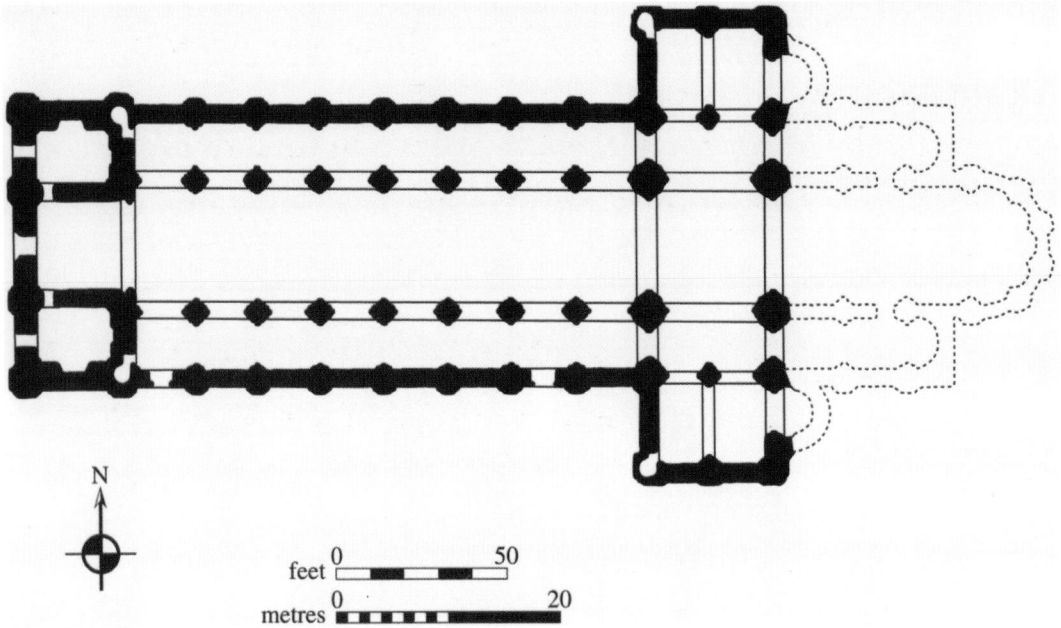

feet 0 ___ 50

metres 0 ___ 20

Figure 3. Caen, Saint-Étienne, mid-1060s to 1080s.

so that English medieval cathedrals as they are today are renowned for the variety of periods in their fabric, as at Ely, which has a Norman nave of around 1100, an east end of the 13th century, and a crossing of the 14th. This contrasts with France, where cathedrals such as those at Reims and Amiens are noteworthy for their unitary character (again acknowledging the existence of exceptions).

What is perhaps most surprising about this distinction between Anglo-Saxon and Norman approaches, between the additive and the integrated, is that it still applies, as, for example, in the following ways (substituting the British state for the Anglo-Saxon). There is the manner of the introduction of the metric system into Britain, which can be accurately described as additive, as the Metrication Board operated only from 1969 to 1981, leaving much of the change largely voluntary. This resulted in the imperial and metric systems being used together, evident in the survival of pints, miles and timber sizes. In the realm of philosophy, British empiricism with its ad hoc methods contrasts with the French love of theory, and especially holistic theory.[9] The difference is also evident in respective attitudes to constitutional contradictions. In 2003 the British government devolved various powers to the Scottish parliament, which meant that, while MPs of English constituencies could not vote on matters solely affecting Scotland, Scottish MPs at Westminster could vote on matters which only affected English citizens. This was pointed out by Tam Dalyell and hence is known from the

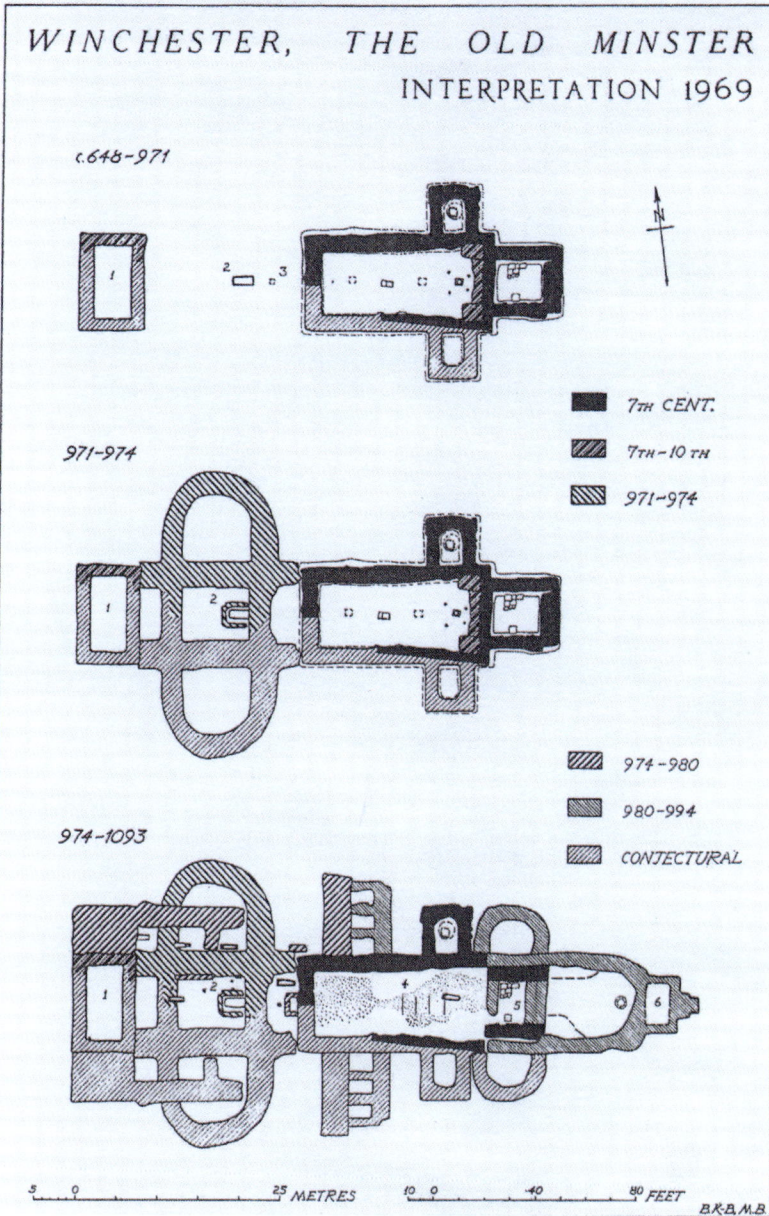

Figure 4. Winchester Cathedral, seventh to tenth centuries. Plan by Martin Biddle and Birthe Kjølbe-Biddle, 1970 (see note 2).

name of his constituency as the West Lothian question. I am no expert in the workings of the French constitution, but I am nonetheless certain that a similar contradiction would not have been allowed to happen in France. However, before I go any further out on that particular limb, let me turn to the next subject, namely length.

c. Length

The earliest Norman replacements of the Anglo-Saxon cathedrals and major abbey churches were on the same scale as their predecessors and models in Normandy, the design of Lanfranc's Canterbury, for example, begun in 1070, being based on that of Saint-Étienne in Caen, begun a few years earlier. But then the 1070s saw an extraordinary development, in which the longest church kept being surpassed by a new longer one, as, following Lanfranc's Canterbury, at St Augustine's, York, St Albans and Winchester (Table 2).

What is the explanation for the increase in the lengths of these churches? It has been suggested that size was determined by practical need, arising from increased numbers of monks or canons. As already noted, there were such increases: for example, the Winchester annals record that Bishop Walchelin increased the number of monks.[10] These would affect the east arm, but the increases in length include the nave as well. This could be explained by an interest in maintaining the proportional relationship between the lengths of the east and west arms, so this is a possible solution. The increases in numbers could, of course, have been due to competition between institutions, and that raises the possibility that the increases in length were as well. As Christopher Brooke succinctly said of churches being smaller in Normandy and larger in England: 'In Normandy their rulers were counts or dukes at most, in England kings'.[11]

Of course such behaviour, 'my building is longer than yours', is ridiculous, but then many human pursuits are. I call in evidence the ex-sacrist of Tewkesbury who, describing the church in the 1920s, noted with pride that the interior of its crossing tower was one square foot larger than the equivalent space at St Albans.[12] Then there are the skyscrapers in 20th-century America, where the Chrysler Building was erected in 1929 as the world's tallest structure; it was surpassed shortly after by the Empire State, in response to which the owners of the Chrysler Building added a radio aerial. Now we have the Burj Khalifa in Dubai, the Petronas Towers in Kuala Lumpur and, just over the Thames from the Tower of London, the Shard.

The claim of competition in lengths between Norman great churches raises a multitude of questions. In particular, how did they know how

Canterbury (Lanfranc)	1070	80 m	262 ft
Canterbury, St Augustine's	1073	89 m	292 ft
York	1075	102 m	335 ft
St Albans	1077	109 m	358 ft
Winchester	1079	133 m	436 ft

Table 2. Lengths of selected Norman churches begun from 1070 to 1079, from the chord of the apse to the interior of the façade, in order of date and length.

long the preceding building was going to be, when it had been begun only two or three years before? The answer could be that plans would have been available, that patrons, before construction commenced, arranged for the surveying of the site of the whole building, and, most important, that they would have wanted the length to be known.[13] Speed of response is supported by the numerous examples in the period of buildings adopting aspects of others begun only a few years before, as with the example of Canterbury and Caen mentioned above. I think, therefore, that questions such as this can be answered, and that competition was the motive.

This conclusion receives substantial support from what happened next, after Winchester, begun in 1079. I have left a gap in Table 2 between it and the earlier examples in order to stress the extent of the increase in its length over the preceding buildings, and because Winchester establishes a plateau, as from then on the largest buildings, those at St Paul's, Anselm's Canterbury, Durham and Bury St Edmunds, approximate to the length of Winchester, rather than surpassing it (Table 3).[14]

Why did they stop increasing the length of the buildings beyond that of Winchester? It could be because the cost was becoming too great. We are, on the other hand, dealing with a very select handful of buildings, and if the super-rich want to compete then they will find the money. One can in fact prove the point, at Bury St Edmunds, where competition was definitely a factor. The abbey church there was begun after 1081, the east arm of which survives at crypt level, and then in the 1090s it was hugely enlarged, almost certainly because it was in competition with the new cathedral of Norwich, begun in 1096 on the same scale as the 1080s design at Bury (Figure 5).[15] The west front of the enlarged building is one of the widest and most massive ever built: if they had wanted to make the nave longer but felt that they could not afford it, they could simply have reduced the width of the façade and used the money for the extra bays. The reason is rather that, along with Winchester and the

Canterbury (Lanfranc)	1070	80 m	262 ft
Canterbury, St Augustine's	1073	89 m	292 ft
York	1075	102 m	335 ft
St Albans	1077	109 m	358 ft
Canterbury (Anselm)	1093	119 m	391 ft
Durham Cathedral	1093	121 m	397 ft
London, St Paul's	1087	122 m	400 ft
Bury St Edmunds II	1095	131 m	430 ft
Winchester	1079	133 m	436 ft

Table 3. Lengths of selected Norman churches begun from 1070 to the 1090s, from the chord of the apse to the interior of the façade, in order of length.

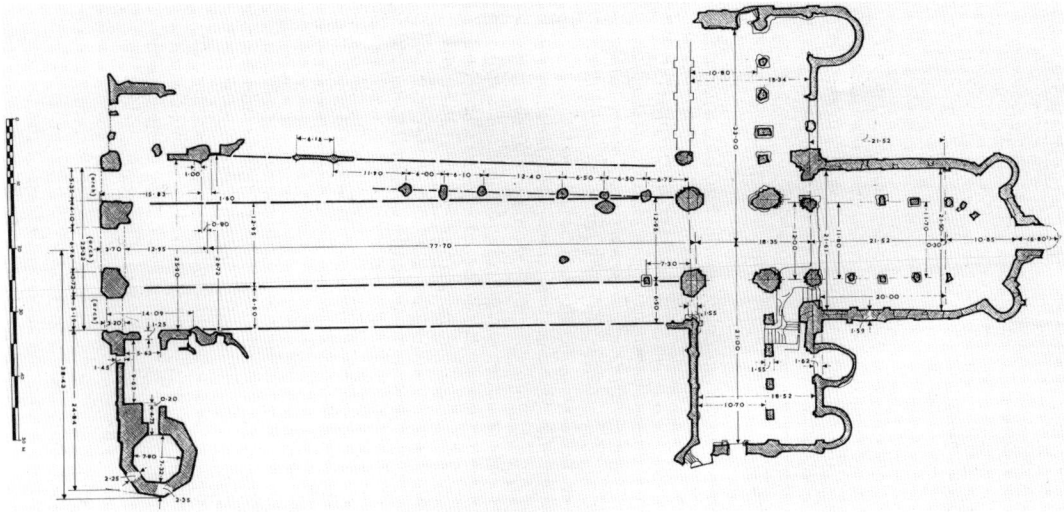

Figure 5. Bury St
Edmunds, abbey church,
after 1081, enlarged in
the 1090s.

Canterbury (Lanfranc)	1070	80 m	262 ft
Canterbury, St Augustine's	1073	89 m	292 ft
York	1075	102 m	335 ft
St Albans	1077	109 m	358 ft
Canterbury (Anselm)	1093	119 m	391 ft
Durham Cathedral	1093	121 m	397 ft
London, St Paul's	1087	122 m	400 ft
Rome, Peter's	320 s	124 m	407 ft
Bury St Edmunds II	1095	131 m	430 ft
Winchester	1079	133 m	436 ft

Table 4. Lengths of selected Norman churches begun from 1070 to the 1090s, with
Rome St Peter's, from the chord of the apse to the interior of the façade, in order of
length.

other buildings, they had reached the size of a historic parallel, the most
important building in the Latin Church, St Peter's in Rome, built in the
320s by the Emperor Constantine (Table 4).[16]

The parallel with St Peter's raises the question: were there other
examples of this practice, outside Norman England? The answer is yes,
but it is a surprising yes. From the end of late Antiquity in the sixth or
seventh century to 1079 there was one, and only one, example.[17] That,
however, was Speyer, a new cathedral founded by the emperor Conrad
II as the burial place of his new Salian dynasty, begun in 1030 and
consecrated in 1061, so certainly topical at the time of the planning of

Canterbury (Lanfranc)	1070	80 m	262 ft
Canterbury, St Augustine's	1073	89 m	292 ft
York	1075	102 m	335 ft
St Albans	1077	109 m	358 ft
Canterbury (Anselm)	1093	119 m	391 ft
Speyer	1030	120 m	394 ft
Durham Cathedral	1093	121 m	397 ft
London, St Paul's	1087	122 m	400 ft
Rome, Peter's	320 s	124 m	407 ft
Bury St Edmunds II	1095	131 m	430 ft
Winchester	1079	133 m	436 ft

Table 5. Lengths of selected Norman churches begun from 1070 to the 1090s, with Rome St Peter's and Speyer, from the chord of the apse to the interior of the façade, in order of length.

Winchester (Table 5) (Figures 6 and 7).[18] Since Speyer is the only church before Winchester with a length based on that of St Peter's, it is difficult to believe that the patrons and architect of Winchester did not intend their building to be compared with it, along with St Peter's.

d. William the Conqueror

This is the point at which to move to the final category in the case for change, namely William the Conqueror. The immediate patron of Winchester was Walchelin, bishop of the see, but it is also right to see William the Conqueror as important in this regard, given that he identified himself with Winchester significantly more than with anywhere else: he kept the treasury there, resided there at Easter in almost all years when he was in England, wore the crown there at Easter, arranged for the three important church councils of 1070, 1072 and 1076 to be held there, and had Domesday run from there.[19] In the late 1070s, when Winchester was being designed, he was heavily preoccupied in Normandy, yet there can be little doubt that Walchelin would have known either explicitly what William wanted or how to satisfy his standards and preferences.[20]

William's standing in the international context is well documented. In 1075, for example, Hugh, bishop of Langres in eastern France, predicted that he would become emperor.[21] He also involved himself in the politics of the kingdom of Leon-Castile, first in the 1070s in negotiations over the marriage of Adelida, his oldest daughter, and, in all likelihood, in a conspiracy of the mid-1080s to gain control of the sub-kingdom of Galicia, a part of Leon-Castile (Figure 8).[22]

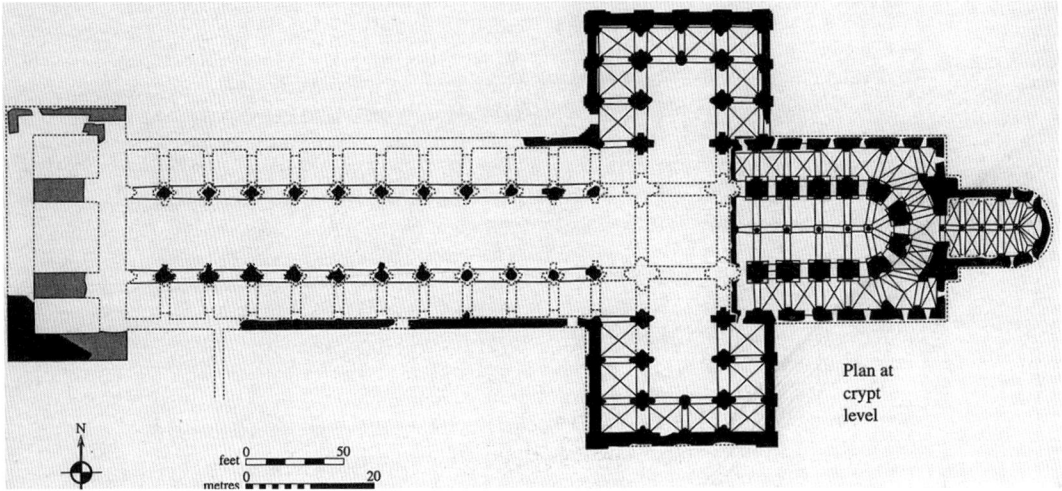

Figure 6. Winchester Cathedral, the Norman building, 1079 to early 12th century.

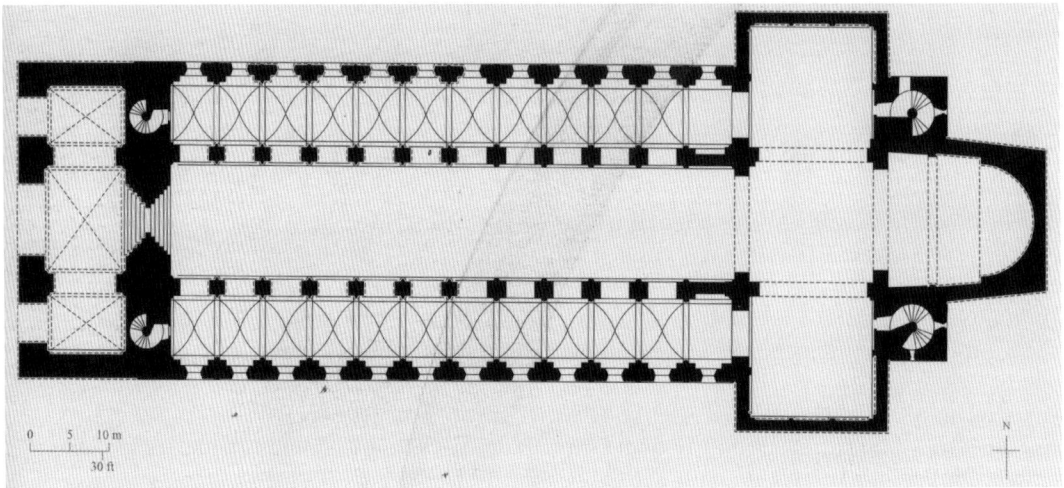

Figure 7. Speyer Cathedral, 1030–61.

Why might he have been interested in acquiring Galicia? The answer to that is the cathedral of Santiago de Compostela, after Jerusalem and Rome the third most important pilgrimage centre in Christendom.[23] There is even a possible architectural element in this proposed link. I refer to the new church begun there in 1078, with its aisles round all three sides of each transept arm, a feature also found at Winchester (Figure 9). The history of this feature in the 11th century is certainly complex, as there are examples in France and the Empire in addition to those in Galicia and England, but, acknowledging that, I believe it

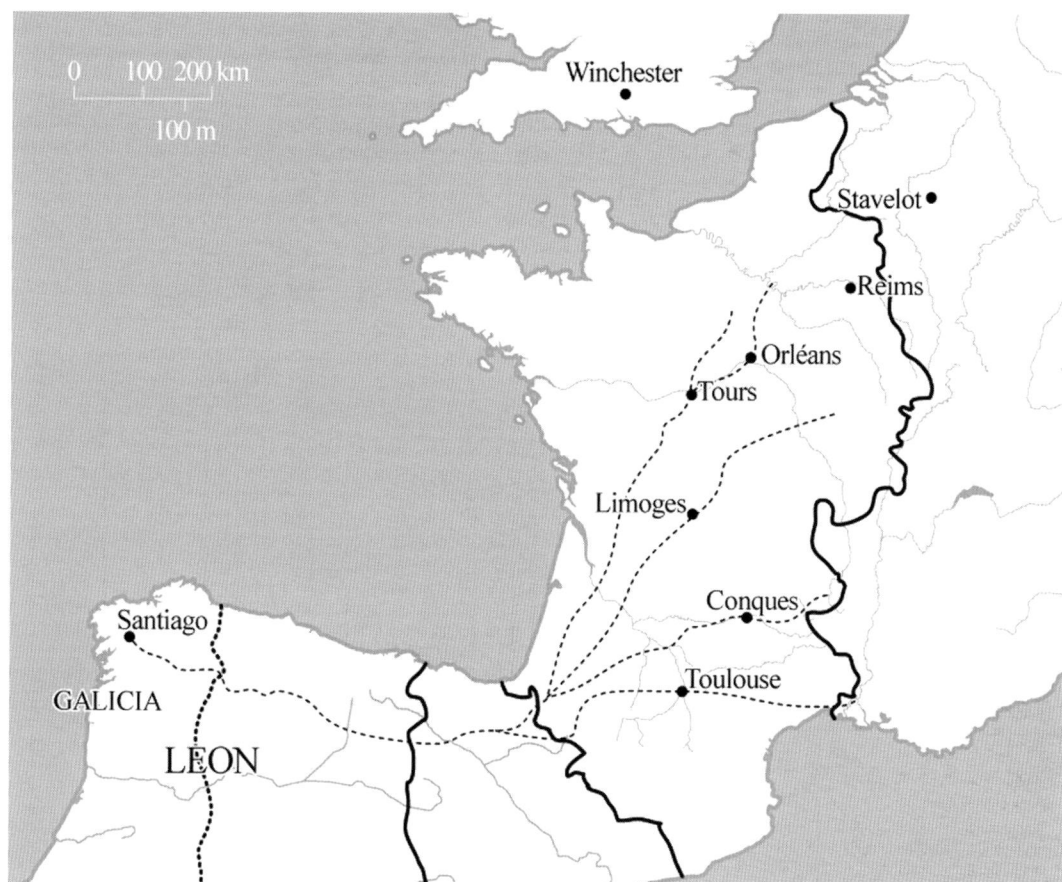

Figure 8. Leon and Galicia in the 1070s.

is possible that the use of the feature at Winchester was derived from Santiago, which was being planned between 1075 and 1077.[24]

I shall end the case for great change there and turn to the evidence for continuity.

II. The case for continuity

I know of six arguments which can be proposed in support of continuity and which, therefore, call into question the case for great change presented above. They concern saints, churchmen, the liturgy, Westminster Abbey, decoration and an Anglo-Norman style.

a. Saints

After Lanfranc's initial tantrum many Anglo-Saxon saints, and especially the most important ones, were fully accepted by the Normans, as exemplified by Swithun at Winchester, Ætheldreda at Ely, Edmund at Bury and Cuthbert at Durham.[25] The Norman treatment of these

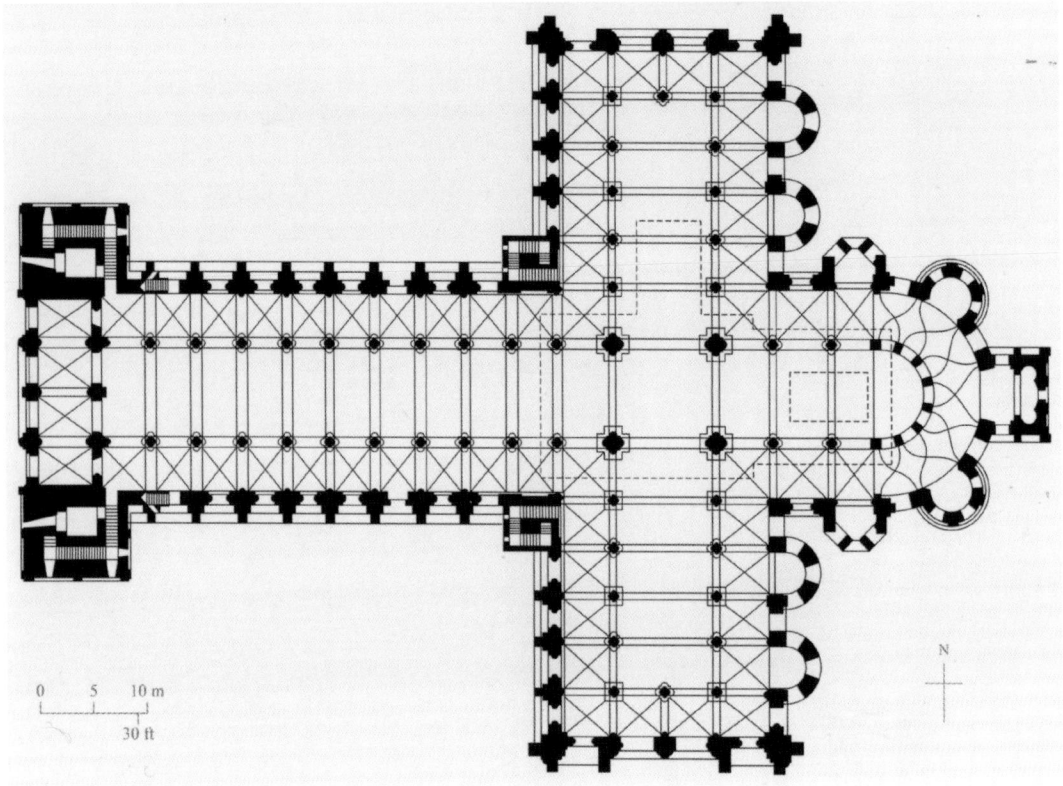

Figure 9. Santiago de Compostela, cathedral, 1078 to early 12th century.

Anglo-Saxon saints is a clear element of continuity, especially as, being dedicatees, they were very closely associated with the buildings. Nonetheless they have no obvious effect on the form of their churches and therefore do not weaken the claim of profound change in the architecture.

b. Churchmen

Anglo-Saxon churchmen were replaced with Norman appointees much more slowly than their secular equivalents, in most cases retaining their position until they died.[26] They were, therefore, an element of continuity, but the Anglo-Saxons who remained in office appear to have had little or no impact on the architecture of the major buildings. Even Wulfstan, who roundly criticised the fashion for rebuilding churches, when he came to rebuild his own at Worcester approved a design of Norman character.[27]

c. Liturgy

The tenth-century reform of the liturgy in England, recorded in the *Regularis Concordia*, included two things which continued after the

Conquest. One is the Anglo-Saxon oddity of the monastic cathedral, unknown on the continent except for the 12th-century Norman cathedral of Monreale in Sicily. This is a clear element of continuity, but again, as with the saints and the churchmen, the point is institutional rather than anything to do with the scale or character of the buildings. The second is the presence of certain rooms which occur not only in Anglo-Saxon churches but also in Norman ones in England, suggesting continuity.[28] Yet it needs to be borne in mind that the *Regularis Concordia* was the Anglo-Saxon manifestation of a reform movement in the northwestern parts of the Empire and the north of France. It is, therefore, no surprise that some of these elements were used not only in Norman buildings in England after the Conquest, but also in Norman buildings built in Normandy before the Conquest. For example, the abbey church of Jumièges, begun in the 1040s or 1050s, has transept platforms which are well placed for antiphonal singing as enjoined by the *Regularis Concordia*, and a sanctuary over the west door, providing what the *Regularis Concordia* refers to as one of the options for a second choir.[29] The presence of Anglo-Saxon liturgical features in churches of the Norman period can, therefore, be explained by them having been imported by the Normans without reference to Anglo-Saxon models.

d. *Westminster Abbey*

Everything we know about Edward the Confessor's Westminster Abbey, at least half of which was built during his reign between 1042 and 1066, is Norman in character, from the overall layout to the alternating supports and the profiles of the bases, and from William of Malmesbury, who describes it as being 'in a new style of architecture'.[30] It is therefore a Norman church in England before the Conquest, happening because Edward was raised in Normandy. There is also an aspect of Westminster which looks forward to what happens after the Conquest, namely its length, for at 96 m (315 feet) it is longer than any church in Normandy of the 11th century (see for example Rouen Cathedral and Saint-Étienne in Caen at around 80 m or 262 feet), and vies with the lengths of buildings of the mid-1070s in England, lying between St Augustine's and York in Table 2. The explanation for this is presumably (as noted by Christopher Brooke, above) that Westminster was built for a king rather than a duke.

Westminster is therefore definitely relevant, something to put in the continuity tray of the balance, but there is no evidence of people copying even aspects of it while it was being built in the years before 1066.

e. *Decoration*

Next is the use of Anglo-Saxon decorative elements in Norman buildings in England. This is to be expected in the smaller buildings of the post-Conquest period. Such elements do not, however, occur in the larger buildings of the 1070s and 1080s, which are in any case noticeably short of decoration, and it is only in the 1090s and the early 12th century that there is a marked increase in the decoration of such churches. Anglo-Saxon features form part of this, such as the interlaced arches at Durham, derived from manuscripts, arch mouldings in the second phase of building at Ely, and piers in the nave of Rochester Cathedral and clerestory of Waltham Abbey, both of the 1120s, which closely resemble those of Great Paxton, built around 1060.[31] It is possible that elements such as these formed part of a continuing Anglo-Saxon tradition in smaller buildings in the intervening decades, but it is just as likely that the Normans simply used them because they were searching for variety in the new, richly decorated phase of Norman architecture.

e. An Anglo-Norman style

The large churches built by the Normans in England differed from their equivalents in Normandy, so it is tempting to describe them as 'Anglo-Norman'. The use of Norman in the term is fully justified, as the basic elements of Norman great churches in England were imported from Normandy. The problem lies with Anglo-, as it implies an Anglo-Saxon contribution alongside that of Normandy. As indicated in the discussion of decoration, there is no evidence for this until the 1090s, and what is primarily new about the great churches of the 1070s and 1080s is their size and the number of elements which have a continental origin other than Normandy. These include the raised crypt and sanctuary in Lanfranc's Canterbury from Lombardy, cushion capitals from the Empire, York's aisleless plan from Angers, Tewkesbury's giant order from western France, and the unusual tangential ambulatory chapels of Anselm's Canterbury from Cologne, to mention only a few.[32] Norman architecture in England can only be called 'Anglo-Norman' because it was England which provided the royal context that can be used to explain this broadened area of interest.

Conclusion

To sum up, there are elements of continuity in the post-Conquest ecclesiastical architecture of the powerful which need to be taken into account, although in every instance there is a mitigating factor. Anglo-Saxon saints, while in some cases offering clear evidence of continuity, are not directly involved in the variations in the designs, and Anglo-Saxon churchmen follow the lead of their Norman-appointed colleagues. The liturgy is a possibility in the case of some elements, but their sources are for the most part Norman or continental, and there are few if any elements where an Anglo-Saxon source is definitely more likely. Westminster is very much involved, but, while it is an Anglo-Saxon building in political and chronological terms, it is a Norman one in terms of its architecture, so it is only with difficulty that one can claim it as a sign of Anglo-Saxon architectural continuity across the Conquest. Aspects of the decoration offer a clear example of the use of Anglo-Saxon forms after the Conquest, but only after a gap of a quarter of a century. A posited Anglo-Norman character of post-Conquest buildings is not a sign of continuity, because the term describes the Norman introduction of the changes to Norman architecture in England and not because those changes were in any way Anglo-Saxon. The strongest and clearest case is, therefore, that of the decoration, but the delay in the appearance of Anglo-Saxon elements means that the key decades of the 1070s and 1080s remain those of an architecture which is in almost all respects very different from that of the Anglo-Saxons.

In my view these aspects of continuity pale into insignificance beside what I am inclined to call the onslaught of building following the Conquest: the replacement of every Anglo-Saxon cathedral and most of the major abbey churches; the abandoning of the additive approach to both the designing and altering of churches; the dramatic increases in length; and with those increases the buildings competing first with each other in Norman England and then in an international context across the Latin Church.

Except perhaps for the areas of the *reconquista* in the Iberian peninsula, I know of no change in church architecture on this scale anywhere else in medieval Europe.

13

The aristocracy of conquered England

Judith A. Green

For many of us thinking of the conquering Normans, the prevailing image is of those short-haired warriors on horseback on the Bayeux Tapestry, throwing up a castle at Hastings even before the battle. We know they spoke French, which became the language of the social elite, and they often used French surnames which were passed down through the male line. The idea that a family 'came over with the Conqueror' has beguiled genealogists for centuries and has taken on a new life with the construction of family trees online. The establishment of that new elite was undoubtedly one of the most fundamental changes wrought by the Conquest, but it was clearly much more complicated than the simple paradigm outlined above.

The most obvious point to make about research in the last few years is the sheer volume of work on individuals, on their careers and kins-folk, on the construction of lordships, and on networks and regions. New approaches, such as prosopography, or collective biography, have added both to the overall picture and to our knowledge of individ-uals.[1] We know much more precisely, for example, from which regions of Normandy most of the newcomers came, and we can appreciate more fully the nature of the Breton contribution to the conquest.[2] The newcomers secured the levers of power through the sheriffs' office, and the transition from English to Norman sheriffs was sometimes facilitated through judicious intermarriage.[3] The power of the great men of the Conquest over the land settlement has become clearer. When, inevit-ably, the Conqueror had to turn his attention to other pressing issues, the great men and their followers were well placed to benefit – men like Robert d'Ouilly, first constable of Oxford castle and, it appears, an agent of Odo, bishop of Bayeux, King William's half-brother.[4] Roger Bigod similarly may have owed his start to a connection with the bishop.[5] As men established themselves in the regions, we can trace their alliances with their new neighbours, and their patronage of monastic houses, both old and new. In west Kent, for instance, the Norman bishop, Gundulf, appointed in 1077, came to be at the heart of a network of benefactors, Norman and English, of Rochester Cathedral priory.[6] Thus we know much more about the new aristocracy than before, and added to the growth of knowledge is the rise of new approaches, arranged here under the headings of lordship, material culture and mental world. The resulting picture is much more complex, changing over time and according to political and familial circumstances, than used to be thought.

Lordship

The study of lordship, the key to aristocratic power, has undergone an important change. The focus used to be on dependent land tenure, or feudalism, on its influence on land law, on the obligation to military service and relations between the crown and the aristocracy.[7] The idea of a feudal pyramid with everyone holding land of someone else who held it of the king still persists in popular history, long after most historians have stopped writing about 'feudalism' as a Norman import into England.[8] Put crudely, it was thought that William the Conqueror 'introduced feudalism into England', transforming the basis of land law and social relations. Land remains at the heart of discussions of the new aristocracy simply because of the scale of the transfer at the top of society.[9] The most important recent contributions to the subject have been by George Garnett and John Maddicott. The former has argued that the premise on which the land transfer was based was the result of a renegotiation of relations between bishops, abbots and the king so that the churchmen recognised that they held their land of the king in return for loyalty and service. This new contract was then extended to lay lords.[10] The latter has studied how political assemblies before 1066 evolved into the great councils of the Norman kings, for no king, however powerful, could afford to act without the backing of the great men.[11]

Historians have also turned their attention to the personal aspects of lordship, to ideas of honour and shame, to the role of rituals in creating and sustaining a lord–man relationship, and to their mutual expectations.[12] Ideas about the ethics of war were in flux. The conquest of England had pitted Christians against other Christians. Those who had participated in the campaigns of 1066 and the years that followed probably felt in special need of forgiveness. A papal legate, Ermenfrid of Sion, laid down a scale of penances for those involved in the fighting. Penitence supplied a strong motive for Normans to give churches they acquired with their lands to monasteries.[13] Not only that, but reformers were teaching that it was wrong for laymen to possess churches.

The early campaigns after 1066 were unrelenting as the Normans fought to establish themselves against Englishmen and their Scandinavian allies. It seems that in the long term, however, the newcomers were less brutal towards their defeated enemies than the English had been, preferring to ransom their captives taken from among the aristocratic elite than to kill or mutilate them. This, it has been suggested, was a sign of a shift in ideas about the ethics of warfare, moving away from older ideas to a more 'chivalrous' approach.[14]

Lordship involved hierarchy, and the newcomers, mainly from Normandy but also from other regions of France, arrived with their own ideas about rank and status. The title of count, or *comes*, was transferred into England.[15] The term was used as the translation of the pre-Conquest title earl, whilst the *vicecomes*, or deputy count, was used for the shire-reeve, or sheriff.[16] The title *baro*, or baron, came to be used of the greater tenants-in-chief whose lands were passed on as entities, or baronies.[17] The word *fidelis*, sworn man, was used of those who had sworn allegiance, but did not necessarily hold land of the king.[18] Beneath the very top level of the new elite, made up mainly of men related by blood to William the Conqueror, the number of newcomers was relatively small.[19] It has been shown that at lower levels many Englishmen in fact remained in place as tenants. This factor helps to explain why there was not more resistance and disruption than there was.[20]

Lordship pervaded all social levels, and working out exactly how the Conquest affected relations between lords and peasants has been a major preoccupation in recent years. The picture obviously varied from region to region. In the north during the harrying by William's army in 1069–70 there was massive dislocation, hardship, starvation and even, it was said, cannibalism.[21] After the harrying, lordships were set up in much of Yorkshire, but elsewhere in the north lordships took longer to establish and more native families evidently remained in place.[22]

Some estates passed to new lords without major structural change. Even so, many peasants were subjected to increased burdens in the form of higher rents or heavier services, or they suffered by being downgraded from free to unfree status.[23] The most unfree were called *servi*, or slaves.[24] There were slaves and a slave trade in 11th-century England. The first wife of Earl Godwine was later said to have sent slave girls to Denmark.[25] Church reformers were trying to stamp out the practice, and the slave trade did die away in England over the century following the Conquest.[26] The Latin word *servus* came to mean not slave in the classical sense but the serf or peasant, the villein who was not allowed to leave the estate or to marry without permission.[27] It has been argued that the emergence of serfdom or villeinage as a legal category took a decisive step forward after 1066.[28] Others suggest that this was a much longer process, and that serfdom essentially came to be defined during the legal developments of Henry II's reign.[29]

The difficulty is in seeing how far the Conquest itself triggered changes in rural society.[30] Some would see the changes associated with peasant status as a reflection of longer term trends in rural society by which open fields and nucleated villages were established across a great swathe of England.[31] Here, it seems, between the middle Saxon period and the 12th century great estates were broken up into smaller units, or manors, many with resident lords, a local church and open fields. The study of fields, settlements and land use reveals a complex picture and a lengthy period of change in which new lords, a rising population and environmental considerations all played a part.

Some estates remained in the hands of ecclesiastical landlords with relatively few changes. Lands in lay control were more likely to be broken up.[32] The new lords assembled new complexes, known as 'honours'.[33] It was at one of their principal manors that they established their main residences. In some instances they simply moved into the buildings of their predecessors, perhaps strengthening the defences.[34] Sometimes they built on new sites, with a fortified mound and enclosure, the motte and bailey castle. Sometimes they built from the first in stone, for example, at Richmond in Yorkshire. Form and conception varied and, as has been argued recently, prestige and display were in many cases intrinsic to their design from the start.[35] Far from being utilitarian defensive forts, many were conceived of from the first as residences intended to convey power, wealth and status.

That the new lords did not in many cases live in heavily defended encampments is a consideration which keys into a bigger discussion about the degree of force by which the newcomers were established. Historians have been divided on this topic: some point to the evidence of discontinuity, and to references to arbitrary and illegal seizures of land mentioned in Domesday Book.[36] Others point to an apparently peaceful transfer.[37] There was clearly a good deal of reorganisation. Paul Dalton's study of Yorkshire showed how, after the Conqueror's harrying of 1069–70, new lordships were set up, some of which by 1086 were evidently much more developed than others.[38] Yet other scholars have demonstrated, on the one hand, how the core of new lordships had existed before 1066, and, on the other, new lords took over not just the demesne lands of a named predecessor or predecessors but also his tenants as well.[39]

Finally, it seems that the process was dominated by a relatively small number of new lords who in turn gave out lands to their followers. After this first wave of migration, there were further arrivals into the top levels of the aristocracy, as the Norman kings sought to reward their allies and their 'new men'.[40] This was not, as far as we know, a sizeable and sustained migration.

It is usually assumed that the new lords, enriched beyond their wildest dreams, simply drew as much revenue as they could from their estates – that they were, in other words, a class of *rentiers*.[41] The study of estate profiles has thrown light on landlord priorities, those who wanted large home farms (demesnes), perhaps with parks (for deer) and warrens (for rabbits), with locally resident peasant workforces.[42] Other regions were devoted to sheep-farming, or open tracts of moorland. New wealth could of course simply be spent in conspicuous consumption, about which more below, and it could be given to the church. At first such gifts were frequently made to monastic houses in Normandy, which then often established English priories.[43] Over time new and independent foundations were established to which lords and their tenants made gifts, and it was here that they were often buried, rather than being taken 'back home' to Normandy.[44]

Family strategies continued to lie at the heart of politics. There has been a good deal of discussion about the extent to which the Normans brought with them an idea of family more strongly orientated towards lineage and male primogeniture, reflected in hereditary naming patterns.[45] It used to be argued that this was very different from Anglo-Saxon custom, according to which it seems there was greater provision for all sons, not just the eldest, but the evidence does not support such a sharp contrast. What did often happen was that in the first generation lands were divided at the Channel, for fathers had more freedom to dispose of lands they had acquired as they wished than their inherited lands, where family claims were stronger.[46] Some chose to pass their lands to one heir, and new cross-Channel complexes came into being. Women played a particularly important role as channels through which land could be transferred between families.[47] There was still a degree of latitude for families in making arrangements for their lands, as well as opportunities for kings to assign individuals as heirs or heiresses, and so to reward their allies.

As well as women, the issue of gender has also been raised.[48] The Conquest was pre-eminently a man's affair: the Bayeux Tapestry famously shows only three women, the mysterious Ælfgyva (apparently involved in a sexual affair), Queen Edith at the bedside of the dying Edward the Confessor, and the woman with her child burned out of her home by the Normans: sinner, widow and victim, in other words. To be a successful man, one had to be a warrior. Warrior bishops, like Odo of Bayeux who was at the Battle of Hastings, thus blurred social categories. Hair came into it, too. The English thegns with their long hair seemed suspiciously like women, and for the hostile observer it might have seemed as though they deserved to be defeated.[49]

Material culture

The English aristocracy, then, looked different from the Normans.[50] How long did this contrast persist, given we live in a world when fashions change so quickly? Did the Normans prefer to keep their own fashions to make sure they were distinguished from their defeated enemies? We know certainly that by the reign of William Rufus the young men at his court liked to wear their hair long and to have shoes with exaggerated points.[51] The king himself had a taste for fine shoes.[52] What we do not hear about is the Normans taking up the English fashion for tattoos and arm-rings.

It seems, too, that the newcomers may have taken to a more exotic diet with their new-found wealth. One of the more interesting developments in recent research has been into changes in diet through the analysis of middens on castle sites.[53] The Normans may have eaten more pork, game and exotic species than their predecessors.[54] The lay elite is thought to have imported new species such as fallow deer and possibly peafowl and rabbits.[55] They enjoyed eating cetaceans, especially whales, and constructed fishponds near their castles.[56] The newly rich Normans evidently enjoyed lavish meals, with some dishes elaborately prepared for the table.

In particular the Normans ate more venison. Hunting and hawking were a form of recreation, a way of providing food for the table, a means of exercising skills of horsemanship and experiencing comradeship, and, once again, a way of displaying wealth and status by the possession of valuable hawks, hounds and horses. They were thus crucial to the lifestyle of the aristocracy at several levels. In early 11th-century Normandy the dukes and their great nobles enjoyed hunting.[57] There were two main methods of hunting deer, either by driving them into enclosures or, more excitingly but dangerously, chasing them across open ground.[58] As yet there is no evidence to suggest that the dukes were at odds with other lords over hunting rights. It seems most likely that each had their own hunting grounds.

The Normans brought their own rituals to the hunting of red deer over open land (*par force*). Moreover, William the Conqueror famously loved the red deer as if he were their father, and banned their hunting, as well as that of the boar.[59] This meant that in designated areas, such as the New Forest, local landowners did not have the right to hunt these animals.[60] In some cases there were precedents, in others the king was asserting rights over what would later be called common land, but he or his officials could also place land under forest law by an act of will.[61] The king's rights were contentious from the first because, it seems, it had earlier been the case that lords could hunt freely on their own land, provided they respected the king's right to do the same on his land.[62] English nobles and thegns (and, allegedly, the monks of Canterbury) had enjoyed hunting and hawking, and had established hays and deer parks for the management of deer.[63]

The author of the Anglo-Saxon Chronicle in his obituary of William the Conqueror lamented the forest laws, and in 1088, when William Rufus was facing rebellion and needed English support, he sent out letters promising them lighter tribute (geld) and free hunting.[64] In terms of diet and lifestyle, therefore, the gulf between the diet of the lay elite and the poor had widened, and this is reflected in animal remains and also survivals in the landscape.

Mental world

Previously the settlement of the new aristocracy, its accommodation with the natives and, finally, its self-identification as English, has been viewed as a one-way process. Analysis of the construction and reshaping of identities has benefitted, however, from close analysis of narrative texts, from charters and from subjects such as patterns of religious patronage and places of burial. When did the Normans, or Flemings or Bretons, in England begin to identify with their new country?[65] For how long and how strongly were ties to the homeland felt? How far did location make a difference to a sense of identity, if spending long periods at court or at the remoter edges of the kingdom?[66] The term colonisation has been used in connection with the Normans in England, but implicit in that term is that the newcomers were exporting Norman culture and institutions to England.[67] Should we regard the Normans in England as one strand in a diaspora stretching from Scotland to Spain and from Italy to Antioch?

Given that we cannot write the biographies of individual members of the new elite, and personal details are few, what evidence is there that bears on the construction of identity? One criterion is the way different peoples were addressed in charters, as 'French and English' or as 'Normans and English.'[68] Another is the importance of legal status, given the idea that law was thought to have belonged to a people. In the earliest decades the French and the English were regarded as having their own laws, but this distinction seems to have faded away in the early 12th century.[69]

In terms of a wider cultural context, there is the evidence of language and literature, art and architecture. Old French became the language associated with elite status, while old English remained the language of the majority and Latin the language of the church, of charters, and of Domesday Book.[70] How far was there a snobbery about the ability to speak French? Here the story of Brictric the parish priest of Hazelbury in Somerset in the 1130s is sometimes mentioned: he could not speak French and so was excluded from talking to the archdeacon and the bishop.[71] Were the English despised by their new lords? The 12th-century chronicler Orderic Vitalis, elsewhere critical of the morality of the Conquest, painted a cheerful picture of English and Normans living peacefully together, and of shops full of French goods bought by the English 'completely transformed by foreign fashion.'[72] There are indications, however, that the Normans may have despised the English, for instance, in the nicknames 'Godric' and 'Godgifu' given to Henry I and his English wife Matilda.[73] Eadmer, the English monk–historian of Canterbury, was very bitter about the lack of promotion prospects for Englishmen in the church in the early 12th century.[74] The Normans and the English obviously intermingled, especially in the towns and in the church. Normans had to get to grips with old English laws, for these had not been abolished, and churchmen had to be able to understand and possibly translate Anglo-Saxon homilies; what how is less clear is how far old English culture was valued by the newcomers.[75]

To sum up: there was no simple linear process by which the new elite became absorbed into and identified with England. Much depended on personal situation and dynastic accident for the preservation or breaking of family ties with the Continent. Those whose interests were most strongly associated with the court had a natural interest in the maintenance of the bond between England and Normandy. Those who settled in the far north of England, for instance, or on the marches of Wales, were more likely to be in a small minority and, rather than imposing their culture on the locals, to have 'gone native'.[76]

Moreover, just as the new elite was composite, so was English society in 1066. There were different regions with different histories, different population mixes and even different languages. One of the topics my own recent work has addressed is the chronology of the formation of the kingdom between the tenth and the twelfth centuries, and both the integrative forces as well as surviving regionalism. In recent years reservations have been expressed about the idea of a tenth-century 'reconquest' of the Midlands and the north from the Danes by the monarchy; in other words, of a process driven by the vigorous West Saxon monarchy.[77] English society in 1066 was obviously far from unified and the north, itself composed of different ethnic groups, was semi-detached. The arrival of a new elite, whose most powerful members did hold land further south, was therefore a force for integration. So far as East Anglia is concerned, Andrew Wareham argued a few years ago that important social changes by which great kinship groups were already breaking up in favour of families defined by lineage.[78] The Normans in Cornwall arrived in another region only loosely tied into the English kingdom, and with its own language.[79]

Finally, our approach to the aristocracy of conquered England has profited greatly from a comparative approach which highlights both the similarities and the differences between what was happening in England and northern France. Debate has concentrated on how far lordship in England after 1066 differed from that in northern France because of the strength of royal government: how far could lords establish effectively autonomous zones of power in their own localities?[80] How far was lordship in Normandy transformed by the situation in England? Or, to put it another way, was the kind of lordship established in England by William the Conqueror exported to Normandy, rather than the other way round? Understanding more about Norman (as well as Flemish and Breton) societies will all throw light on the situation in England.

A wider angle and a longer timeframe thus help to contextualise the aristocracy of Norman England. New approaches, whether analysing the gendered language of narratives or subjecting bones from spoil heaps to close study, will continue to enlarge our understanding. Going back, then, to the question I posed at the start of this article, should we still see the introduction of a new aristocracy as one of the decisive changes of the Norman Conquest? The answer surely is yes: most of the individuals were newcomers, in a new relationship with the king, with a different view of their rights over land, speaking a different language, and many living in strongly defended residences literally pigging out on lavish meals.

14

1066 and the landscape

Oliver H. Creighton

For the most part, the rural landscape of Norman England probably looked very much like the rural landscape of late Anglo-Saxon
England – but with the people in it working a little bit harder. While
this might sound like a throwaway remark, it probably encapsulates
the broad reality of life for many people in the English countryside in
the generation or two after 1066. While the phrase 'the Norman landscape' conjures up images of imposing elite sites synonymous with the
projection of Norman power and authority – towering castles, great
cathedrals and a proliferation of new abbeys and priories – this chapter
digs a little deeper to consider the realities of what political takeover
meant on the ground, and to reflect on how it affected the experiences
of the peasantry, who of course comprised the vast majority – perhaps
over 90 per cent – of England's population of around two million. The
stark fact is that the Conquest was achieved and imposed upon this
indigenous population by a military force usually estimated to comprise
no more than 10,000 men and consolidated by an immigrant population of no more than a couple of tens of thousands more, although the
ways in which the English and Normans subsequently assimilated and
ethnic divisions were broken down after initial hostility is an equally
important dimension to the post-Conquest story (see Williams, this
volume).[1]

1066: a landscape perspective

Two essential pieces of context are required before we engage with the
question of what the Norman Conquest meant for the English countryside. First, the character of the landscape was so varied that Norman
influence was bound to be felt very differently in different places.
Second, the 'Conquest' was a complex multi-phase process rather than
a single event, carried out by a social group that was far from homo-
genous, meaning once again a variety of experiences on the ground.

The English landscape on the eve of the Norman Conquest was well developed and wealthy by European standards, and had not suffered significant and widespread disruption through war for half a century or more. It was also a landscape whose appearance and texture varied profoundly and intricately. The character of England's *pays* – districts with certain landscape character and distinctive and sometimes unique types of communities – was already well defined by 1066.[2] Regional landscape character was manifest not only in the physical qualities of terrain, but also in distinctive systems of agriculture and patterns of human settlement. A mosaic-like rural landscape saw differences between areas of upland, lowland, moorland and fen; between zones characterised by villages and more scattered hamlets and farms; and between regions of pastoral, arable and mixed agriculture. The Conquest naturally had differential effects across these zones, including in areas that witnessed bloody military campaigns and rebellions, others where Norman authority loomed especially large or where new landlords saw particular need or potential to intervene and reorganise, and others still bypassed by the flow of conflict.

The character of England's varied landscape and the experiences of its inhabitants outside the social elite are alluded to only tangentially in the contemporary narrative sources of the late 11th century. For Norman or Anglo-Norman chroniclers, the landscape was the backcloth to military campaigns, with the challenging nature of physical geography used to magnify William the Conqueror's achievements in traversing wild countryside and putting down revolts, as in the north in 1069–70. In contrast, the peasantry surface only occasionally in narrative accounts, mainly as mute victims of military devastation. Glimpses of everyday life in the countryside in the wake of the Conquest are rare, although Orderic Vitalis records that in 1070: 'You could see many villages or town markets filled with displays of French wares and merchandise, and observe the English, who had previously seemed contemptible to the French in their native dress, completely transformed by foreign fashions'.[3] This snapshot of integration and cultural assimilation among everyday folk a mere four years after 1066 is followed by the observation that 'everyone cultivated his own fields in safety and lived contentedly with his neighbour', but it is notable that the writer uses this anecdote to magnify the drama of the violent revolts that directly follow it in the narrative.

Accordingly, we must take on board the contribution of archaeology in order to come to grips with the lived experiences of the majority in the late 11th century. While great bodies of scholarly literature have addressed the high-status components of Norman landscapes – most obviously castles and monasteries, but also parks and forests – and pools of ink have been spilt deconstructing the 'tenurial revolution' of 1066–86, whereby patterns of lordship and administration were radically reconfigured, as captured within the folios of Domesday Book, only now have we started to consider the totality of what happened on the ground. It is only recently that scholars have started to explore the fuller potential of this information – about rural settlements, manorial sites, local church-building, sculpture, burial practices and portable material culture – and to assess not only whether change is observable in the wake of 1066, but also whether it can be attributed to Norman agency, despite the considerable challenges involved in dating the sites and material culture in question.[4]

Another important consideration in exploring the extent to which 1066 transformed the English landscape is that the 'Norman Conquest' was not a single nationwide event but a more protracted and regionally distinctive process.[5] Nor was the conquest entirely 'Norman'; the incoming population included Bretons, Flemings and other Frenchmen. Ethnically distinct incoming groups sometimes settled in particular regions, with the prominent Flemish role in the settlement of Holderness and south Wales a clear case in point.[6]

To the historian John Le Patourel the Norman Conquest had two essential elements: a military phase, followed by a colonisation phase.[7] As Le Patourel observed, these phases overlapped chronologically, but they also impacted upon different regions over very different timescales. In terms of its effects upon the English landscape, the Norman Conquest is best seen not as a discrete horizon that signalled rapid and widespread transformation, but as a high-level political, ecclesiastical and mercantile takeover that interacted in complex ways with longer-term trajectories of change already in train, including, for instance, the formation of villages, the growth of lordship and the rebuilding of local churches. Accordingly, we can most appropriately understand the 'landscape signature' of the Norman Conquest not as a new template imposed on the countryside from above; rather, it acted to accelerate certain trends that were already in progress, while arresting others, and sending others still off in new and different directions.

Figure 1 maps the principal military phases of the Norman Conquest between 1066 and 1070. It makes very clear that campaigning, raiding and revolts affected some very widely separated parts of the kingdom in a relatively short space of time. It also shows how the zone under Norman control expanded progressively but unevenly across England – although we must, of course, remember that at the time this process was not somehow natural or inevitable. Between 1066 and 1070 England possessed a series of fluid and temporary internal borders, initially around the core zone of southeast England that was subdued first, before the zone of Norman influence spread to the southwest in 1068, from which point Anglo-Norman relationships took on an altogether different and confrontational aspect, and then into the Midlands and the north.[8] Progress was not always smooth and the Norman settlement was certainly not complete by 1070 or even by the time of the Domesday survey in 1086. The conquest and settlement of northern England was

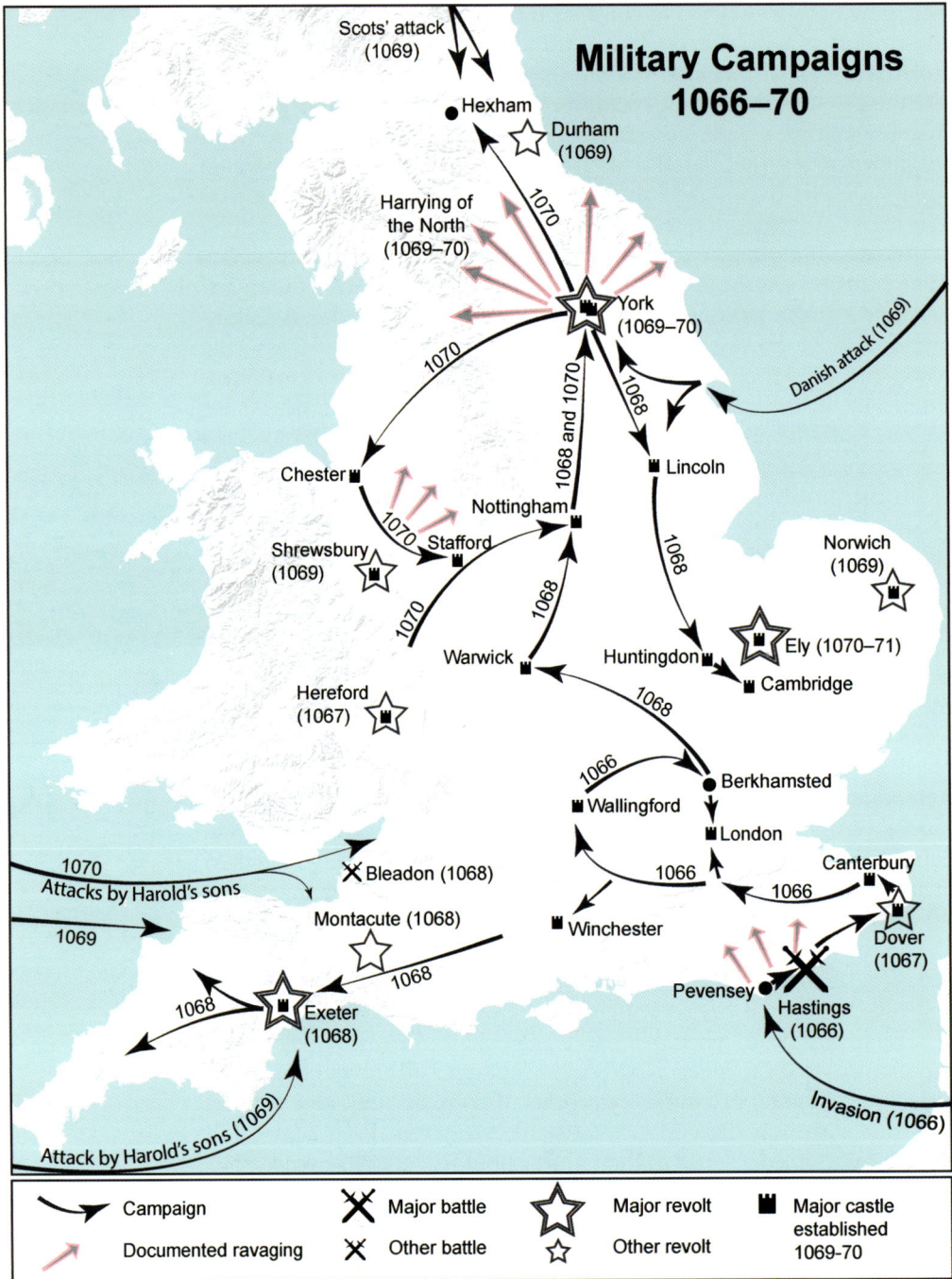

Figure 1. Principal military campaigns and events in England, 1066–70. Map by Oliver Creighton.

especially protracted: as late as 1092 William II despatched colonists to settle the area around Carlisle in Cumbria after building a castle there, sending 'very many peasants there with women and with livestock to live there to till the land', as recorded in the Anglo-Saxon Chronicle.[9]

Entries of waste manors in Domesday Book have been seen as direct evidence of the 'Conqueror's footprints',[10] even given the period of time (up to 20 years) that had elapsed between these military events and the survey. Historians and historical geographers have long urged caution in equating Domesday entries for 'waste' with areas of landscape devastation. A 'waste' manor in Domesday Book could have multiple meanings and origins, including an estate that was economically if not physically waste (particularly where it lacked significant arable production), or a place where inadequate data was available.[11] In Yorkshire, we have to explain away the concentration of waste manors on the flanks of the Pennines (Figure 2): either this is where rebels were hunted down, or else it was these areas that were depopulated to fill the newly created settlements in the Vale of York. It is also instructive that in parts of the country many manors were already waste in 1066.

As the second best-known event of the Norman Conquest, William I's Harrying of the North has received particular academic attention: historians have argued for maximalist and minimalist views of the event's destructive impact and argued over whether its severity transgressed the rules of contemporary warfare;[12] historical geographers have mapped the evidence of 'waste' in Domesday Book (Figure 2) and investigated links between devastated areas and zones of planned villages;[13] while archaeologists have started to investigate its long-term consequences for the region's development and identity.[14] The narrative sources are unanimous in stressing the scale and severity of the harrying: in general terms they talk of the ruination and destruction of Yorkshire; in human terms about refugees and starvation that led to a massive death toll and even cannibalism among the survivors; and in terms of the landscape about great tracts of the countryside and villages left abandoned.[15] It has long been recognised that a cluster of hoards in North Yorkshire probably marks the campaign around the 'Harrying of the North' or the lead-up to it.[16] The patterns probably reflect both that the depositors of coin hoards were killed or displaced before they could return to retrieve their buried treasure and that people were simply more likely to bury coins in periods of public fear and insecurity.

The focus on the Harrying of the North has, however, meant that other episodes of ravaging are not as fully appreciated or studied, such as William's ravaging in the northwest, for example.[17] While it is easy to see these events as the epitome of Norman influence – involving conquest and subjugation by aggressive and superior forces – it is important to understand that landscape devastation in the wake of the Conquest was not just by Norman armies. From the campaign of 1068 we can be sure that William's armies contained English soldiers, while

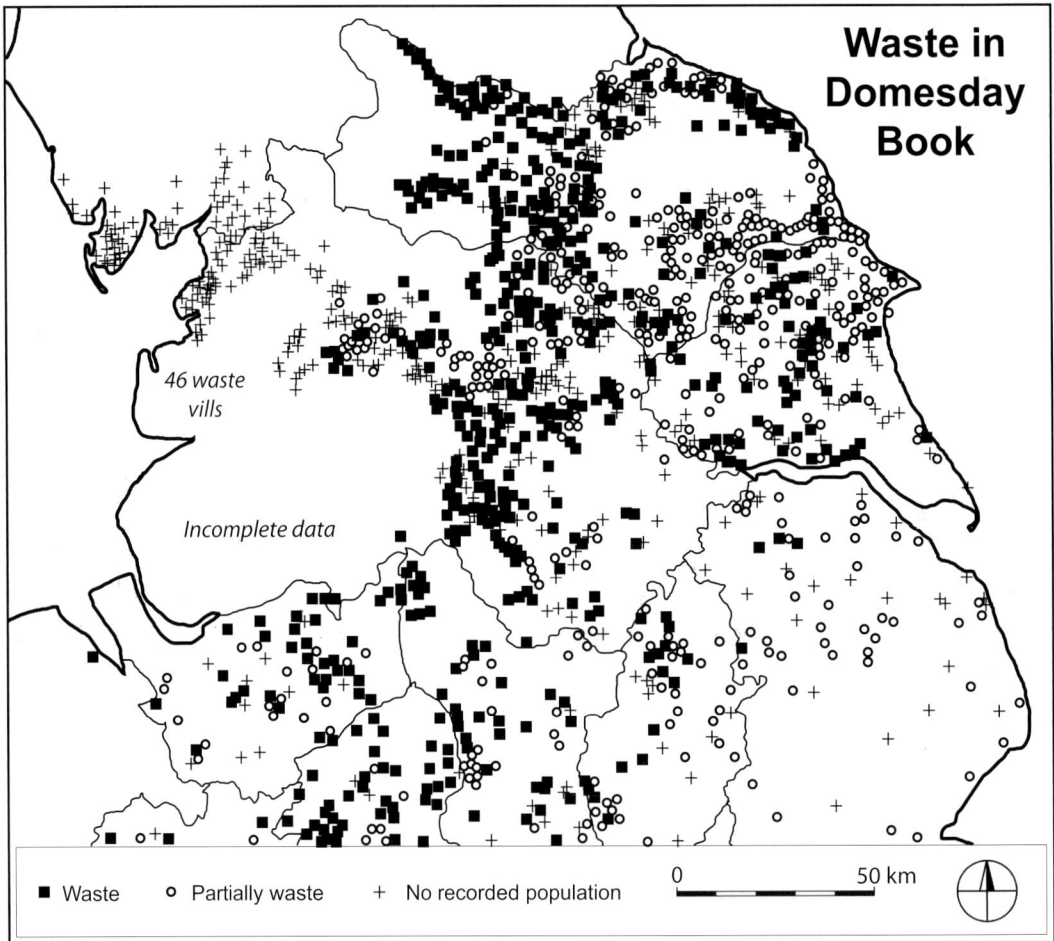

Figure 2. Domesday waste in the north of England. Re-drawn from Darby, H. C., 1977, *Domesday England*, Cambridge: Cambridge University Press, Fig. 83. Map by Oliver Creighton.

ravaging was also carried out by Danish forces attacking the east coast, by forces loyal to Harold's sons assaulting the southwest, by the Scots from the north and the Welsh from the west (Figure 1). To some extent these events were an extension of the 'normal' pattern of medieval warfare, although the sheer volume of military activity in a short space of time is striking and cannot fail to have impacted negatively upon local economies.

It is worth pausing briefly to consider the actual physical consequences of the actions by William's armies. That the Harrying was carried out in the pit of the winter of 1070 is essential to understanding its severity. Images of burning fields are inappropriate. Targets of opportunity would have included livestock, which Norman armies could also requisition as foodstuffs, and settlement infrastructure (primarily in the form of vernacular timber buildings susceptible to burning). But for military

forces deliberately targeting the economic base of the north, more sensible targets were the ox plough teams whose replacement (involving not
only acquisition, but also training) would have been especially challenging, as well as granaries containing seed-corn for the future. Part of the
reason why we should not underestimate the viciousness and thoroughness with which Norman armies ravaged the landscape is that these
actions were deliberate and sometimes politically motivated as opposed
to representing 'collateral damage' inflicted by over-enthusiastic or
poorly disciplined soldiers. Armies needed to live off the land, of course,
but the wasting of a rival's estates had great symbolic importance as it
proclaimed to populations the impotence of their lords and rulers to
protect them. The wasting of the Sussex coast before Hastings might be
seen in exactly this light, while the Harrying of the North was a punitive
measure and a personalised attack by William himself, besides having
the added military rationale of denying economic resources to Danish
armies, from which further attacks were anticipated.

Elite landscapes: estate centres and hunting

Castles were the most obvious symbol of Norman power and it a
truism that they dominated the landscape.[18] In the couple of decades
following 1066 this may have been perfectly true in the towns, but not
the countryside. With castle-building at first strategically focused in the
old *burhs* and shire centres – at places such as Canterbury, London,
Nottingham, Warwick and Wallingford, for example, which saw new
royal castles established – and at the *capita* of major magnates, most of
which were similarly associated with towns, precious few peasants in
the years immediately after 1066 lived under their shadow of a castle;
indeed many must never have seen one.

But this urban focus on the initial impact of the Norman regime
was counterbalanced by another trend: the Conquest signalled a move
in the interests of aristocrats *away* from the towns and *towards* the
countryside. The thegns (or aristocrats) of Anglo-Saxon England had
maintained strong urban interests, holding property within *burhs* and
founding churches within them, for example.[19] In contrast, with the
major urban centres dominated by royal castles and presence, the post-
Conquest aristocracy became increasingly focused on the countryside,
which highlights one frequently overlooked point of difference with
the broader northwest European world. It was on rural estates that the
residences, fortifications, patronage, leisure interests and energies of the
Anglo-Norman aristocracy were overwhelmingly directed.

Early Norman castles were strikingly varied in scale and in terms
of the technologies used in their construction, ranging from expansive and imposing edifices of stone to earth and timber fortifications
built for lords of the manor. The inconsistency with which Domesday
Book records around 50 castles, mainly in the towns, and the text of the

Prologue to the *Inquistio Eliensis* (which details what the commissioners should enquire into), indicates that William probably made no mention of castles at all when he ordered the survey.[20] Overall, no more than 100 castles are documented in England and Wales in the period before about 1100. Many other Norman castles have no recorded history at all, however, including numerous motte and baileys (where an artificial mound is adjoined by an enclosed courtyard) and ringworks (the principal alternative type of site, comprising a fortified enclosure defined by a bank and ditch). Indeed, in many English counties the number of completely undocumented early castles is much higher than the number recorded in historical sources in some way. But attempts to estimate the total number of castles built in the late 11th and early 12th centuries are bedevilled by the large number of 'possible', 'probable' and 'alleged' sites where it is impossible to judge for sure whether a surviving field monument was, in fact, a castle. Several different landscape features of alternative origin can be mistaken for early castles; for example, some supposed mottes are instead misidentified prehistoric burial mounds, medieval windmill mounds or post-medieval prospect (or viewing) mounds. Equally, however, there are also many examples of sites where Norman motte-builders re-used earlier features, and where castle earthworks were re-purposed in post-military phases. Marlborough Castle, Wiltshire, displays both scenarios: its vast 18 m-high motte was formed from a large prehistoric monument, and it was later adapted as a grand post-medieval garden feature.[21] We also have to consider 'vanished' castle sites, whose existence is attested in documentary sources but where no physical evidence survives, and other types of fortification that stretch the definition of 'castle', including siege castles (or 'counter castles', built to blockade an enemy castle or town) and fortified churches and monasteries. A total distribution map of all sites that have been identified as early castles is offered in Figure 3.

These caveats aside, the best estimates are that as a minimum perhaps around 950–1,150 castles were built in England and Wales before 1200, but, critically, only a proportion of these will have been active at any one point in time.[22] The overall density of early castles in England's landscape was certainly far lower than in contemporary France. While Figure 3 highlights how early castles clustered most thickly on the disputed Anglo-Welsh borderlands, equally significant is the broad evenness of their distribution elsewhere. The distribution may be a little thicker in prime wealthy arable districts and lower on exposed uplands and low-lying fen, and the general impression is that most of these early castles were established as manorial centres tied to the land rather than their distribution reflecting any overarching military strategy or rationale. Another perennial issue remains uncertainty over the dating of the numerous undocumented mottes and ringworks. Important debates concern how many of these sites relate to, variously, the initial phase of Norman conquest, the subsequent consolidation of estates by

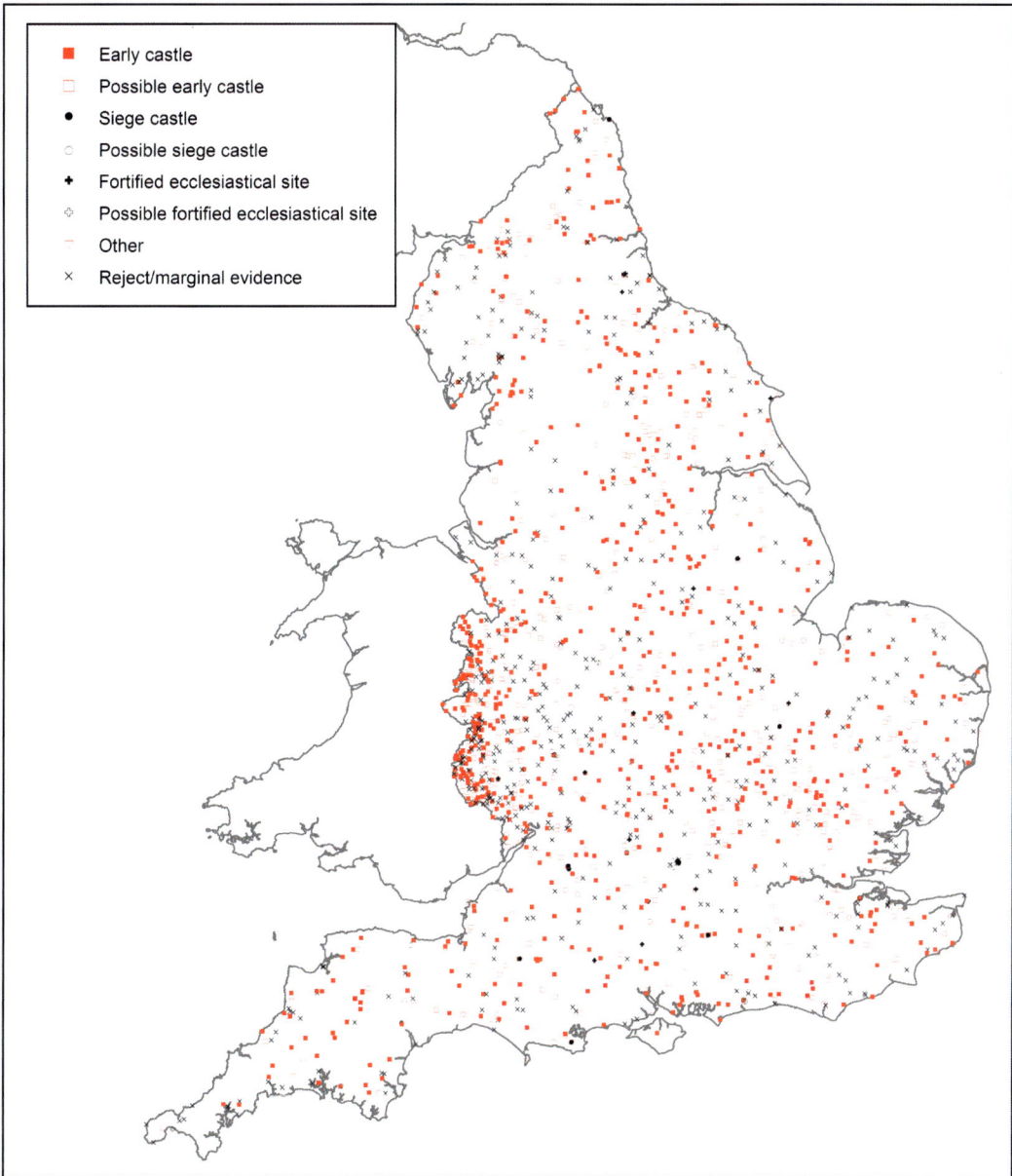

Figure 3. Distribution map of castles built in England before c.1200, also showing possible sites, siege castles, fortified ecclesiastical sites and other 'reject' sites where evidence for an early castle is marginal or mistaken. Based on Creighton, O. H. and Wright, D. W., 2016, *The Anarchy: War and Status in 12th-century landscapes of conflict*, Liverpool: Liverpool University Press, plate 6. © Anarchy? War and Status Project. Map by Steven Trick.

private lords, and, perhaps most problematically, the upsurge of private castle-building in times of war – most notably the so-called 'Anarchy' of Stephen's reign in the mid-12th century.[23] The likelihood is that the distribution map of early castles filled out gradually and in piecemeal fashion after a slow start, primarily as the result of local initiatives on the ground and the intensification of lordship; it saw redundancies as well as new foundations, but also short sharp bursts of intensive castle-building in specific contexts, including during the civil war of the late 1130s, 1140s and early 1150s.

But to understand the effects of Norman castle-building on England's landscape we have to consider more than the number of sites that were built or active at any point in the late 11th and early 12th century. Castles were part and parcel of the repertoire of lordship and need to be understood as such; these were not purely military installations isolated from the wider world, but lordly edifices bound up with the projection of power, the control of territory and the administration of estates. Equally important is the visual presence of castles that loomed far larger over the rural populace than the lordship sites of late Anglo-Saxon thegns. In particular, the donjon (or great tower) served as a highly visual and permanent embodiment of authority in an era when lords were more likely to be absent than present in their castles. Although the idea that these great towers served as places of last refuge in the event of a siege is enduring, these were multifunctional buildings, many of which served ceremonial and ritual purposes as theatres of lordship intended to impress and overawe contemporaries.[24] Detailed analysis of the locations and landscape contexts of Norman donjons shows that lords were acutely aware of the visual opportunities provided by their sites – both in terms of the visibility of these structures from afar and the outward-looking views they provided – but it is striking how often the most highly visible locations within the immediate area were not selected, with castles instead exploiting particular types of visual opportunity, such as dominating a specific locality or views from a particular route or community.[25]

From the perspective of the history of the English landscape, we therefore need to appreciate that most new Norman castles were estate centres intimately bound up to the land and its exploitation and administration, as well as fortresses. Behind their defences many castles hosted manorial courts from which justice was administered under the close eye of their lords; some were in effect working farms containing, for example, stables, barns and granaries, and all were components within local settlement patterns.[26] In the case of Hen Domen, Montgomeryshire, which is our foremost example of an early Norman timber castle subject to thorough excavation, the relatively humble nature of the site's everyday material culture in the 12th century has led the archaeologists to suggest that its lord's wealth might have been tied up with cattle, not portable wealth.[27] At Sandal Castle, West Yorkshire, environmental archaeological evidence from the site (including from animal bones, pollen, charred plant remains and molluscs) highlights the intensification of cattle and sheep farming around the site at the expense of woodland, which was progressively opened up through the 12th century and beyond.[28]

Where early Norman castles within villages have been thoroughly excavated it is not unusual to see that motte and bailey or ringwork castles developed on the sites of earlier enclosed or defensible Anglo-Saxon noble residences – the type site being Goltho in Lincolnshire.[29] Again, the impression is not so much of the sudden imposition of authority upon communities; rather that lordship was intensifying, given a visual makeover and a more military aspect. Display was not entirely absent in manorial complexes of the tenth and early eleventh centuries, however, as evident in the placement of buildings and their churches in relation to routes of approach.[30] The status of castles as vehicles for the expression of seigneurial status was accentuated further by the frequent association between castle and other symbols of rural lordship – not just the estate church, but also the mill, dovecote and rabbit warren. It is important to underline that this view of early timber castles as part of the machinery of rural lordship rather than stark fortresses is not purely the product of revisionist scholarship: the great pioneer of Norman castle studies, Ella Armitage, commented in her 1912 volume *The Early Norman Castles of the British Isles* that the reasons for the placement of mottes in the landscape were 'manorial rather than military'.[31]

Equally fundamental to the imprint of the Norman regime was the proliferation of new monasteries whose estate management strategies pioneered or intensified exploitation across their extensive properties. But, again, the immediate upsurge in activity in the years after 1066 mainly impacted upon the urban world, which saw the foundation of several important Benedictine houses.[32] Few major or successful rural houses were established at first: instead, Norman magnates retained responsibility for monasteries they had founded in their homeland, and it is in these establishments that many of them chose to be buried. The Cluniac houses of the 1070s and 1080s were mainly found in association with baronial castles and the order failed to achieve lasting success because of its haphazard growth and inadequately endowed establishments.[33] It was not until the middle years of the 12th century that the full impact of the reformed orders was felt in the countryside; the 19 years of Stephen's reign saw the number of monastic houses in England and Wales grow by 50 per cent, as lords founded abbeys and priories out of penance and to put down territorial markers amidst the political turmoil, and even then it was decades before acts of monastic foundation translated into permanent buildings and well-established communities with the capacity to transform local landscapes.[34]

Estate churches were other crucial elements in the developing repertoire of lordship. Their sculpture displayed elite patronage while within their cemeteries tomb slabs were further manifestations of seigneurial identity.[35] At Raunds in Northamptonshire we have clear archaeological evidence that the cemetery of an Anglo-Saxon church was cleared by the incoming Norman lord, but this was probably unusual.[36] The disruption of cemeteries through castle-building was mainly restricted to the towns, as witnessed at Barnstaple, Norwich and Worcester, for example.[37] The construction of new stone churches in the countryside and the reconstruction of old timber ones in stone was another phenomenon rooted in the late Anglo-Saxon period given impetus by Norman lords. Likewise, the breaking up of the large territories of minster churches into smaller parishes was a slow process which the Norman Conquest sat in the middle of. The frequent juxtaposition of Norman castle and church in some senses perpetuated an Anglo-Saxon phenomenon. Especially characteristic of local power projection in the tenth and early eleventh centuries were 'tower-nave churches' (freestanding towers containing chapels but without naves) built by high-ranking Anglo-Saxon lords at their estate centres, typically within or just outside the enclosures that embraced their halls.[38] The Norman Conquest and consolidation saw the same essential repertoire repeated, but with a more military and imposing character. Some churches adjacent to early castles lay within heavily defended bailey enclosures, so that the rural population would have had to come through the castle gate to worship (Figure 4). Seen from a longer-term perspective, the powers of rural lords had been intensifying since the late Anglo-Saxon period; the significance of the Norman Conquest is that this process was ratcheted up a couple of extra notches in a very short space of time.

The Norman love of hunting and the centrality of this activity to elite identity are well known and well studied. Through the imposition of strategies designed to protect game and to create or maintain environments conducive to the chase, hunting also held the capacity to alter the landscape. Just as importantly, it also impacted upon how large tracts of the countryside could be accessed and by whom. The signature environments for hunting were the park (a privately owned and enclosed space), the forest (not always a wooded area, but an extensive zone where stringent game protection laws applied), and the chase (a private hunting territory). As with other aspects of the Norman influence on England's countryside, changes to hunting landscapes represented evolution rather than revolution; control over precious and prestigious hunting resources was increased and its jurisdiction extended, rather than 1066 signalling a clean point of departure from previous practice. After all, not only is hunting well attested as a royal and noble pastime in the Anglo-Saxon period; as a means of displaying power it was a more or less universal strategy among European medieval rulers.[39]

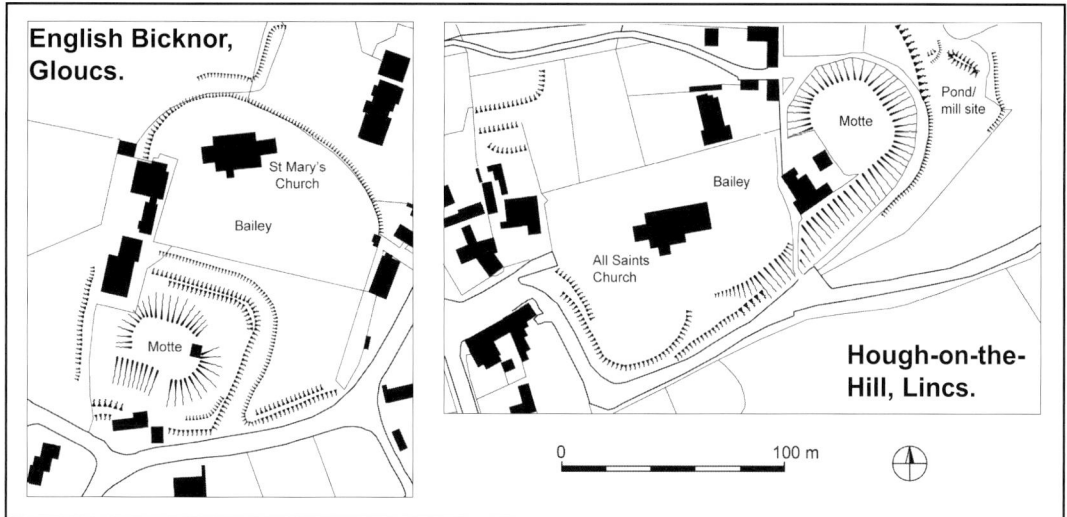

Figure 4. Early castles with churches inside their bailey enclosures. At Hough-on-the-Hill the church contains Late-Saxon fabric, indicating a pre-castle foundation; at English Bicknor the earliest phase of the church dates to the mid-12th century. Map by Oliver Creighton.

Deer parks are sporadically documented in Domesday Book, several of them properties of the king in royal forests. Thirty-seven are recorded, using the terms *parcus* (park) or *haga/haia* ('hay' or enclosure), although this figure demonstrably under-represents the total in existence at the time.[40] Some of these units had their origins before 1066 and continued in use into the Anglo-Norman period, as at Ongar, Essex, where a *derhage* (or 'deer hedge') is mentioned in a will of 1045.[41] How often this sequence is repeated is exceptionally difficult to tell, however. The sources in which references to deer parks can occur become more plentiful and varied through time, but we can still be sure that the number of parks increased dramatically after the Norman Conquest. The precise chronology is difficult to establish, given that few licences exist for the period before about 1200, and a park's creation will very often predate its first reference in documentary sources.[42] The strong likelihood is that park creation in the post-Conquest period gained momentum only gradually through the late 11th and 12th centuries, as lords consolidated their positions and developed their estates, rather comprising a sudden early burst of activity. As far as we can tell, early Norman parks were mainly constructed for the king and major magnates, especially in southern and southeast England; for lesser lords it was the century and a half after 1200 that was the 'great age of the medieval park'.[43]

We also understand the form of the Norman deer park only hazily,[44] although the indications are that many were more closely physically associated with elite residences than their Anglo-Saxon counterparts, and characteristically lobe-shaped in a way that made for efficiencies of enclosure but which also cut across the grain of the landscape (Figure 5). As large bounded entities to which access was tightly controlled, parks

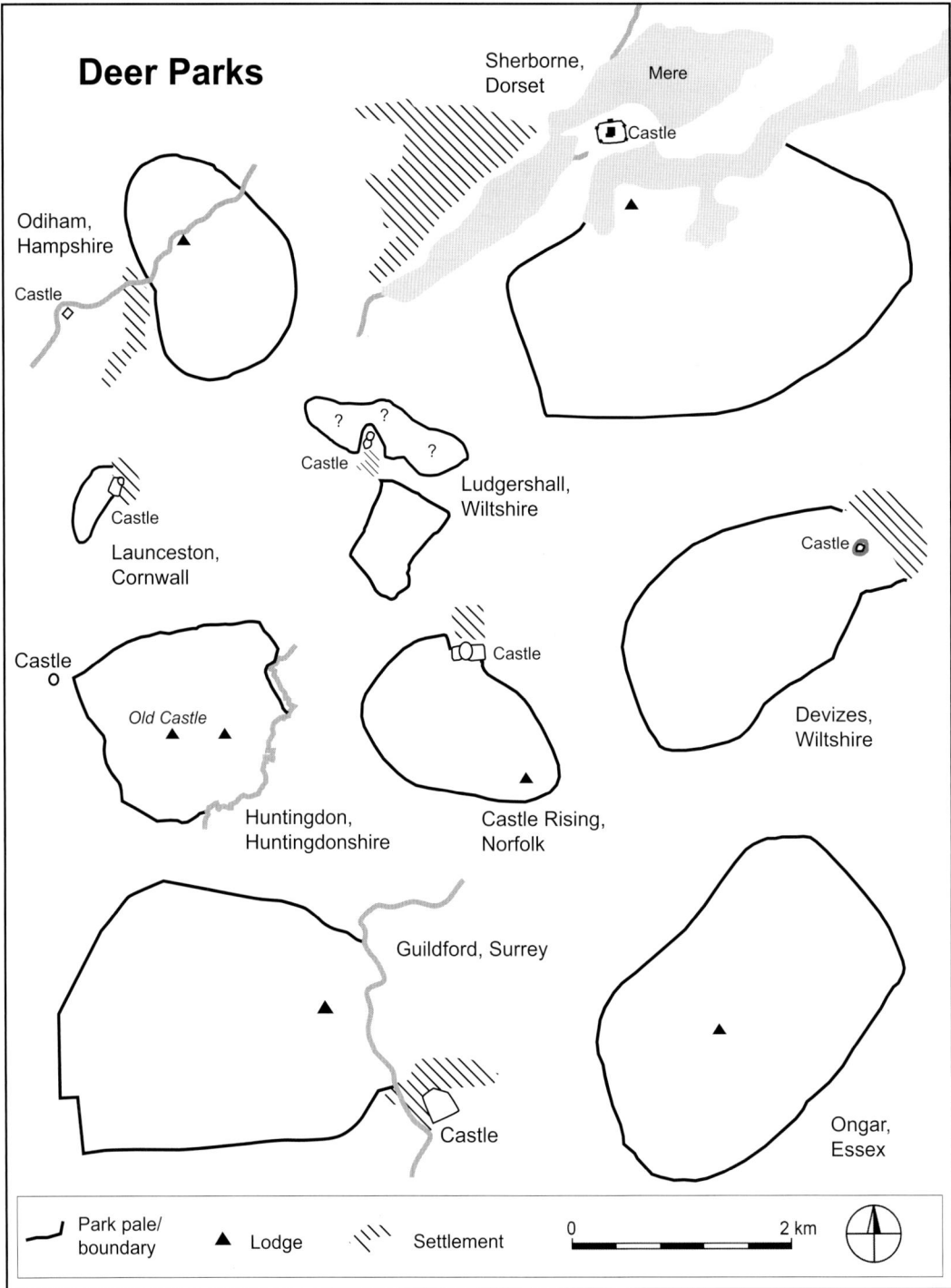

Figure 5. Topographies of selected Norman deer parks founded in the late 11th and 12th centuries, showing their relationships with early castles and settlements. Map by Oliver Creighton and Mike Rouillard.

had profound impacts on landscape development, not least in taking large swathes of land out of production, sometimes entailing the re-routing of roads and influencing the longer-term pattern of settlement growth. Some formed elements within wider schemes of landscape re-planning involving newly established boroughs, with the scheme of a castle bracketed on one side by a planned settlement and on the other by a park a recurring theme, although this seems to have been character-istic of the mid-12th century rather than the immediate post-Conquest period.[45] There is a debate over whether such schemes can be seen as early examples of 'designed landscapes' that show aesthetic sensibilities as well as projecting power.[46] It was also within parks that the Normans established the horse studs essential to breeding and training warhorses. While the Anglo-Saxon period saw horses used for military purposes on a limited scale (albeit with little or no evidence that warriors fought on horseback), the Norman Conquest saw a quantum leap in horse breeding that extended to the introduction of Spanish bloodstock.[47]

The type of game most closely associated with the park was the fallow deer. Rather than having been imported to England from Normandy, as once thought, it now seems that fallow deer were introduced via Sicily shortly after the Conquest, although it took decades before it was firmly established as the 'premier park species'.[48] Early examples would have been kept for show as prized exotica in exclusive menageries rather than running free in parks; the remains of one enormous early male spe-cimen from the Norman castle at Trowbridge, Wiltshire, might be a first generation import – perhaps from Turkey or Greece.[49] Likewise, while the Normans introduced other exotic species including the peacock and pheasant, these are exceptionally rare in animal bone assemblages from archaeological sites before the mid-12th century, while the rabbit seems to have been a late-12th-century introduction.[50]

The policies of the Norman kings of restricting hunting activities and conserving wild game in forests affected far larger tracts of territory than deer parks, although these built on precedents set by Anglo-Saxon rulers to protect their hunting resources, which in turn drew upon Frankish traditions. While the practice of protecting hunting rights was, therefore, nothing new, the legal framework to enforce them – the des-ignation of areas as subject to forest law and the related system of forest courts – was, and took the association between kingship and hunting to a higher level and applied it to far larger areas. Twenty-five forests are mentioned in Domesday Book; by 1200 there were 150, many of them in the hands of magnates.[51] The application of forest law in England cer-tainly took a very different path to the situation in Normandy: forests in England were both more extensive and exclusive, containing great swathes of non-royal demesne.[52]

Studies of forest development reveal a myriad of patterns on the ground, as Norman forest law was imposed on landscapes of sharply different character with distinctive histories of landholding. Unlike parks, forests were not physically enclosed, and their perimeters were typically irregular, with settlements scattered around their fringes. In Wessex – the heartland of English kingship – forests were established in areas where rulers had long-established hunting interests, so that Anglo-Saxon royal estates with extensive demesne woodland formed the cores of Norman forests.[53] At Cheddar, Somerset, archaeological excavation has shown how an Anglo-Saxon timber palace favoured as a hunting seat was rebuilt as a grand royal hunting lodge within Mendip Forest and used by the crown up to the early 13th century.[54] Domesday Book also records hunting grounds in several upland regions that the Normans repurposed as forests, including devastated lands on the Anglo-Welsh border used for hunting in 1066, and Exmoor, where three foresters held land at Withypool in 1066.[55] Pollen sequences from areas that were subject to forest law provide one important means of illuminating any major ecological changes that took place. Although well-dated sequences are few and far between, there are indications from sites in the New Forest, Hampshire, and Epping Forest, Essex, that there was little appreciable change in land management strategies from the early medieval period through the post-Conquest centuries.[56]

We should also not forget the productive role of the vast swathes of the countryside subject to forest law; these areas yielded a wide variety of resources such as pasture and timber for building, as did deer parks, which also contained fishponds and rabbit warrens and were venues for hawking.[57] In certain cases, however, the imposition of forest law might adversely affect local economies and populations, at least temporarily. A particular debate has focused on the impact of afforestation on the area of the New Forest. While William of Malmesbury criticised William I for a policy which saw settlements abandoned and a productive region turned over to wild game, the claims were probably exaggerated.[58] Historians and historical geographers have debated whether entries in a special section of the Domesday folios for Hampshire that detail holdings under forest law attest large-scale depopulation, although most now agree that the area, with its thin poor soils, was sparsely populated in 1066 and that the overall scale of evictions across some 30–40 settlements was probably quite modest, if real enough for those involved.[59]

Estates and agriculture

It was the urban rather than the rural world that felt the first pulse of Normanisation. Alongside castle-building it was manifested in great campaigns of cathedral construction and reconstruction in the Romanesque style, as seen at Winchester and Lincoln, for example (see Fernie, this volume). Townscapes such as Norwich and Nottingham were transformed through the planning of new markets and the settlement of merchant–colonists, while the phenomenon of new town plantation was kick-started by Norman lords keen to develop their estates and raise revenues.[60] While these horizons provide clear markers of Norman activity and influence in towns, it is often profoundly difficult to date change in the countryside with the levels of precision necessary to meaningfully feed into historical debate. It is not that the countryside didn't witness change; the question is over what tangible impact this had, and over what sort of timescale, on settlements, field systems and agricultural regimes.

The Norman 'settlement' has usually been understood and studied in terms of the actions of the great magnates who received or seized English estates and carved out their lordships; far less attention has focused on settlement at a non-noble level – knights, sergeants, merchants, peasant-colonists – and how these groups interacted with their English counterparts.[61] By 1086 virtually every peasant had a new landlord, but whether the replacement of one overlord with another had real consequences on the ground depended once again on geographical context. For the most part, new lords had little immediate motivation to intervene and alter agricultural regimes attuned to local landscapes or to ring radical changes to the ways that rents were collected and services owed. That reeves (officials overseeing a landowner's estate) seem to have remained in place was another important reason for underlying continuity. The most profound changes to the administration of England's landscape occurred in those areas of the country, especially the north and on the borderlands with Wales, where estates were grouped into great units under the jurisdiction of a single powerful super-magnate. This contrasted with the predominant pattern over much of central and southern England whereby the pattern of land ownership was much more fragmented, with more loosely grouped parcels of estates and the assets of an overlord typically distributed over several shires.

We see the formation of the larger tenurial units in areas where it was in William I's strategic interest. All were centred on castles. Thus, in Yorkshire, devastated and vulnerable not only from the Scots but also to an enduring Viking threat, the northern powerhouses of Norman colonisation were the honours of Blyth-Tickhill, Holderness, Pontefract and Richmond, and the Palatinate of Durham. The large number of Domesday manors in the north disputed between different lords indicates that in some areas lords may have been acting quasi-autonomously in the 1070s and early 1080s to carve out their possessions, making for a free-for-all land-grab motivated by private enterprise as opposed to a centralised redistribution of land – what has been termed a 'kleptocracy'.[62] The strategically crucial southeast coast, linking the kingdom to Normandy via its ports, saw the creation of five contiguous 'rapes' (the word is derived from the Anglo-Saxon for 'rope', meaning an area that was marked out): (from west to east) Chichester, Arundel, Bramber, Lewes and Pevensey. The borderlands with Wales were dominated by three Earldoms: (from south to north) Hereford, Shrewsbury and

Chester; while in the far southwest Cornwall was in the hands of the Count of Mortain, William the Conqueror's half-brother. That this massive reorganisation cut across ancient tenurial patterns must have contributed – sometimes alongside military devastation – to the fall in manorial values between 1066 and 1086 that is characteristic of many such regions.[63] Such a shakeup could have profound consequences on the ground, especially where it cut long-established economic and administrative interconnections between different zones of landscape. To give one example: the creation of the rapes of Sussex ensured that links were severed between manors and their outlying colonies or assets in the Weald.[64]

The key piece of evidence that new Norman overlords were pumping their estates for revenues far harder than their Anglo-Saxon predecessors lies in Domesday Book: south of the River Trent we see a general rise in the value of manors between the time these estates were acquired by their lords and the year of the survey.[65] Fourteen shires show increasing values in the period 1066–86, six of them by 20 per cent or more.[66] The short space of time over which these rises took place suggests that they cannot be explained by large-scale agricultural reorganisation. Instead, explanation can be sought in Norman lords increasing rents and imposing taxes.[67] The detail of strategies varied depending on context.

In East Anglia, in the Honour of Clare, rises in manorial values might be explained by an increase in demesne livestock, especially sheep, with most demesne manors showing dramatic rises in the number of sheep between 1066 and 1086 – at Clare itself the increase was from 60 to 480, although this might reflect how tenants were turning to sheep farming and the promise of cash payments in order to meet increased overheads, rather than some lordly master plan.[68] In the marshlands of Kent, Domesday Book indicates dramatic intensification of marshland exploitation in the two decades after 1066; the evidence is particularly compelling for the deep and expansive marshes around Romney, where salt-panning and fishing by tenants combined with settlement and pastoralism helped to transform this distinctive environment.[69]

In the north and east of England sokemen in particular were pressed for higher payments; many were reduced in status to villeins subject to lords, and sokelands could become 'berewicks' attached to the lord's demesne.[70] The grouping of rural populations more tightly around the seigneurial core might be more characteristic of the immediate post-Conquest period than we realise, although arrangements are not widely documented until the 12th century. Owing heavy service rents sometimes known as 'worklands', such populations could be directed to the most labour-intensive tasks as lords increased production on their demesnes.[71] They would have maintained high-status elements of manorial infrastructure – digging fishponds and moats around the *curia* (or manorial enclosure), or working the lord's garden, for example. Nor did the abolition of slavery as a result of Norman religious sensibilities see greater freedom in the countryside; rather, the same individuals did more or less the same work but within a different social category. Many slaves became bordars, allocated smallholdings around the lord's demesne for which they owed labour rent. While these widespread changes in peasant status were a signature of the Norman Conquest, we also need to appreciate that, viewed over the *longue durée*, the greater levels of control that new lords wielded over rural populations only accelerated a longer-term trend that had been in train since the late Anglo-Saxon period.

Archaeological evidence shows that most of the more important trends in the production and consumption of key foodstuffs around the time of the Norman Conquest were similarly longer-term processes that continued into the 12th century and beyond: the shift in cereal cultivation away from barley and towards wheat; the move from cattle to sheep/goat; and the growth in the consumption of maritime fish.[72] If Norman culinary tastes saw shifts in what was eaten, and how, then it was at an elite level. Particularly important in this respect are post-Conquest changes in the consumption of fowl (towards chicken, and occasionally other exotic species such as peacock, and away from duck); in the slaughter of pigs (a favoured aristocratic foodstuff) at an earlier age; and in the introduction of more exotic herbs and spices (including mustard, for example) into cooking.[73] Perhaps slightly more visible in the countryside of post-Conquest England was the rise in viticulture that responded to Norman elite tastes. Domesday Book records 42 vineyards in southern England, the majority of them in the hands of lay lords; 10 are listed as new or only partially yielding, suggesting an upsurge in viticulture in the post-Conquest decades.[74]

In his landmark regional study *The Norman Conquest of the North*, William Kapelle made a powerful argument that the initial extent of Norman colonisation in the north (that is, by c.1100) was influenced by the 'oat bread line' – a historical agricultural dividing line between the east coast plain, where arable cultivation was dominated by wheat and rye, and the west, where oats and barley were the characteristic crop.[75] The argument is that the Normans prioritised for settlement land that could support the production of bread made from wheat, which was both a major element of their diet and whose consumption was a symbol of social status. We should also recognise, however, how the organisation of several northern honours ensured access to different landscapes type, including upland zones for hunting. It is striking how major honorial castles in the north such as Richmond, North Yorkshire, and Barnard Castle, County Durham, for example, were sited at the interface between upland and lowland pays.[76]

Settlement landscapes

Few peasants of the late 11th century lived in settlements with new Norman-French names. This might initially seem like an insignificant observation, but it marks a major point of comparison between the Norman Conquest and the invasion and settlement of Anglo-Saxons in the fifth and sixth centuries and the Vikings in the ninth and tenth centuries, both of which were, to an extent, folk-movements that transformed the place-name landscape. The English landscape contains a tiny handful of Norman-French place names from the late 11th and early 12th centuries and these are with few exceptions associated with elite sites or settlements – primarily new castles and the towns that grew up around them (for example, Belvoir ('beautiful view'), Leicestershire, and Richmond ('strong hill'), North Yorkshire), and occasionally hunting resources (for example, Beaumont ('beautiful hill') Chase, Rutland).[77] Striking is the way that many of these new names referenced the qualities of the landscape itself, often in a positive way, with some names clearly transplanted from the homeland to appropriate new contexts. Evidence that an old Anglo-Saxon place-name was replaced with a new Norman one is rare, although the Gloucestershire name Miserden, first documented in the 12th century (as Musarden, referencing the Musard family who held the manor in 1086) and replacing the Anglo-Saxon name *Greenhampstead* is one example.[78] On the western edge of Shropshire the place-name Montgomery was implanted by Earl Roger before 1086 to name his new castle, as listed in Domesday Book. Remembering his hometown in Normandy, we can only guess to as to whether this proclaimed some aggressive colonial statement to the Welsh, or was borne out of nostalgia.[79] 'Manorial affixes' to place-names, whereby the identity of a magnate family became associated with a place to distinguish it from another with the same name (for example, Kingston Lacy, Dorset), were mainly much later in date and have little to do with the earlier phases of Norman colonisation. It is also instructive how the Conquest left virtually no trace on England's field names, unlike the earlier Scandinavian settlement,[80] testifying once again to its limited impact on the workaday farming world.

Unpicking the impact of the Norman Conquest on England's rural settlements is rendered hugely challenging by the difficulties of dating evidence of change to the periods before and after 1066. We certainly see no horizon of 'Norman' material culture in the archaeological record of rural England; instead the term 'Saxo-Norman' is used to characterise the pottery of the 11th and 12th centuries, just as it describes the transitional architecture of parish churches around this time. The issue is especially acute in the west and north of England, parts of which were effectively aceramic (that is, without pottery) until well into the 12th century. Everyday artefacts of the period are so scare on rural sites that it is difficult to come to grips with the material culture of the 'Norman' peasantry; dress accessories – such as brooches, buckles and finger rings – are especially scant, with the 11th century representing a gap in the chronology of some classes of artefact.[81] All this means that a simple 'before and after' picture' of rural life is close to impossible.

One area where continuity seems clear is in the technologies used in everyday housing. The earliest surviving medieval domestic buildings date only from the mid- to late 12th century (a good early example being the stone-built manor house at Boothby Pagnell, Northamptonshire), but from the archaeological record we can be quite sure that the essential building methods and appearance of peasant housing remained unchanged either side of 1066. It was not until about 1200 that 'earthfast' timber building technologies (whereby the principal posts are set in post-holes) were gradually replaced by 'timber-framing' (where a building's strength relies on jointing), although the transition was neither sudden nor even across England.[82]

Turning to the origins and structures of settlements, it is important to underline that England's medieval landscape did not witness a single definable 'village moment' that saw the widespread formation of nucleated settlements around the same time. Instead, we see a mosaic of nucleation processes, affecting some but by no means all regions, in train between the ninth and twelfth centuries, so that villages were still forming and being planned either side of the Norman Conquest.[83] The enduring tendency of medieval settlement historians to focus attention on the question of when and why nucleated villages came into existence, at the expense of understanding the full range of settlement forms (including scattered hamlets and farmsteads and mixed forms), has gradually given way.[84] The weight of accumulated studies since the growth of the subject in the 1950s show no clear horizon of widespread settlement reorganisation across England in the wake of 1066, although this is not to say that the period saw stasis; rather, the Norman impact can only be discerned through detailed study of individual settlements and regions.[85] Even in the cases of the most thoroughly excavated villages, however, correlating evidence of settlement change with historically significant watersheds is hazardous in the extreme, as the case of Wharram Percy, East Yorkshire – arguably the most fully studied regular village in England – shows. An integrated and evolving research programme of excavation, fieldwork and documentary research has worked wonders to elucidate the settlement's complex biography.[86] But while it is generally accepted that the village's form relates to an episode of planning, it remains an open question as to when this occurred; reorganisation after the Norman Conquest is one possible context among others, which also include the Middle Saxon and Scandinavian periods.[87]

The Norman Conquest and colonisation saw little or no impact upon the rural settlement pattern as a product of direct immigration, which was mainly limited to the towns. Through Domesday Book we can glimpse the presence of some likely first-generation immigrants to the countryside, but only on a very modest scale, in the form of Frenchmen (*Francigenae*). Over 250 are listed, sometimes in groups attached to castles but sometimes not, pointing to immigration at the non-elite level, as they appear mixed in with the rest of the rural population and might be best understood as free tenants.[88]

These issues of dating and chronology aside, it is possible to identify some of the key processes of settlement growth and identify areas that may be attributable to the Norman Conquest, either directly or indirectly. Where rural settlements grew or were re-shaped in the late 11th and early 12th centuries this was often the result of direct policies by lords. In certain places Domesday Book captures the commercialisation of the countryside as newly established Norman lords set up markets at or even within their castles. The entry for Hoxne, Suffolk, explains that William Malet had set up a Saturday market at his castle at Eye that had superseded one controlled by the bishop, while Exon Domesday records parallel processes in the Count of Mortain's castles at Launceston and Trematon, Cornwall.[89] Domesday Book also specifies that some rural castles were built on waste, as colonising ventures, as at Clifford's castle, Herefordshire, and Rockingham, Northamptonshire, while the land that formed the castelry of Caerleon was waste in 1066.[90]

Archaeology shows that the lordly planning of villages occurred from the late Anglo-Saxon period onwards, although this was one potential motor among many in settlement nucleation. At the sites of Shapwick, Somerset, and Raunds, Northamptonshire, for example, manorial lords were involved in the creation of structured and hierarchical settlements within which lordship sites were clearly differentiated in the ninth and tenth centuries.[91] While the identification and dating of episodes of seigneurially driven village planning are fraught with problems, there is certainly no clear evidence for an upsurge of such activity as a result of the Conquest. Indeed, if the evidence points in any direction it is to the 12th century as the key 'era of planned development' (for examples, see Figure 6).[92] The influence of contemporary new town planning, population growth and the growth of the market network might be important factors here as lords consolidated their positions. What might be thought of as the most characteristically type of 'Norman' village of all, the fortified village embraced within the outer defences of the castle, seems to be characteristic of the so-called 'Anarchy' of the 1130s, 1140s and 1150s rather than the years after 1066; Boteler's Castle in Warwickshire is a clear example.[93]

We should also remember that non-nucleated settlement landscapes could be the product of top-down planning. One instructive example is a study of the Vale of Montgomery, on the borderlands between England and Wales, where a pattern of 12 isolated mottes has been interpreted as evidence of deliberate re-settlement in the wake of landscape devastation in the late 11th century.[94] There are very few instances where settlement abandonment appears to be the direct result of Norman

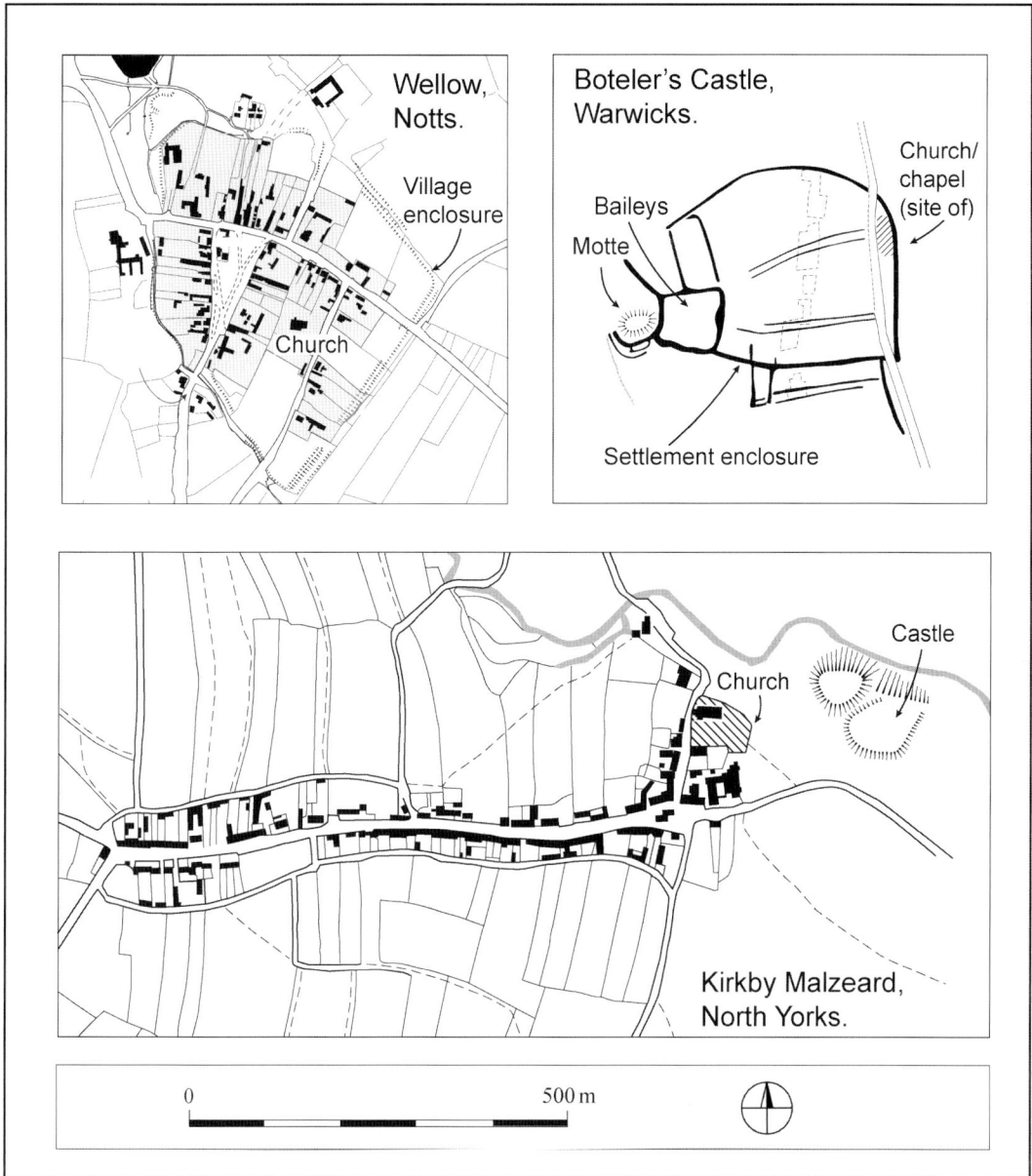

Figure 6. Planned villages. Wellow is an enclosed village that seems to have been founded by the Cistercians in the mid-12th century when the estate was reorganised. Boteler's Castle is a fortified village attached to a castle; it was founded in the mid-12th century, as demonstrated by excavation, and abandoned early in the 13th century. Kirkby Malzeard is a northern planned village whose reorganisation may date to the early to mid-12th century, when the castle emerged at the head of a local lordship. Map by Oliver Creighton and Mike Rouillard.

lordship. The development of the New Forest (see above) is one case in point where tenants might have been forcibly evicted in a scheme of land clearance, while the Domesday entry for Carisbrooke on the Isle of Wight represents an unusual case of a manor with a reduced geld assessment that is attributed to castle-building.[95] During the middle years of the 12th century some castle-building in Stephen's reign seems to have caused local dislocation to settlements, as attested at Eaton Socon, Cambridgeshire, where a castle was superimposed on a village and church.[96]

Particular debate has focused on William the Conqueror's Harrying of the North in 1069–70 as a catalyst for village planning in the north. Proof that these events cleared the way for widespread village planning is hard to find. Excavations of medieval tenements within the city of Durham have revealed evidence of houses fired and the collapse of the pottery supply that has been tentatively linked to the Harrying of the North,[97] but potential physical evidence of the event is elusive in the countryside. Archaeological evidence for northern planned villages shows that their origins could stretch into the 12th century and beyond.[98] Pollen cores can potentially help. One shows forest regeneration that has been linked to the wake of Norman devastation.[99] Rather than looking for discrete events, we might instead search for longer-term processes that reflect the Normanisation of the north.

Conclusion: a Normanised landscape?

Overall, this assessment of change in the English landscape after 1066 presents a complex and incomplete picture, and there is plenty of room for future research. We arguably have little appreciation of the overall character of the 'Norman landscape' nor its regionally distinctive signature, as academic study has focused on the higher status components of the countryside rather than the totality, and on the immediate impacts of the Conquest rather than longer-term trajectories of change.

In conclusion, it seems clear that the rupture with the past at a political level heralded by 1066 was not matched by equally profound change in the English landscape, at least initially. In the major urban centres townsfolk witnessed energetic programmes of castle- and church-building that stamped the Norman presence on these environments, but the essential rhythms of life for most English peasants remained essentially unchanged by the Conquest. Despite the imposition by an alien regime of a new aristocracy keen to squeeze revenues from their freshly acquired estates, the fabric of the countryside continued to develop, as before, only gradually and over much longer timescales – a 'long, slow, quiet revolution ... the product of small steps and individual actions',[100] rather than a transformation imposed from above.

The most obvious internal changes within settlements attributable to the Conquest were the castle-building projects that saw lordship take on a more militarised and imposing aspect. But we should be cautious in assuming that a peasantry under increased pressure in the late 11th and 12th centuries was a product of the Norman Conquest alone, as the progressive ratcheting up of lordly control over rural populations can be traced back to the late Anglo-Saxon period. The overwhelming impression is that in the countryside we see change accelerated rather than initiated, including in church-building and the protection of hunting rights. It is arguably not until the middle years of the 12th century that what we might see as the elements of the classic 'Norman landscape' were in place. This century saw the highpoint of afforestation and the peak of castle-building, parish church-building, monastic foundation and perhaps village planning by private lords. In the countryside, Normanisation was a slow, cumulative process that took a century or so of private enterprise and brokerage, in the wake of centralised policy, to materialise.

15

Writing about William the Conqueror

━━━━━━━

David Bates

Introduction

When I passed the manuscript of *William the Conqueror* to Yale University Press I explicitly acknowledged that there were many subjects that I was going to continue to think about and about which I needed to learn more (x).[1] This statement in part stemmed from the controversial and complex nature of the book's much written about subject and from the decision that the book would be a biography and not a treatment of the so-called Norman Conquest of England (14). It also resulted from the amount of new material the book contained and from the changes I was arguing needed to be made to what I had once thought well-established narratives. It was, however, also very much a consequence of an awareness of the ethical complexities of the world of power in which William operated and that his life was, and is, relevant not just to the interpretation of history of the Middle Ages, but to the history of humanity across the centuries. This was ultimately because an 11th-century ruler was the heart of a social, cultural and political organism – or probably I should write organisms – on which an almost infinite number of expectations converged, many of them irreconcilably contradictory yet frequently having to be in some way resolved.

It was with all this in mind that I wrote that 'William's life is ultimately a parable on the eternal moral conundrum of the legitimacy of violence used to achieve what its perpetrators believe to be a justifiable end' (513). Writing this derived from a deepening awareness that his life was as controversial for his contemporaries and for the generations that followed immediately afterwards as it remains today, often for the same reasons albeit within a different setting. In consequence, in both *William* and my Ford Lectures, delivered and published as *The Normans and Empire*, I drew on anthropology and other social sciences to create a framework to define cultural norms, scripts and rules in order to write biography and to analyse power.[2] In doing so, I was making a deliberate attempt to modernise my subjects as well as to create a framework that permitted as much objectivity as was possible. William's life is, of course, also relevant to understanding England's and Britain's long-term relationship with Europe (and not just with France). The North Sea world and relations with Scandinavia that went back at least into the ninth century are a central part of this.

I have often been asked how long it took me to write *William the Conqueror*. Having signed the contract in 2000, in terms of actual writing, the response is 'approximately 16 years'. But 'approximately 50 years' and 'approximately three years' are also meaningful answers to the question. The rationale for the first is that David Douglas's *William the Conqueror* and the problems of writing a biography of a medieval king featured a lot in the supervision I received from Frank Barlow while I was a research student at the University of Exeter between 1966 and 1970. It was also at that time that I began to realise the potential to be derived from immersing myself in French historiography and from working on charters in the archives in Normandy and France. I was, in particular, fascinated to learn from Lucien Musset's publications that discoveries were possible and, from him and from Marie Fauroux's then-recently published edition of the pre-1066 charters of the Norman rulers, how work of that kind could be done.[3] For the second, the answer is that it was only in 2013 that I truly grasped how I could complete the book in a way that I found morally satisfactory and intellectually convincing. This involved the recognition that while the Conquest could not – for obvious reasons – be entirely omitted, the book's purpose was to use biography as a means of understanding the individual at its heart, together with the society and cultures that shaped his actions and thoughts and those of the individuals and communities who supported and opposed him.

The personal significance of the work in the archives of northern France remains as important to me as it was when I undertook it. When I published my edition of William's charters for the period between 1066 and 1087, I announced that it contained 74 charters not listed in the calendar it was intended to replace, a statistic that is actually misleading since I located a lot more material that was then unknown or scarcely known.[4] Fully aware as I nonetheless was that I was ultimately no more than one participant in a centuries-long tradition of Anglophone scholars who have worked in France, it is nonetheless personally very gratifying to have observed other contemporaries and subsequent scholars working in France and to be involved in the sharing of information across the Channel that is nowadays a regular practice. New William charters have also been discovered and major cartularies have been published.[5] What we used to call 'the facts' are constantly being increased in number. The passions of my youth have not subsided. How can we possibly think we can understand such a supposedly well-known subject without knowing the documents on which interpretation has to be based? And not setting out to discover more and make those we think we know more accessible? The archives always beckon and should continue to do so for all with a serious interest in the subject.

My work on charters notwithstanding, writing the book made me think a lot more about the main narrative sources than I had expected. This is an area where important publications have appeared since *William* went to press.[6] My reflections related both to those who wrote about William during his lifetime and to the great 12th-century historians writing in both England and Normandy, and above all to William of Malmesbury, Orderic Vitalis, Henry of Huntingdon, Robert of Torigni and Wace. Inheriting, as they did, conflicting opinions about William and the Conquest from their sources, they also had their experiences of the following 50 years to draw on as well as a long-term awareness of England's history that took in the conquest of 1016 and went back to before the time of Bede.[7] Work since writing *William* has made me even more aware that they were part of the process they were writing about. Outstandingly gifted as they were, they nonetheless distort, albeit often unconsciously, and, in doing so, they frequently illuminate. Never more is that profound platitude that historians are the products of their times relevant than in their case. It is irresistibly tempting to write that an 11th- and 12th-century equivalent of Ian Wood's *The Modern Origins of the Early Middle Ages* is needed, but that there could profitably also be a companion volume entitled *The Twelfth-Century Origins of the Life of William the Conqueror and his Times*.[8]

While it is especially gratifying to me that others are now writing about Normandy and England, William, and 1066-related matters across broad chronological periods which have 1066 neither as a starting-point nor an end-point, I am nonetheless left with the feeling that my observation that the chronological perspective necessary to understanding William the Conqueror's life and place in history must encompass the period from about 900 to about 1250 (507, 511) requires me to write another book.[9] Ideally such a book will be very wide-ranging and treat of the themes of diversity, gender, identity, cultural transfer, migration, national, regional, local and individual experience and change. In very idealistic moments, I think that this should be a history written from the bottom up (as they say). Impossible as this may be, there remain compelling reasons to try. The book must certainly be located within the history of Europe and of the North Sea world and must start from the widely accepted conclusion that Normandy and England were participants in the political culture that was prevalent throughout the post-Carolingian medieval west, albeit with significant differences in the way in which it was applied.[10] It was with this in mind that I wrote in *William* that we must think of the conquest of England as 'the take-over of one state by another one' (525).

William's life must also be located within the intense 11th-century debates about when war was required to bring about peace. This was a world of profound paradoxes.[11] In the lay world violence was culturally structured. Kings and other rulers (such as a duke of Normandy) were expected to maintain peace while, at the same time, the threat of violence, or an actual resort to violence, were expected of them in certain circumstances, as it had been for many centuries before the 11th century. Additionally, while the 11th-century Church preached and taught ideals that were intended to produce a better and peaceful world, the form that that world should take was deeply controversial, so much so that in a recent book by Jehangir Yezdi Malegam it has been referred to as 'this seemingly schizophrenic period'.[12] William's life and his conquests were part of this, both because of their violence and the determined efforts he made to have his actions externally legitimated and because of how he deliberately set out to place his conquests and actions on a European stage. Hence the controversies that his life engendered and the diametrically opposed opinions of his methods and achievements produced by contemporaries.[13]

As the essays in this book show, debates around subjects such as chivalry and ecclesiastical and secular architecture raise issues concerning the transfer of cultural values across the lands that William and his successors ruled. The same applies to the history of law. Analyses built around 'empire', as defined in *The Normans and Empire*, and around life-histories and migration make it certain that 1066 brought about radical change. England's, Britain's and Europe's histories would have been very different had William lost the Battle of Hastings. The subject's complexity and the range of factors in play have, however, made me think that words like 'continuity' and 'change' are utterly inadequate for the subject we are dealing with. In relation to the interdisciplinarity and the intellectual cross-fertilisation that are essential to a full analysis, essays in a recent publication have done much to bring archaeology's contribution into clearer focus alongside the publications on, for example, ecclesiastical architecture, coins, manuscripts and castles that are referred to in *William* and in this book.[14] These thoughts have grown stronger ever since *William* was published. In trying to appraise William in an interdisciplinary way, I can only hope that I have made a small contribution to their realisation.

Writing the narrative

Specific facts and episodes in William's life that I believe I have reinterpreted are multiple, far too many to list in an article of this kind. I will, therefore, focus on what I regard as the most significant. In terms of trying to understand William's personality, the reappraisal of his supposed 'illegitimate' birth surely has to be among the most important of them. Since *William* was published, a book by Sara McDougall has put his birth and early years into the required context. By pointing out that it was not until the turn of the 13th century that the ecclesiastical authorities adopted a new and standardised definition of marriage and that the terms *nothus* and *bastardus* refer to someone born of a woman of lower social standing, she affirms even more strongly than I did that

William was politically legitimate.[15] Additionally, Elisabeth van Houts' study of Orderic Vitalis's attitude to his own childhood is a further valuable insight into why he wrote about William's early years in the way he did.[16] I would, therefore, now emphasise even more than I did that the starting-point for understanding William's personality has to be that his life was always intended to be that of an aristocrat. Pushed hard, the evidence might even indicate that he was an only and much-loved son singled out early by his parents for advancement. It is, therefore, irresistible to say that, for me, those who continue to refer to him as 'William the Bastard' and 'Guillaume le Bâtard' must at the least be asked to define what they mean.

The introduction into the analysis of the frequently occurring phenomenon of child rulership shows that it was as good as certain that there would be turbulence during William's early years as duke. It nonetheless still seems to me that William was well supported both personally and politically during his childhood and adolescence; the European perspective I adopted reinforces this. The same issues are, of course, also relevant to how we interpret what happened in England in the first days of the year 1066, and arguably in the decade before. Why was Edgar the Ætheling passed over when William was not, especially since Edgar in 1066 was several years older than William was in 1035? In terms of general context, the North Sea world and the politics of northern France are ever-present defining factors in William's life; the ramifications of the 1016 conquest continued to influence his policies right up until the end. Likewise, the precision brought to understanding of William's post-1066 itinerary by editing his charters, and, above all, to thereby grasping just how much of his time was spent in Normandy and France after 1072 makes a big difference. As an event within a process, the takeover of the county of Maine in 1062–3 and William's subsequent visits and military campaigns there have to be as centrally important to England's history as they are to Normandy's and France's. For England and the British Isles, they created the need for structures that supported rule *in absentia*. As already noted, the values and aims of churchmen and general developments within the Church are also a central contextualising factor.

All these are relevant to the way we should assess the first years of William's rule as king of the English that is pivotal to the whole book, and the associated rejection of the 'cherished dream' of 'an Anglo-Norman kingdom', a dream that either never existed or was in practice extremely limited in its operational implications. I have also undertaken further work on William's attitude to Wessex that is very illuminating in relation to his longer-term performance of kingship in England, something to which I will return.

More specific reinterpretations derive from many other aspects of William's story. First, from the discovery that Guy of Brionne was effectively an orphan deposited at the Norman court to be educated.

Second, from the argument that Archbishop Robert of Canterbury's visit to Normandy took place late in 1052 rather than in 1051. Third, from the reinstatement of the traditional date of 1052–3 for William's and Matilda's marriage as against the well-nigh universally accepted 1051. Fourth, from the appearance together in the 1056 Flemish charter of Harold, earl of Wessex, and Guy, count of Ponthieu. Fifth, from the narrative of William's relations with Ralph, count of Amiens, Valois and the Vexin and his son Simon based above all on the previously unpublished charter by which Simon restored Gisors to Rouen cathedral. Sixth, from the introduction of environmental history and the life-cycle of oxen into the discussion of the Harrying of the North. Seventh, from the insertion of the Ramsey Benedictional as a source for William's 'second coronation' and the grant of the papal banner. Eighth, from adjustments to the narrative of the years 1075–6. Ninth, from the discovery of Matilda's period acting on William's behalf in England in 1081–2. And tenth, from the affirmation of Domesday Book's location within the documentary cultures of the medieval west and the argument for its potential role in peace-making.

Each of the above does, I think, change the narrative in significant ways that I am not going to repeat, except as required to illustrate continuing personal thought and to comment on recent publications. Thus, the re-dating of Archbishop Robert's visit is not incompatible with Tom Licence's recent interpretation of the 'succession question'; the way in which it re-shapes the narrative actually makes significant individuals' behaviour more logical, notably that of Count Baldwin of Flanders which has previously been wrongly neglected. Both our approaches can be fitted into a scenario in which all knew that there was going to be a crisis when Edward the Confessor died and that, whatever others may have been aiming for, William's intentions were widely known across northern Europe. By foregrounding Hariulf of Saint-Riquier's chronicle more than I did, he arguably makes Count Guy of Ponthieu's and Harold's presence together in 1056 at Saint-Omer and Guy's consequential knowledge of the issues relating to the English succession an even more significant element in the narrative. The deliberate sidelining of Edgar the Ætheling by both Harold and William arguably makes Harold's behaviour either an act of betrayal or the recognition that a serious crisis demanded the leadership of a competent adult male, and William's a rejection of Edward the Confessor's right to change his mind.[17] It may also be significant that the author of the *Carmen de Hastingae Proelio*, Guy, then archdeacon, and later bishop, of Amiens, was present at Saint-Omer. Awareness of the issues involved could have influenced what he wrote and, perhaps, even the decision to write the poem.

The revival of the traditional date of 1052–3 for William's and Matilda's marriage suggests to me that they and their supporters worked hard to secure papal agreement to the marriage and that they did so within the prevailing contemporary norms. Even though the issue of their marrying within the prohibited degrees did occasionally re-surface, all that could possibly have been done was done in order to remove a potential weakness and to legitimate. The episode draws attention to the existence from a relatively early date of both the thoroughness that characterises so many of William's actions and, like so much else, the determination on his part to combine getting his own way with being able to argue that what he was doing was ethically and politically justified. It in all likelihood explains the high esteem in which successive popes apparently held him. Yet it is exactly a narrative of this kind that fuels the ambivalence about William that was present for contemporaries and which many have subsequently felt. The negotiations that were conducted pinpoint those seemingly contradictory elements in William's behaviour and character that are perplexing not just for a biographer but for anyone who thinks seriously about his life; namely the apparent contrasts between, on the one hand, the drive to conform to some kind of legal and normative framework and the capacity to gain and retain loyalty and support and, on the other, the occasions when he resorted to extreme violence and treated rebels with extreme severity. This chemical behavioural compound, already evident by his mid-20s, has to be at the heart of his achievements and his reputation.

Matilda's period acting on William's behalf in England not only affirms the book's theme of her role as queen, trusted partner, and peace-weaver within the family, it illustrates how multi-faceted women's political and social roles could be and how important women's history is to understanding the gendered 11th-century world. Always prominent, she moved even closer to centre-stage at the time when her family was in danger of falling apart. Elizabeth Tyler's recent excellent analysis of royal women as literary patrons strikingly shows that, unlike her predecessors and her successors, Matilda is not known to have played this role. Yet arguably this was because there was no need to be one. There was no need for any *apologia* to be written. Unlike Queen Emma, she had not created potential conflict between her children and, unlike Queen Edith, she had borne children and, therefore, not apparently played a part in the crisis like the one that blew everything apart in 1066. She does, however, fit the conventional role model by ensuring that her daughters were well educated.[18] Since publishing *William*, further work has made me even more aware of how important Matilda was.

The work on William and Wessex that I have undertaken since publishing the book has enabled me to further develop this and other points. Among other things, it has involved looking closely at the way in which the existing danegeld exemptions on royal lands within Wessex were exploited and expanded to fund William's itinerary and crown-wearings in England.[19] It has also made me more aware of how prominent William's family was there. Matilda's role within the western Wessex shires is part of this, but so too is the (probably short) life of her and William's one child, about whom little is known – their daughter Matilda, who looks to have been educated in England. All this and more can legitimately be seen as representing a display of continuity from before 1066 intended to demonstrate legitimacy, as well as also resembling the arrangements that Cnut made in Wessex and around Winchester.[20] As I wrote in the book, they may also have been a consequence of the region's convenience for the crossing to and from Normandy, an argument that becomes even more convincing when patterns of land-holding in Wessex are examined. All of this was ultimately central to William's capacity to have a presence in England while being physically away on the other side of the Channel for so much of the time after 1072. An article by Rebecca Browett published since *William* went into production has shown that major ecclesiastical figures within Wessex were set on belittling distinguished English saints, albeit to little long-term effect.[21] This suggests that there may well have been differences between William and some of his closest associates about their responsibilities to the English people and their traditions, a point to which I will return.

Since 2016 I have come to think even more strongly that it is William's actions and the events of the period between 1066 and 1070 that do most to explain both his later reputation and the outcome of conquest. Like Chapters 1 and 2, Chapters 7 and 8 are the pivots on which everything swings. The starting-point for an understanding of what shaped William's first years as king of the English has to be to discover what it was about him that made so many people willing to commit in 1066 to what was ultimately a very risky enterprise, and then to remain committed when it became clear that a battle and serious military campaigning were pretty well certain. The crucial factors must surely have been his recognised competence as a general and a capacity to sustain morale. With his abilities as a soldier needing nowadays to be set within a historiography that accepts that battle was a matter of last resort and that war-leaders usually avoided one if possible, Hastings must to an extent be put aside. With personal prowess and a consistent capacity to organise quickly and very efficiently and to catch opponents off-balance being points that consistently emerge in my narrative and which are, of course, crucial to sustaining morale, it is other aspects of those qualities that require some further comment. Among these, the dedication of the abbey church of La Trinité of Caen and the enclosure there of his and Matilda's daughter Cecilia as a child oblate have an importance that needs to be emphasised. The personal sacrifice – it was seen as such – was intended to propitiate the deity and to persuade the world that William and Matilda knew the ethical and religious dimensions of what they were asking thousands of people to undertake on their behalf.

To further comprehend these times, William of Poitiers' *Gesta Guillelmi* must be treated as being uniquely informative on the apparatus of leadership that created this confidence. With full recognition given to it being a panegyric intended to demonstrate William's legitimacy, read carefully and interpreted as answering criticisms of excesses that we can find set out by other contemporaries, among other things it becomes a manual for a war-leader that deals with the practice and ethics of war; its author had, of course, been a soldier before becoming a cleric. To treat it simply as 'propaganda' or to describe it with adjectives such as 'sycophantic' is seriously to under-value it as an example of a literary genre; as is being increasingly emphasised, it was ultimately a work of rhetoric that must be located within a centuries-old tradition of such historical writing about kings.[22] The *Gesta Guillelmi*'s statement that 'foreign knights flocked to help him in great numbers, attracted partly by the well-known liberality of the duke, but all fully confident of the justice of his cause' foregrounds so many of the contradictory values that have to be analysed to assess William. For me, it has become a key text for understanding how the world was shaped in and after 1066. How could appropriate rewards be given to the thousands who were risking their lives and souls without contravening the supplement to William's coronation oath on which Archbishop Ealdred of York, the man who crowned William, had insisted; namely, to treat all his people justly? And how could their security not only to enjoy these rewards, but to live peacefully and normally, be guaranteed?[23]

The way in which these contradictions came into the open very rapidly after William's coronation is shown by the two statements about the year 1067 made by Poitiers and by the anonymous author of the relevant section of the 'D' version of the Anglo-Saxon Chronicle. The former wrote that before leaving England for Normandy in the spring William both made just laws and granted lands and the custody of castles to trusted men from France; the latter that the English people were oppressed by the construction of castles and the levying of very heavy taxation.[24] What for one were the requirements of security, reward and legitimate peaceful rule were for the other the instruments of oppression, extortion and injustice. Since William of Poitiers was one of William's chaplains, a man who might have heard his confession, and the second someone close to Archbishop Ealdred, we can see how William's conduct immediately polarised opinion among those who were at the centre of events. We surely also have, through them, an insight into conversations that were taking place and which must have influenced behaviour.

Indications of the presence from the start of divergent opinions about William, as Thomas O'Donnell has recently emphasised, also surface in the *Carmen de Hastingae Proelio*, part of whose purpose he sees as being to supply a commentary on the ambiguities inherent in William's conduct; the author was thereby enabled to praise William and also to write about 'the uneven case for William's candidacy and the bloody means by which he pursued it'.[25] Paul Dalton's subtle analysis of the time between the Battle of Hastings and William's departure for Normandy in the spring of 1067 may be couched in terms of 'peace-making', but he does also use the word 'intimidate'; the two are, of course, not incompatible routes to an end, but, as we are seeing, contemporaries were profoundly ambivalent about their proportionate use thereof in 1066–7.[26] The section in Edward Impey's second essay in this book (Chapter 6) that draws attention to the large baileys of the castle-sites developed at this point underlines just how cogent was the need to maintain security for the victors and how disruptive it was for the defeated.

I will always ponder whether William could have acted differently in the first years of his reign in England. Was there a point when different decisions might have been taken? It became ever clearer to me as I wrote the two relevant chapters just how much of the crucial redistribution of England's lands and resources and the decisive relocation of real power took place during this early period. For all that many pre-1066 sheriffs and abbots and others remained in office, the dominance and intrusiveness of the new elite is the factor of central importance.[27] As the essays in this volume show, outstanding work has been done on the prosopography and the life-histories of the English, the Normans and the French and on the redistribution of estates. However, the history that an attempt nonetheless ought to be made to write is one of how people experienced victory and defeat at this time, with the interdisciplinary and comparative parallels surely lying in other cases of sudden political collapse.[28] We must certainly think of William operating at the heart of a swirling whirlpool of emotions, expectations and opinions.

The coincidence in 1069 of a revolt in northern England that was combined with invasions from Scotland and Denmark and the rebellion that overthrew William's rule in Maine needs to be kept in the forefront of our thoughts in interpreting the events of 1069–70. Arguably they together created the greatest crisis of William's life; it was the moment when all he had achieved must have seemed closest to ruin. The Harrying of the North of 1069–70 can surely be seen as William's direct personal response to it. I found the introduction of environmental history alongside the statistics and the geography of ravaging that derive from analyses of Domesday Book into the discussion helpful in terms of understanding the policy that was followed. It was valuable above all in relation to the deliberate destruction of thousands of individual livelihoods and to understanding why the recovery of northern England was apparently so slow. But I am left thinking that further work is needed to understand the cultural context in which the decision to undertake such extensive destruction seemed permissible. Medieval attitudes to the treatment of non-combatants are an important subject that needs to be looked at more deeply and talked about much more; the issue is not just one of conduct in war but of political punishment for rebellion. What levels of violence could a medieval state employ in order to maintain its power? The Harrying also says a lot about the resilience of the people who subsequently rebuilt their lives; it is here that archaeology and the study of buildings are taking the subject forward very effectively.[29]

The contrast between William's conduct in England and Maine at this time is also significant. When control over Maine was eventually recovered in 1073, the countryside was ravaged during the campaign that brought it about. But although no aristocrat from Maine was given lands in England, no one of any significant social status there had their lands confiscated because they had rebelled. Power was re-imposed, but the extreme savagery of the Harrying was not involved. On the other hand, the absence of an integrative strategy has to be very important. We are dealing here with the foundations of the cross-Channel empire that endured until 1204; their place in the history of its troubles and achievements is one of a multitude of reasons why a biography of William the Conqueror is an important subject.

Pope Alexander II's grant of a banner to accompany the 1066 expedition is another aspect of that year and of the first years of William's reign as king of the English that has been much discussed. Based as it is on a statement in the *Gesta Guillelmi*, it has again become controversial. As far as I am concerned, the 'second coronation' of 1070 and the evidence of the Ramsey Benedictional (plate 7) reinforce the argument that the banner was granted; the regular visits as legate of Bishop Ermenfrid of Sion and his role in the so-called Penitential Ordinance also support this view. We also need, however, to stop thinking in simplified institutional terms about William and his kingdom's and duchy's relations with 'the papacy'. Different popes interpreted their responsibilities differently, with Alexander II being in some ways more interventionist, at least in terms of regime change, than the more controversial Gregory VII (1073–85) was later to be. We must also not assume that Alexander granted the banner so that William could carry out the conquest that we know happened; it may have been awarded for what might have seemed the more limited objective of removing a perjured king, surely the case that was argued on William's behalf in Rome.

Relations between William and Alexander II are another subject that merit further investigation. That Gregory VII pushed William and his clergy to keep their distance in ways they had not previously done is well known. One consequence of this has been illustrated in a recent article by Benjamin Savill to the effect that the politically adroit Abbot Baldwin of Bury St Edmunds read the signs and moved away from seeking direct papal support and documentary confirmations after the fashion of pre-1066 English bishops and abbots to organising the forging of charters of William's royal predecessors as a means to obtain confirmations from William and his court.[30]

When it comes to the 12th-century historians who wrote about William, recent publications and work that I have undertaken myself have highlighted the ethical complexities that William's life raised for them, as well as for their treatment of England's pre-11th-century history.[31] This in turn has implications for the narrative of his life and the way in which we should use these writers' testimonies. Emily Winkler has pointed out that William of Malmesbury's and others' verdict on William's legitimacy and rule was generally favourable, albeit with some reservations, mostly about his character. However, William of Malmesbury does this in a way that marginalises a lot of the 'D' and 'E' Chronicles' accounts of William's life and his later years as king and also William of Poitiers.[32] And in his revisions to the later *Gesta Pontificum*, Malmesbury announced that he had to qualify what he had written about William in the *Gesta Regum*. He could still see that circumstances excused William's actions, but rhetorically he wondered whether anyone who robbed the inhabitants of the kingdom to placate his enemies could be truly excused. He also stressed his arrogance and his reluctance to listen to religious advice.[33]

Strikingly, of the other great historians writing in the first half of the 12th century, it is Orderic Vitalis who, while writing in Normandy and like Malmesbury of mixed English and French birth, is the most critical of William. Whether or not he was always writing, as he once announced he was, 'a history of the Normans for the Normans', it is certain that he came to see the Normans as a flawed, turbulent and self-destructive people, a judgement arguably founded in his experience of living in the midst of the wars between William's sons in and around Normandy. Contact between him and William of Malmesbury, a factor too often ignored by modern commentators, had important implications for the way in which they wrote the narrative.[34]

It is certainly significant that Orderic, Malmesbury and others were generally ready to blame 'the Normans' for the conflict and destruction of livelihoods rather than William himself. That they also produced different verdicts on important events is central to the problems of creating a narrative and writing a biography.[35] The way in which William deliberately set out to play on a European stage after 1066 also made the takeover of kingship in England inextricably part of the debates about the nature of peace and the responsibility for upholding it that were central to the arguments within what effectively became a war between Pope Gregory VII and the Emperor Henry IV. With the papacy's espousal of violence and direct intervention being present in the times of Popes Leo IX (1049–54) and Alexander II (1061–73), the granting or otherwise of a papal banner in 1066 makes the support that was indubitably provided an aspect of an extremely important European narrative.[36]

My introduction into the analysis of the historiography of medieval rule devoted to *Spielregeln*, ritual and performance provided insights that opened up many possibilities. We can recognise William's expressions of so-called anger, the one occasion on which he is known to have shed tears in public, his prostrations before ecclesiastics, and other instances of apparently dramatic behaviour as performances, thereby taking them away from any simplifying psychological interpretation. One result is that, in terms of the many narratives that seem to take us close to William, we have to be aware that, at least on the surface, they do not necessarily tell us much more than that he knew the techniques of rule. However, an approach exemplified by Christina Pössel's statement that: 'If ritual doesn't do anything … then the question arises why these actors made these choices' is helpful.[37] Rituals are on the surface. It is the underlying narratives that are crucial to the route from the sources to biography and from there to history.[38] The construction of these narratives must always be the subject of further thought, as must the norms and scripts that produced them.

The William the Conqueror who emerged from this type of analysis seemed to me often to be someone whose interventions frequently produced rational solutions to the issues under discussion. A case in point is the Primacy Dispute between Archbishops Lanfranc and Thomas that opened up immediately after they had been appointed to the two English archbishoprics. The accounts written for the two sides record that William's anger as being directed against both of them, a sign that a solution was paramount for him; the threats made against Thomas in particular were nonetheless so ferocious as to give pause for thought. William's dealings with Wales and the king of Scots also seemed to me to be ultimately determined by the need to reach a *modus vivendi* that emphasised his predominance without any mutual loss of face. Enough was, however, done to show that greatly superior force could be brought to bear if a solution was not found. In relation to issues such as clerical marriage and the slave trade, William can be seen to espouse abolition in both cases, but then to draw back when implementation was deemed difficult because too many livelihoods were threatened or, so William of Malmesbury believed, in the case of the slave trade, the king's finances. This should surely be defined as pragmatism or self-interest; once more the floodgates of debate burst open.

When we are provided with elements of the underlying narrative by more than one writer, as we are in the truly terrible scene when William shed tears as Earl Edwin's decapitated head was brought into his presence by those who had killed him, the commentaries can disagree profoundly. Orderic believed that William was to blame because he had treated Edwin dishonourably. William of Malmesbury, on the other hand, thought Edwin deserved his fate because he was an incorrigible rebel. My explanation in the book was to locate the scene as being a consequence of the undermining of the surviving English elite and, therefore, to place myself close to Orderic. But it may well be that it was Malmesbury who best reflects William's own thinking. Whatever the case, William's shedding of tears shows some recognition on his part of the situation's sensitivity and complexity, albeit that it might be thought to have been a means to extricate himself from culpability or to be a statement that the fate of rebels was his responsibility and not that of Edwin's killers. This one story shows yet again how individual beliefs shaped what later writers wrote about William and the difficulties they create for producing a narrative.

William the Conqueror's place in history

During my life as William's biographer I have heard very many different opinions expressed about him. When I have distributed my amateurish questionnaires to audiences I have addressed, they have produced remarkably contrasting, and often extreme and irreconcilable, verdicts. For some he was a good thing, for some a bad one. Notions of a tyrannical Norman yoke that came close to destroying a quintessential Englishness that only re-emerged a long time later certainly persist. And so do forms of hero-worship and notions of the Normans as a civilising force who rescued England from decadence. The presence of these attitudes and beliefs in what can be loosely defined as cultural memory have also been brought to the surface in the media's coverage of the projected loan of the Bayeux Tapestry to the UK. Thankfully Siobhan Brownlie has conducted surveys and an analysis within the framework of Cultural Memory Studies that has the authority and sophistication that this subject deserves.[39] All are a demonstration that vibrant forces that probably lie beyond the influence of my academic biography are still shaping William's posthumous reputation, as they have been ever since the day he died.

Since completing *William*, I have also been personally reminded of how memory of William's life remains powerfully influential in some places. These include being invited to unveil of a bust of him at Great Berkhamsted on 14 October 2016 at the place where the English submitted to William after Hastings and listening again to Philippe Contamine recounting the story of how he and other children of Caen were taken to the church of Saint-Etienne in 1944 as the Allied bombs fell on the town, and were told that that William was protecting them because the British and their allies would surely not harm them in the church built for the man who had been their king. A visit I made to York produced a huge audience.

Articles by Véronique Gazeau and, more recently, by Brian Golding have also indicated that the forces that have shaped William's modern reputation were different in Normandy and, to a lesser extent, in France. Norman patriotism played a central part in all this, as did the notion of the Normans and their associates as the bringers of civilisation to the barbarian Anglo-Saxons.[40] Having worked and lived on both sides of the Channel, it strikes me that these differences are actually two sides of the same coin, with the modern controversies that swirl around the subject of empire as a phenomenon in human history providing a meaningful framework for analysing them. In the end – of course – we are again left with the conclusion that historical writing is predominantly a product of the historians' own times and of their personal experiences, a topic that has recently been analysed in books about how the medieval past has been understood within the academy and by the wider public.[41]

A glance at the evolution of William's and Charlemagne's posthumous reputations constitutes a final way of bringing what I regard as the central issues into focus. Peace and European integration have arguably become Charlemagne's legacy to his descendants – and, indeed, to humanity – in ways that have produced many remarkable results.[42] William's place within this tradition is exemplified by the anonymous author of the *De Obitu Willelmi*'s opinion that Einhard's *Vita Karoli* was a suitable text to plagiarise to describe William. His omissions will, however, always strike me as being significant, as they did when I published the book (492), including the deliberate removal of the references to intellectual curiosity. While one result of this comparison is to show that we are left with an abundance of evidence for Charlemagne's court as a place of culture and ethical debate and that such material is less plentiful for William's court, it is, of course, possible that the relatively greater quantity and quality of the Carolingian evidence misleads us. My earlier comments about the relationship of the 'D' Chronicle and William of Poitiers' *Gesta Guillelmi* certainly indicate that debates of this kind were taking place. But it is also possible to shift the entire focus of the comparison and suggest that we should debate whether Charlemagne or William has the greater responsibility for bringing more lives to a premature end.

In the case of William's posthumous reputation as it developed and as it has descended to us, Abbot Baldwin of Bury St Edmunds' creative sponsorship of charter writing is just one illustration of how the pre-1066 past started to be reworked very soon after 1066, with William's confirmation of Baldwin's efforts making him an actor at the heart of the process. After William's death, many religious institutions self-interestedly set out to make his actions suit their own interests. Thus, even his own grandson, Bishop Henry of Winchester, could have another grandson, King Stephen, confirm charters that mispresented William's treatment of the Old Minster, Winchester.[43] The readiness to adjust and to invent William's role became more frequent as the 12th and 13th centuries advanced.[44] Disreputable stories about him were also in circulation, with a recent article demonstrating that a rumour rejected by William of Malmesbury to the effect that William had killed Matilda was being widely reproduced in Icelandic literature in the 13th century.[45] Yet on the other hand, William's daughters, the nun and abbess Cecilia and Adela, countess of Blois-Chartres, were assiduous agents of the perpetration of a good memory. And his son King William Rufus honoured his father by financing a magnificent tomb at Caen and going to York to dig the first sod of the earth so that the abbey of St Mary's could be built, an act of atonement for what all would have recognised as one of William the Conqueror's worst deeds. It has also become much clearer to me since writing *William* how much the making and subsequent use of Domesday Book and the writings of the great 12th-century historians have distorted the place of the so-called Norman Conquest in England's history.[46] We have here another subject worthy of further investigation and about which I intend to write more.

William the Conqueror is surely a man for all ages. We must now return to 'the parable' mentioned earlier. William was supremely good at legitimating his actions and persuading others to do that for him. On the other hand, he was responsible for acts of extreme violence. His rule in England evolved from those first years that I have dwelt on to a final decade that can be seen as mostly characterised by peace, acts of patronage, a new architectural grandeur and the righting of wrongs. Winchester cathedral and the Domesday survey's peace-keeping and legitimating role exemplify much of this. On the book's final pages, I tried to make it clear that William's life must be debated in terms of ethical values that are the foundations of civilised society. His contemporaries knew this and we should think in the same terms; hence, the reference to the poetic flattery of Fulcoius of Beauvais writing in about 1075 that 'he heals where he wounds; both war and peace obey him sympathetically' (526). I used the word 'empire' with a similar purpose in *The Normans and Empire*. Empires are by their very nature controversial. But, as they are nowadays often written about, they require us to think about the interplay of cultures and peoples, thereby bringing into play crucial wider perspectives.

William the Conqueror's life must be written about as a distinct historical episode, hence the need to keep searching for charters and reinterpreting the known evidence. However, it also has its place within the history of humanity. It shows why the study of the Middle Ages matters as much as it always has. And why old controversies matter and why they must be re-shaped to fit with 21st century concerns.

Notes

Introduction

1 Bartlett, *The Making of Europe*, 313.
2 For comment along these lines, see Bates, *The Normans and Empire*, 186–7.
3 Thus, Dyer and Hadley (eds.), *The Archaeology of the 11th Century*.
4 Bates, *William the Conqueror*, 507, 511.

1 Normandy before 1066

1 Nortier, M., 1967, 'Histoire politique', 'Bibliographie normande 1966', *AN* 17, 118–26 ('Les travaux français ont toutefois restés des publications assez sommaires (si l'on ne s'en tient qu'à ceux qui ont vu le jour en 1966), alors que, du côté anglais, nous sont venues plusieurs savantes études parfois passionnées', at 118).
2 Douglas, D. C., 1967, 'Les réussites normandes (1050–1100)', *Revue historique* 237, 1–16 (paper given at the Conférence franco-anglaise d'historiens, London, 1 October 1966) and Le Patourel, J., 1967, 'L'Empire Normand', *Revue historique de droit français et étranger*, 399–400 (abstract of a paper given in the Journées d'histoire du droit et des institutions de l'Ouest at Avranches, 31 May–3 June 1966): see Nortier, M., 1968, 'Bibliographie normande 1967', *AN* 18, 205–10, at 206.
3 For fuller treatments see Bates, *Normandy before 1066* and *William the Conqueror*, especially for the decades before the Conquest. See also Hagger, *Norman Rule in Normandy, 911–1144*, Woodbridge, Boydell Press, 2017.
4 For an overview, see Bauduin, P., 2003, 'Les sources de l'histoire du duché. Publications et inventaires récents', *Tabularia 'Études'* 3, 29–55.
5 A major work that reflects on the many studies published over almost 30 years is Pohl, *Dudo of Saint-Quentin*. Pierre Bouet, who has written many papers on Dudo, is working on a new edition of the text.
6 See, among others, Potts, C., 1992, 'The Early Norman Charters: A New Perspective on an Old Debate', in Hicks, C. (ed.), *England in the Eleventh Century: Proceedings of the 1990 Harlaxton Symposium*, Stamford, 25–40; Bates, D., 2000, *Re-ordering the Past and Negotiating the Present in Stenton's 'First Century'*, Reading, 12–15; Bates, D., 2003, 'La "mutation documentaire" et le royaume anglo-normand (seconde moitié du XIe siècle – début du XIIe siècle)',

in Gasse-Grandjean, M.-J. and Tock, B.-M. (eds.), *Les actes comme expression du pouvoir au Haut Moyen Âge. Actes de la Table Ronde de Nancy, 26–27 novembre 1999*, Turnhout, 33–49; Van Torhoudt, É., 2007, 'L'écrit et la justice au Mont Saint-Michel: les notices narratives (vers 1060–1150)', *Tabularia 'Études'* 7, 107–37.

7 Nortier, G., 1971, *Les bibliothèques médiévales des abbayes bénédictines de Normandie*, Paris; Lecouteux, S., 2015, 'Réseaux de confraternité et histoire des bibliothèques: l'exemple de l'abbaye bénédictine de la Trinité de Fécamp', unpublished doctoral thesis, Université de Caen Normandie; for Mont-Saint-Michel, see the project, 'Bibliothèque virtuelle du Mont Saint-Michel': www.unicaen.fr/bvmsm/.

8 See note 7 for manuscripts. Concerning charters, see SCRIPTA (Site Caennais de Recherche Informatique et de Publication des Textes Anciens): www.unicaen.fr/scripta/.

9 Mainly at the CRAM of Caen (becoming CRAHAM: Centre de recherches archéologiques et historiques médiévales, UMR 6273 University of Caen/CNRS), founded by Michel de Boüard in the mid-1950s. The latter founded the 'Château Gaillard' conferences in 1962, which are still held every two years in different European countries. See also the journal *Archéologie médiévale*, founded in 1971.

10 Coupland, S., 1998, 'From poachers to gamekeepers: Scandinavian warlords and Carolingian kings', *EME* 7, 85–114; Bauduin, *Le monde franc et les Vikings*.

11 Bauduin, *La première Normandie (X^e–XIe siècles)*; Bauduin, P., 2005, 'Chefs normands et élites franques fin IXe–début Xe siècle', in Bauduin, P. (ed.), *Les fondations scandinaves en Occident et les débuts du duché de Normandie*, Actes du colloque de Cerisy-la-Salle (25–29 septembre 2002), Caen, 181–94.

12 Carpentier, V., 2014, 'Du mythe colonisateur à l'histoire environnementale des côtes de la Normandie à l'époque viking: l'exemple de l'estuaire de la Dives (France, Calvados), IXe–XIe siècles', in Bauduin, P. and Musin, A. (eds.), *Vers l'Orient et vers l'Occident: regards croisés sur les dynamiques et les transferts culturels des Vikings à la Rous ancienne/Eastwards and Westwards: Multiple Perspectives on the Dynamics and Cultural Transfers from the Vikings to the Early Rus'*, Caen, 199–213; Carpentier, V., 2017, 'L'immigration scandinave sur le continent au Xe siècle: un invisible archéologique?', in Garcia, D. and Le Bras, H. (eds.), *Archéologie des migrations*, Paris, 255–65.

13 Abrams, L., 2013, 'Early Normandy', *ANS* 35, 45–64; Abrams, L., [forthcoming], 'The Study of Scandinavian Settlement in the Viking Age: Historiographical Perspectives on the Application of Place-Names in England and Normandy', in Bauduin, P. and D'Angelo, E. (eds.), *Les historiographies des mondes normands, XVIIe–XXIe*

siècle: construction, influence, évolution, Actes du colloque international d'Ariano Irpino (9–10 mai 2016) [forthcoming].

14 Carpentier, 'Du mythe colonisateur'.

15 Van Torhoudt, É., 2008, 'Centralité et marginalité en Neustrie et dans le duché de Normandie. Maîtrise du territoire et pouvoirs locaux dans l'Avranchin, le Bessin et le Cotentin (VIe–XIe siècles)', unpublished doctoral thesis, Université Denis Diderot (Paris VII).

16 Abrams, L., 2012, 'Diaspora and Identity in the Viking Age', *EME* 20, 17–38; Jesch, J., 2015, *The Viking Diaspora*, London and New York.

17 For a recent overview, see Moesgaard, J. C., 2012, 'Les ateliers monétaires normands dans la tourmente viking', in Chameroy, J. and Guihard, P.-M. (eds.), *Circulations monétaires et réseaux d'échanges en Normandie et dans le Nord-Ouest européen (Antiquité–Moyen Âge)*, Caen, 155–72.

18 For this kind of discussion based on sources from the late Anglo-Saxon period, see Lestremau, A., 2013, 'Pratiques anthroponymiques et identités sociales en Angleterre du milieu du Xe à la fin du XIe siècle', unpublished doctoral thesis, Université de Paris Panthéon Sorbonne.

19 Nissen-Jaubert, A., 2005, 'Implantations scandinaves et traces matérielles en Normandie. Que pouvons-nous attendre?', in Bauduin (ed.), *Les fondations scandinaves en Occident*, 209–23.

20 Kershaw, J., 2013, *Viking Identities: Scandinavian Jewellery in England*, Oxford; Richards, J. D. and Taylor, J., 2010, 'The Metal Detector and the Viking Age in England', in Ó Corráin, D. and Sheehan, J. (eds.), *The Viking Age: Ireland and the West*, papers from the proceedings of the Fifteenth Viking Congress, Cork, 18–27 August 2005, Cork, 338–52, at 349–50.

21 Coumert, M., 2014, 'Les récits d'origine et la tradition historiographique normande', in Bauduin, P. and Lucas-Avenel, M.-A. (eds.), *L'Historiographie médiévale normande et ses sources antiques. Actes du colloque de Cerisy-la-Salle et du Scriptorial d'Avranches (8–11 octobre 2009)*, Caen, 137–54.

22 Bauduin, P., 2001, 'Autour d'une construction identitaire: la naissance d'une historiographie normande à la charnière des Xe–XIe siècles', in Nagy, P. (ed.), *Conquête, acculturation, identité: des Normands aux Hongrois. Les traces de la conquête*, Rouen, 79–91.

23 Pohl, *Dudo of Saint-Quentin*, 199–216.

24 van Houts, E., 2016, 'Qui étaient les Normands? Quelques observations sur des liens entre la Normandie, l'Angleterre et l'Italie au début du XIe siècle', in Bates, D. and Bauduin, P. (eds.), *911–2011. Penser les mondes normands médiévaux. Actes du colloque de Caen et Cerisy-la-Salle (29 septembre–2 octobre 2011)*, Caen, 129–46.

25 Thomas, *The English and the Normans*; Webber, N., 2005, *The Evolution of Norman Identity, 911–1154*, Woodbridge.

26 Davis, R. H. C., 1976, *The Normans and Their Myth*, London; Loud, G., 1981, 'The "*Gens Normannorum*" – myth or reality?', *ANS* 4, 104–16, 204–9; Lucas-Avenel, M.-A., 2008, 'La *gens Normannorum* en Italie du Sud d'après les chroniques normandes du XIᵉ siècle', in Gazeau, V., Bauduin, P. and Modéran, Y. (eds), *Identité et ethnicité: concepts, débats historiographiques, exemples*, Caen, 233–64.

27 Barthélemy, D., 1994, *La mutation de l'an mil a-t-elle eu lieu: servage et chevalerie dans la France des Xᵉ et XIᵉ siècles*, Paris.

28 Barthélemy, D., 2012, *La chevalerie. De la Germanie antique à la France du XIIᵉ siècle*, Paris, 257 ('la mutation chevaleresque est une mutation des usages de la lance'). For Normandy, see 223–63; Stafford, P., 1998, '"La Mutation Familiale": A Suitable Case for Caution', in *The Community, the Family and the Saint. Patterns of Power in Early Medieval Europe*, Turnhout, 103–25.

29 Bates, D., 2000, 'England and the "Feudal Revolution"', in *Il Feudalesimo nell'Alto Medioevo*, vol. 2, Spoleto, 611–46 (Settimane di studio del Centro Italiano di Studi sull' nell'Alto Medioevo, 47 (8–12 aprile 1999)), 611–49, at 625; see also Bates, D., 2003, 'Writing a New Biography of William the Conqueror', in Kondo, K. (ed.), *State and Empire in British History*, Proceedings of the Anglo-Japanese Conference of Historians, Kyoto, 10–12 September 2003, Tokyo, 9–20, at 12.

30 Bates, D., 2003, 'The Conqueror's Adolescence', *ANS* 25, 1–18.

31 See, for example, Debord, A., 1992, 'Remarques à propos des châtelains normands aux XIᵉ et XIIᵉ siècles', *Recueil d'études offert à Gabriel Désert* (Cahier des Annales de Normandie, n° 24), Caen, 327–36.

32 Arnoux, M., 1992, 'Classe agricole, pouvoir seigneurial et autorité ducale. L'évolution de la Normandie féodale d'après le témoignage des chroniqueurs (Xᵉ–XIIᵉ siècles)', *Le Moyen Age* 98, 35–60, at 52; Arnoux, M., 2000, '*Rustici* et *homines liberi*: où sont passés les serfs normands?', *Mélanges de l'Ecole Française de Rome – Moyen Age* 112, 563–77; Arnoux, M. and Maneuvrier, C., 2003, 'Le pays normand. Paysages et peuplement (IXᵉ–XIIIᵉ siècles)', *Tabularia 'Etudes'* 3, 1–27; Arnoux, M., 2012, *Le temps des laboureurs. Travail, ordre social et croissance en Europe (XIᵉ–XIVᵉ siècle)*, Paris, 115–25. See also Gowers, B., 2013, '996 and All That: The Norman Peasants' Revolt Reconsidered', *EME* 21, 71–98.

33 Arnoux, M., 2006, 'I Normanni prima della conquista. Costruzione politica e identità nazionale', in Licinio, R., and Violante, F., (eds.), *I caratteri originari della conquista normanna. Diversità e identita nel Mezzogiorno (1030–1130)*, Atti delle XVI giornate normanno-sveve (Bari, 5–8 ottobre 2004), Bari, 52–66, at 63.

34 Le Jan, R., 2005, 'Le royaume franc vers 900: un pouvoir en muta-tion?', in Bauduin (ed.), *Les fondations scandinaves en Occident*, 83–95, at 91.

35 And perhaps it was part of the ability of William to gain the confidence of his men. On this ability, see Bates, *William the Conqueror*, 219, 517.

36 Bauduin, P., [forthcoming], 'Ombres et silences d'un règne: Richard II dans les *Gesta Normannorum ducum* de Guillaume de Jumièges', paper given at the Journée d'étude 'Les silences de l'historien' (Caen, 26 février 2016).

37 Kamp, H., (2001), 'Die Macht der Zeichen und Gesten. Öffentliches Verhalten bei Dudon von Saint-Quentin', in Althoff, G. (ed.), *Formen und Funktionen. Öffentlicher Kommunikation im Mittelalter*, Stuttgart, 125–55.

38 Koziol, G., 1992, *Begging Pardon and Favor. Ritual and Political Order in Early Medieval France*, Ithaca and London, 147–59: 'Dudo was fairly obsessed by the ritual' (at 151); 'For Dudo, supplication was a concentrated symbol of good lordship, an emblem of "good faith" that maintained peace' (at 152).

39 Koziol, *Begging Pardon*, 271–5.

40 Bauduin, 'Chefs normands et élites franques'.

41 Bauduin, P., 2003, 'L'insertion des Normands dans le monde franc fin ixe–début xe siècle: l'exemple des pratiques matrimoniales', in Flambard Héricher, A.-M. (ed.), *La progression des Vikings, des raids à la colonisation*, Mont-Saint-Aignan, 105–17.

42 Bates, *Normandy Before 1066*, 112–13.

43 Bauduin, P., 2006, 'Observations sur les structures familiales de l'aristocratie normande au xie siècle', in Bates, D., Gazeau, V., Anceau, É., Lachaud, F. and Ruggiu, F.-J. (eds.), *Liens personnels, réseaux, solidarités en France et dans les îles Britanniques (xie–xxe siècle)/Personal Links, Networks and Solidarities in France and the British Isles (11th–20th Century)*, Paris, 15–27.

44 Van Houts, E., 1999, 'Countess Gunnor of Normandy (c.950–1031)', *Collegium medievale* 12, 7–24; Stafford, *Queen Emma and Queen Edith*; van Houts, E., 1986, 'The Origins of Herleva, Mother of William the Conqueror', *EHR* 101, 399–404; Thompson, K., 2011, 'Being the Ducal Sister: The Role of Adelaide of Aumale', in Crouch and Thompson (eds.), *Normandy and Its Neighbours*, 61–76.

45 Bauduin, P., 2002, 'Du bon usage de la *dos* dans la Normandie ducale (X^e–début XIIe siècle)', in Bougard, F., Feller, L. and Le Jan, R. (eds.), *Dots et douaires dans le haut Moyen Age*, Rome, 429–65; Van Houts, E., 1999, *Memory and Gender in Medieval Europe, 900–1200*, Basingstoke and London; Quirk, K., 2001, 'Men, Women and Miracles in Normandy, 1050–1150', in Van Houts, E. (ed.), *Medieval Memories. Men, Women and the Past, 700–1300*, Harlow, 53–71.

46 Musset, L., 1976, 'L'aristocratie normande au XIe siècle', in Contamine, P. (ed.), *La noblesse au Moyen Age, XIe–XVe siècles, Essais à la mémoire de Robert Boutruche*, Paris, 71–96; Musset,

L., 1959, 'A-t-il existé en Normandie au XIe siècle une aristocratie d'argent? Une enquête sommaire sur l'argent considéré comme moyen d'ascension sociale', *AN* 9, 285–99.

47 Bauduin, *La première Normandie*, 232–7; Van Torhoudt, É., 2006, 'Les sièges du pouvoir des Néel, vicomtes dans le Cotentin', in Flambard Héricher, A.-M. (ed.), *Les lieux de pouvoir au Moyen Âge en Normandie et sur ses marges*, Caen, 7–35.

48 OV, iii. 330–5.

49 Van Torhoudt, 'Centralité et marginalité', 550 onwards, 561, 563 onwards, 594.

50 Green, J. A., 1984, 'Lords of the Norman Vexin', in Gillingham, J. and Holt, J. C. (eds.), *War and Government in the Middle Age, Essays in Honour of J. O. Prestwich*, Woodbridge, 46–63; Louise, G., 1992–3, *La Seigneurie de Bellême X^e–XIIe siècles, dévolution des pouvoirs territoriaux et construction d'une seigneurie de frontière aux confins de la Normandie et du Maine à la charnière de l'An mil*, 2 vols., ed. Le Pays Bas-Normand, 1990 (n° 3–4); 1991 (n° 1–2), Flers; Bauduin, *La première Normandie*; Power, D., 2004, *The Norman Frontier in the Twelfth and Early Thirteenth Centuries*, Cambridge.

51 Spear, D., 2006, *The Personnel of the Norman Cathedrals During the Ducal Period, 911–1204*, Fasti Ecclesiae Anglicanae, London.

52 Bouet, P. and Neveux, F. (eds.), 1995, *Les évêques normands du XIe siècle, Actes du colloque de Cerisy-la-Salle (30 sept.–3 oct. 1993)*, Caen; Allen, R., 2009, 'The Norman Episcopate 989–1110', unpublished PhD thesis, University of Glasgow, 2009.

53 Gazeau, V., 2007, *Normannia Monastica (X^e–XIIe siècle)* 2 vols.: Vol 1, *Princes normands et abbés bénédictins*; Vol. 2, *Prosopographie des abbés bénédictins*, Caen.

54 Gazeau, *Normannia Monastica*, i, 98.

55 Gazeau, *Normannia Monastica*, i, 102.

56 Gazeau, *Normannia Monastica*, i, 198–219.

57 Bulst, N., 1973, *Untersuchungen zu den Klosterreformen Wilhelms von Dijon 962–1031*, Bonn; Gazeau, V., 2002, 'Guillaume de Volpiano en Normandie: état des questions', *Tabularia 'Études'* n° 2, 35–46.

58 Gazeau, *Normannia Monastica*, ii, 333–5.

59 Allen, R., 2015, 'Avant Lanfranc. Un réexamen de la carrière de Mauger, archevêque de Rouen (1037–1054/55)', in Barrow, J. S., Delivré, F. and Gazeau, V. (eds.), *Autour de Lanfranc (1010–2010). Réforme et réformateurs dans l'Europe du Nord-Ouest*, Caen, 131–52, at 134–5.

60 See, for example, Mancia, L., 2014, 'Reading Augustine's *Confessions* in Normandy in the 11th and 12th Centuries', *Tabularia 'Études'* n° 14, 195–233; Mancia, L., 2015, 'John of Fécamp and Affective Reform in Eleventh-Century Normandy', *ANS* 37, 161–80; Foulon,

J.-H., 2012, 'Le chevalier Herluin et la fondation de l'abbaye du Bec: un dossier complexe entre tentation érémitique et normalisation cénobitique', *Revue historique* 314, 563–608.

61 Bates, 'The Conqueror's Adolescence', 11–12; Bates, *William the Conqueror*, 74–8; Allen, 'Avant Lanfranc. Un réexamen de la carrière de Mauger'.

62 Gibson, M., 1978, *Lanfranc of Bec*, Oxford; Cowdrey, H. E. J., 2003, *Lanfranc: Scholar, Monk, and Archbishop*, Oxford; Barrow et al., *Autour de Lanfranc*.

63 Barlow, F., 1965, 'A View of Archbishop Lanfranc', *JEH* 16, 163–77 (reprinted in Barlow, F., 1983, *The Norman Conquest and Beyond*, London, 223–38, at 233).

64 Allen, R., 2009, 'The *Acta archiepiscoporum Rotomagensium*: Study and Edition', *Tabularia, 'Documents'* 9, 1–66, at 39–40.

65 Fernie, E., 2016, 'De la Normandie aux États latins d'Orient: l'architecture normande ou l'architecture des Normands?', in Bates and Bauduin, *911–2011. Penser les mondes*, 309–24.

66 Lecouteux, 'Réseaux de confraternité et histoire des bibliothèques'; Lecouteux, S., 2016, 'Deux fragments d'un nécrologe de la Trinité de Fécamp (XIᵉ–XIIᵉ siècles). Étude et édition critique d'un document mémoriel exceptionnel', *Tabularia. 'Documents'* 16, 1–89, at 35–51.

67 Lecouteux, 'Réseaux de confraternité et histoire des bibliothèques', i, 512–13.

68 Lecouteux, 'Réseaux de confraternité', i, 493.

69 Haskins, C. H., 1915, *The Normans in European History*, Boston and New York, 82.

70 Musset, L., 1970, 'Naissance de la Normandie (Vᵉ–XIᵉ siècles)', in de Boüard, M. (ed.), *Histoire de la Normandie*, Toulouse, 106; Musset, L., 1977, 'Les apports anglais en Normandie de Rollon à Guillaume le Conquérant (911–1066)', *Publications de l'Association des Médiévistes Anglicistes de l'Enseignement Supérieur* 4, 59–82.

71 d'Onofrio, M. (ed.), 1994, *Les Normands, peuples d'Europe, 1030–1200*, Paris.

2 England before 1066

1 Barlow, *Edward the Confessor*.

2 Garnett, *Conquered England*.

3 Bates, *William the Conqueror*, 108–19; Licence, T., 2013, 'Robert of Jumièges, Archbishop in Exile (1052–5)', *ASE* 42, 311–29.

4 Barlow, *Edward the Confessor*, 251–3.

5 Baxter, 'Edward the Confessor and the Succession Question'; Licence, 'Edward the Confessor and the Succession Question'.

6 Maddicott, J. R., 2004, 'Edward the Confessor's Return to England in 1041', *EHR* 119, 650–66.

7 Wormald, P., 2006, *The Times of Bede: Studies in Early English Christian Society and its Historian*, Baxter, S. (ed.), Oxford, 106–34.

8 *EHD* I, no. 104, no. 1 (ASC, *sub anno 900*).

9 Keynes, S., 1998, 'King Alfred and the Mercians', in Blackburn, M. A. S. and Dumville, D. N. (eds.), *Kings, Currency and Alliances: History and Coinage of Southern England in the Ninth Century*, Woodbridge, 1–45, at 24–45; Keynes, S., 2001, 'Edward, King of the Anglo-Saxons', in Higham, N. J. and Hill, D. H. (eds.), *Edward the Elder 899–924*, London, 40–66.

10 Lapidge, M., 1993, *Anglo-Latin Literature, 900–1066*, London, 77.

11 *EHD 1*, no. 104.

12 Molyneaux, G., 2011, 'Why Were Some Tenth-Century English Kings Presented as Rulers of Britain?', *TRHS* 6th ser., 21, 59–91.

13 Foot, *Æthelstan*.

14 Scragg, D. (ed.), 2008, *Edgar, King of the English 959–975*, Woodbridge.

15 Stenton, F. M., 1971 (3rd ed.), *Anglo-Saxon England*, Oxford, 368.

16 Molyneaux, *Formation*, esp. 182–94.

17 Keynes, S., 2012, 'The Cult of King Edward the Martyr During the Reign of King Æthelred the Unready', in Nelson, Reynolds and Johns (eds.), *Gender and Historiography*, 115–25; Roach, *Æthelred the Unready*, 68–77, 167–74.

18 *EHD* I, no. 1.

19 Molyneaux, 'Why?'.

20 McGuigan, N., 2015, 'Neither Scotland nor England: Middle Britain, c.850–1150', unpublished PhD dissertation, University of St Andrews, 82–135.

21 Wickham, C., 2009, 'Problems in Doing Comparative History', in Skinner, P. (ed.), *Challenging the Boundaries of Medieval History: The Legacy of Timothy Reuter*, Turnhout, 5–28, at 20–3.

22 Campbell, *The Anglo-Saxon State*; Baxter, S., 2009. 'The Limits of the Late Anglo-Saxon State', in Pohl, W. and Wieser, V. (eds.), *Der frühmittelalterliche Staat – europäische Perspektiven*, Vienna, 503–14.

23 See chapters 9, 13 and 15.

24 Roach, *Kingship and Consent*, 122–46.

25 Whitelock, D., 1974 (2nd ed.), *The Beginnings of English Society*, London; Loyn, H. R., 1991 (2nd ed.), *Anglo-Saxon England and the Norman Conquest*, London, 194–202, 351–67.

26 Baxter, *Earls of Mercia*, 61–124; Baxter, S. and Blair, J., 2006, 'Land Tenure and Royal Patronage in the Early English Kingdom: A Model and a Case Study', *ANS* 28, 19–46.

27 Wickham, 'Problems', 16–22.

28 *EHD* I, nos. 1 and 118.

29 Loyn, H. R., 1955, 'Gesiths and Thegns in Anglo-Saxon England from the Seventh to the Tenth Century', *EHR*, 70, 529–49.

30 Williams, A., 1997, 'A West-Country Magnate of the Eleventh Century: The Family, Estates and Patronage of Beorhtric Son of Ælfgar', in Keats-Rohan, K. S. B. (ed.), *Family Trees and the Roots of Politics: the Prosopography of Britain and France from the Tenth to the Twelfth Century*, Woodbridge, 41–68; Williams, *The World before Domesday*; Senecal, C., 2001, 'Keeping up With the Godwinesons: In Pursuit of Aristocratic Status in Late Anglo-Saxon England', *ANS* 23, 251–66; Clarke, *The English Nobility*.

31 Baxter, *Earls of Mercia*, 128–38.

32 Lavelle, R., 2007, *Royal Estates in Anglo-Saxon Wessex: Land, Politics and Family Strategies*, Oxford.

33 Naismith, R., 2017, 'The Ely Memoranda and the Economy of the Late Anglo-Saxon Fenland', *ASE* 45, 331–75.

34 Baxter, *Earls of Mercia*, 204–69.

35 Innes, M., 2000, *State and Society in the Early Middle Ages: The Middle Rhine Valley, 400–1000*, Cambridge, 4–12.

36 Roach, *Kingship and Consent*; Maddicott, *Origins*, 1–56.

37 Harmer, *Anglo-Saxon Writs*.

38 Molyneaux, *Formation*, 155–72.

39 Tinti, F., 2010, *Sustaining Belief: The Church of Worcester from c.870 to c.1100*, Farnham, 85–125.

40 Molyneaux, *Formation*, 141–55.

41 Molyneaux, *Formation*, 182–214.

42 Naismith, R., 2014, 'Prelude to Reform: Tenth-Century English Coinage in Perspective', in Naismith, R., Allen, M., and Screen, E. (eds.), *Early Medieval Monetary History: Studies in Memory of Mark Blackburn*, Farnham, 39–84.

43 Naismith, R., 2016, 'The Coinage of Æthelred II: A New Evaluation', *English Studies* 97, 117–39.

44 Keynes, S. and Naismith, R., 2011, 'The *Agnus Dei* Pennies of King Æthelred the Unready', *ASE* 40, 175–223.

45 Roach, *Kingship and Consent*, 216–17.

46 Naismith, R., 2017, *Medieval European Coinage, with a Catalogue of the Coins in the Fitzwilliam Museum, Cambridge. 8: Britain and Ireland c.400–1066*, Cambridge, 253–8.

47 Keynes, S., 1991, 'The Historical Context of the Battle of Maldon', in Scragg, D. (ed.), *The Battle of Maldon AD 991*, Oxford, 81–113, at 99–102.

48 *EHD* II, no. 1.

49 Keynes, S., 2008, 'The Massacre of St Brice's Day (13 November 1002)', in Lund, N. (ed.), *Beretning fra seksogtyvende tværfaglige vikingesymposium*, Moesgaard, 32–66; Roach, *Æthelred*, 191–200.

50 Jesch, J., 2015, *The Viking Diaspora*, London, 183–90.

51 Reynolds, S., 1985, 'What Do We Mean by "Anglo-Saxon" and "Anglo-Saxons"?', *Journal of British Studies* 24, 395–414; Foot,

S., 1996, 'The Making of Angelcynn: English Identity Before the Norman Conquest', *TRHS* 6th ser., 6, 25–49; Wormald, *Legal Culture*, 359–82.

52 Pratt, D., 2007, *The Political Thought of King Alfred the Great*, Cambridge, 105–7.

53 *EHD* I, no. 226.

54 Foot, S., 2005. 'The Historiography of the Anglo-Saxon "Nation-State"', in Scales, L. and Zimmer, O. (eds.), *Power and the Nation in European History*, Cambridge, 125–42; Wormald, P., 2005, 'Germanic Power Structures: The Early English Experience', in Scales and Zimmer (eds.), *Power and the Nation*, 105–12.

55 Molyneaux, *Formation*, 6–7.

56 See the papers in Lavelle and Roffey (eds.), *Danes in Wessex*; with Williams, A., 2017, 'Of Danes and Thegns and Domesday Book: Scandinavian Settlement in Eleventh-Century Berkshire', *ANS* 39, 219–35; and Williams, A., 1986, '"Cockles Amongst the Wheat": Danes and English in the Western Midlands in the First Half of the Eleventh Century', *Midland History* 11, 1–22.

57 *EHD* I, no. 105.

58 Hadley, D., 2002, 'Viking and Native: Re-thinking Identity in the Danelaw', *EME* 11, 45–70.

59 Stafford, P., 2008, '"The Annals of Æthelflæd": Annals, History and Politics in Early Tenth-Century England', in Barrow, J. and Wareham, A. (eds.), *Myth, Rulership, Church and Charters: Essays in Honour of Nicholas Brooks*, Aldershot, 101–16.

60 *EHD* I, no. 1 (*sub anno* 1007).

61 Moore, R. I., 2007 (2nd ed.), *The Formation of a Persecuting Society: Authority and Deviance in Western Europe, 950–1250*, Oxford.

62 Scragg, D., 1991, 'The Battle of Maldon', in Scragg (ed.), *Battle of Maldon*, 1–36, at 21 and 31.

63 *EHD* II, no. 1 (*sub anno* 1066).

3 William the Conqueror and the capture of London in 1066

1 *Carmen*, 38–9, lines 653–4.

2 Morton and Muntz, xv; Barlow, *Carmen*, xxiv–v (re attribution); xl–xli (date). For how the poem might have ended, Barlow, *Carmen*, xc.

3 Morton and Muntz, l; Barlow, *Carmen*, xxxvi.

4 See Morton and Muntz, L, n5.

5 The voyage from Saint-Valéry would have been little longer than that from Dives to Saint-Valéry. Presumably the need to transport horses made the shortest route the more attractive.

6 See the interesting discussion in Higham, N. J., *The Norman Conquest*, 1998, 50–52.

7 *GG*, 142–3 (*Subegit autem urbes Anglorum cunctas dux Guillelmus copiis Normanniae uno die ab hora tertia in vesperum …*).
8 *Carmen*, 36–7, lines 596–7; see Dalton, P., 2015, 'William the Peacemaker: The Submission of the English to the Duke of Normandy, October 1066–January 1067', in Dalton, P. and Luscombe, D. (eds.), 2015, *Rulership and Rebellion in the Anglo-Norman World, c.1066–c.1216: Essays in Honour of Professor Edmund King*, Farnham and Burlington VT, 21–44, at 23.
9 Bates, *William the Conqueror*, 247; ASC 'D', 1066 (Swanton, 200).
10 *GG*, 146–7.
11 *GG*, 164–5; *Carmen*, 36–7. And also by William's construction of a castle there (*intra moenia munitionem construxit*) and its bestowal on William fitz Osbern; Bates, *William the Conqueror*, 250.
12 *GG*, 142–3.
13 *GG*, 144–5.
14 *GG*, 144–5; *Carmen*, 36–7, line 558. Neither the ASC nor the *GND* makes reference to the Dover sojourn.
15 *GG*, 142–3.
16 *GG*, 144–5 (*ubi populum innumerabilem congregatum acceperat*).
17 *Carmen*, 36–7.
18 At least, eight days after its submission: how long he took to capture the place is not explained (*GG*, 142–3, 144–5).
19 *Carmen*, 36–7, line 623.
20 *GG*, 144–5. On the 'broken tower', see Parfitt, K., 2004, 'The Broken Tower', *Kent Archaeological Review* 156, 130–2; Ward, A., 2004, 'A brief note on the "broken tower"', *Kent Archaeological Review* 157, 156–8.
21 *Carmen*, 36–7, 38–9. On context, Morton and Muntz, xlvii–xlviii. See also Dalton, 'William the Peacemaker', 25.
22 As others have concluded: see e.g. Douglas, *William the Conqueror*, 205; Dalton, 'William the Peacemaker', 25.
23 *GND*, ii, 170–1 (*Mane … autem illucesscente, spoliis hostium distractis et corporibus suorum carorum sepultis, iter arripuit quod Londoniam tendit*).
24 *Carmen*, 38–9, line 636 (*Quo populosa nitet Londona vertit iter*).
25 *GG*, 146–7 (*copioso ac praestantia military famoso incolatu abundant*).
26 *GG*, 146–7.
27 *Carmen*, 38–9, lines 641–2 (*Hanc bello superata petit gens improba, sperans/Vivere per longum libera tempus in hac*).
28 *Roman de Rou*, 286, lines 8859–66; on Wace as a historian, see van Houts, E., 1997, 'Wace as Historian,' in Keats-Rohan, K. S. B. (ed.), *Medieval Prosopography: The Roots and Branches of Power in France and England from the Tenth to the Twelfth Centuries*, Woodbridge, 103–32 (reprinted in van Houts, *History and Family Traditions*, chapter X).

29 Below, p.40.

30 *Carmen*, 38–9 (*Urbs est ampla nimis, perversis plena colonis/Et regni reliquis dicior est opibus*). For later sources, *Breuis Relatio*, 33 ('not waiting there for long, he began to go towards London, the principal city of England, and in this way to conquer the land of the English itself. Then, shortly afterwards, very many of the English began to come to him and make peace').

31 Stenton, F. M., 1971 (3rd ed.), *Anglo-Saxon England*, 390–3.

32 *Roman de Rou*, 244–5.

33 *Roman de Rou*, 266–7, 268–9.

34 *GG*, 120–21.

35 English, B., 1995, 'Towns, Mottes and Ringworks of the Norman Conquest', in Ayton, A. and Price, J. L., *The Medieval Military Revolution*, London, 45–61, at 45.

36 Bates, D., 1982, *Normandy Before 1066*, London and New York, 178–9; Jean-Marie, L., 2001, *Caen aux XIe et XIIe siècles. Espace urbain, pouvoirs et société*, Paris, 27–35.

37 Douglas, *William the Conqueror*, 182.

38 Morton and Muntz, 43 n4; *Carmen*, 40, lines 671–2 (*Nam veluti patrum testantur gesta priorum/Ex solito reges hic diadema ferunt*).

39 Sheldon, H. L. and Tyers, I., 1983, 'Recent Dendrochronological Work in Southwark and its Implications', *London Archaeologist* 4, no. 14, 355–61, 359–61; Vince, A., 1990, *Saxon London: An Archaeological Investigation*, London, 77; Hill, C. et al., 1980, *The Roman Riverside Wall and Monumental Arch in London*, LAMAS Special Paper no. 3, London, 70.

40 In the context of the 'rebuilding' of the city which the ASC places in 886. Keene, D. J., 2003, 'Alfred and London', in Reuter, T. A. (ed.), *Alfred the Great: Papers from the Eleventh-Centenary Conferences*, Aldershot, 246; Keynes, 1998, 23; ASC 'E', 886 (*recte* 885) (Swanton, 81); Keynes, S. and Lapidge, M. (ed. and trans.), 1983, *Alfred the Great: Asser's Life of King Alfred and Other Contemporary Sources*, London, 97–8. See Vince, *Saxon London*, 85, for discussion of date. Alfred 'honourably rebuilt the city of London, made it habitable, and gave it into the custody of Æthelred, ealdorman of Mercia'.

41 Vince, *Saxon London*, 80, 92; Kingsford, J. (ed.), 1971, *John Stow: A Survey of London*, Oxford, 35.

42 Stenton, *Anglo-Saxon England*, 391–2; ASC 'D', 1016 (Swanton, 149).

43 *Carmen*, 38–9, line 639.

44 For *turres*, see *Carmen*, 40–41, 42–3, lines 677, 699.

45 *Carmen*, 40–41, line 677, 42–3, line 699.

46 *Carmen*, 40–41, line 678.

47 *GND*, ii, 170–71.

48 Hilbert, 'Adelae Comitissa', 163, line 529 ('*Hostis adest*' aliqui clamant a turribus altis).

49 ASC 'D', 1066 (Swanton, 199, 201)

50 JW, ii, 606–7.

51 *GG*, 146–7.

52 *GG*, 100–101.

53 Bates, *William the Conqueror*, 216; Stafford, P., 2011, 'Archbishop Ealdred and the D Chronicle', in Crouch, D. and Thompson, K., 2011, *Normandy and its Neighbours, 900–1250: Essays for David Bates*, Turnhout, 135–56, at 139; Dalton, 'William the Peacemaker', 30.

54 *GG*, 146–7.

55 JW, ii, 604–5 ('When they heard of his [Harold's] death, Earls Edwin and Morkar, who had slipped away from the battle with their men and came to London'; *Cuius morte audita, comites Eduuinus et Morkarus, qui se cum suis certamini substraxere, Lundoniam venere*).

56 *GG*, 146–7; *GND*, ii, 180–81 (re. 1069); *Carmen*, 38–9, line 647.

57 *Carmen*, 38–9, lines 645, 649.

58 *Carmen*, 38–9, lines 645–52 (*rectores atque potentes/Tali consilio consuluere sibi:/Scilicet ut puerum natum de traduce regis/In regem sacrent, ne sine rege forent/Autumat insipiens uulgus se posse tueri/Regali solo nomine, non opere./In statuam regis puer est electus ab illis/Cuius presidium contulit exicium*).

59 ASC 'D', 1066 (Swanton 199): 'Aldred the Archbishop and the citizens of London wanted to have Edgar Cild as king, as was his proper due'. On Ealdred and links with ASC 'D', see Stafford, 2011, 'Archbishop Ealdred and the D Chronicle'.

60 ASC 'D', 1066 (Swanton, 199).

61 JW, ii, 604–7 (*Aldredus autem Eboracensis archiepiscopus, et idem comites, cum civibus Lundoniensibus et butsecarlis clitonem Eadgarum, Eadmundi regis Ferrei Lateris nepotem, in regem levare voluere*: 'However, Ealdred, archbishop of York, and those earls with the citizens of London and the seamen, wished to raise to the throne the ætheling Edgar, grandson of King Edmund Ironside').

62 *GG*, 146–7.

63 The verb used in *GG* is *statuere*, i.e. to establish, decide on, or 'chose' as Davis and Chibnall translate it.

64 *Carmen*, 38–9, line 648.

65 *Carmen*, 38–9, line 648.

66 See, for example, Higham, *The Death*, 214.

67 *senden him þa to Ædgar æðeling. forðan þet þe landfolc wendon þæt he sceolde cyng wurðen se æðeling hit him geatte þa bliþolice* ('... and sent him to the ætheling Edgar because the local people thought he ought to become king, and the ætheling happily agreed it for him'), ASC 'E', 1066 (Swanton, 199).

68 Knowles, Dom D., Brooke, C. N. L. and London, V., 1972, *The Heads of Religious Houses in England and Wales 940–1216*, Cambridge, 60; Dalton, 'William the Peacemaker', 41.

69 Higham, *The Death*, 215.

70 Baring, F. H., 1909, *Domesday Tables for the Counties of Surrey, Berkshire, Middlesex, Hertford, Buckingham and Bedford and for the New Forest, with an Appendix on the Battle of Hastings*, London.

71 Palmer, J. J. N., 1995, 'The Conqueror's Footsteps in Domesday Book', in Ayton, A. and Price, J. (eds.), *The Medieval Military Revolution*, London, 23–44; Bates, *William the Conqueror*, 249.

72 *GG*, 146–7 (*ubi frequentiorem audivit eorum conventum, non longe a Lundonia consedit*).

73 Not Westminster as supposed by Morton and Muntz, li.

74 *GG*, 147–8.

75 *GG*, 146–7 (*cremantes quicquid aedificiorum citra flumen invenere*).

76 E.g. Douglas, *William the Conqueror*, 206; Bates, *William the Conqueror*, 249.

77 Gower, G., 1996, '*Brixges Stane*', *the Meeting Place of the Hundred of Brixton*, London, 1.

78 And perhaps as early as the 870s or 880s (Vince, *Saxon London*, 87).

79 Watson, B., Brigham, T. and Dyson, T., 2001, *London Bridge: 2000 Years of a River Crossing*, Museum of London Archaeology Service Monograph, 8, London, 53.

80 ASC 'C', 1016 (Swanton, 148); and Watson, B. et al., 2001, 54.

81 Watson, B., 2001, 53–4 and Fig. 27.

82 Bates, *William the Conqueror*, 249.

83 *GG*, 146–7; *GND*, ii, 170–71.

84 Grayson, A. J., 2010, 'Thames Crossings near Wallingford from Roman to Early Norman Times', *Oxoniensia* 75, 1–14, at 11; ASC 'E', 1013 (Swanton, 143–4).

85 Grayson, 'Thames Crossings', 1; Phillips, G., 1981, *Thames Crossings: Bridges, Tunnels and Ferries*, Newton Abbot, 69; Dalton, 'William the Peacemaker', 26.

86 Grayson, A. J., 1981, 11. Otherwise the first documentary evidence for a bridge dates from 1141 (Grayson, 1981).

87 *GG*, 146–7.

88 The west side, as the river flows due south at this point.

89 Roffe, D., 2015, 'An English Legacy: The Liberty of the Honour of Wallingford', in Keats-Rohan, K. S. B. (ed.), *Wallingford: The Castle and the Town in Context*, Oxford, 28–32, 29.

90 Grayson, A. J., 1981, 7–8.

91 Grayson, A. J., 1981, 11.

92 Grayson, 'Thames Crossings', 6–12.

93 JW, ii, 606–7.

94 *GG*, 146–7; Dalton, 'William the Peacemaker', 27.

95 *GG*, 146–7 (*Hinc procedenti statim ut Lundonia conspectui patebat, obviam exeunt principes civitatis; sese cunctamque civitatem in obsequium illius, quemadmodum ante Cantuarii, tradunt*).

96 JW, ii, 606–7.

97 Baring, *Domesday Tables*, 212; see Palmer, J. J. N., 'The Conqueror's Footprints in Domesday Book', 1998, 33–4.

98 Palmer, 'The Conqueror's Footsteps', 33–4; Clarke, *The English Nobility*, 280–81; Green, *The Aristocracy*, 55.

99 ASC 'D', 1066 (Swanton, 200).

100 *GG*, 146–7 (as above, n96).

101 *GG*, 146–7.

102 *GR*, i, 460–61.

103 HH, 394 (*Willelmus vero tanta potitus victoria, susceptus a Lundoniensibus pacifice*).

104 OV, ii, 182 (*Lundonii nichilominus utile consilium percipientes sese in obsequium ducis tradiderunt et obsides quot et quos imperarat adduxerunt. Edgarus Adelinus qui rex constitutus fuerat ab Anglis resistere diffidens humiliter Guillelmo se regnumque contulit*: 'The Londoners also took the wise course and surrendered to the Duke, bringing him all the hostages he named and required. Edgar Atheling, who had been proclaimed king by the English, hesitated to take up arms and humbly submitted himself and the kingdom to William').

105 Stenton, *Anglo-Saxon England*, 597.

106 GND, ii, 170–71 (*Inde vero profectus Londoniam est agressus, ubi precursores milites venientes in platea urbis plurimos invenerunt rebelles resistere toto conamine decertantes. Cum quibus protinus congressi non minimum luctum intulerunt urbi ob filiorum ac civium suorum funera plurima. Videntes demum Londonii se diutius contra stare non posse, datis obsidibus se suaque omnia nobilissimo victori suo hereditario domino subposuere*).

107 *Carmen*, 38–9, lines 659–64 (*Comperit ut factum fatuis quod non erat equum,/Prescripte muros urbis adire iubet./Paruit extimplo celeri velocius aura/Agmen belligerum castra locare sibi/Densatis castris a leva menia cinxit,/Et bellis hostes esse dedit vigiles*).

108 *Carmen*, 40–41, lines 673–7 (*Edificat moles, veruecis cornua ferro/Fabricat et talpas, urbis ad excidium/Intonat inde minas, penas et bella minatur/Iurans quod, licitum si sibi sit spacium/Menia dissoluet, turres equabit harenis/Elatam turrem destruet aggerie*). On the possible meaning of the last line see Barlow, *Carmen*, 41 n4; Morton and Muntz, 43 n5. It may be that Guy assumed all great cities to have great towers, as did his own home town of Amiens (Impey, E., 2008, 'The Ancestry of the White Tower', in Impey, E. (ed.), *The White Tower*, 225–41, at 235–6).

109 Guy of Amiens's authorship and the early date of the work have been reaffirmed by Elisabeth van Houts, ('Latin Poetry and the Anglo-Norman Court, 1066–1135: the *Carmen de Hastingae Proelio*', *Journal of Medieval History* 15 (1989), 39–62, at 53–4; Barlow (ed.), *Carmen*, 39 n4; and Orlandi, 1996, 'Some afterthoughts on the *Carmen de Hastingae Proelio*', in Nip, R. I. A. et al. (eds.), 1996, *Media Latinitatis: A Collection of Essays to Mark the Occasion of the Retirement of L. F. Engels*, Instrumenta Patristica 28, Turnhout, 117–27.

110 *GND*, i, xxxv.

111 *GG*, xx; Davis, R. H. C., 1981, 'William of Poitiers and his History of William the Conqueror', in Davis and Wallace-Hadrill, J. M. (eds.), 1981, *The Writing of History in the Middle Ages: Essays Presented to Richard William Southern*, Oxford, 71–100, 74.

112 For William of Poitiers' use of the *Carmen*, see Morton and Muntz, xviii–xix.

113 Support for Edgar: *Carmen*, the 'men ... defeated in battle', or the 'foolish mob' elected Edgar (*Carmen*, 38); ASC 'D', 1066 (Swanton, 199).

114 *GG*, 146–7; Dalton, 'William the Peacemaker', 27.

115 ASC 'D', 1066 (Swanton, 200).

116 See Stenton, *Anglo-Saxon England*, 464–5, 660; Williams, A., 2000, 13; Dalton, 'William the Peacemaker', 37; Taylor, P., 1992, 'The Endowment and Military Obligations of the See of London: A Reassessment of Three Sources', *Anglo-Norman Studies* 14, 287–312, 304.

117 ASC 'D', 1066 (Swanton 199–200).

118 Higham, *The Death*, 217.

119 See Morton and Muntz, liii n3; Harmer, F. E., 1952, 342, 560–61; Stenton, *Anglo-Saxon England*, 640.

120 The visit of 'Count William from overseas with a great troop of Frenchmen' in 1051 is recorded in the ASC 'D', 1051 (Swanton, 176). On this, see Bates, 2016, 113: 'At the very least, therefore, there is no decisively compelling reason to reject the statement in the 'D' Chronicle that William visited England in 1051'. See also Douglas, D. C., 1953, 'Edward the Confessor, Duke William of Normandy and the English Succession' *English Historical Review*, lxviiii, 526–45; Oleson, T. J., 1957, 'Edward the Confessor's Promise of the Throne to Duke William of Normandy', *English Historical Review*, lxxii, 221–8.

121 Crucially, see Clarke, *The English*, 37, 46, 114 for examples. Almost all held by Geoffrey de Mandeville in 1086 (154).

122 Brooke, C. N. L. and Keir, G., 1975, *London 800–1216: The Shaping of a City*, London, 193; Harmer, *Writs*, 342, no. 75 ('Easgar stallere').

123 On the office of *Stallere* see Stenton, *Anglo-Saxon England*, 420, 632; Harmer, *Writs*, 50–1; Williams, A., *Kingship and Government in pre-Conquest England*, Macmillan, 126–7; Clarke, *The English Nobility*, 135–6.

124 *Carmen*, 40–41, lines 681–3 (*contractus debilitate/Renum sicque pedum segnis, ab officio/Vulnera pro patria quoniam numerosa receipt*).

125 Freeman, E. A., 1870–79 (2nd ed.), *The History of the Norman Conquest of England*, vol. 3, 500–1: '... and Ansgar, the valiant Staller, was borne back to London, his body disabled by honourable wounds, but his heart still stout and his wit still keen to keep up resistance to the last'. Freeman cites Guy of Amiens, who does *not* say that Ansgar was at Hastings, and has therefore simply assumed it. See also Freeman, E. A., 1870–79 (2nd ed.), *The History of the Norman Conquest of England*, 6 vols., Oxford, vol.

3, 524: 'Before long the wounded sheriff Ansgar contrived to make his way thither from the hill of slaughter'.

126 *Roman de Rou*, 266, lines 7825–30 (*Cil de Londres, par dreite fei,/ deivent garder le corps le rei,/tot entor lui deivent ester/e l'estandart deivent garder;/cil furentr mis a l'estandart*: 'The men from London, in true faith, were to protect the king's person, stand all round him and protect the standard'. (Burgess, G. S. (trans.), 2004, 179).

127 Clarke, *The English Nobility*, 154; Green, *The Aristocracy*, 37: *Carmen*, 44; Harmer, *Writs*, 560–61; Blake (ed.), *Liber Eliensis*, 165 (Fairweather (trans.), *Liber Eliensis*, 197).

128 *Carmen*, 40–1, lines 685–6 (*Omnibus ille tamen primatibus imperat urbis/Eius et auxilio publica res agitur*).

129 *Carmen*, 42–3, 44–5.

130 Blake (ed.), *Liber Eliensis*, 165, c.96 (*cadendus est, Normannis Dei iudicio Angliam bello citius optinentibus, qui usque ad diem mortis eius cum pluribus aliis in ergastulo carceris ferro astrictus mox retrudendus erat*) (Fairweather (trans.), *Liber Eliensis*, 197: Ansgar 'was inevitably to fall into scandal and disgrace, when the Normans, by the judgement of God, very quickly gained possession of England in war, and soon he was to be thrust, with a number of others, into the dungeon of a prison, bound with iron, right until the day of his death').

131 Note that the earls are not named amongst the part offering surrender in the *Carmen*.

132 *ASC* 'D' (Swanton, 200); *GG*, 147–8; JW, ii, 606–7.

133 Brooke and Keir, *London*, 193; their source appears to be Harmer, *Writs*, 344, no. 77.

134 Brooke and Keir, *London*, 196.

135 Harmer, *Writs*, no. 51.

136 Harmer, *Writs*, no. 105.

137 *VCH Kent*, iii, 208; Brooke and Keir, *London*, 372.

138 Harmer, *Writs*, nos. 105–6, 370–72.

139 Brooke and Keir, *London*, 29.

140 Harmer, *Writs*, no. 75, 342.

141 *Carmen*, 42–3, lines 698–703: *Cernitis oppressos valido certamine muros/Et circumseptos cladibus innumeris/Molis et erecte transcendit machina turres/Ictibus et lapidum menia scissa ruunt./ Casibus a multis, ex omnia parte ruina/Eminet...*

142 *Carmen*, 42–3, 44–5, lines 731, 739–40.

143 *Carmen*, 44–5, lines 743–5 (*Vultibus in terra deflexis, regis ad aulam/Cum puero pergunt agmine composito./Reddere per claves urbem, sedare furorem/Oblato querunt munere cum manibus*).

144 Hilbert, 'Adelae Comitissae', 163, line 529 ('*Hostis adest*' aliqui clamant a turribus altis) and 162, line 494 (*Septaque munivit moenia rarus homo*).

4 The armour and weapons of the Anglo-Saxons and Normans

1 Wijnhoven Martijn, A., 2015, 'La túnica de hierro de Vimose (Fionia, Dinamarca): nuevas investigaciones en torno a la confección de cotas de malla', *Gladius* 35, 77–104. Earlier solid links were made by punching rather than forge welding, see Jouttijärvi, A., 'The manufacture of chain mail', Early Iron: http://www.gnom.dk/projekter/ringbrynjehistorie.pdf

2 Adams, N., 2010, 'Rethinking the Sutton Hoo Shoulder Clasps and Armour', in Entwistle, C. and Adams, N. (eds.), *Intelligible Beauty: Recent Research on Byzantine Jewellery*, London, 83–112.

3 Burges, W. and C. A. de Cosson, 1880, 'Catalogue of the Exhibition of Ancient Helmets and Examples of Mail', *The Archaeological Journal*, 37, 455–594.

4 Gilmour, B. J., 1999, 'The Mail Shirt', in Niblett, R. (ed.), *The Excavation of a Ceremonial Site at Folly Lane, Verulamium*, London, 159–67. See Wyley, S. F. 'The Gjermundbu Mail Shirt' http://www.angelfire.com/wy/svenskildbiter/armsandarmour/mailshrt.html.

5 Bravermanova, M., 2012, 'The So-Called Armour of St Wenceslaus – A Historical Introduction', *Acta Militaria Medievalia* 8, 213–19; Checksfield, N., Edge, D. and Williams, A., 2012, 'Examination and Assessment of the Wenceslaus Mail Hauberk,' *Acta Militaria Medievalia* 8, 229–41.

6 Musset, 2002, *The Bayeux Tapestry*, Woodbridge, 46.

7 For all these examples see Tweddle, D., 1992, *The Anglian Helmet from Coppergate*, York, passim.

8 British Library, Harley MS 603, fo. 69r; Lavelle, R., 2012, *Alfred's Wars*, Woodbridge, 283.

9 Peirce, I., 1988, 'Arms, Armour and Warfare in the Eleventh Century', *ANS* 10, 237–57.

10 See Glover, 1996, 'English Warfare in 1066', in Morillo, S. (ed.), *The Battle of Hastings: Sources and Interpretations*, Woodbridge, 174–88, at 176–7; and Bradbury, 2010, *The Battle of Hastings*, Stroud, 60.

11 See Allen, V., 2009, 'On the Nature of Things in the Bayeux Tapestry and its World', in Foys, M. K., Overbey, K. E. and Terkla, D. (eds.), *The Bayeux Tapestry: New Interpretations*, Woodbridge, 51–70, at 51; and Caviness, M. H., 2009, 'Anglo-Saxon Women, Norman Knights and a "Third Sex" in the Bayeux Embroidery', in Foys et al. (eds.), *The Bayeux Tapestry*, 85–118, at 96, although with regards to the latter area of study it is worth remembering that it has been stated that 'in Old Norse *sverð* [sword] also means penis' (Hjardar, K. and Vike, V., 2016, *Vikings at War*, Oxford, 157, 168).

12 A sword which was claimed to have been possibly 'taken … at Hastings' as well as belonging to the de Bohun family allegedly also saw action at the battles of Stamford Bridge (1066), Bannockburn (1314) and Boroughbridge (1322). The 11th-century blade was described as 'probably used at Hastings' (Christie's Second Annual Sale of Rare and Extraordinary Works of Art and Objects Celebrating All Things Unusual, South Kensington, 3 September 2014, Sale 5263, Lot 134) and as being 'an extremely rare late medieval broadsword, with earlier Viking blade … The sword's illustrious story begins in the eleventh century where it was possibly captured at the Battle of Hastings by Humphrey De Bohun and later remounted to become a family sword.' Almost needless to say, despite this amazing provenance and an estimate of £120,000, the sword failed to sell.

13 A reputed 'battle-axe' from the Battle of Hastings is displayed at the Battle Museum of Local History. Found in 1951, in Marley Lane, Battle, it has been identified by some in the last few years as a 'battle-axe' (see www.battlelocalhistory.com/1066-battlemuseum-1.html, accessed 8 August 2017). The present author would suggest that it is a woodcutter's axe of indeterminate pre-modern date, as previously identified. It was originally dated to between the ninth and thirteenth centuries, but all recent dating techniques have only confirmed that it was made before 1600. Mention has also been made of another axe-head, of the throwing or 'Francisca' type, which it is claimed was found 'on the field of Hastings some ten years ago' in about 1976 (Peirce, 'Arms, Armour and Warfare', 246–7), but the whereabouts of this piece and its exact find spot are currently unknown. An undocumented axe-head, stated to have previously been in the possession of Ian Peirce and currently in another private collection, is said to have been 'found in the environs of Battle.' Described by Peirce as 'an 11th century Danish axe-head', this is of a type that would have been used at Hastings and, if the find spot could be confirmed, it could potentially be a unique and important surviving weapon from the battle itself or at least 'associated' with it. Finally the existence of a seax, also in possession of the Battle Museum, should be noted. The seax, also previously owned by Ian Peirce, dates to about the eighth century and so clearly predates the battle. The alleged find-spot, in Battle itself, is a doubtful one.

14 Such as the purported discovery and evidence of a crossbow (Austin, N., 2012, *Secrets of the Norman Invasion*, Crowhurst, 278–91). Another weapon that should also be mentioned is a spear-head allegedly found by a dog-walker on Caldbec Hill. This weapon, however, has since been lost and despite some 'experts' claiming it 'could be medieval' an existing photograph of it shows that is almost certainly of African origin and nothing to do with the battle.

15 The skeleton ('180') was originally linked to the Battle of Hastings (see www.bbc.co.uk/news/uk-england-sussex-27446020, accessed

7 August 2017) but by 2015 re-dating had proved it to possibly be connected with the much later Battle of Lewes, some 20 miles and 188 years (1264) away from Hastings (see www.sussexexpress.co.uk/news/yesterday-channel-reveals-grisly-mass-graves-of-lewes-1-6707150, accessed 7 August 2017). Sites of what are claimed to be possible mass graves of 'French dead' have been suggested, but these have not been confirmed (see Lawson, 2007, illus. 65, 66, 67 and 73).

16 See Lewis, M. J., 2005, *The Archaeological Authority of the Bayeux Tapestry*, BAR British Series, no. 404, 41, 56.

17 Mann, J., 1965, 'Arms and Armour', in Stenton, F. M. (ed.), *The Bayeux Tapestry: A Comprehensive Survey* (2nd ed.), London, 56–69, at 57.

18 For discussions on the reliability of the Bayeux Tapestry as a source see, for example, Brooks, N. P. and Walker, H. E., 1979, 'The Authority and Interpretation of the Bayeux Tapestry', *ANS*, i, 1–34; Bernstein, D. J., 1986, *The Mystery of the Bayeux Tapestry*, London, 110–11; Lewis, *The Archaeological Authority*, xi, 15–16; Lewis, M. J., 2008, *The Real World of the Bayeux Tapestry*, Stroud, 113, 125; Lewis, M. J., 2009, 'Embroidery Errors in the Bayeux Tapestry', in Foys et al. (eds.), 130–40; Flambard Héricher, A.-M., 2004, 'Archaeology and the Bayeux Tapestry', in Bouet et al. (eds.), *The Bayeux Tapestry*, 261–87, at 262; Brown, S. A., 2013, *The Bayeux Tapestry. Bayeux, Médiathèque Municipale: MS. 1 A Sourcebook*, Turnhout, lxxxvi–ii. The criticism that earlier studies 'considered the Tapestry "our best authority for the arms and armour of the period" even though some eleventh-century weapons do survive' (Lewis, *The Archaeological Authority*, 15) illustrates the problem; indeed, only 'some' have survived and so the contemporaneous Bayeux Tapestry does indeed provide a resource, albeit one to be used critically. As Barlow pithily points out: 'Modern canons of historical accuracy and objectivity governed none of the literary accounts of the Norman invasion nor the design of the Bayeux Tapestry ... A review of the sources for the campaign and battle shows that, although all can be called in evidence, none is likely to be completely reliable ... [however] the Tapestry can be regarded as more factual than any of the literal accounts' (*Carmen*, xxvi, lx).

19 See Mann, 'Arms and Armour', 56–7; Bradbury, *Battle of Hastings*, 62. The Bayeux Tapestry has quite rightly been called 'the most important and informative source for any investigation into the armour and weapons employed in the second half of the eleventh century' (Peirce, 'Arms, Armour and Warfare', 237), and 'It is undoubtedly an extremely valuable source for the military equipment of the age' (France, J., 2004, 'The Importance of the Bayeux Tapestry for the History of War', in Bouet et al. (eds.), *The Bayeux Tapestry*, 290–9, at 295).

20 See Ellis Davidson, H. R., *The Sword in Anglo-Saxon England: Its Archaeology and Literature*, Woodbridge, 39, 106–7.

21 Lobated pommels were an older form but are depicted alongside swords with disc pommels in second-quarter 11th-century manuscript illustrations (i.e. 'The Army of the Four Kings defeats the Army of the Five Kings', *Ælfric's preface to Æthelwærd*, British Library, MS Cotton Claudius B IV, f. 24v). Despite it being claimed that one 'three-lobed' pommel is depicted in the Bayeux Tapestry (Lewis, *The Archaeological Authority*, 47 n294; Lewis, *The Real World*, 117), this is not clear or certain, and if the pommel is indeed of that type it was very much 'going out of fashion' during the 11th century (Lewis, *The Archaeological Authority*, 51). It might be worth noting that this particular sword is held by the only swordsman in the tapestry depicted bearing two swords (see note 36 below). Although it has been suggested that the representation of disc pommels on the Bayeux Tapestry might be due to distorted ('irregularly drawn') representations of 'recumbent D' or 'brazil-nut' pommels and that such pommels were 'unlikely to have been commonplace before the end of the eleventh century' (Lewis, *The Archaeological Authority*, 135), and that this type appeared later (Lewis, *The Real World*, 118), these assumptions appear incorrect. Disc pommels had been in existence since at least the late tenth century (Oakeshott, E., 1994(a), *The Archaeology of Weapons: Arms and Armour from Prehistory to the Age of Chivalry*, Woodbridge, 176–7; Oakeshott, E., 1994(b), *The Sword in the Age of Chivalry*, Woodbridge, 95), although it must be pointed out that the figure Oakeshott uses in particular as evidence of this is misattributed and misdated to 983–1; it actually comes from the *Codex Aureus of Echternach* (Nuremberg, Germanisches Nationalmuseum, GNM Hs.156142, fo. 18v), and is actually of about 1030–50, which is, of course, still well before the Conquest). As has also been noted, disc pommels 'are commonplace in Romanesque manuscripts' (Lewis, *The Archaeological Authority*, 52, 324).

22 Oakeshott, *The Sword in the Age of Chivalry*, 80.

23 See Ellis Davidson, *The Sword*, 75, 184 (who discusses the use of such wrist loops in Viking sagas), Gravett, C. and Nicolle, D., 2006, *The Normans*, Botley, 79; Short, W. R., 2009, *Viking Weapons and Combat Techniques*, Yardley, Pennsylvania, 123–4.

24 For a detailed and still useful discussion on the making of swords, even though this work concentrates on earlier swords, see Ellis Davidson, *The Sword*, 15–103. See also Peirce, 'Arms, Armour and Warfare', 250; Moilanen, M., 2015, *Marks of Fire, Value and Faith: Swords with Ferrous Inlays in Finland During the Late Iron Age (ca. 700–1200AD)*, Turku, Archaeologia Medii Aevi Finlandiae 21, 208–16.

25 Ellis Davidson, *The Sword*, 28.

26 Moilanen, *Marks of Fire*, 12.

27 For an informed discussion regarding this group of sword blades see Stalsberg, A., 2008, '*The Vlfberht Sword Blades Reevaluated*', Stavanger, 2008; www.jenny-rita.org/Annestamanus.pdf, accessed 1 January 2017.

28 Notker the Stammerer, *De Carolo Magno*, about 883–4, in Thorpe, L. (ed. and trans.), 1983, *Einhard and Notker the Stammerer: Two Lives of Charlemagne*, Harmondsworth, 167–8.

29 Ellis Davidson, *The Sword*, 113–14 and 164–5.

30 It is quite conceivable that the naming of arms continued into this period, and the battle of Hastings, given that Harald Hardrada (d.1066) had a mail shirt called 'Emma'.

31 Anon, about 1200, in Pàlsson, H. and Edwards, P. (eds. and trans.), 1981, *Orkneyinga Saga: The History of the Earls of Orkney*, Harmondsworth, 210–11.

32 *Egil's Saga*, about 1200–50, in Óskarsdóttir, S. (ed. and trans.), 2004, *Egil's Saga*, Harmondsworth, 141.

33 Blöndal, S., 2007, *The Varangians of Byzantium: An Aspect of Byzantine Military History*, Cambridge, 207; Mann, 'Arms and Armour', 66.

34 *Roman de Rou*, about 1170–74, 176.

35 *GG*, 135.

36 Peirce, 'Arms, Armour and Warfare', 250.

37 *Carmen*, 30–31.

38 It has also been suggested that the scene depicts the impalement of the Norman by the Anglo-Saxon's sword (Kiff, J., 1985, 'Images of War: Illustrations of Warfare in Early Eleventh-Century England' *ANS* 7, 177–94, at 192), but given the position of the sword, and it being consistent with the depiction of many other armoured warriors similarly armed with swords (BT 51 and 56, for example), it seems totally unreasonable not to assume that it is the Norman's own sword, still sheathed, at his side. Otherwise this would make the Norman the only two-sword-wielding warrior in the Tapestry (a curious point first noted by Kiff, 'Images of War', 192–3). For discussions about warriors, mostly mythological, bearing two swords, see Ellis Davidson, *The Sword*, 201–2, 209; Pollington, S., 2002, *The English Warrior: From Earliest Times to 1066*, Hockwold-cum-Wilton, 132–7. See also Cowdrey, H. E. J., 1988, 'Towards an Interpretation of the Bayeux Tapestry', *ANS* 10, 49–65, at 60, who sees the killing of the 'defenceless' man as an act of shame. As for the Anglo-Saxon not being armoured, there are examples of those elsewhere on the Bayeux Tapestry (i.e. BT 66–7). For a different and perhaps not altogether convincing discussion of this scene, see Bernstein, *The Mystery*, 145, 166, 171–4, 177. See also *Carmen*, lxxxiii.

39 Kiff, 'The Image', 192.

40 The looting of the enemy by the Normans is also mentioned in GND 171.

41 Although some argue that the 'use of baldrics seems to have disappeared by the mid 11th century' (Gravett, C., *The Norman Knight 950–1204AD*, London, 54), such a baldric is clearly depicted being worn by 'Goliath' in *The Tiberius Psalter*, English (Winchester), about 1050 (British Library, MS Cotton Tiberius C VI, fo. 9).

42 Stephenson, I. P., 2006, *The Late Anglo-Saxon Army*, Stroud, 94; Gravett, *Norman Knight*, 14.

43 Two Normans hold sheathed swords to which belts with buckles are already attached. One is also shown wearing a waist-belt. This raises the question of whether the Normans also suspended, in some way, their swords from the waist-belts they already wore. This is not impossible; as has been noted, 'Originally the sweord-fetelt was a leather strap ... attached directly to the sheath, girt about the waist, and fastened with a buckle' (Keller, M. L., 1906, *The Anglo-Saxon Weapon Names Treated Archaeologically and Etymologically*, Heidelberg, 47) and it is something like this that appears to be depicted in the Tapestry (see also Ellis Davidson, *The Sword*, 118–20, 142; Stephenson, *The Late Anglo-Saxon Army*, 94).

44 Norman, A. V. B., 1971, *The Medieval Soldier: Crowell Medieval Life Series*, New York, 238.

45 Stephenson, *The Late Anglo-Saxon Army*, 97.

46 *Beowulf*, XXXVII, lines 2702–4; see www.heorot.dk/beowulf-rede-text.html, accessed 8 December 2017.

47 For a detailed discussion of staff weapons see Troso, M., 1988, *Le Armi in Asta delle Fanterie Europee (1000–1500)*, Novara.

48 *Roman de Rou*, 177.

49 Underwood, R., 1999, *Anglo-Saxon Weapons and Warfare*, Stroud, 39.

50 See Hewitt, J., 1855, *Ancient Armour and Weapons in Europe*, vol. I, Oxford and London, 28; Keller, *Anglo-Saxon Weapon Names*, 128–9; Hill, P., 2012, *The Anglo-Saxons at War 800–1066*, Barnsley, 149.

51 DeVries, K., 1999, *The Norwegian Invasion of England in 1066*, Woodbridge, 218.

52 *Egil's Saga*, about 1200–50, in Óskarsdóttir (ed. and trans.), 96.

53 Although it has also been stated that at Hastings 'It is unlikely that spears were barbed or had lugs in reality' (Gravett, *The Norman Knight*, 13).

54 See Peirce, 'Arms, Armour and Warfare', 245; Wilson, *The Bayeux Tapestry*, 224. Regarding rivet heads, it may be worth noting that a complete Viking spear from between 825 and 950, with birch haft, recovered in 1974 and held by the Archaeological Museum, Oslo (C34256), has only a very small iron nail for attachment

(see http://secretsoftheice.com/news/2017/11/29/spear/, accessed 8 December 2017. I would like to thank my colleague Keith Dowen for bringing this spear to my attention). The lugged spears have also been described as 'contemporary' weapons but with certain 'fossilised' elements (Lewis, *The Archaeological Authority*, 46, 56).

55 See Troso, *Le Armi*, 105–6 for two examples dated to the 11th century and another example in Nicolle, D., 1987, *The Normans*, London, 4, dated to the 11th–12th century.

56 Such 'winged' spears are illustrated in the British Library, MS Cotton Cleopatra C VIII fo. 10v and fo. 11r, of the late 10th to early 11th century.

57 Anglo-Saxons appear to be preparing to hurl what might be described as 'javelins' at the oncoming Norman cavalry on at least two occasions in the Bayeux Tapestry (BT 61 and 62), and one is famously depicted as flying through the air towards the Normans (BT 61). Interestingly, in the same scene one 'javelin' is depicted that appears to indicate it was thrown by a mounted Norman soldier (BT 61), although many other Normans on horseback also give the impression that they may be about to cast their 'javelin' or light spear/lance (i.e. BT 59).

58 *GG*, 129; *Carmen*, 25.

59 *Carmen*, 28–9 and 30–31.

60 One does find them depicted elsewhere, such as in 'The Army of the Four Kings defeats the Army of the Five Kings', *Ælfric's preface to Æthelwærd*, British Library, MS Cotton Claudius B IV, fo. 24v; second quarter of the 11th century.

61 Although such barbed heads have been described as making 'little sense' (Lewis, *The Real World*, 120) the present author disagrees with this contention for the reasons given above.

62 See Peirce, 'Arms, Armour and Warfare', 244. Such lances (and spears) with hafts of ash and applewood are described in the 11th–12th century *Song of Roland*, 185, line 2537; 'Burning the lances of ash and apple-beam' (Sayers, D. L. (ed. and trans.), 1957, *The Song of Roland*, Harmondsworth, 148).

63 See Brown, R. A., 1996, 'The Battle of Hastings' in Morillo (ed.), *The Battle of Hastings*, 195–218, at 208–10, for a detailed discussion on the use of the lance.

64 See Strickland, M., 1997, 'Military Technology and Conquest: The Anomaly of Anglo-Saxon England', *ANS* 19, 353–82, at 361, for a succinct discussion about the variety of lance techniques as well as about the duration of the so-called 'development' of the 'couched' lance.

65 *Roman de Rou*, 177.

66 See Glover, 'English Warfare', 184–5 n54 for a further interesting discussion on what the Normans might, or might not, have been capable of regarding the use of the lance.

67 This is in opposition to what has been suggested by other writers who suggest that, in fact, there is at least one scene in the Bayeux Tapestry (BT 53) which depicts 'three Normans, with couched lances, have them placed diagonally across the neck of their horses' (Peirce, 'Arms, Armour and Warfare', 245 and see Wilson, G., 1987, 'Norman Arms and Armour' in Wilson, G. (ed.), *England under the Normans, 1066–1154, A British History Illustrated Special*, 8–12, at 10). This interpretation of the scene is in fact wishful thinking and it is simply not at all clear if that is actually what they are being portrayed as doing. One must also consider, however, that the probably more importantly regarded horse was embroidered first and then the lance was simply stitched across its neck with no regard for, or understanding of, true perspective. As to the rider whose lance *may* be crossed over the neck of his horse (BT 20), the stitched line of the lance is in line with the neck and head of the horse and so it is unclear if it has actually been passed over the horse.

68 This point is touched upon, but not sufficiently followed through, when it is was suggested that 'it is only surprising that at Hastings they [the Normans] apparently used against a dismounted enemy a style of charge ideally suited for unhorsing opposing cavalry' (Peirce, I. G., 1986, 'The Knight, his Arms and Armour, in the Eleventh and Twelfth Centuries', in Harper-Bill, C. and Harvey, R. (eds.), *The Ideals and Practice of Medieval Knighthood: Papers From the First and Second Strawberry Hill Conferences*, Woodbridge, 152–64, at 162). Peirce appears to have been following Brown, who had made the point previously that 'the new tactic was developed ... for the unhorsing of horsed opponents of whom there were none at Hastings' (Brown, The Battle of Hastings', 210). However, Strickland is quite clear, and correct, in forcefully stating that the couched lance was 'designed primarily for fighting against other cavalry' (Strickland, 'Military Technology', 363).

69 Brown, 'The Battle of Hastings', 210.

70 See Strickland, 'Military Technology', 366 n53, referring to the First Crusade, and a single early depiction of a lance crossing over a horse's neck is found in 'carvings on Modena Cathedral of about 1099–1106' (Norman, *The Medieval Soldier*, 232), in the mounted figure of King Arthur on the *Porta della Pescheria*, although a later, but still debated, date of 1120–40 has been more recently suggested (Stokstad, M., 1991, 'Modena Archivolt', in Lacy, N. J. (ed.), *The New Arthurian Encyclopedia*, New York, 324–6). It might be fair to describe what is depicted in the Bayeux Tapestry as, in fact, 'semi-couched' lances, and the appearance of combat with the 'couched' lance has even been stated as appearing in Europe as late as 'the mid-twelfth century' (Williams, A., Edge, D. and Capwell, T., 2016, 'An Experimental Investigation of Late medieval Combat with the

Couched Lance', *Journal of the Arms and Armour Society* 22, 1–16). Even the famous Tristan I embroidery from Wienhausen, of about 1300, depicts lances both placed over the horses neck and not, illustrating and confirming what appears to be a long period of transition. For a nimble discussion of the various suggested origins of 'mounted shock combat' see DeVries, K. and Smith, R. D., 2012, *Medieval Military Technology*, Toronto, 13.

71 These thicker lances have been noted previously (Brown, 'The Battle of Hastings', 210) but another writer stated that 'Most of the spears are spindly, except for a few, and it is not possible to suggest why they are exceptions' (France, 'The Importance of the Bayeux Tapestry', 296). The present author's observation contradicts the earlier assertion of another writer: 'The only difference visible in contemporary illustrations between infantry and cavalry spears is that infantry spears sometimes appear thicker in the haft' (Wilson, 'Norman Arms and Armour', 10). It is also surprising that another writer incorrectly noted 'That the lances and spears are quite light is shown by the fact that they are always depicted by a single line of stitches, as though they had length, but very little thickness', whilst at the same time noting the different treatment accorded to other wooden staves, such as those of axes (Mann, 'Arms and Armour', 66–7). This, as the present writer has shown, is simply not the case and the stated lack of any distinction between weapons ('two types of spear – a distinction not recognized or portrayed by the Tapestry designer' (Wilson, *The Bayeux Tapestry*, 225)) is incorrect.

72 *Carmen*, 24–5.

73 *GG*, 138–9. It has been suggested that the broken lance is indicative of the lance having been broken upon striking the enemy (Brown, R. A., 1985, *The Normans and the Norman Conquest*, Woodbridge, 147).

74 *Roman de Rou*, 185.

75 See Davis, R. H. C., 1988, 'The Warhorses of the Normans', *ANS* 10, 67–81, at 68, 79; Strickland, 'Military Technology', 366.

76 *Carmen*, 28–9 (it must be said that 'makes many a corpse' is a better translation of this line; see *Carmen*, 29 n2).

77 *Roman de Rou*, 185.

78 *Roman de Rou*, 186.

79 See Mann, 'Arms and Armour', 66; Wilson, *The Bayeux Tapestry*, 225.

80 Pollington, *The English Warrior*, 150.

81 'Norwegian', as Burgess, *Roman de Rou*, 184, has it.

82 Norman, *The Medieval Soldier*, 96; Mann, 'Arms and Armour', 66.

83 *Roman de Rou*, 186.

84 *Roman de Rou*, 189.

85 *Roman de Rou*, 184.

86 See Stephenson, *The Late Anglo-Saxon Army*, 101. With reference to this act it is worth pointing out the mounted Norman famously depicted being attacked by an axe-wielding Anglo-Saxon on the Bayeux Tapestry, his horse struck on the head (BT 65).

87 Thompson, L., 2004, *Ancient Weapons in Britain*, Barnsley, 102–5.

88 *Roman de Rou*, 188.

89 Peirce, 'Arms, Armour and Warfare', 246.

90 See Lewis, *The Real World*, 120; Brown, S. A., 2009, '*Auctoritas, Consilium et Auxilium*: Images of Authority in the Bayeux Tapestry', in Foys et al. (eds.), 25–35, at 27–8. Such axes are described as a 'metaphor for power and rule' (Brown, '*Auctoritas*', 27). See elsewhere for claims it is a 'mark' or 'symbol of martial prowess' (Stephenson, *The Late Anglo-Saxon Army*, 39, 103). See also Wilson, *The Bayeux Tapestry*, 225.

91 See Glover, 'English Warfare', 185 n57.

92 Stephenson, *The Late Anglo-Saxon Army*, 98.

93 DeVries, *The Norwegian Invasion*, 218, but see note 11.

94 *GG*, 129.

95 Gravett, *The Norman Knight*, 14. In fact it has been pointed out that only one true mace is depicted (BT 54) (Mann, 'Arms and Armour', 66), and this might well be indicative of their comparative rareness.

96 *Roman de Rou*, 185.

97 *GG*, 129.

98 For a short discussion, see Neveux, F., 2004, 'The Bayeux Tapestry as Original Source', in Bouet et al. (eds.), 172–95, at 184–5.

99 Duggan, L. G., 2013, *Armsbearing and the Clergy in the History and Canon Law of Western Christianity*, Woodbridge, 15.

100 Duggan, *Armsbearing*, 15.

101 D'Israeli, I., 1807 (5th ed.), *Curiosities of Literature, in Three Volumes*, vol. 1, London, 281.

102 Bernstein, *The Mystery*, 142, 217–8.

103 Duggan, *Armsbearing*, 99.

104 Duggan, *Armsbearing*, 22.

105 Duggan, *Armsbearing*, 23 (incorrectly giving the date as 1080).

106 Thorne, P. J., 1982, 'Clubs and Maces in the Bayeux Tapestry', *History Today* 32, issue 10, 48–50, at 49; Wilson, *The Bayeux Tapestry*, 225; Cowdrey, 'Towards an Interpretation' 51; Duggan, *Armsbearing*, 15.

107 See Thorne, 'Clubs and Maces', 49. It perhaps also worth reiterating that these wooden *baculum* are also different from the wooden clubs or beaters that three huntsman are depicted using (BT 7 and 13) (Cowdrey, 'Towards an Interpretation', 51 n6).

108 Thorne, 'Clubs and Maces'; Wilson, *The Bayeux Tapestry*, 226; Cowdrey, 'Towards an Interpretation', 51; Gravett, *The Norman*

Knight, 15; Jones, R. W., 2010, *Bloodied Banners: Martial Display on the Medieval Battlefield*, Woodbridge, 134–5.

109 Hewitt, J., 1860, *Ancient Armour and Weapons in Europe*, Supplement, Oxford and London, 404–6.

110 Strickland, M. and Hardy, R., 2005, *The Great Warbow: From Hastings to the Mary Rose*, Stroud, 53, 67.

111 Strickland and Hardy, *The Great Warbow*, 64.

112 Wilson, *The Bayeux Tapestry*, 225; Stephenson, *The Late Anglo-Saxon Army*, 52–8.

113 Six archers are depicted in the main frieze and 23 in the lower border. None of them are depicted with crossbows despite the claim that some are (Austin, *Secrets*, 278–311).

114 Strickland, 'Military Technology', 355.

115 See Wilson, *The Bayeux Tapestry*, 225; Jessop, O., 1996, 'A New Artefact Typology for the Study of Medieval Arrowheads', *Medieval Archaeology* 40, 192–205, at 195 (Fig. 2).

116 A group of Norman archers in the lower border (69, 70) are depicted with quivers full of arrows in front of them. This could indicate that quivers were removed before shooting or they depict 'a new supply of arrows brought up from the rear' (Peirce, 'Arms, Armour, and Warfare', 248).

117 Strickland and Hardy, *The Great Warbow*, 48. About the types of bow used see, for instance, Mann, 'Arms and Armour', 67–8; Lewis, *The Real World*, 120; and in particular Peirce, 'Arms, Armour and Warfare', 248, who by stating that the bows were 'drawn to the chest only … unlike the successful longbow of later centuries' seemingly, and perhaps somewhat disingenuously, implies that they are 'shortbows'. It has been simply stated that 'The so called "short-bow" is a myth' (Stephenson, *The Late Anglo-Saxon Army*, 109). See also Strickland, 'Military Technology', 355 n11.

118 Strickland and Hardy, *The Great Warbow*, 33–48.

119 *GG*, 127 (the translation would make better sense if it read 'bows [or self-bows] and cross-bows').

120 *Carmen*, 24–5 (again the translation would make better sense if 'darts' was substituted with either 'arrows' or 'shafts', which were carried in quivers; 'darts', i.e. javelins, were not).

121 *Roman de Rou*, 183. *Wibetes* has been translated as 'mosquitoes' but could mean any insect that bites or stings, such as a midge, or it could be a reference to the sound the arrows made, like the annoying buzzing of such insects. *Wibete* or *Vibete* has also been described as simply being an English word, deriving perhaps from Old English, meaning 'arrow' (Keller, *Anglo-Saxon Weapon Names*, 215). Thorpe confusingly, and erroneously, refers to them as 'billets' (Thorpe, L., 1973, *The Bayeux Tapestry and the Norman Invasion: with an introduction and a translation from the contemporary account of William of Poitiers*, London, 29).

122 Blair, C., 1962, *European and American Arms c.1100–1850*, London, 35.

123 See Bradbury, J., 1985, *The Medieval Archer*, Woodbridge, 27; Morton and Muntz, 114.

124 *GG*, 127.

125 *Carmen*, 20–1, 24–5. For a discussion regarding the use of the crossbow at the battle of Hastings see in particular Morton and Muntz, 112–15.

126 Crossbow bolts, 'quarrels', are specifically described: *quadratis iaculis*, *Carmen*, 24–5. See also Gravett, C., 1992, *Hastings 1066: The Fall of Saxon England*, London, 25; Morillo, *Battle of Hastings*, 47 n4; Morton and Muntz, 113.

127 Stephenson, *The Late Anglo-Saxon Army*, 112–13; Underwood, *Anglo-Saxon Weapons*, 18.

128 Darlington and McGurk, *Chronicle*, 605 ('*fundibalariorum*'). See also Gravett, *Hastings 1066*, 17, 25, 34; Strickland and Hardy, *The Great Warbow*, 64. The depictions of slings are also found in contemporary Biblical illustrations, such as 'David and Goliath' in the 'Harley Psalter' (British Library, Harley MS 603, fo. 73v), though illustrating a Biblical event does not confirm or deny its presence on the battlefield.

129 Keller, *Anglo-Saxon Weapon Names*, 62–3; Hill, *The Anglo-Saxons at War*, 167.

130 *Carmen*, 10–11.

131 See Morris, M., *The Norman Conquest*, 174; Lawson, *Battle of Hastings*, 194. For the use of fire in ravaging generally see Rogers, C. J., 2010, 'Fire', in Rogers, C. J. (ed.), *The Oxford Encyclopedia of Medieval Warfare and Military Technology*, Oxford, 50–1.

132 One of the best and most recent discussions about the death of Harold is found in Foys, M. K., 2009, 'Pulling the Arrow Out: The Legend of Harold's Death and the Bayeux Tapestry', in Foys et al. (eds.), *The Bayeux Tapestry*, 158–75; summarised in Foys, M. K., 2016, 'Shot Through the Eye and Who's to Blame?', *History Today* 66, issue 10, 6–7.

133 *Carmen*, 32–3.

134 Bernstein, *The Mystery*, 160; Morillo, *Battle of Hastings*, 51 n26.

135 Foys, 'Pulling the Arrow Out', 174–5.

5 Myths and mysteries of the Bayeux Tapestry

1 The most complete surveys of the Bayeux Tapestry probably remain Stenton, F. M. (ed.), 1957, *The Bayeux Tapestry: A Comprehensive Survey*, London, and Wilson, D. M., 1985, *The Bayeux Tapestry: The Complete Tapestry in Colour with Introduction, Description and Commentary*, London. See also Bouet, P. and Neveux, F., 2013, *La*

Tapisserie de Bayeux: révélations et mystères d'une broderie du Moyen Âge, Rennes, 168–9.

2 Stukeley, W., 1743, *Palaographia Britannica*, London, vol. 2, 90–91.

3 Hicks, C., 2006, *The Bayeux Tapestry: The Life Story of a Masterpiece*, London, 95–104.

4 Hicks, *Bayeux Tapestry*, 205–31; Brown, *Bayeux Tapestry*, 17–20.

5 Boris Johnson, 17 May 2016.

6 Gibbs-Smith, C. H., 1973, *The Bayeux Tapestry*, London, 4; Grape, W., 1994, *The Bayeux Tapestry*, Munich and New York, 23.

7 Bouet and Neveux, *Tapisserie de Bayeux*, 168–9.

8 Caen, Archives Départementales du Calvados, Manuscrits du Chapitre de la cathédrale de Bayeux, MS 199 (after Brown, *Bayeux Tapestry*, 161).

9 Brown, *Bayeux Tapestry*, 3–6.

10 De Montfaucon, B., 1730, 'La Conquête de l'Angleterre par Guillaume le Bâtard, Duc de Normandie, dit le Conquérant', *Les Monumens de la Monarchie Françoise*, vol. 2, Paris, 1–31.

11 Hicks, C., 2011, 'The Patronage of Queen Edith', in Lewis et al. (eds.), *The Bayeux Tapestry*, 8.

12 Lyttleton, G., 1769, *The History of the Life of King Henry the Second, and the Age in which he lived …*, vol. 1, London, 353–5.

13 De la Rue, G., 1811, 'Sur la tapisserie de Bayeux', *Rapport général sur travaux, Académie des sciences, arts et belles-lettres de Caen*, vol. 2, 184.

14 Delauney, H. F., 1824, *Origine de la Tapisserie de Bayeux prouvée par elle-même*, Caen.

15 Bates, D. R., 1970, 'Odo Bishop of Bayeux 1049–1097', University of Exeter, unpublished PhD thesis, 49, 88. See also Bates, D. R., 1975, 'The Character and Career of Odo, Bishop of Bayeux (1049/50–1097)', *Speculum* 50, 1–20.

16 For his estates, see GDB and LDB.

17 First proposed by Lancelot, A., 1732, 'Suite, de l'explication d'un monument de Guillaume le Conquérant', *Mémoires de literature tirés des registres de l'Académie royale des Inscriptions et Belles-Lettres depuis l'année MDCCXXVI jusques et compris l'année MDCCXXX*, vol. 7, 602–68. Also see Fowke, F. R., 1898, *The Bayeux Tapestry*, London, 23.

18 McNulty, J. B., 1989, *The Narrative Art of the Bayeux Tapestry*, New York, 76.

19 Corney, B., 1838, *Researches and Conjectures on the Bayeux Tapestry*, London; Tsurushima, H., 2011, '*Hic Est Miles*: Some Images of Three Knights: Turold, Wadard and Vital', in Lewis, Owen-Crocker and Terkla (eds.), *Bayeux Tapestry*, 81–91.

20 Brooks, N. P. and Walker, H. E., 1979, 'The Authority and Interpretation of the Bayeux Tapestry', *ANS* 1, 1–34, at 8.

21 *GG*, 70–71; OV, ii, 134–5.

22 Lewis, M. J., 2016, 'Ecclesiastics in the Bayeux Tapestry', in Henderson, A. C. and Owen-Crocker, G. R. (eds.), *Making Sense of the Bayeux Tapestry: Readings and Reworkings*, Manchester, 86–7.

23 Pastan, E. C. and White, S. D., 2014, *The Bayeux Tapestry and its Contexts: A Reassessment*, Woodbridge.

24 Hicks, 'Queen Edith', 5–9, and Stephenson, P., 'Where a Cleric and Ælfgyva …', 71–4, in Lewis et al. (eds.), *Bayeux Tapestry*.

25 See Bridgeford, A., 2004, *1066: The Hidden History of the Bayeux Tapestry*, London and New York, 191–9, 304–9.

26 Keats-Rohan, K. S. B., 2012, 'Through the Eye of the Needle: Stigand, the Bayeux Tapestry and the Beginnings of the *Historia Anglorum*', in Roffe, D. (ed.), *The English and their Legacy, 900–1200: Essays in Honour of Ann Williams*, Woodbridge, 159–74.

27 *GG*, 176–7.

28 Bertrand, S., 1966, *La Tapisserie de Bayeux et la manière de vivre au onzième siècle*, La Pierre-qui-Vire, 49; Musset, *The Bayeux Tapestry*, 21, 24–5; Wilson, *Bayeux Tapestry*, 204–6; Wingfield Digby, G., 1957, 'Technique and Production', in Stenton, *Bayeux Tapestry*, 48–9.

29 Herren, M. W. (trans.), 1988, Baudri de Bourgeuil, *Adelae Comitissae*, in Brown, *Bayeux Tapestry*, 167–77.

30 Budny, M., 1991, 'The Byrhtnoth Tapestry of Embroidery' in Scragg, D. (ed.), *The Battle of Maldon*, Oxford, 263–78, though this might not have been an illustrated historical account.

31 Dodwell, C. R., 1993, *The Pictorial Arts of the West 800–1200*, New Haven and London, 26.

32 See in particular Hart, C., 2000, 'The Bayeux Tapestry and Schools of Illumination in Canterbury', *ANS* 22, 117–67.

33 Van der Horst, K., Noel, W. and Wüstefeld, W. C. M. (eds.), 1996, *The Utrecht Psalter in Medieval Art: Picturing the Psalms of David*, 't Goy-Houten, 121–65.

34 Wormald, F., 1957, 'Style and Design', in Stenton, *Bayeux Tapestry*, 31.

35 Dodwell, C. R. and Clemoes, P., 1974, *The Old English Illustrated Hexateuch*, Early English Manuscripts in Facsimile 18, Copenhagen.

36 Gameson, R., 1997, *The Study of the Bayeux Tapestry*, Woodbridge, 170.

37 Wormald, 'Style', 32.

38 Lewis, M. J., 2011, 'The Bayeux Tapestry and Oxford, Bodleian Library, Junius 11', in Lewis et al. (eds.), *Bayeux Tapestry*, 105–11.

39 Wilson, *Bayeux Tapestry*, 204. An alternative view is offered by Short, I., 2001, 'The Language of the Bayeux Tapestry Inscription', *ANS* 23, 268–74.

40 Brooks and Walker, 'Authority and Interpretation', 10; Gameson, *Bayeux Tapestry*, 184.

41 Gameson, *Bayeux Tapestry*, 182–91.

42 Grape, *The Bayeux Tapestry*, 47–8.

43 Beech, G., 2005, *Was the Bayeux Tapestry Made in France? The Case for Saint-Florent of Saumur*, London and New York.

44 Gameson, *Bayeux Tapestry*, 172; Pastan and White, *Bayeux Tapestry*, 121.

45 Lewis, M. J., [forthcoming], 'La Tapisserie de Bayeux et l'art anglo-saxon'.

46 Henige, C., 2005, 'Putting the Bayeux Tapestry in its Place', in Owen-Crocker, G. R. (ed.), *King Harold II and the Bayeux Tapestry*, Woodbridge, 125–37.

47 Gibbs-Smith, *Bayeux Tapestry*, 4. For an alternative view, Bouet, P., 2004, 'Is the Bayeux Tapestry Pro-English?', in Bouet, P. et al. (eds.), *The Bayeux Tapestry*, 197–215.

48 See, for example, discussion within Bouet, P. and Neveux, F., 2011, 'Edward the Confessor's Succession According to the Bayeux Tapestry', in Lewis, Owen-Crocker and Terkla (eds.), *Bayeux Tapestry*, 59–65.

49 Lewis, M. J., 2007, 'Identity and Status in the Bayeux Tapestry: The Iconographic and Artefactual Evidence', *ANS* 29, 100–20, at 115.

50 Bouet and Neveux, 'Succession', 63.

51 *VEdR*, 123–5.

52 Barlow, *The Godwins*, 91.

53 Gibbs-Smith, C. H., 1957, 'Notes on the Plates', in Stenton, *Bayeux Tapestry*, 169; Hill, D., 1998, 'The Bayeux Tapestry: The Case of the Phantom Fleet', *Bulletin of the John Rylands Library* 80, 23–31, at 27–8.

54 Stenton, *Bayeux Tapestry*, 9.

55 Gravett, C., 1996, *Hastings 1066: The Fall of Saxon England*, London, 68–76.

56 See, for example, Stephenson, 'Where a Cleric and Ælfgyva …', 71–4.

57 *GG*, 176–7.

58 Gibbs-Smith, 'Notes', 171; Bouet and Neveux, *La Tapisserie de Bayeux*, 56.

59 *GG*, 176–7.

60 Maclagan, E., 1945, *The Bayeux Tapestry*, London and New York, 12; Bertrand, S., 1978, *The Bayeux Tapestry*, Rennes, 20.

61 Bouet and Neveux, 'Succession', 59.

62 See discussion in Owen-Crocker, G. R., 2007, 'Gesture in the Bayeux Tapestry', *ANS* 29, 145–78, at 151.

63 Rule, ed., *Eadmer*, 6 (Bosanquet (trans.), 8).

64 Hart, 'Schools of Illumination', 129–30.

65 *VEdR*, 119.

66 Bouet and Neveux, 'Succession', 65.

67 Beech, *Bayeux Tapestry*, 61.

68 *GG*, 176–7.

69 Beech responds to these criticisms in Beech, G., 2011, 'The Breton Campaign and the Possibility that the Bayeux Tapestry was Produced

in the Loire Valley', in Lewis et al. (eds.), *Bayeux Tapestry*, 10–16, at 14–16.

70 Walker, I. W., 1997, *Harold: The Last Anglo-Saxon King*, Stroud, 103–12, 152–65; Lewis, M. J., 2008, *The Real World of the Bayeux Tapestry*, Stroud, 46–7.

71 Bachrach, B. S., 1986, 'Some Observations on the Military Administration of the Norman Conquest', *ANS* 8, 1–25, at 9; Walker, *Harold*, 166.

72 Bradbury, J., 1998, *The Battle of Hastings*, Stroud, 139.

73 Brooks and Walker, 'Authority and Interpretation', 23–34.

74 Hill, D. and McSween, J., 2011, 'The Storage Chest and the Repairs and Changes in the Bayeux Tapestry', in Lewis et al. (eds.), *Bayeux Tapestry*, 44–51.

75 Foys, M. K., 2009, 'Pulling the Arrow Out: The Legend of Harold's Death and the Bayeux Tapestry', in Foys, M. K., Overbey, K. E. and Terkla, D. (eds.), *The Bayeux Tapestry: New Interpretations*, Woodbridge, 158–75.

76 Grape, *Bayeux Tapestry*, 69.

77 Gameson, *Bayeux Tapestry*, 194.

78 Maclagan, *Bayeux Tapestry*, 22.

79 Lewis, 'Identity and Status', 119; Lewis, *Real World*, 181–2.

80 Lewis, 'Identity and Status', 119.

81 Lewis, *Real World*, 188.

82 Lewis, 'Authority and Status', 103–7.

83 Lewis, M. J., 2016, 'Intertextuality in the Bayeux Tapestry: The Form and Function of Dress and Clothing', in Hyer, M. C. and Frederick, J. (eds.), *Textiles, Text, Intertext: Essays in Honour of Gale R. Owen-Crocker*, Woodbridge, 69–84, at 78–80. Significant numbers (over 60) of late Anglo-Saxon brooches have been recorded by the Portable Antiquities Scheme (see www.finds.org.uk).

84 Lewis, 'Authority and Status', 105.

85 Lewis, *Real World*, 183–9.

86 Lewis, M. J., 2009, 'Embroidery Errors in the Bayeux Tapestry and their Relevance for Understanding its Design and Production', in Foys, Overbey and Terkla (eds.), *Bayeux Tapestry*, 130–40.

87 Although the general consensus is that the Bayeux Tapestry was made in England, it is possible (albeit less likely) that a Norman was its designer, though clearly inspired by Anglo-Saxon art.

88 The author observed such while witnessing a photographic study of the Bayeux Tapestry in January 2017. See also Gameson, *Bayeux Tapestry*, 193, who inferred that the design would have been sketched out.

89 Levé, A., 1919, *La Tapisserie de la reine Mathilde, dite la Tapisserie de Bayeux*, Paris, 148–9; Gibbs-Smith, *Bayeux Tapestry*, 6.

90 Messent, J., 1999, *The Bayeux Tapestry Embroiderers' Story*, Thirsk, 48.

91 Lewis, 'Embroidery Errors', lists the errors in the Bayeux Tapestry.

92 Musset, *Bayeux Tapestry*, 72.

93 See discussion in Pastan and White, *Bayeux Tapestry*, 159–61, 171–82. Also see Bernstein, D. J., 1986, *The Mystery of the Bayeux Tapestry*, London, 124–35; McNulty, J. B., 1989, *The Narrative Art of the Bayeux Tapestry Master*, New York, 2–3.

94 Grape, *Bayeux Tapestry*, 41–3; Musset, *Bayeux Tapestry*, 72–5; Lewis, *Real World*, 9.

95 Bertrand, S. and Lemagnen, S., 1996, *The Bayeux Tapestry*, Rennes, 13; Bouet and Neveux, *Tapisserie de Bayeux*, 29, noted that the peacocks are colour-coded to match William and Harold.

96 Bernstein, *Bayeux Tapestry*, 128–34; Pastan and White, *Bayeux Tapestry*, 154–82.

97 Wormald, 'Style and Design', 28; Bouet and Neveux, *Tapisserie de Bayeux*, 142; Musset, *Bayeux Tapestry*, 114; Bernstein, *Bayeux Tapestry*, 74–8.

98 Wormald, 'Style and Design', 27–8; Grape, *Bayeux Tapestry*, 43.

99 Grape, *Bayeux Tapestry*, 79, suggested that such 'erotic detail' was a 'durable feature of French religious art', though his parallels are of much later date than the Bayeux Tapestry.

100 Clarke, H., 2013, 'The Identity of the Designer of the Bayeux Tapestry', *ANS* 35, 119–39. See also Pastan and White, *Bayeux Tapestry*, 121–2, 194–5, for a general discussion of Scotland's involvement in the Tapestry.

101 Lewis, *Real World*, 179.

102 Bernstein, *Bayeux Tapestry*, 82–8, 192–5; Terkla, D., 1995, 'Cut on the Norman Bias: Fabulous Borders and Visual Glosses on the Bayeux Tapestry', *Word & Image* 11, 264–90.

103 Pastan and White, *Bayeux* Tapestry, 171–82 provided a 'revisionist view' of the significance of the borders as part of their hypothesis that the Tapestry was produced by the community of St Augustine's in the context of Anglo-Norman politics following the Conquest.

104 Bertrand, S., 1957, 'The History of the Bayeux Tapestry', in Stenton, *Bayeux Tapestry*, 82.

105 As observed by Gurney, H., 1817, 'Observations of the Bayeux Tapestry', *Archaeologia* 18, 359. See also Hicks, *Bayeux Tapestry*, 118–19; Brown, *Bayeux Tapestry*, 13.

106 Bertrand and Lemagnen, *Bayeux Tapestry*, 29; Bouet and Neveux, *Tapisserie de Bayeux*, 89; Lewis, *Real World*, 31.

107 Messent, *Embroiderers' Story*, 76–7.

6 William the Conqueror and London's early castles

1 *GG*, 162 (*Vidit enim inprimis necessarium magnopere Lundonienses coerceri*).

2 Bates, *William the Conqueror*, 254.

3 *GG*, 150.

4 *GG*, 158; Dalton, P., 2015, 'William the Peacemaker: The Submission of the English to the Duke of Normandy, October 1066–January 1067', in Dalton, P. and Luscombe, D. (eds.), 2015, *Rulership and Rebellion in the Anglo-Norman World, c.1066–c.1216: Essays in Honour of Professor Edmund King*, Farnham and Burlington VT, 21–44, at 39.

5 *GG*, 158–9; *Acta*, no. 180. On the writ see also Bates, *William the Conqueror*, 269, 270–1.

6 Irvine, S., 2004 (ed.), *Anglo-Saxon Chronicle, a Collaborative Edition: Volume 7, ms. E: A Semi-Diplomatic Edition with Introduction and Indices*, 108 (*weall þe hi worhton onbutan þone tur*); Swanton, 234 ('the wall which they constructed around the Tower').

7 Hinted at in Stenton, F. M., 1935, *Norman London*, London, 5.

8 *OV*, ii, 194–5 (*Egressus Lundonia rex dies aliquot in propinquo loco Bercingis morabatur dum firmamenta quaedem ... perficerentur*).

9 *GG*, 114 (*Normanni prima munitione Penevessellum, altera Hastingas occupavere*).

10 *GND*, ii, 166 (*ubi statim firmissimo vallo castrum condidit*).

11 Taylor, A. J., 1969, 'Evidence for a pre-Conquest Origin for the Chapels in Hastings and Pevensey Castles', *Chateau-Gaillard* 3, 144–51, at 150–1.

12 Fulford, M. and Rippon, S., 2011, *Pevensey Castle: Excavations in the Roman Fort and Medieval Keep, 1993–5*, Wessex Archaeology. Archaeological evidence for William's interventions, however, is lacking.

13 Above, p.37.

14 On this, see for example Bouet, P., 2016, 'Châteaux et residences princières dans la Tapisserie de Bayeux', in Davies, J. A., Riley, A., Levesque, J.-M. and Lapiche, C., 135–46, 39.

15 *GG*, 144. The *Carmen*, 36, line 607, has the men of Dover surrender the keys to the *castrum* while en route from Hastings, and makes no mention of building fortifications.

16 Brown, R. A., 1969, 'The Norman Conquest and the Genesis of English Castles', *Château Gaillard* 3, 1–14.

17 Creighton, O. H., 2005, *Castles and Landscapes: Power, Community and Fortification in Medieval England*, Sheffield, 280.

18 *GG*, 164 (*intra moenia munitionem construxit*); Barlow, F., 1964, 'Guenta', Appendix to Biddle, M., 1964, 'Excavations at Winchester, 1962–4', *Antiquaries Journal*, xliv, 188–219, 217–19.

19 *GG*, 160, 162 (*dum firmamenta quaedam in urbe contra mobilitatem ingentis ac feri populi perficerentur. Vidit enim inprimis necessarium magnopere Lundonienses coerceri*).

20 I am grateful to David Bates for making these points.

21 *GG*, 148 (*Praemisit ergo Lundoniam qui munitionem in ipsa construerent urbe*).

22 *GG*, 10 (*Nam praeter alia firmamenta, quae moliri consuevit belli necessitudo*).

23 *GG*, 34 (*editius firmamentum occupavit*). Normally *editus*.

24 *GG*, 62.

25 E.g. Stenton, F. M., 1971 (3rd ed.), *Anglo-Saxon England*, 599; Hugh Braun suggested in 1937 – alas, not believably – that William of Poitiers was referring to 'Barking Hill', which he believed to have been the name of the eminence occupied by the church of All Hallows Barking: Braun, H., 1937, 'London's First Castle', *Transactions of the London and Middlesex Archaeological Society* 7, 445–51, at 447.

26 E.g. Douglas, *William the Conqueror*, 207 (but see also ibid, n3). Or it is deftly omitted (Bates, D., 1989, *William the Conqueror*, London; Matthew, D. J. A., 1966, *The Norman Conquest*, London).

27 Very little has been written on the Confessor's palace. See Wilson, C., 2015, 'A Monument to St Edward the Confessor: Henry III's Great Chamber at Westminster and its Paintings', in Rodwell, W. and Tatton-Brown, T., 2015, 152–86 at 154; Crook, J. and Harris, R., 2002, 'Reconstructing the Lesser Hall: An Interim Report from the Medieval Palace of Westminster Research Project', *Parliamentary History* 21, 22–61, 24–7.

28 *VCH Essex*, ii, 116; DB Essex IX.7.

29 Dalton, 'William the Peacemaker', 40.

30 Wolstenholme, J., 1855, *Two Lectures on the History and Antiquities of Berkhamsted*, London. 80; Ekwall, E., 1960, *Concise Oxford Dictionary of English Place Names*, 39.

31 Although Bates, *William the Conqueror*, 266, suggests that 'decisions at this time' – i.e. after the meeting of Christmas 1066 – 'would have had the solemnity that had not been present before the coronation'.

32 Turner, G. T., 1912, 'William the Conqueror's March to London in 1066', *EHR* 27, 209–25, at 224; Douglas, *William the Conqueror*, 207 n3.

33 Orderic in *GND*, ii, 208.

34 OV, ii, 214 (*Locum vero intra moenia ad extruendum castellum delegit*); Colvin, H. M., Brown, R. A. and Taylor, A. (eds.), 1963, *History of the King's Works*, 6 vols., 196382, I, 20–1.

35 On the last point see Drage, C., 1987, 'Urban Castles', in Schofield, J. and Leech, R. (eds.), *Urban Archaeology in Britain*, 117–32, at 117, 119; Armitage, E., 1912, *Early Norman Castles of the British Isles*, 95–6.

36 Impey, E., 2002, 'The Donjon at Avranches (Normandy),' *The Archaeological Journal* 159, 249–57.

37 Delacompagne, F., 2006, 'Une maison urbaine à Bayeux (IXᵉ–XVIIIᵉ siècle). De la maison canoniale à la maison de la fabrique', in Bouet,

P. and Neveux, F. (eds.), *Les Villes normandes au Moyen Âge: renaissance, essor, crise*, Caen, 159–76, at 159, Fig. 1.

38 Gauthiez, B., 1992, 'Hypothèses sur la fortification de Rouen au onzième siècle. Le donjon, la tour de Richard II, et l'enceinte de Guillaume', *ANS* 14, 61–76, at 63–9.

39 Biddle, M., 1987, 'Early Norman Winchester', in Holt (ed.), *Domesday Studies*, at 311–31, at 312–14; Barlow, F., 1964, 'Guenta', *Antiquaries Journal* 44, 217–19.

40 Drage, 'Urban Castles', 119; Davison, B., 1967, 'Three Eleventh-Century Earthworks in England: Their Excavation and Implications', *Château Gaillard* 1, 39–48 at 41; Parsons, D., 2004, 'Urban Castles and Late Anglo-Saxon Towns', in Lindley, P., 2004, 30–40, at 36, Fig. 6; Fox, A., 1952, *Roman Exeter (Isca Dumnoniorum). Excavations in the War-Damaged Areas, 1945–47*, Manchester, 2, Fig. a.

41 Darvill, T., 1988, 'Excavations on the Site of the Early Norman Castle at Gloucester, 1983–84', *Medieval Archaeology* 32, 1–49, at 1–3 and Fig. 1.

42 Stocker, D., 2004, The Two Early Castles of Lincoln', in Lindley, P., *The Early History of Lincoln Castle*, Occasional Papers in Lincolnshire History and Archaeology, 12, Lincoln, 9–22, at 9. In this case, though, the remainder of the Roman enclosure served as the outer bailey.

43 Roffe, D., 2015, 'Introduction', in Keats-Rohan, K. S. B., 2015, 1–8, at 3.

44 Pounds, N. G. J., 1990, 7.

45 Haslam, J., 1988, 'Parishes, Churches, Wards and Gates in Eastern London, 35–44, 35–41, in Blair, W. J., *Minsters and Parish Churches: The Local Church in Transition, 900–1200*, Oxford, puts forward a more detailed and confident account.

46 Derek Keene, personal comment; see also Haslam, 'Parishes', 35.

47 Lincoln (160 houses), York (an entire shire or ward), Shrewsbury (51 houses). Destruction on a smaller scale occurred also at Cambridge, Gloucester, Huntingdon, Stamford, Wallingford and Warwick. For a useful summary see English, B., 1995, 'Towns, Mottes and Ringworks of the Conquest', in Ayton, A. and Price, J. L. (eds.), *The Medieval Military Revolution*, London, 45–61, at 47.

48 Fradley, M., 2015, 'Urban Castles in the Middle Ages: Wallingford in Context', in Keats-Rohan, K., 2015, 20–7, at 25; for Oxford, see also Dodd, A. (ed.), 2003, *Oxford Before the University. The Late Saxon and Norman Archaeology of the Thames Crossing, the Defences and the Town*, Oxford Archaeology, Thames Valley Landscapes Monograph No. 17, at 41, with references to excavation archives.

49 Davison, B. K., 1967, 'Three Eleventh-Century Earthworks in England: Their Excavation and Implications', *Château Gaillard* 1, 39–48, 40, and Figs. 1 and 2.

50 Harold Sands suggested to Ella Armitage that the first castle 'may simply have been a bank and palisade across the angle of the Roman wall' (Armitage, E., 1913, *The Early Norman Castles of the British Isles*, New York 22 n2); Clapham, A. W. and Godfrey, W., 1912, *Some Famous Buildings and Their Story*, 32–3; Colvin, H. M., 1963, *The History of the King's Works*, vol. 2, 709.

51 Parnell, G., 1983, 'The Western Defences of the Inmost Ward, Tower of London', *Transactions of the London and Middlesex Archaeological Society*, vol. 34, 107–50, 111–13; Parnell, G., 1993, *The Tower of London*, London, 17; on the pottery see Redknapp, M., 1983, 'The Pottery', in Parnell, G., 1983, 120–49, 135–49.

52 King, D. J. C. and Alcock, L., 1969, 'Ringworks of England and Wales', *Château Gaillard* 3, 90–127, at 93–4.

53 Liddiard, R., 2005, *Castles in Context: Power, Symbolism and Landscape*, 19.

54 King and Alcock, 'Ringworks of England and Wales', *Château Gaillard* 3, 90–127, at 117 (re. Tower: Exeter and Winchester are not included in their list).

55 Hodgett, G. A. J. (ed.), 1971, *The Cartulary of Holy Trinity Aldgate*, London Record Society, London, 190, no. 964; 191, no. 966; Neininger, F. (ed.), 1999, *English Episcopal Acta 15: London, 1076–1187*, Oxford, 28–9, no. 38.

56 Glasgow University Library, MS Hunter U.2.6, fo. 171v; see also Brooke, C. N. L. and Keir, G., 1975, *London 800–1216: The Shaping of a City*, London. The text: *Anno incarnatione dominice M C LVII anno scilicet III Henrici iunioris tempore Radulfi prioris et Hugonis de Mateni archidiaconi orta est dissensio quedam inter nos et presbiterum ecclesie sancti Petri de Ballivo de parte quondam parochialis ecclesie sancti Bothulfi foris Algate.*

57 *Calendar of Liberate Rolls Henry III*, 1916, vol. 1 (1226–4), London, 258; *Calendar of Close Rolls Henry III*, 1908, vol. 3, 1234–7, London, 424.

58 *Calendar of Liberate Rolls Henry III*, 1916, vol. 1 (1226–4), London, 396.

59 *Calendar of Liberate Rolls Henry III*, 1916, vol. 1 (1226–4), London, 444, 449.

60 Ducange, Sieur de, 1883–7, *Glossarium medie et infimae latinitatis*, 10 vols., Paris, x, 539; Latham, R. E. and Howlett, D. R. et al. (eds.), 1975–2013, *Dictionary of Medieval Latin from British Sources*, 17 vols., Oxford, i, 175–6.

61 Foster, C. W. (ed.), 1931–73, *Registrum Antiquissimum of the Cathedral Church of Lincoln*, 10 vols., Lincoln Record Society, Hereford, ix, 217–18, no. 2629; 203, no. 2611.

62 Popescu, E., 2004, 'Norwich Castle Fee', *Medieval Archaeology* 68, 209–19, at 213–14. St Martin's was demolished in 1562 (Messent, C. J., 1932, *The City Churches of Norwich*, Norwich, 63–4).

63 The church was given to St Frideswide's in 1122, Wigram, S. R. (ed.), 1895–6, *Cartulary of the Monastery of St Frideswide at Oxford*, 2 vols., Oxford, i, 11 (*sancti petri ad castrum*). It stood at the junction of Queen Street and New Inn Hall Street.

64 Stocker, 'The Two Early Castles', 9 and Fig. 1.

65 Popescu, E. S., 2009, *Norwich Castle: Excavations and Historical Survey, 1987–98*, 2 vols., Norwich, ii, 980, Table 12; Popescu, E., 2016, 'Norwich Castle', in Davies, J. A., Riley, A., Levesque, J.-M. and Lapiche, C., 2016, *Castles and the Anglo-Norman World*, Oxford, 3–30, at 14, Fig. 1.9; 18, Fig. 1.13; and 27.

66 Re. Nottingham: Marshall and Foulds, 1997, 'The Royal Castle', in *A Centenary History of Nottingham*, Beckett, J. (ed.), Manchester, 44.

67 Re. Rochester, see Gomme, 1887, 183; Flight and Harrison, 1978, 'Rochester Castle 1976', *Archaeologia Cantiana* 104, 27–60, at 28, Fig. 1.

68 Re. Chester, see Pounds, N. J. G., 1990, *The Medieval Castle in England and Wales*, 211, and Morris, R., c.1893, *Chester in the Plantagenet and Tudor Reigns*, Chester, 107–8.

69 Fournier, G., 1964, 'Le Château de Puiset au debut du XIIe siècle et sa place dans l'evolution de l'architecture militaire', *Bulletin Monumental* 122, 355–74, at 361–3.

70 Stocker, 'The Two Early Castles', 17 and Fig. 7.

71 Popescu, 'Norwich Castle Fee', 209–15; for the charter of Edward III, Hudson, J. and Tingley, J., 1906, *The Records of the City of Norwich*, 2 vols., Norwich, i, 23–7.

72 Drage, C., 1990, *Nottingham Castle: A Place Full Royal*, Nottingham, 28 and Fig. 4.

73 Cronne, H. A. and Davis, R. H. C. (eds.), 1968, *Regesta regum anglo-normannorum, vol. 3, Regesta Regis Stephani ac Mathildis Imperatricis ac Gaufridi et Henrici Ducum Normannorum, 1135–1154*, Oxford, iii, 99, no. 274 (*et concede illi ... Custodiam turris Londonie cum parvo castello quod fuit Ravengeri*). See also Colvin, H. M., Brown, R. A. and Taylor, A. (eds.), *History of the King's Works*, 6 vols., 1963–82, vol. 2, 707.

74 For a discussion of the terms and their meaning, see Round, J. H., 1892, *Geoffrey de Mandeville: A Study of the Anarchy*, London, Appendix O, 328–46; in the case of Colchester, Gloucester, Hereford and Worcester see *Geoffrey*, 328–9, citing charters. On Gloucester, see also Cronne and Davis (eds.), *Regesta*, iii, 149, no. 387. Arques, Caen and Torigny are also mentioned in *Geoffrey* (333, 331, 334), the source for Arques and Torigny being Howlett, R. (ed.), 1884–9, Robert of Torigny, 'Chronica', in *Chronicles of Stephen, Henry II and Richard*, Rolls Series, 4 vols., London, iv, 81–315, at 106, 161. The source relating to Caen is Stapleton, T. (ed.), 1844, *Magni Rotuli scaccarii Normanniae sub Regibus Angliae*, 2 vols., i, 56.

75 Hodgett (ed.), *The Cartulary of Holy Trinity Aldgate*, 228; re. earlier passages, Derek Keene, personal communication.

76 '*a porta de Algate usque ad portam Ballii Turris que nuncupatur Cungata et tota venella vocata Chykenlane versus Berkyngchirche usque ad cimiterium*', Hodgett (ed.), *The Cartulary of Holy Trinity Aldgate*, 228.

77 On the plan, see Keay, A., 2001, *The Elizabethan Tower of London: the Haiward and Gascoyne plan of 1597*, London Topographical Society, London, no. 158.

78 At or after the demise of the bailey, the name seems to have become attached to a gate called the 'Congate', described in 1340 as 'beside the chapel', and thus opening through the Roman wall close to the White Tower chapel, near or beside the Wardrobe Tower (TNA, E 101 470/8). I am grateful to Jeremy Ashbee for this information and interpretation.

79 De Boüard, M., 1979, *Le Château de Caen*, 10–11.

80 ASC (Swanton (trans.)), 234.

81 Colvin, H. M., Brown, R. A. and Taylor, A. (eds.), *History of the King's Works*, 6 vols., 1963–82, HMSO, ii, 712.

82 Gibbs, M. (ed.), 1939, *Early Charters of the Cathedral Church of St Paul*, Camden 3rd ser., 58, London, 22–3; Johnson, C. and Cronne, H. A. (eds.), 1956, *Regesta Regum Anglo-Normannorum, vol. ii, Regesta Regis Henrici Primi, 1100–1135*, Oxford, 102, no. 991.

83 P.155; Robertson, J. C. (ed.), 1875–85, *Materials for the History of Thomas Becket, Archbishop of Canterbury*, 7 vols., Rolls Series, London, vol. 3, 1–15, iii, 220–1 (*Habet ab Oriente arcem palatinam, maximam et fortissimam, cuius et area et muri a fundamento profundissimo exurgunt; caemento cum sanguine animalium temperato. Ab Occidente duo castella munitissima*).

84 Stenton, F. M., 1990, *Norman London by William Fitz Stephen*, New York, 8. The full text is printed in Bateson, 1902, 'A London Municipal Collection of the Reign of King John', *English Historical Review* 17, 480–511, 707–30, 485–6.

85 See Bentley, D., 1987, 'The Western Stream Reconsidered: An Enigma in the Landscape', *London Archaeologist*, v, no. 12, 328–34, Fig. 1.

86 Bentley, 'The Western Stream', 328–32 and Fig. 1. See also Tyler, 2000, 24; Gaimster, D. and Bradley, J., 2002, 'Medieval Britain and Ireland, 2000', *Medieval Archaeology* 46, 163, 1246–64.

87 Gibbs (ed.), 1938, *Early Charters of the Cathedral Church of St Paul, London*, Camden 3rd ser., 59, London, 137–8, no. 179; Moore, N., 1918, *The History of St Bartholomew's Hospital*, 2 vols., vol. 1, 213 (*ballio extra Ludgate*); Maxwell-Lyte, 1890–1915, *A Descriptive Catalogue of Ancient Deeds in the Public Record Office: Prepared under the Superintendence of the Deputy Keeper of the Records*, 6 vols., London, vol. 4, 177 A 7499 (*in ballio*). The church occurs as Sancti Petri de Ballio in 1253, in a confirmation charter of Roger

of Salisbury's grant of the church to St Bartholomew's Priory, and so very probably reproducing a suffix it had had since the 12th century (*Cartae antiquae*, Conway Davies, no. 340, 14). The dedication itself supplanted an earlier one to St Edmund. See Harben, H. A., 1918, *A Dictionary of London: Being Notes Topographical and Historical Relating to the Streets and Principal Buildings in the City of London*, London, 523–4, for later examples.

88 McCann, B., 1993, *Fleet Valley Project*, interim report, Museum of London, 51 and Figs. 18, 21 and 22.

89 Derek Keene, personal communication.

90 Based on a 14th-century description of the boundaries of the Soke of Robert FitzWalter, Riley, H. T. (ed.), 1859–62, 'Liber Custumarum', in *Munimenta Gildhallae Londoniensis*, 4 vols., Rolls Series, London, ii, part 1, 150; Keene, D., 2004, 'Alfred and London', in *Alfred the Great: Papers from the Eleventh-Centenary Conferences*, Reuter, T. A., Aldershot.

91 Mortimer, R., 1989, 'The Baynards of Baynard's Castle', in Harper-Bill, C. and Harvey, R. (eds.), *The Ideals and Practice of Medieval Knighthood*, Woodbridge et al., 241–53, at 252; Johnson and Cronne (eds.), *Regesta regum anglo normannorum, vol ii*, no. 749, 52–3.

92 *DP*, i, 327; Mortimer, 'The Baynards', 241.

93 The *Chronicon* (British Library, MS Cotton Cleopatra C3) is not published, but excerpts are given by Dugdale, *Monasticon* (Caley, Ellis and Bulkeley Bandinel (eds.), vi, 147). Little Dunmow was the Essex seat of the Baynards, who had founded the priory in 1106. The chronicle was begun by Nicholas de Brompfield, Canon of Little Dunmow, in 1259 (*VCH Essex*, ii, 150). William Baynard forfeited for rebellion (ASC, Swanton (trans.), 243; HH, 457).

94 ASC (Swanton (trans.), 219).

95 Gibbs (ed.), *Early Charters*, 15, no. 13.

96 Gibbs (ed.), *Early Charters*, 23–4 (*tantum de fossato mei castelli ex parte Tamesis ad meridiem quantum opus fuerit ad faciendum murum eiusdem ecclesie tantum de eodem fossato quantum sufficiat ad faciendum viam extra murum ex altera parte ecclesie ad aquilonem quantum predictus episcopus de eodem fossato diruit*: 'as much of the ditch of my castle (*castellum*) on the south side [of St Paul's] as was needed to make a [precinct] wall of St Paul's, and as much of the ditch as was required for making a way outside the wall, and on the north side of the church, as much as the bishop destroyed of the same ditch').

97 Derek Keene, personal communication.

98 Stenton, *Norman London*, 8. See above, note 83, for references to the printed full text.

99 Cathcart King, D. J., 1988, *Castellarium Anglicanum: An Index and Bibliography of the Castles in England, Wales, and the Island*, 2 vols., New York, 8.

100 Chibnall, M., 1996, *Anglo-Norman England, 1066–1166*, 11; *GG*, 142, mentions no name, but notes '*dispositaque custodia Hastingas cum strenuo praefecto*'. His identity as Humphrey of Tilleul is given by Orderic (OV, ii, 220): Humphrey, '*qui Hastingas a prima die constructionis ad custodiendum susceperat*'; see also Loyd, L. C., 1951, *The Origins of Some Anglo-Norman Families*, Harleian Society Publications, 103, Leeds, 85.
101 *GG*, 164; Barlow, 'Guenta', 219.
102 *GG*, 164.
103 *DP*, 226–7; Green, J. A., 1983, 'The Sheriffs of the Conqueror', *ANS* 5, 129–43, at 131–2.
104 Clarke, *The English Nobility*, 154; Green, *The Aristocracy*, 37; Round, *Geoffrey de Mandeville*, 37 and n2.
105 Green, 'The Sheriffs', 131–2.
106 Ravengar had held land in Ramsden (DB Essex 18.6), in Wheatley and Wickford (DB Essex 18.7), all three of Odo of Bayeux, at Bulphan (DB Essex 9.2) of St Mary's Barking, and in West Tilbury (DB Essex 30.21), of Geoffrey de Mandeville. See also *VCH Essex*, vol. 1, London 1903, 508 n7.
107 DB Essex 30.21.
108 Mortimer, 'The Baynards', 251–2.
109 Ashbee, J., 2008, 'The Function of the White Tower Under the Normans', in Impey, E. (ed.), *The White Tower*, London and New Haven, 125–40, at 128–36.
110 *GG*, 164.

7 1066 and warfare: the context and place (Senlac) of the Battle of Hastings

1 And possibly a third if Adam of Bremen's report of an Irish king being killed at Stamford Bridge is correct, cited by van Houts, E., 1995, 'The Norman Conquest Through European Eyes', *EHR* 110, 832–53, at 836 (reprinted in van Houts, *History and Family Traditions*, chapter 8).
2 Reuter, T., 1999, 'Carolingian and Ottonian Warfare', in Keen, M. (ed.), *Medieval Warfare: A History*, Oxford, 13–35, 18–19. The wars of the 1070s between Henry IV and the Saxons were to generate a similarly rich literature.
3 In addition to other, much shorter, contemporary Norman and English accounts, notably in the *Gesta Normannorum Ducum* by William of Jumièges and in the 'D' and 'E' versions of the Anglo-Saxon Chronicle.
4 I have followed the numbering of the BT scenes in Lucien Musset, *The Bayeux Tapestry*.
5 Keegan, J., 1976, *The Face of Battle*, Harmondsworth, 13–77.

6 Bachrach, B. S. and Bachrach, D. S., 2017, *Warfare in Medieval Europe c.400–c.1453*, London, 13.

7 Abels, R., 2008, 'Cultural Representation and the Practice of War in the Middle Ages', *Journal of Medieval Military History* 6, 1–31.

8 Though WP did twice, once only allusively, refer to them; *GG*, ii.8, 25, 113–15, 141.

9 Crossbowmen are not shown at all, and the role of heavily armed infantry seriously underplayed; France, J., 2004, 'The importance of the Bayeux Tapestry for the history of war', in Bouet, P. et al. (eds.), *The Bayeux Tapestry*, 289–99, 293.

10 Bennett, M., 1998, 'The Myth of the Military Supremacy of Knightly Cavalry', in Strickland, M. (ed.), *Armies, Chivalry and Warfare in Medieval Britain and France*, Stamford, 304–16; France, J., 1999, *Western Warfare in the Age of the Crusades 1000–1300*, London, 53–63, 150–86.

11 Although, as scene 49 shows, the designer was capable of fitting a hill into his main register. On the difficulties faced by cavalry attacking uphill, see Bachrach and Bachrach, *Warfare*, 294.

12 See, for example, the role played by a hillock in both the Tapestry (scenes 53–4) and in *GR*, i, 454–5. The hillock appears also in Wace (*Roman de Rou*, 282–3, line 8613), but only after he had already written more than 600 lines on the battle. Although Wace knew that Harold's banner had been raised where Battle Abbey later stood (248–9, lines 6964–6), and where as victor William raised his own (286–7, lines 8881–6), for him the hill was a place up which the clergy and servants climbed in order to watch the battle (268–9, lines 7941–8). The 'hillock' does not appear on the detailed contour map in Hare, J., 1985, *Battle Abbey: The Eastern Range and the Excavations of 1978–80*, London.

13 In any case there is no reference to *bellum de Hastinges* in Domesday Sussex.

14 He has William disembarking at Hastings and Harold heading straight for Hastings, *GR*, i, 416–17, 448–53. Equally influenced by BT is the text of Henry of Huntingdon, HH, 388–9. ASC 'D' and 'E' reported that William landed or built a castle there.

15 *GG*, 172–3.

16 The 'C' Chronicle ends with Stamford Bridge.

17 Wace's belief that the English 'made a ditch to one side which ran through the fields' is just one of the ways in which his long narrative reflects good 12th- century battle practice, not the realities on the ground at Battle; *Roman de Rou*, 258–9, lines 7487–8. See Bennett, M., 1989, 'Wace and Warfare', *ANS* 11, 37–58 (reprinted in Strickland, *Anglo-Norman Warfare*, 230–50).

18 *GR*, i, 434–5, here describing William's defence of Normandy in 1054. But it may be, as Richard Abels has argued, that, unlike

William, Harold lived within a battle-seeking military culture; Abels, R., 2001, 'From Alfred to Harold II: The Military Failure of the Late Anglo-Saxon State', in Abels, R. and Bachrach, B. S. (eds.), *The Normans and Their Adversaries at War*, Woodbridge, 15–30, at 30. Not until the 12th century do we find accounts suggesting that Harold was advised to leave the fighting to others.

19 Scenes 49–50.

20 *GG*, 14–15, 24–7, 114–17.

21 Marianus Scotus, *Chronicon*, MGH Scriptores v, 559. Cited in van Houts, 'The Norman Conquest Through European Eyes', 839.

22 *GG*, 116–17, 126–7. William of Malmesbury knew that some people exaggerated English numbers, *GR*, i, 422–3.

23 Bachrach, B. S., 1986, 'Some Observations on the Military Administration of the Norman Conquest', *ANS* 8, 1–25, at 2.

24 In any case, both 'occupying' and 'crest of a ridge' are imprecise and subjective concepts.

25 Bates, *William the Conqueror*, 229.

26 Only an author living far away, Amato of Monte Cassino, offered numbers, but this in a text that survives only in a 14th-century French translation of a Latin original. Cited by van Houts, 'The Norman Conquest Through European Eyes', 849 n4.

27 Strickland, M. and Hardy, R., 2005, *The Great Warbow: From Hastings to the Mary Rose*, Stroud, 6; Strickland, M., 1997, 'Military Technology and Conquest: The Anomaly of Anglo-Saxon England', *ANS* 19, 353–82, at 355–9.

28 HH, 392–3, and see chapter 4.

29 Although Guy of Amiens asserted that shields were of little use against crossbow bolts, he mentioned missilemen only early in his 230 lines on the battle; *Carmen*, 20–1, 24–5, lines 337–40 and 381–2. WP also wrote them into the start of the battle, *GG*, 126–9, and then mentioned then only once more, after the Normans had won the upper hand and the badly weakened English 'took their punishment', 132–3.

30 HH, 394–5. Given that arrows gain in velocity and inflict higher casualties the greater the height from which they descend, it seems likely that the Norman archers did their best to loft their arrows from the start. On the ballistics, see Bowlus, C. R., 2006, *The Battle of Lechfeld*, Aldershot, 30–6.

31 *GR*, 454–7; HH, 394–5. The same motif is in line 463 of Baudri of Bourgueil's poem, 'To Countess Adela', addressed to the Conqueror's daughter Adela, and thought to have been written before 1107 when he became archbishop of Dol, Otter, M., 1996, 'Baudri of Bourgueil, "To Countess Adela"', *Exemplaria* 8, 60–141. This is to discount Amato of Monte Cassino, whose lost Latin text, written c.1080, might also have included it.

32 For discussion of this, see Gillingham, J., 2007, 'Holding to the Rules of War (*Bellica iura tenentes*): Right Conduct Before, During

and After Battle in North-Western Europe in the Eleventh Century', *ANS* 29, 1–15.

33 *GND*, i, 168–9. He completed this work in 1070.

34 *GND*, i, 168–9. Given this, it is plain that WJ cannot, in the immediately preceding sentence, have written that Harold was killed in the first attack. Most likely the word 'first' came from the pen of a careless copyist – and an early one, since the word is in all the surviving manuscripts.

35 Porter, R., 2012, '"On the Very Spot": In Defence of Battle', *English Heritage Historical Review* 7, 5–17.

36 ASC 'E', 1087.

37 'on the site of the battle in memory of this victory and for the absolution of the sins of all who were killed', *Brevis Relatio*, 33.

38 Freeman, E. A., 1873, *History of the Norman Conquest*, revised edn., vol. 3, New York and Oxford, 297. Whether or not Freeman was right to envisage the lower ground on either side as a quagmire in October, the 'isthmus' acts as a watershed for streams running east and west.

39 Hare, J. N., 1981, 'The Buildings of Battle Abbey: A Preliminary Survey', *ANS* 3, 78–95, at 80.

40 For example, Brown, R. A., 1981, puts the ridge at 6–800 yards, with troops drawn up 400 yards to the west of Harold's standard and 200–400 yards to the east; 'The Battle of Hastings', *ANS* 3, 1–21, at 10 (reprinted, Strickland, *Anglo-Norman Warfare*, 161–81, at 170).

41 Although great abbeys certainly had the power to divert roads, it is unlikely that this happened here, since there was little reason why the earlier route should have climbed to the top of the hill only to come down again almost immediately. On this point see Lawson, M. K., 2002, *The Battle of Hastings 1066*, Stroud, 59 n29.

42 Only if the Normans had tried to go right round the English left so as to attack them from the rear would they have found 'slopes so steep as to be unassailable', Ramsay, J., 1898, *The Foundations of England*, 2 vols., vol. 2, 29. But to outflank the English left as conventionally reconstructed, they would not have had far to go.

43 While noting that this 'deployment has been ignored or skated over by nearly all historians, but must have given William some anxious thought', Lemmon reckoned that an earlier deployment and advance in line 'was precluded by the broken nature of the ground and the two marshy valleys', Lemmon, C. H., 1956, *The Field of Hastings*, St Leonards-on-Sea, 23, 41–2.

44 Since Lemmon wrote, ideas about what medieval chivalry entailed have changed hugely. For a recent survey, see Kaeuper, R., 2016, *Medieval Chivalry*, Cambridge.

45 By contrast it was the commander of the Norman right, Robert de Beaumont, whom he praised for his achievement that day. True, WP

had Beaumont connections, but given the lie of the land it is also likely that a right flanking attack, in best Vegetian fashion, gave the invaders their best chance. *GG*, 128–31; Milner, N. P. (trans.), 1993, Vegetius, *Epitome of Military Science*, Liverpool, 98.

46 Bates, *William the Conqueror*, 240.

47 JW, ii, 604–5 (*quia arto in loco constituti furerant Angli, de acie se multi subtraxere*).

48 *GG*, 128–33.

49 *Carmen*, 24, line 415 (*densissima turba*); 26, line 421 (*spissum nemus*: 'the dense forest of the English'); 26, line 428 (*spissa silva*: 'thick wood').

50 *Breuis Relatio*, 31.

51 Unless we take seriously the possibility that the English were there in the tens of thousands; Lawson, *Battle of Hastings*, 150.

52 Martin, D., Martin, B. and Whittick, C., 2016, *Child of Conquest. Building Battle Town. An Architectural History, 1066–1750*, Burgess Hil, 2–8, esp. Figs. 1.4 and 1.5.

53 OV, ii. 92–3, 214–15, 304–5.

54 OV, ii. xxi, xxvi, xxxix for his presence at English monasteries – where William of Malmesbury may have picked up his tracks. My thanks to David Bates for drawing attention to this point.

55 *GG*, 126–33 (ii.15, 17, 20–21); *Carmen*, 22–3, 26–9, lines 369, 423–4, 443–61. For pre-1066 cavalry warfare under Duke William, see Gillingham. J., 1989, 'William the Bastard at War', in Harper-Bill C. et al. (eds.), *Studies in Medieval History presented to R. Allen Brown*, Woodbridge, 141–58 (reprinted in Strickland, *Anglo-Norman Warfare*, 143–60).

56 The pros and cons of active royal participation in fighting are discussed in some of the essays in Clauss, M., Stieldorf, A. and Weller, T. (eds.), 2015, *Der König als Krieger. Zum Verhältnis von Königtum und Krieg im Mittelalter*, Bamberg.

57 Strickland, 'Military Technology', 382.

58 *GND*, ii, 170–71.

59 *GG*, 138–41. Cf. 'The greatest part of the English nobility was killed there together with Harold and his two brothers', *Breuis Relatio*, 32.

60 Strickland, M., 1992, 'Slaughter, Slavery or Ransom: The Impact of the Conquest on Conduct in Warfare', in Hicks, C. (ed.), *England in the Eleventh Century*, Stamford, 41–59; Strickland, *War and Chivalry*; Barthélemy, D., 2007, *La Chevalerie*, Paris, 189–96.

61 OV, ii, 169–70.

62 Those named were a bishop of Dorchester, an abbot of Ramsey and four ealdormen.

63 ASC 937, 1004, 1010. Hence, 'Had he [William] rather than Harold been killed or had he failed to rally his men when the Breton left collapsed at a crucial stage, the outcome could have been a bloody

slaughter of the invader, as had occurred at Stamford Bridge', Strickland, 'Military Technology', 368–9.

64 Strickland, 'Slaughter, Slavery', 47. Cf. Wyatt, D., 2009, *Slaves and Warriors in Medieval Britain and Ireland, 800–1200*, Leiden; Gillingham, J., [forthcoming], 'Cultures of Conquest: Warfare and Enslavement in Britain Before and After 1066', in Ashe, L. (ed.), *Conquest 1016 and 1066*.

65 Ralph Glaber on the battle of Nouy in 1044 between Count Geoffrey Martel and Count Theobald of Blois, discussed in Gillingham, J., 2007, 'Fontenoy and After: Pursuing Enemies to their Death in France Between the Ninth and Eleventh Centuries', in Fouracre, P. and Ganz, D. (eds.), *Frankland: The Franks and the World of the Early Middle Ages. Essays in Honour of Dame Jinty Nelson*, Manchester, 242–65, at 260–62.

66 In 11th-century France we get the first clear evidence of the practice of ransoming captives; Strickland, M., 2001, 'Killing or Clemency? Ransom, Chivalry and Changing Attitudes to Defeated Opponents in Britain and Northern France, 7–12th Centuries', in Kortüm, H.-H. (ed.), *Krieg im Mittelalter*, Berlin, 93–122; Barthélemy, D., 2009, 'The Chivalric Transformation and the Origins of Tournament as seen through Norman Chroniclers', *HSJ* 20, 141–60.

67 Pope Gregory VII even came under fire because back in 1066 he had, while still a cardinal, lent his support to an enterprise that came to involve killing on a shocking scale; van Houts, 'The Norman Conquest Through European Eyes', 850–51.

68 Tschan, F. J. (trans.), 1959, *History of the Archbishops of Hamburg-Bremen by Adam of Bremen*, New York, 158–9.

69 Gillingham, 'Holding to the Rules', 14.

70 It was 'the largest and most bloody engagement they would ever experience, fought in a desperate war of conquest against men felt to be beyond the behavioural restraints in operation between members of the Norman knighthood itself', Strickland, 'Slavery and Slaughter', 59.

71 In WP's view, the men of Kent were less savage than the other English, being improved by their proximity to Gaul; *GG*, 128–9, 164–5.

72 'As victor, he could have killed the English magnates … but he preferred to act more moderately and rule with greater clemency', *GG*, 143–4.

73 Gillingham, J., 1994, '1066 and the Introduction of Chivalry into England', in Garnett, G. and Hudson, J., *Law and Government in Medieval England and Normandy: Essays in Honour of Sir James Holt*, Cambridge, 31–55 (reprinted in Gillingham, J., 2000, *The English in the Twelfth Century: Imperialism, National Identity, and Political Values*, Woodbridge, 202–29).

74 Gillingham, 'William the Bastard at War'.

75 Morris, *William I*, 87.
76 Bachrach and Bachrach, *Warfare*, 365.
77 *GG*, 109–10. And see below, note 80.
78 *GR*, i, 422–3; Bates, *William the Conqueror*, 233.
79 OV, ii, 232–7.
80 *CS*, 582–4; EHD II, 649–50. No penance was laid down for plundering, only for killing in pursuit of plunder.

8 1066 and the English

1 Thomas, *The English and the Normans*; Williams, *The English*.
2 Stenton, F. M., 1971, (3rd. ed.), *Anglo-Saxon England*, Oxford, 626. Stenton included only Thorkell and Colswein; for Gospatric and Edward, see Williams, *The English*, 26, 40, 99, 105–7. The hidage (carucage in the north) is a tax assessment, not a measure of physical size.
3 GDB 142: *DB Herts* 38, 1–2 (Edgar; both held of him by Godwine, another Englishman); GDB 160r: *DB Oxon* 54, 1; GDB 238, 244: *DB Warks* B2; 43, 1–3 (Christina). For Harold son of Earl Ralph's land, see GDB 169: *DB Gloucs* 61, 1–2; GDB 177: *DB Worcs* 22, 1; GDB 238, 244: *DB Warks* B2; 38, 1–2 (Harold).
4 For Ead/Ealdgifu, who may have been connected with the earls of Mercia, see GDB, 172r, 178r: *DB Worcs* 28, 1; Baxter, *Earls of Mercia*, 171–2 and n88, 252. For William Leofric, see GDB 61: *DB Berks* 28, 1–3; GDB 167v: *DB Gloucs* 38, 1–5: LDB 93, 103: *DB Essex* 59, 1; he also held just under 3½ hides in Oxfordshire, for which no pre-Conquest tenant is given (GDB 160: *DB Oxon* 46, 1). In the Berkshire folios he is mistakenly called William fitzRichard, but comparison with the Wiltshire entry for land attached to Coleshill (Berkshire) shows that William Leofric is intended (GDB 72v: *DB Wilts* 49, 1 and note); Williams, A., 1989, 'An Introduction to the Gloucestershire Domesday', in Erskine, R. W. H. and Williams, A. (eds.), *The Gloucestershire Domesday*, London, 24–5.
5 For Thorkell, see Green, *English Sheriffs*, 83; for Colswain (Kolsveinn), see Roffe, D., 2012, 'Hidden Lives: English Lords in Post-Conquest Lincolnshire and Beyond', in Roffe, D. (ed), *The English and their Legacy, 900–1200: Essays in Honour of Ann Williams*, Woodbridge, 206–7.
6 For Godric, see LDB 202r–205v: *DB Nf* 12, 1–45; LDB 355v–356r: *DB Sf* 13, 1–7; Williams, *The English*, 108–9; for Kolgrimr, see GDB 370r–370v: *DB Lincs* 67, 1–27; Roffe, 'Hidden Lives', 208–9.
7 GDB 153: *DB Bucks* 55, 1 (Alric's manor of Steeple Claydon), 56, 1–3 (Alsige's three tenements). For Alvred Wigot's nephew, see GDB 160: *DB Oxon* 43, 1–2; Williams, *The English*, 99–103.
8 Lennard, R., 1959. *Rural England*, Oxford, 67.
9 GDB 148v: *DB Bucks* 17, 16.

10 In Essex, Richard fitz Gilbert had let Thaxted at farm to an unnamed Englishman for £60 a year, but each year 'the renders are deficient by at least £10', because, as the jurors testified, the land rendered only £50 (LDB 38v: *DB Essex* 23, 1). For someone who managed to make the system work in his favour, see Robert Latimer below.

11 ASC 'E', 1087.

12 The legal minimum qualification for thegnhood was possession of five hides of land, and Ailric's manor at Marsh Gibbon was assessed at only four hides, but he probably had other land. He might indeed be identical with the aforementioned Alric the cook (*Alricus coquus*) whose 20 hides lay in Steeple Claydon (GDB 153: *DB Bucks* 55, 1), for both Steeple Claydon and Marsh Gibbon lay in Lamua Hundred, and the Domesday name-form *Alricus* could represent OE Æthelric.

13 Williams, *The World before Domesday*.

14 It has been claimed that Harold and his father Godwine were wealthier than the king, but see Grassi, J., 2002, 'The Lands and Revenues of Edward the Confessor', *EHR* 117, 251–83; Baxter, *Earls of Mercia*, 129.

15 Blake (ed.), *Liber Eliensis*, 167 (Fairweather (trans.), *Liber Eliensis*, 198–9). Peter A. Clarke listed 90 pre-Conquest landowners with land worth £40 or more, while Robin Fleming estimated that 70 individuals had land worth £60 or more (Clarke, *The English Nobility*, 227–370; Fleming, *Kings and Lords*, 65 and n47). More will come to light as identification of pre-Conquest landholders proceeds.

16 II Cn 70–1 (*EHD*, I, 429); 'among the Danes' (that is, in the earldom of Northumbria), the king's thegns were subdivided into 'he who has his soke', and 'he who has a more intimate relationship with the king'.

17 Stenton, F. M., 1970, 'English Families and the Norman Conquest', in Stenton, D. M. (ed.), *Preparatory to Anglo-Saxon England*, Oxford, 325–44, at 333. Stenton believed these regions had 'few attractions for Norman settlers', but the timing of the Norman settlement is probably the key factor (Thomas, *The English and the Normans*, 112–18).

18 They are the English equivalents of another group of modest landholders, entered under the general heading of 'king's servants' (*servientes regis*); the difference is that while most of the *taini* are English, most of the *servientes* are of continental origin. Where they can be traced in later records, the successors of both usually hold by 'sergeanty', that is, by the performance of specific services for the king. See further Williams, *The English*, 109–22; Roffe, D., 2007, *Decoding Domesday*, Woodbridge, 158–9.

19 For Robert and his family, see Tsurushima, H., 1992, 'The Fraternity of Rochester Cathedral Priory', *ANS* 14, 313–37, at 329–31, 333; Williams, *The English*, 84–5.

20 Boulay, F. R. H. du, 1966, *The Lordship of Canterbury*, London, 387.

21 Okasha, E., 1983, 'A Supplement to *Hand-List of Anglo-Saxon Non-Runic Inscriptions*', *ASE* 11, 83–118, at 88–9 (no. 161: Canterbury VII). The memorial also names Eadsige's father Edward.

22 They are listed among the *ministri uicecomitis* in a charter of Bishop Gundulf of Rochester (Tsurushima, 'The Fraternity', 329 n87).

23 Tsurushima, H., 1996, 'Domesday Interpreters', *ANS* 18, 201–22.

24 GDB 10, 12v: *DB Kent* 5, 149 and note; 7, 30. The father's name, Godric *wisce* ('marsh'), is given in the entry for Badlesmere in the contemporary *Excerpta* of St Augustine's, and the abbey claimed to have King Edward's writ and seal for the estate (Ballard, A. (ed.), 1920, *An Eleventh-Century Inquistion of St Augustine's, Canterbury*, Oxford, 4–5).

25 Galbraith, V. H., 1961, *The Making of Domesday Book*, Oxford, 153–5.

26 Both 'tenant-in-chief' and 'mesne-tenant' are modern terms, but too useful to discard.

27 GDB 82v: *DB Dorset* 47, 10 and notes.

28 Williams, A., 1969, 'The Dorset Geld Rolls', in Pugh, A. (ed), *VCH Dorset* iii, 36; GDB 82v: *DB Dorset* 43, 1. The Geld Rolls, bound up with Exon Domesday in the *Liber Exoniensis*, record the taking of a tax contemporaneous with or just before the 1086 survey.

29 Harding *regine pincerna* attests S 1036 (dated 1062) and S 1042 (in 1065); S = Sawyer, P. H., 1968 (ed.), *Anglo-Saxon Charters: An Annotated Hand-List and Bibliography*, London; updated and revised as *The Electronic Sawyer*, www.esawyer.org.uk/about/index.html (accessed 4 May 2017). See Keynes, S., 1988, 'Regenbald the Chancellor (*sic*)', *ANS* 10, 185–222, at 206–7. In 1086, Harding was holding as a *tainus regis* land at Burley (Berkshire) which he had previously held of Queen Edith (GDB 63v: *DB Berks* 65, 17). He is probably identical with Harding of Wilton, who held Cranmore (Somerset) of Glastonbury Abbey both before and after 1066 (GDB 90v: *DB Som* 8, 32 and note), and with the Harding who in 1086 held 27½ hides in Wiltshire as a *tainus regis* in 1086; he had held a further 18½ hides in the same shire, which had passed to Earl Aubrey (GDB 69, 74).

30 Hamilton, N. E. S. A. (ed.), 1886, *Inquisitio Comitatensis Cantabrigiensis*, London, Rolls series. The lists, with those from the Ely Inquest, are printed as appendices in *DB Cambs*.

31 Lewis, C. P., 1993, 'The Domesday Jurors', *HSJ* 5, 17–44.

32 GDB 194v: *DB Cambs* 14, 41 and Appendix K.

33 *DB Cambs*, Appendix L.

34 GDB 195v: *DB Cambs* 14, 71 and Appendix A.

35 Galbraith, *Making of Domesday Book*, 155.

36 The king gave smaller fiefs to Osbern fitzRichard, Ralph de Mortemer, Roger de Lacy, Hugh l'Asne and Nigel the physician,

and the Church, including the bishops of Chester and Hereford, Shrewsbury Abbey, and Much Wenlock, also had land, but the total amount was tiny in comparison with Earl Roger's fief.

37 The same arrangement is found, for the same reasons, in Cheshire under Earl Hugh of Avranches, and in Cornwall where the earl was the king's half-brother, Robert of Mortain, but not in Kent, where the earl was the king's other half-brother, Odo of Bayeux; the difference may turn on the fact that Odo of Bayeux was in jail in 1086, and his lands were in the hands of the king.

38 Williams, *The English*, 91, Table VI.

39 OV, ii, 194–5.

40 Williams, *The English*, 91–3.

41 GDB 252v: *DB Shrops* 3c, 8, 14; Galbraith, V. H., 1929, 'An Episcopal Land-Grant of 1085', *EHR* 44, 371–2, with a facsimile opposite 353 (Barrow, J. (ed.), 1993, *English Episcopal Acta VII: Hereford 1079–1234*, Oxford, no. 2); Mason, J. F. A., 1954, 'Eadric of Bayston', *Transactions of the Shropshire Archaeological Society* 55, 112–18. According to the 12th-century writer Walter Map he had land at Lybury North, held by the bishop in 1086 (GDB, 252; Wright, T. (ed.), 1850, *Walter Map, De Nugis Curialium*, Camden Society, vol. 50, 79–82).

42 Eyton, R. W., 1854–60, *Antiquities of Shropshire*, 12 vols., London, iii, 48–50, iv, 194; GDB 257r: *DB Shrops* 4, 11, 5; 12; 16 and notes.

43 Williams, *The English*, 93–6.

44 Hearne, T. (ed.), 1723, *Hemingi Chartularium Ecclesiae Wigornensis*, Oxford, fo. 38r; GDB 259r: *DB Shrops* 4, 27, 11; 14; 32.

45 GDB 256v, 260, 260v: *DB Shrops* 4, 8, 9; 5, 8–9; 7, 6. Ealdred also held Acton Scott, which had belonged to Eadric TRE, of Earl Roger (GDB 259v: *DB Shrops* 4, 27, 33).

46 OV, iii, 6–7.

47 Rees, U. (ed.), 1975, *The Shrewsbury Cartulary*, Aberystwyth, i, x–xii and no. 19, ii, no. 256.

48 Orderic describes Edward as *consobrinus* of King David, literally 'cousin on the mother's side' (OV iv, 276–7). King David's mother, Queen Margaret, was a granddaughter of King Edmund II Ironside, himself a full brother of Eadgyth, grandmother of Edward's father Siward (Williams, *The English*, 95–6; Barrow, G. W. S., 2003, 'The Companions of the Ætheling', *ANS* 25, 35–45, at 40–41).

49 Thomas, *The English and the Normans*, 161–80. For the free tenants, including riding-men (mounted escorts and messengers), see Faith, R., 1997, *The English Peasantry and the Growth of Lordship*, Leicester, 94–8, 121–5.

50 Williams, A.,1999, 'The Abbey Tenants and Servants in the Twelfth Century', in Keen, L. (ed.), *Studies in the Early History of Shaftesbury Abbey*, Dorchester, 131–60.

51 Orderic names his father, Odelerius of Orleans, but not his mother, OV, ii, 256–7.

52 LDB 232: *DB Nf* 21, 13.

53 Thomas, 'English Women and Norman Men', in *The English and the Normans*, 138–60.

54 Moore, J., 1994, 'Family-Entries in English *Libri Vitae*, c.1050–c.1530', *Nomina* 16, 99–128. For the *libri vitae*, see Keynes, S. (ed.), 1996, *The Liber Vitae of the New Minster and Hyde Abbey Winchester, British Library Stowe 944*, Copenhagen; Rollason, D. and Rollason, L. (eds.), 2007, *The Durham Liber Vitae, London, British Library, MS Cotton Domitian A. VII. Edition and Digital Facsimile with Introduction, Codicological, Prosopographical and Linguistic Commentary, and Indexes*, London, 3 vols.; Rollason, L. (ed.), 2015, *The Thorney Liber Vitae: London, British Library, Additional MS 40,000, fols 1–12r: Edition, Facsimile and Study*, Woodbridge.

55 Keynes (ed.), *Liber Vitae of the New Minster*, 98, 101–2 and fols. 29r, 41r.

56 GDB 45v: *DB Hants*, 23, 33–4. Teotselin's lands lay in Boarhunt, held TRE by Leofsige and Merewine as two manors, and *Aplestede*, formerly held by Goding; one of them may have been Ealdgyth's father.

57 Keynes (ed.), *Liber Vitae of the New Minster*, 97 and fo. 28v; GDB 50v: *DB Hants* 69, 41. For a survey of intermarriage over the whole of the 11th and early 12th centuries, see van Houts, E., 2011, 'Intermarriage in Eleventh-Century England', in Crouch, D. and Thompson, K. (eds.), *Normandy and its Neighbours, 900–1250: Essays for David Bates*, Turnhout, 241–76.

58 In a charter from 1100–16, Godric and his wife Ingreda gave St Benet's Holme land at Little Melton (*EHD*, II, 842–3). It had been bequeathed to St Benet's by Godric's English predecessor Edwin (LDB 20: *DB Norfolk* 12, 32), and St Benet's remembered Edwin and Ingreda as the benefactors (West, J. R. (ed.), 1932, *The Register of the Abbey of St Benet Holme*, Norwich, no. 62). Perhaps Ingreda was Edwin's daughter, in which case the 'continental' marriage belongs to the previous generation (*DP*, 219).

59 Clark, C., 1991, 'Onomastics', in Blake, N. (ed.), *The Cambridge History of the English Language ii, 1066–1476*, Cambridge, 551–87. Elisabeth van Houts rejects the marriage of Walter Scot on the grounds that he might have been an Englishman who had taken a Norman name ('Intermarriage', 251 n25). This is, of course, possible, although his appearance as one of 'the men of the abbot' in the diploma of Abbot Rhiwallon might equally well be taken to imply that he was an incomer.

60 Feilitzen, Olof von, 1976, 'The Personal Names and Bynames in the Winton Domesday' in Biddle, M. (ed.), *Winchester in the Early*

Middle Ages: An Edition and Discussion of the Winton Domesday, Oxford, 189.

61 Williams, *The English*, 198–9.

62 Keene, D., 'Henry fitzAilwin (d.1212)', *ODNB*, available online (subscription required) at http://dx.doi.org/10.1093/ref:odnb/9526; Williams, *The English*, 205–6.

63 Feilitzen, 'Personal Names and Bynames', 190, Fig. 2; Urry, W., 1967, *Canterbury Under the Angevin Kings*, London, 170–71, 226–49; Clark, C., 1995, 'People and Languages in Post-Conquest Canterbury', *JMH* 2, reprinted in Jackson, P. (ed.), *Words, Names and History, Selected Papers of Cecily Clark*, Woodbridge, 179–206.

64 Stacy, N. E. (ed.), 2000, *Charters and Custumals of Shaftesbury Abbey 1089–1216*, Oxford, 32; Clark, C., 1987, '*Willelmus rex? Vel alius Willemlmus*', *Nomina* 11, reprinted in Jackson, *Words, Names and History*, 280–98.

65 The father of Thorkell (ODan Þorkil) of Warwick bore the OE name Æthelwine (Williams, A., 1989, 'A Vice-Comital Family in Warwickshire in the Eleventh Century', *ANS* 11, 279–95). For Scandinavian names in 11th-century England, see Fellows-Jensen, G., 1994, 'Danish Personal Names and Place-Names in England', in Rumble, A. R. (ed.), *The Reign of Cnut*, London, 125–40; Fellow-Jensen, G., 1995, *The Vikings and their Victims: The Evidence of Names*, London, Dorothea Coke Memorial Lecture 1993.

66 Clark, C., 1978, 'Women's Names in Post-Conquest England: Observations and Speculations', *Speculum* 53, reprinted in Jackson, *Words, Names and History*, 117–43.

67 Clark, 'Onomastics', 555–6, 567–9. Some later surnames incorporate OE personal names, like Aylmer (Æthelmaer), Edrich (Eadric), Goodwin (Godwine), Wooldridge (Wulfric) and Elphick (Ælfric).

68 Roffe, 'Hidden Lives', 205–28. Illuminating studies of the effects of the Conquest in the north include Aird, W., 1998, *St Cuthbert and the Normans: The Church of Durham, 1071–1153*, Woodbridge, and Phythian-Adams, C., 1996, *Land of the Cumbrians: A Study in British Provincial Origins*, Aldershot.

69 Amt, E. and Church, S. (eds.), 2007, *Dialogus de Scaccario: Constitutio Domus Regis: The Dialogue of the Exchequer, and The Disposition of the Royal Household*, Oxford, 82.

70 Garnett, G., 2004, 'Review of Thomas, *The English and the Normans*', *Times Literary Supplement* 30 July, 11.

71 The arguments for 'early' and 'late' are set out in Williams, *The English*, and Thomas, *The English and the Normans* respectively.

72 Amt and Church, *Dialogus de Scaccario*, 80.

73 ASC 'E', 1086.

9 1066 and government

1 Stenton, F. M., 1908, *William the Conqueror and the Rule of the Normans*, London, 1–62 (quotations at 14, 18, 21–2 and 62).

2 Stenton, F. M., 1971 (first ed. 1943), *Anglo-Saxon England*, Oxford, chapters 11–15.

3 A landmark study was Dolley, R. H. M. and Metcalf, D. M., 1961, 'The Reform of the English Coinage under Eadgar', in Dolley, R. H. M. (ed.), *Anglo-Saxon Coins: Studies Presented to F. M. Stenton on the Occasion of His 80th Birthday*, London, 136–68. Important among subsequent surveys are: Metcalf, D. M., 1998, *An Atlas of Anglo-Saxon and Anglo-Norman Coin Finds, c.973–1086*, London; Allen, M., 2012, *Mints and Money in Medieval England*, Cambridge, 1–40; Naismith, R., 2016, *Medieval European Coinage with a Catalogue of the Coins in the Fitzwilliam Museum, Cambridge 8: Britain and Ireland c.400–1066*, Cambridge, 211–77.

4 Hill, D. and Rumble, A. (eds.), 1996, *The Defence of Wessex: The Burghal Hidage and Anglo-Saxon Fortifications*, Manchester; and see now Baker, J. T. and Brooks, S., 2013, *Beyond the Burghal Hidage: Anglo-Saxon Civil Defence in the Viking Age*, Leiden.

5 Hollister, C. W., 1962, *Anglo-Saxon Military Institutions*, Oxford.

6 Lawson, M. K., 1984, 'The Collection of the Danegeld and Heregeld in the Reigns of Æthelred II and Cnut', *EHR* 94, 721–38; Lawson, M. K., 1989, 'Those Stories Look True': Levels of Taxation in the Reigns of Æthelred II and Cnut', *EHR* 104, 385–406; Lawson, M. K., 1990, 'Danegeld and Heregeld Once More', *EHR* 105, 951–61; Gillingham, J., 1989, ' "The Most Precious Jewel in the English Crown": Levels of Danegeld and Heregeld in the Early Eleventh Century', *EHR* 104, 373–84; Gillingham, J., 1990, 'Chronicles and Coins as Evidence for the Levels of Tribute and Taxation in the Late Tenth- and Early Eleventh-Century England', *EHR* 105, 939–50.

7 Keynes, S., 1980, *The Diplomas of King Æthelred 'The Unready' 978–1016*, Cambridge, 14–153; and most recently, Keynes, S., 2013, 'Church Councils, Royal Assemblies, and Anglo-Saxon Royal Diplomas', in Owen-Crocker, G. R. and Schneider, B. W. (eds.), 2013, *Kingship, Legislation and Power in Anglo-Saxon England*, Woodbridge, 17–182.

8 Keynes, S., 1990, 'Royal Government and the Written Word in Late Anglo-Saxon England', in McKitterick, R. (ed.), *The Uses of Literacy in Early Mediaeval Europe*, 226–57; Kelly, S., 1990, 'Anglo-Saxon Lay Society and the Written Word', in McKitterick, *The Uses of Literacy*, 36–62.

9 Maddicott, *Origins of the English Parliament*, Oxford, 1–56.

10 Wormald, *Legal Culture in the Early Medieval West*; Wormald, *The Making of English Law*; Wormald, *Papers Preparatory to the Making of English Law*. Important contributions to the ensuing debate include Hyams, *Rancor and Reconciliation*, 3–154; Hudson, *The Oxford History of the Laws of England*, 17–92, 161–99, 244–55; Lambert, *Law and Order*.

11 See, for example, Campbell, J., 2000, 'The United Kingdom of England: The Anglo-Saxon Achievement', in his *The Anglo-Saxon State*, 31–53; Wormald, P., 1999, '*Engla Lond*: The Making of an Allegiance', in his *Legal Culture*, 359–82; Foot, S., 1996, 'The Making of *Angelcynn*: English Identity Before the Norman Conquest', *TRHS* 6th ser., 6, 25–49; Molyneaux, G., 2014, 'Did the English Really Think They Were God's Elect in the Anglo-Saxon Period?', *JEH* 65, 721–37.

12 Harvey, S. P. J., 1971, 'Domesday Book and its Predecessors', *EHR* 76, 753–73; and see now Harvey, *Domesday: Book of Judgment*, 7–31.

13 Campbell, J., 1986, 'Observations on English Government from the Tenth to the Twelfth Century', in his *Essays in Anglo-Saxon History*, 155–70; Campbell, J., 1986, 'The Significance of the Anglo-Norman State in the Administrative History of Western Europe', in his *Essays in Anglo-Saxon History*, 171–90; Campbell, J., 2000, 'The Late Anglo-Saxon State: A Maximum View', in his *The Anglo-Saxon State*, 1–31.

14 Molyneaux, *Formation*.

15 See, for example, Stafford, *Unification and Conquest*, v–vi, 57–68, 83–101; John, E., 1991, *Reassessing Anglo-Saxon England*, Manchester, 139–95; Fleming, *Kings and Lords*, 21–103; Garnett, G., 1990, 'Conquered England, 1066–1215', in Saul, N. (ed.), *The Oxford Illustrated History of Medieval England*, Oxford, 61–101, at 65–8.

16 Sawyer, P. H., 1965, 'The Wealth of England in the Eleventh Century', *TRHS* 5th ser., 15, 145–64; see now Sawyer, *The Wealth of Anglo-Saxon England*.

17 Campbell, J., 2000, 'Was it Infancy in England? Some Questions of Comparison', in *The Anglo-Saxon State*, 179–200.

18 Harvey, S. P. J., 1988, 'Domesday England', Hallam, H. E. (ed.), *The Agrarian History of England and Wales II. 1042–c.1350*, Cambridge, 45–136; Faith, *The English Peasantry*.

19 Faith, R. and Banham, D., 2013, *Anglo-Saxon Farms and Farming*, Oxford, 294–5.

20 Fairbairn, H., 2013, 'The Nature and Limits of the Money Economy in Late Anglo-Saxon and Early Norman England', unpublished PhD thesis, King's College, London; Naismith, R., 2013, 'The English Monetary Economy, c.973–1100: the Contribution of Single Finds', *Economic History Review* 66, 198–225.

21 Fleming, R., 2001, 'The New Wealth, the New Rich, and the New Political Style in Late Anglo-Saxon England', *ANS* 23, 1–22.

22 Dodwell, C. R., 1982, *Anglo-Saxon Art: A New Perspective*, Manchester, 198–215.

23 Williams, A., 2002, 'Thegnly Piety and Ecclesiastical Patronage in the Late Old English Kingdom', *ANS* 24, 1–24; Baxter, *The Earls of Mercia*, 162–203.

24 Blair, J., 2015, 'The Making of the English House', *Anglo-Saxon Studies in Archaeology and History* 19, 184–206; and Fernie, E. in this volume.

25 Fleming, R., 2010, *Britain after Rome: The Fall and the Rise, 400 to 1070*, London, 241–317; Hamerow, H. et al. (eds.), 2011, *The Oxford Handbook of Anglo-Saxon Archaeology*, Oxford, especially chapters 12 (on the settlement pattern), 17–21 on food production, 22–5 on craft production and technology, and 26–31 on trade, exchange and urbanisation.

26 Metcalf, *Atlas*, 18–21, and maps 1–14; see also the searchable *Early Medieval Corpus of Coin Finds*, https://emc.fitzmuseum.cam.ac.uk.

27 Sawyer, 'Wealth of England', 161–3; Campbell, 'Was it Infancy in England?', 196–7.

28 ASC 'C', 'D', 'E', 1018, 'D', 1066, 1067.

29 Reuter, T., 2006, 'Assembly Politics in Western Europe from the Eighth Century to the Twelfth', in Nelson, J. L. (ed.), *Medieval Polities and Modern Mentalities*, Cambridge, 193–216.

30 Wickham, C., 2005, *Problems in Doing Comparative History*, The Reuter Lecture 2004, Southampton; reprinted in Skinner, P. (ed.), 2009, *Challenging the Boundaries of Medieval History: The Legacy of Timothy Reuter*, Turnhout, 5–28.

31 S, no. 1003.

32 Keynes, 'Church Councils, Royal Assemblies, and Anglo-Saxon Royal Diplomas', 62–92.

33 Keynes, S., 2002, *An Atlas of Attestations of Anglo-Saxon Charters, c.670–1066*, Cambridge, now accessible online through *Kemble: The Anglo-Saxon Charters Website*, currently at http://dk.usertest.mws3.csx.cam.ac.uk/node/115, Tables 71–5.

34 Maddicott, *Origins of the English Parliament*, 57–67.

35 Baxter, S. and Blair, J. 2006, 'Land Tenure and Royal Patronage in the Early English Kingdom: A Model and a Case Study', *ANS* 28, 19–46; Baxter, *Earls of Mercia*, 125–51.

36 Distribution maps of all Domesday landholders can now be consulted through Baxter (ed.), *PASE Domesday* (http://domesday.pase.ac.uk).

37 *VEdR*, 76.

38 Baxter, S., 2007, 'MS C of the Anglo-Saxon Chronicle and the Politics of Mid-Eleventh-Century England', *EHR* 122, 1189–227.

39 ASC MS 'D' *s.a.* 1051; Cubbin, G. P., 1996, *The Anglo-Saxon Chronicle, a Collaborative Edition, Volume 6, MS. D: A Semi-Diplomatic Edition with Introduction and Indices*, 70.

40 ASC 'CD' *s.a.* 1052; Cubbin (ed.), 73.

41 VEdR, 80 (*in eadem gente horrebat quasi bellum ciuile*).

42 ASC 'CDE' *s.a.* 1065, 1066; *VEdR*, 74–83; Baxter, *Earls of Mercia*, 48–57.

43 Bates, *Normandy before 1066*, 2–43, 147–88; Hagger, *Norman Rule in Normandy*; Loud, G. A., 2000, *The Age of Robert Guiscard: Southern Italy and the Norman Conquest*, Harlow, 234–95; Takayama, H., 1993, *The Administration of the Norman Kingdom of Sicily*, Leiden; Johns, J., 2002, *Arabic Administration in Norman Sicily: The Royal Dīwān*, Cambridge.

44 Dolley, M., 1966, *The Norman Conquest and the English Coinage*, London; Williams, G., 2012, 'Monetary Contacts Between England and Normandy, c.973–1180: A Numismatic Perspective', Chameroy, J. and Guihard, P.-M. (eds.), *Circulations monétaires et réseaux d'échanges en Normandie et dans le Nord-Ouest européen (Antiquité–Moyen Age)*, Caen, 251–62; Allen, M., 2014, 'Coinage and Currency under William I and William II', in Naismith R., Allen, M. and Screen, E. (eds.), *Early Medieval Monetary History: Studies in Memory of Mark Blackburn*, Farnham, 85–112; Naismith, R., [forthcoming], 'Currency and Conquest in Eleventh-Century England' (I am grateful to Dr Naismith for sight of this paper prior to publication).

45 Dumas, F., 1979, 'Les monnaies normandes', *Revue numismatique* 6th ser., 21, 84–140; Moesgaard, J.-C., 2009, 'La monnaie au temps de Guillaume le Conquérant', in Lemagnen, S. (ed.), *La tapisserie de Bayeux: une chronique des temps vikings? Actes du colloque international de Bayeux, 29 et 30 mars 2007*, Bonsecours, 89–99; Moesgaard, J.-C., 2015, 'Saints, Dukes and Bishops: Coinage in Ducal Normandy, c.930–c.1150', in Gasper, G. and Gullbekk, S. (eds.), *Money and the Church in Medieval Europe, 1000–1200: Practice, Morality and Thought*, Farnham, 197–207.

46 Dolley, *Norman Conquest and the English Coinage*, 11–12.

47 Allen, M., 2012. 'The Mints and Moneyers of England and Wales, 1066–1158', *British Numismatic Journal* 82, 54–120; Allen, 'Coinage and Currency', 86; Naismith, 'Currency and Conquest'.

48 Grierson, P., 1985, 'Domesday Book, the Geld *De Moneta* and *Monetagium*: a Forgotten Minting Reform', *British Numismatic Journal* 55, 84–94; Metcalf, D. M., 1987, 'The Taxation of Moneyers under Edward the Confessor and in 1086', Holt, J. C. (ed.), *Domesday Studies*, Woodbridge, 279–94; Allen, 'Coinage and Currency', 86–9.

49 Allen, *Mints and Money*, 23–7.

50 Allen, 'Coinage and Currency', 96–7; Fairbairn, 'The Nature and Limits of the Money Economy', 229.

51 Spufford, P., 1988, *Money and its Uses in Medieval Europe*, Cambridge, 95–7.

52 *GRA*, i, 384–7.

53 Williams, 'Monetary Contacts Between England and Normandy', 183.

54 Keynes, S., 1988, 'Regenbald the Chancellor (*sic*)', ANS 10, 185–222; Sharpe, R., 2004, 'The Use of Writs in the Eleventh Century', *ASE* 32, 247–91; *Acta of William I*, 43–62.

55 For estimates of the value of the holdings of sheriffs in 1066 and 1086, see (respectively): Wormald, *Papers Preparatory to the Making of English Law*, 200; Green, J. A., 1983, 'The Sheriffs of William the Conqueror', ANS 5, 129–45, at 140–1.

56 Sharpe, R., 2016, 'The Earliest Norman Sheriffs', *History* 101, 485–94; Sharpe, R., [forthcoming], 'Earls and the Shires in Anglo-Norman England'. I am grateful to Professor Sharpe for sight of this paper and for fruitful conversation on this subject. See also Fleming, *Kings and Lords*, 45–82.

57 Pratt, D., 2013, 'Demesne Exemption from Royal Taxation in Anglo-Saxon and Anglo-Norman England', *EHR* 128, 1–34; and a forthcoming analysis of the Exon geld accounts by C. P. Lewis.

58 Wl Art, 2 and 8 (Liebermann, F. (ed.), 1903–16, *Die Gesetze der Angelsachsen*, 3 vols., Halle, i, 486, 488); Wormald, *Making of English Law*, 398–415; Wormald, *Papers Preparatory*, 161–91.

59 Wl lad 1–3 and Wl Art, 3–4, 6 (*Gesetze*, i, 483, 487); Garnett, G., 1986, '*Franci et Angli*: The Legal Distinctions Between Peoples After the Conquest', ANS 8, 109–37.

60 Maddicott, *Origins of the English Parliament*, 57–67.

61 *Acta of William I*, 75–84.

62 Bates, *William the Conqueror*, 281–450.

63 GDB, fo. 345v (*DB Lincolnshire*, 7, 55).

64 Baxter, S. and Lewis, C. P., [forthcoming], 'Domesday Book and the Transformation of English Landed Society', *ASE*.

65 Maddicott, *Origins of the English Parliament*, 76–86, 442–4.

66 What follows is a provisional sketch of the findings from a collaborative research project concerned with Exeter Cathedral Library MS 3500 (aka Exon Domesday) currently in progress: 'The Conqueror's commissioners: unlocking the Domesday survey of south-western England', funded between 2014 and 2017 by the Arts and Humanities Research Council, reference number AH/L013975/1. The project aims to make to make facsimile images, text, translation, and a comprehensive palaeographical and codicological description of the manuscript freely available online at www.exondomesday.ac.uk;

and in due course to publish a printed volume of the edition and translation of the text, and a monograph exploring its significance. A fuller, though again provisional, statement of the argument sketched here can be found in Baxter, S., [forthcoming], 'The Domesday Controversy', *HSJ*. References here are therefore kept to a minimum.

67 ASC 'E', *s.a.* 1085.
68 Flight, C., 2006, *The Survey of the Whole of England: Studies of the Documentation Resulting from the Survey Conducted in 1086*, Oxford, 38–59.
69 ASC 'E' *s.a.* 1085; Irvine, S. (ed.), 2004, *The Anglo-Saxon Chronicle, A Collaborative Edition, Volume 7: MS. E, A Semi-Diplomatic Edition with Indices and Notes*, Cambridge, 93.
70 *ASC* 'E' *s.a.* 1086.
71 Holt, J. C., 1987, '1086', *Domesday Studies*, 41–64.
72 Baxter, 'Domesday Controversy', with references cited there.
73 Galbraith, V. H., 1961, *The Making of Domesday Book*, Oxford.
74 Holt, '1086'.
75 Higham, N. J., 1993, 'The Domesday Survey: Context and Purpose', *History* 78, 7–19; Maddicott, J., 2007, 'Responses to the Threat of Invasion, 1085', *EHR* 122, 986–97. There is now a growing consensus that Domesday served multiple purposes (see, for example, Harvey, *Domesday*, and Bates, *William the Conqueror*, 462–80).
76 Roffe, D., 2000, *Domesday: The Inquest and the Book*, Oxford, 224–51.
77 Green, J. A. (ed.), 2012, *The Pipe Roll of 31 Henry I*, Pipe Roll Society 95, London.
78 Harvey, *Domesday*, 271–328.
79 Davis, R. H. C., 1987, 'Domesday Book: Continental Parallels', in Holt (ed.), *Domesday Studies*, 15–39; Campbell, 'Observations on English Government', 163–7; Nelson, J., 2007, 'Henry Loyn and the Context of Anglo-Saxon England', *HSJ* 19, 154–70, at 164–9.
80 Bates, D., 1998, 'Les chartes de confirmation et les pancartes normandes du règne de Guillaume le Conquérant', in Parisse, M., Pégeot, P. and Tock, B.-M. (eds.), *Pancartes monastiques*, Turnhout, 95–109.
81 ASC 'E' *s.a.* 1086.
82 Winterbottom and Thomson (eds.), William of Malmesbury, *Vita Wulfstani*, 130.
83 GDB, fo. 148v (*DB Bucks*, 17, 16).
84 Percival, J., 1985, 'The Precursors of Domesday: Roman and Carolingian Land Registers', Sawyer, P. H. (ed.), *Domesday Book: A Reassessment*, 5–27.

10 1066 and the Church

1 *VEdR*, 117.

2 The consensus that formed around Susan Ridyard's article held that Norman bishops were more sympathetic than was once supposed. For statements of this view, see Ridyard, S. J., 1987, '*Condigna Veneratio*: Post-Conquest Attitudes to the Saints of the Anglo-Saxons', *ANS* 9, 176–206; Pfaff, R. W., 1992, 'Lanfranc's Supposed Purge of the Anglo-Saxon Calendar', in Reuter, T. (ed.), *Warriors and Churchmen in the High Middle Ages: Essays Presented to Karl Leyser*, London, 95–108. For recent, more sceptical perspectives, see Hayward, P., 1999, 'Translation-Narratives in Post-Conquest Hagiography and English Resistance to the Norman Conquest', *ANS* 21, 67–93; Licence, T., 2014, 'The Cult of St Edmund', in *Bury St Edmunds and the Norman Conquest*, Licence, T. (ed.), Woodbridge, 104–30.

3 Ridyard, '*Condigna Veneratio*', 206.

4 *EHD* I, 928–34, at 930.

5 Winterbottom, M. (ed. and trans.), 1978, Gildas, *The Ruin of Britain and Other Works*.

6 Gretsch, M., 1999, *The Intellectual Foundations of the English Benedictine Reform*, Cambridge.

7 Knowles, M. D., 1963 (2nd ed.), *The Monastic Order in England*, Cambridge.

8 Gransden, A., 1989, 'Traditionalism and Continuity During the Last Century of Anglo-Saxon Monasticism', *JEH* 4, 159–207, at 207.

9 Loyn, H. R., 2000, *The English Church, 940–1154*, Harlow, 66, citing Barlow, F., 1979 (2nd ed.), *The English Church 1000–1066*, London, 27.

10 Rushforth, R., 2008, *Saints in English Kalendars before AD 1100*, Henry Bradshaw Society, 117.

11 GDB fo. 280r (*DB Derbys.*, B).

12 GDB fo. 252r (*DB Shrops.* [C]).

13 LDB fos. 290r–v, 392b, 394r–v, 421v (*DB Suffolk*, 1.122a–b; 25.52; 25.62; 38.3).

14 LDB fos. 116r–117v (*DB Norfolk*, 1.61).

15 LDB fos, 223r, 227r (*DB Norfolk*, 19.11, 13; 20.2, 8).

16 Williams, A., 2002, 'Thegnly piety and ecclesiastical patronage in the late Old English kingdom', *ANS* 24, 1–24.

17 Blair, *The Church in Anglo-Saxon Society*, 443.

18 *EHD* I, 431.

19 Campbell, J., 1996, 'The East Anglian Sees Before the Conquest', in Atherton, I., Fernie, E., Harper-Bill, C. and Smith, H. (eds.), *Norwich Cathedral: Church, City and Diocese 1096–1996*, London and Rio Grande, 3–21, at 20.

20 LDB fo. 118v (*DB Norfolk*, 1.69).

21 Campbell, J., 1975, *Historic Towns Atlas 2: Norwich*, Lobel, M. D. (ed.), London, 4 and n42.

22 Taylor, H. M. and Taylor, J., 1965, *Anglo-Saxon Architecture*, 2 vols., Cambridge, I at xxv, uses the designation C3 to indicate buildings they believe date from 1050–1100. Of their nine groups it comprises the largest number of churches.

23 Fernie, E., 1982, *The Architecture of the Anglo-Saxons*, London, 121–3.

24 Taylor and Taylor, *Architecture*, ii, 688–93, and i, 209–11, provide measurements; Williams, A., 1997, 'Land, Piety and Politics: The Family and Career of Odda of Deerhurst', Deerhurst Lecture 1996, Deerhurst.

25 Taylor and Taylor, *Architecture*, i, 262–4.

26 Ayers, B., 1985, *Excavation Within the North-East Bailey of Norwich Castle, 1979*, East Anglian Archaeology 28, Norwich, Norfolk Archaeological Unit, 7–26.

27 Blockley, K., Sparks, M. and Tatton-Brown, T., 1997, *Canterbury Cathedral Nave: Archaeology, History and Architecture*, Canterbury, Dean and Chapter of Canterbury Cathedral and Canterbury Archaeological Trust; Fernie, *Architecture of the Anglo-Saxons*, 97–101; Gem, R., 1997, *English Heritage Book of St. Augustine's Abbey Canterbury*, London, 90–111.

28 Lapidge, M., 2003, *The Cult of St Swithun*, Oxford, 374–5 (an edition and translation of the 'Narratio metrica de sancto Swithuno' by Wulfstan of Winchester).

29 Winterbottom and Thomson, William of Malmesbury, *Saints' Lives*, 122–3.

30 Baxter, *Earls of Mercia*, 199, and see also 201.

31 Dodwell, C. R., 1982, *Anglo-Saxon Art: A New Perspective*, Manchester, esp. chapters 2, 6, 7. On secular displays of wealth, see Fleming, R., 2001, 'The New Wealth, the New Rich and the New Political Style in Late Anglo-Saxon England', ANS 23, 1–22; Williams, A., 2011, 'How to be Rich: The Presentation of Earl Harold in the Early Sections of the Bayeux Tapestry', in Lewis, M. J., Owen-Crocker, G. R. and Terkla, D. (eds.), *The Bayeux Tapestry: New Approaches*, Oxford, 66–70.

32 On the Church's early ability to tap the wealth of the Anglo-Saxon aristocracy, see Wormald, P., 1978, 'Bede, *Beowulf*, and the Conversion of the Anglo-Saxon Aristocracy', in Farrell, R. T. (ed.), *Bede and Anglo-Saxon England*, BAR British series 46, 32–95.

33 Hurst, D. (ed.), 1969, Bede, *De templo*, Corpus Christianorum Series Latina 119A, Turnhout, 143–234, at 212–13.

34 On the part played by the liturgy, see Bradford Bedingfield, M., 2002, *The Dramatic Liturgy of Anglo-Saxon England*, Woodbridge, 8–11.

35 Bynum, C. W., 2011, *Christian Materiality: An Essay on Religion in Late Medieval Europe*, Brooklyn.

36 Dodwell, *Anglo-Saxon Art*, 210–15; Watkiss, L. and Chibnall, M. (eds. and trans.), 1994, *The Waltham Chronicle: An account of the discovery of our holy cross at Montacute and its conveyance to Waltham*, OMT, Oxford, 22; Raw, B. C., 1990, *Anglo-Saxon Crucifixion Iconography and the Art of the Monastic Revival*, Cambridge, 41–2; Baxter, *Earls of Mercia*, 198. There is a useful conspectus of relevant texts in Lehmann-Brockhaus, O., 1955–60, *Lateinische Schriftquellen zur Kunst in England, Wales und Schottland, vom Jahre 901 bis zum Jahre 1307*, 5 vols., Munich.

37 Goscelin, *Historia, miracula et translatio s. Augustini*, in *Acta Sanctorum*, Bolland, J. et al. (eds.), 67 vols. (Antwerp and Brussels, 1643–), *Maii* VI, 375–443, at 442; Lapidge, M. (ed.), 2003, *Miracula s. Swithuni*, in Lapidge, *The Cult of St Swithun*, Winchester studies 4.ii, Oxford, 641–97, at 678–80.

38 Dodwell, *Anglo-Saxon Art*, especially chapters 2, 6, 7. For a string of examples and references see Baxter, *Earls of Mercia*, 189–201.

39 For Goscelin's style and manner of depicting saints, see Hamilton, T. J., 1973, 'Goscelin of Canterbury, a Critical Study of his Life, Works and Accomplishments', unpublished PhD thesis, University of Virginia; Love, R. C. (ed.), 1996, *Three Eleventh-Century Anglo-Latin Saints' Lives*, OMT, Oxford, xc–ci; and Love, R. C. (ed.), 2004, Goscelin of Saint-Bertin, *The Hagiography of the Female Saints of Ely*, OMT, Oxford, lv–lxxx.

40 Wilmart, A. (ed.), 1938, Goscelin of Saint-Bertin, 'La légende de ste Édith en prose et vers par le moine Goscelin', *Analecta Bollandiana* 56, 5–101, 265–307, at 296.

41 Napier, A. S., 1907–10, 'An Old English Vision of Leofric, Earl of Mercia', *Transactions of the Philological Society*, 180–88; Stokes, P. A., 2012, 'The Vision of Leofric: Manuscript, Text and Context', *The Review of English Studies* 63, 529–50.

42 Watkiss and Chibnall (eds.), *The Waltham Chronicle*, 22 et seq.

43 Baxter, *Earls of Mercia*, 196 and references.

44 On Peter's cult in context, see Ortenberg, V., 1992, *The English Church and the Continent in the Tenth and Eleventh Centuries: Cultural, Spiritual, and Artistic Exchanges*, Oxford, 165–9.

45 Rogers, N., 1992, 'The Waltham Abbey Relic-List', in Hicks, C. (ed.), *England in the Eleventh-Century: Proceedings of the 1990 Harlaxton Symposium*, Stamford, 157–81.

46 Jones, L., 2009, 'Emma's Greek *Scrine*', in Baxter, S., Karkov, C., Nelson, J. L. and Pelteret, D. (eds.), *Early Medieval Studies in Memory of Patrick Wormald*, London, 499–507.

47 Backhouse, J., Turner, D. H. and Webster, L. (eds.), 1984, *The Golden Age of Anglo-Saxon Art*, London: The British Museum, cats. 126–8; Raw, *Crucifixion Iconography*, plates IIIa, IIIb and IVa for six examples. The closest analogies are small Byzantine 'steatite' icons.

48 Gibson, M., 1978, *Lanfranc of Bec*, Oxford, 165–6.

49 '*Aue alma crux quæ mundi pretium portasti, quæ uexilla regis æterni ferebas. In te enim xpc* [for Christus] *triumphauit; per te et ego miser et peccator famulus tuus, N.*': BL, MS Cotton Tiberius A iii, fo. 59r. The prayer also appears in the New Minster register: Birch, W. de G. (ed.), 1892, *Liber vitae: register and martyrology of New Minster and Hyde abbey, Winchester*, Hampshire Record Society, London, 280.

50 Cott. Tib. A iii, fos. 59v–60r. The tract is edited from this manuscript and Ælfwine's book (Titus D xxvii, fo. 70r–v) in Raw, *Crucifixion Iconography*, 64.

51 Backhouse, J., Turner, D. H. and Webster, L. (eds.), 1984, *The Golden Age of Anglo-Saxon Art*, London: British Museum, no. 125.

52 Respectively Cambridge, University Library MS Ff 1.23 and Corpus Christi College MS 421: Raw, *Crucifixion Iconography*, plates X and XI. The date of the latter is probably mid-century rather than first half.

53 Judith married Tostig in 1051 and they left England in 1065, which indicates the likely date limits of the illumination. The same model for Christ on the Cross was used in two later Winchester Psalters: BL MS Cotton Tiberius C vi. fo. 13r and BL MS Arundel 60, fo. 52v, the former illuminated probably in the late 1060s, the latter in 1072–4; Kidd, P., 2000, 'A Re-Examination of the Date of an Eleventh-Century Psalter from Winchester (British Library MS Arundel 60)', in Cassidy, B. and Wright, R. M. (eds.), *Studies in the Illustration of the Psalter*, Stamford, 42–54.

54 Bestul, T., 1983, 'St Anselm, the Monastic Community at Canterbury, and Devotional Writing in Late Anglo-Saxon England', in *Anselm Studies: An Occasional Journal* 1, 186–98, at 190–91; Whatley, E. G., 1996–2006, 'Late Old English Hagiography, ca. 950–1150', in *Corpus Christianorum, Hagiographies*, Guy Philippart (ed.), 4 vols., Turnhout, ii, 429–99, at 438; Ker, N. R., 1957, *Catalogue of Manuscripts Containing Anglo-Saxon*, Oxford, nos. 73, 297, 310.

55 London, British Library, Cotton Vespasian A i, fo. 160r (*Per te confractum est iugum captiuitatis nostræ. Per te uenit salus mundi et redemptio totius seculi*).

56 For the prayers in the Bury Psalter, see Wilmart, A., 1930, 'The Prayers of the Bury Psalter', *Downside Review* 48, 198–210. On the Psalter, see Rushforth, R. J., 2002, 'The Eleventh- and Early Twelfth-Century Manuscripts of Bury St Edmunds Abbey', unpublished PhD thesis, University of Cambridge, 107–45.

57 Cott. Tiberius A iii, fo. 60r–v (*apud me* … [to defend me] … *intra me sis ut me reficies … circa me sis ut me conserues … ante me …* [to guide me] … *post me sis ut me gubernes … supra me sis ut me benedicas … in me sis ut me ad regnum tuum perducas*).

58 Cott. Tiberius A iii, fos. 58v–59r.

59 Günzel, B. (ed.), 1993, *Ælfwine's Prayerbook: London, British Library, Cotton Titus D. xxvi + xxvii)*, Henry Bradshaw Society 108, London, 46.1–7.

60 Raw, *Crucifixion Iconography*, 61 and references.

61 Bedingfield, *Dramatic Liturgy*, 131: 'totems like the Cross and the Candle frequently stand liturgically for the presence of Christ, and come thereby to absorb much of his divinity'.

62 Napier, A. S. (ed.), 1916, *The Old English version of the enlarged rule of Chrodegang together with the Latin original*, Early English Text Society, o.s. 150, London. Historians sometimes refer to these clerics as 'secular canons' (echoing the language of monks), but the communities discussed here all observed constitutions derived from the Rule of St Chrodegang. In other words, they were 'regulars'.

63 Barlow, F. (ed.), 1972, 'Leofric and his Times', in *Leofric of Exeter: Essays in Commemoration of the Foundation of Exeter Cathedral Library in AD 1072*, Exeter, 1–16, at 8–9.

64 *GP*, 286–8.

65 Salter, H. E. (ed.), 1907–8, *The Cartulary of the Abbey of Eynsham*, Oxford Historical Society 49, 51, Oxford, i, 28.

66 Hart, C. R. (ed.), 1966, *The Early Charters of Eastern England*, Leicester, no. 110.

67 Raine, J. junior (ed.), 1879–94, *The Historians of the Church of York and its Archbishops*, Rolls Series 71, 3 vols., i, 241–2, 344–5.

68 Edwards, K., 1949, *The English Secular Cathedrals in the Middle Ages*, Manchester, 9–10; for Waltham, see Watkiss and Chibnall (eds.), *The Waltham Chronicle*, 32–6.

69 Fernie, *Architecture of the Anglo-Saxons*, 82–4, 111, 129–35, 172. In general, Ortenberg, *The English Church and the Continent*, 57–78.

70 Watkiss and Chibnall (eds.), *The Waltham Chronicle*, 32.

71 Winterbottom and Thomson (eds.), William of Malmesbury, *Saints' Lives*, 34–6.

72 Winterbottom and Thomson (eds.), *Saints' Lives*, 24–6.

73 Licence, T., 2009, 'History and Hagiography in the Late Eleventh Century: The Life and Work of Herman the Archdeacon, Monk of Bury St Edmunds', *EHR* 124, 516–44, at 529.

74 Cott. Tiberius A iii, fos. 88v–93v.

75 Banham, D. (ed. and trans.), 1996, *Monasteriales Indicia: The Anglo-Saxon Monastic Sign Language*, Hockwold-cum-Wilton.

76 Cott. Tiberius A iii, fos. 44r–56v and 94v–97r.

77 Thompson, V., 2005, 'The Pastoral Contract in Late Anglo-Saxon England: Priest and Parishioner in Oxford, Bodleian Library, MS Laud Miscellaneous 482', in Tinti, F. (ed.), *Pastoral Care in Late Anglo-Saxon England*, Woodbridge, 106–20.

78 Wilmart (ed.), 'La légende de ste Édith', 292 (*Hec ... patriis literis sunt mandata*).

79 Lotter, F. and Gäbe, S., 2006, 'Die hagiographische Literatur im deutschen Sprachraum unter den Ottonen und Saliern (ca. 960–1130)', and Philippart, G. and Wagner, A., 2006, 'Hagiographie lorraine (950–1130). Les diocèses de Metz, Toul et Verdun', in *Hagiographies*, Philippart, G. (ed.), IV, 273–521 and 585–744. One or two anonymous Latin hagiographies written in England may date from Edward's era, such as the Life of St Neot; Folcard's Life of St John of Beverley may too, but there are not many contenders in total.

80 We refer to post-Ælfrician works: see Whatley, 'Late Old English Hagiography', 438–9 and 432–3.

81 Ker, *Catalogue*, nos. 21, 48, 49b, 69, 73, 86, 117 (fragments from bindings), 144, 162, 178, 186, 199, 222, 283, 285, 297, 309, 331, 332 and 336. Ker dates about two-thirds of these *s.* xi^{med} and the others in the range *s.* xi$^{3/4}$–*s.* xi$^{2/2}$. Palaeography is not a precise science, but nor should these survivals be taken as a representative sample of what perhaps existed. It is their chronological clustering that is of interest.

82 West, J. R. (ed.), 1932, *St. Benet of Holme, 1020–1210: The Eleventh and Twelfth Century Sections of Cott. MS Galba E. ii*, Norfolk Record Society 2–3, 2 vols. (continuously paginated), 89–90; O'Donovan, M. A. (ed.), 1988, *Charters of Sherborne*, Anglo-Saxon Charters 3, Oxford, lx, no. 22 (S 1032); Hudson, J. (ed.), 2002–7, *Historia Ecclesie Abbendonensis: The History of the Church of Abingdon*, 2 vols., OMT, Oxford, i, 208.

83 Cf. Burton, J. E., 1999, *The Monastic Order in Yorkshire, 1069–1215*, Cambridge. In the north, congregations of hermits went on to form the nuclei of important new monastic communities at York, Durham and Whitby.

84 Hart, *Early Charters of Eastern England*, 86–91.

85 Licence, T., 2011, *Hermits and Recluses in English Society, 950–1100*, Oxford, 82.

86 For the example of Wulfstan of Worcester, see the reference in note 29 above.

11 Women and fear in 1066

1 This chapter is a reworking of material that I published over the last 15 years. I am most grateful to David Bates for his editorial guidance and advice.

2 Strickland, A., 1867, *Lives of the Queens of England from the Norman Conquest*, London.

3 Power, E., 2012, *Medieval Women*, Postan, M. M. (ed.), Cambridge.

4 Clark, C., 1995, 'Women's Names in Post-Conquest England: Observations and Speculations', in *Words, Names and History: Selected Writings by Cecily Clark*, Jackson, P. (ed.), Cambridge,

17–43; and with Fell, C. and Williams, E., 1984, *Women in Anglo-Saxon England and the Impact of 1066*, London, esp. 148–94; Green, *The Aristocracy*, 361–90; Searle, E., 1981, 'Women and the Legitimization of Succession at the Norman Conquest', *ANS* 3, 159–70, 226–32; Stafford, P., 1994, 'Women and the Norman Conquest', *TRHS* 6th ser., 4, 221–49; Stafford, 1989, 'Women in Domesday Book', in *Medieval Women in Southern England*, Reading Medieval Studies 15, Reading, 75–94; Stafford, *Queen Emma and Queen Edith*.

5 Among the burgeoning recent scholarship on the topic, see especially Rosenwein, B. H., 2002, 'Worrying About Emotions in History', *AHR* 107, 821–45; Rosenwein, 2001, 'The History of Emotions: A Debate', *EME* 10, 224–56; Plamper, J., 2010, 'The History of Emotions: An Interview with William Reddy, Barbara Rosenwein and Peter Stearns,' *History and Theory* 49, 237–65.

6 On fear in warriors as a negative characteristic in the Carolingian period, see Stone, R., 2012, *Morality and Masculinity in the Carolingian Empire*, Cambridge, 89–90.

7 *CS*, no. 88, 581–4; translated in Brown, *Norman Conquest*, no. 187, 156–7. For what follows, see also van Houts, E., 2011, 'Intermarriage in Eleventh-Century England', in *Normandy and its Neighbours 900–1250. Essays for David Bates*, Turnhout, 237–70, at 251–2.

8 *CS*, no. 88, 581–4, at 584: clause 10, *De adulteriis et raptibus et fornicationibus quibusdamcumque acsi in patria sua pecassent penitant*; Brown (trans.), *Norman Conquest*, 157.

9 *GG*, 158–9 (*Milites uero mediae nobilitatis atque gregarios, aptissimis edictis coercuit. Tutae erant a ui mulieres, quam saepe amatores inferunt*).

10 OV, ii, 268–9.

11 OV, ii, 202–03 (*inmodicas praedas et incestos raptus*) (my translation).

12 *GG*, 158–9 (*Etiam illa delicta quae fierunt consensus impudicarum, infamiae prohibendae gratia uetabantur*).

13 *Lanfranc Letters*, no. 53.

14 Licence (ed.), *Miracles of St Edmund*, 274–5; van Houts, E., 2014, 'The Women of Bury St Edmunds', in Licence (ed.), *Bury St Edmunds*, Woodbridge, 53–73, at 64–5.

15 Rule, ed., *Eadmer*, 123–4 (Bosanquet (trans.), 127).

16 For what follows, see Brooke, C. N. L., 1989, *The Medieval Idea of Marriage*, Oxford, 39–60; Brundage, J. A., 1990, *Law, Sex, and Christian Society in Medieval Europe*, Chicago and London, 179–203; McDougall, S., 2013, 'The Making of Marriage in Medieval France', *Journal of Family History* 15, 1–19.

17 For what follows, see van Houts, 'Intermarriage', 245.

18 LDB, fo. 232v (*DB Norfolk*, 21.14); Clark, 'Women's Names', 117; Williams, *The English*, 198; van Houts, 'Intermarriage', 265.

19 For the catastrophic impact of loss of land on the English peasant freeholders, see Thomas, H. M., 2003, 'The Significance and Fate of the English Landholders of 1066', *EHR* 118, 303–33, at 322–3; Baxter, S., 2011, 'Lordship and Labour', in Crick and van Houts (eds.), *A Social History*, 98–115 at 105–7.

20 GDB, fo. 74v (*DB Wilts.*, 67.80, 86, 87, 90); Stafford, 'Women in Domesday Book', 80–1.

21 For what follows, see van Houts, 'Women at Bury St Edmunds', 55–9.

22 For Abbot Baldwin, see Bates, D., 2014, 'The Abbey and the Norman Conquest: An Unusual Case?', in Licence (ed.), *Bury St Edmunds*, 5–20.

23 On the Flemish contribution to the Norman Conquest, see Oksanen, E., 2012, *Flanders and the Anglo-Norman World 1066–2012*, Cambridge, 11–18.

24 Van Houts, E., 1988, 'The Ship List of William the Conqueror', *ANS* 10, 159–83 at 176 (reprinted in van Houts, *History and Family Traditions*, chapter VI, and van Houts (trans.), *The Normans in Europe*, no. 37, 130–31).

25 LoPrete, K. A., 2007, *Adela of Blois: Countess and Lord (c.1067–1137)*, Dublin, 23–4.

26 *RADN*, no. 231 (442–6, at 446).

27 OV, iii, 8–10.

28 Bates, *William the Conqueror*, 373–422.

29 On the danger of sea crossings, see Raich, S., 2016, 'Wreck of Sea in Law and Practice in Eleventh- and Twelfth-Century England', *ANS* 38, 141–54.

30 Bates, *The Normans and Empire*, 130–42.

31 This topic has been well explored for the history of the crusades, e.g. Riley-Smith, J., 1997, *The First Crusaders 1095–1131*, Cambridge, 98–9.

32 OV, ii, 218–20; Stafford, 'Women and the Norman Conquest', 248; van Houts, 'Intermarriage', 258–9.

33 For the concept of marital debt, see Brooke, *The Medieval Idea of Marriage*, 48–9.

34 OV, ii, 218–20.

35 *GG*, 156–7; Orderic Vitalis in *GND*, ii, 160–61; OV, ii, 136–7.

36 OV, ii, 138–9, and Orderic in *GND*, ii, 160–63; Baxter, *The Earls of Mercia*, 299–300.

37 OV, i, 214–17.

38 For a full discussion of the failed betrothals of Adeliza (or Adelida), see van Houts, E., 2004, 'The Echo of the Conquest in the Latin Sources: Duchess Matilda, her Daughters and the Enigma of the Golden Child', in Bouet et al. (eds.), *The Bayeux Tapestry*, 135–54 at 141–4.

39 OV, ii, 262–3, 320–23.

40 For a discussion of this problem, see Cownie, *Religious Patronage*, 201–6 and Appendix, 212–5; see also Golding, B., 1986, 'Anglo-Norman Knightly Burials', in Harper-Bill, C. and Harvey, R. (eds.), *The Ideals and Practices of Medieval Knighthood*, Woodbridge, 35–48.

41 For what follows, scc van Houts and Love (ed. and trans.), *The Warenne (Hyde) Chronicle*, Appendix 1, 89–102.

42 For an edition, translation and photograph of Gundrada's tombstone, see van Houts and Love (ed. and trans.), *The Warenne (Hyde) Chronicle*, Appendix 1, 89–94 and plates 1–2.

43 For the foundation of Ste Trinité at Caen for nuns, and St Etienne for monks in the early 1060s, and the penitential reasons for it, see Bates, *William the Conqueror*, 157–61.

44 Cownie, *Religious Patronage*.

45 *CS*, no. 88, 581–4 at 583: Clause 1.

46 For what follows, see van Houts, E., 2016, 'Orderic and his Father Odelerius', in Rozier et al. (eds.), *Orderic Vitalis*, 17–36.

47 OV, iii, 146–7; vi, 552–3.

48 Blair, *The Church*, 361, 493, 520–21.

49 OV, ii, 322–3.

50 Though he was given the label of 'martyr' by William of Malmesbury, *GP*, i, 486–7; Watkins, C., 1996, 'The Cult of Earl Waltheof at Crowland', *Hagiographica* 3, 96–111, at 103.

51 Thompson, S., 1991, *Women Religious: The Founding of English Nunneries after the Norman Conquest*, Oxford, 167, 221.

12 1066 and ecclesiastical architecture

1 The significance of the Conquest has gone from a traditional view that it marked a very important break in England's history, concentrating on the elite, to a more recent one looking at the whole population that sees 1066 as having no special significance. For the latter view see Richardson, H. G. and Sayles G. O., 1963, *The Governance of Medieval England*, Edinburgh, 27: 'for half a century or so from 1066 the English way of life was not sensibly altered', and Rowley, T., 1983, *The Heritage of Norman England, 1066–1200*, London, 7. Rowley was, however, converted to the view that the Conquest marked a significant change to life in England even in the 11th century: Rowley, T., 1998, 'All Change After the Norman Conquest', *British Archaeology* 35, 8–9. See also Bates, *William the Conqueror*, 498: 'For all that England's identity as a kingdom was preserved, so overwhelming was the destruction of the Old English aristocracy that, concretely defined, its Conquest was effectively the take-over of one state by another.'

2 I have addressed aspects of this subject in articles published in 1986, 1994 and 2011 (1986: 'The Effect of the Conquest on Norman

Architectural Patronage', *ANS* 9, 71–85; 1994: 'Architecture and the Effects of the Norman Conquest', in Bates, D. and Curry, A. (eds.), *England and Normandy in the Middle Ages*, London, 105–16; 2011: 'Three Romanesque Great Churches in Germany, France and England, and the Discipline of Architectural History', *Architectural History* 54, 1–22). Some of the points provided in those articles are also presented here, because I consider them essential to the main proposition and because doing so provides an opportunity to respond to contrary arguments that have been presented.

3 These arguments were put forward in discussions following lectures; none of them as far as I know has been published.

4 According to Barry Cunliffe a division between the eastern and western parts of the country goes back to before the Romans (2013, *Britain Begins*, Oxford, 67 and Fig. 2.20).

5 Fernie, E., 1993, *An Architectural History of Norwich Cathedral*, Oxford, 5–10; Fernie, E., 2014, 'The Romanesque Cathedral, 1093–1133', in Brown, D. (ed.), *Durham Cathedral: History, Fabric and Culture*, London, 131–41; the original of this article is Fernie, E., 2007, 'La seconda cattedrale di Durham, 1093–1133', in Quintavalle, A. C. (ed.), 2007, *Medioevo: l'Europa delle Cattedrali*, Milan, 132–40. Figure 14 of the Italian article is a correct diagram of the non-spiral pier in the south transept, incorrectly drawn in Fig. 106 of the English publication.

6 Woodman, F., 1981, *The Architectural History of Canterbury Cathedral*, London, 28.

7 Taylor, H. and Taylor, J., 1965, *Anglo-Saxon Architecture*, Cambridge, 214–17 (Dover), 584–93 (Stow).

8 Biddle, M., 1970, *The Old Minster: Excavations Near Winchester Cathedral 1961–69*, Winchester, 82, Fig. 2: 'The Old Minster: the sequence of construction as interpreted from documentary and archaeological evidence, 1962–69.'

9 Jackson, J., 2015, review of Sudhir Hazareesingh, *How the French Think*, 2015, *Times Literary Supplement*, 17 July, 4–5. Jackson quotes Hazareesingh as saying that, among the French ways of interpreting the world, the first is 'a passion for holism'.

10 Willis, R., 1846, 'The Architectural History of Winchester Cathedral', *Architectural History of Some English Cathedrals*, Part I, Chicheley, 1972, 18.

11 Brooke, C. N. L., 1980, *The Normans as Cathedral Builders*, Winchester, 92.

12 Fernie, E., 1985, 'A Historiography of Tewkesbury Abbey', in Heslop, T. A. and Sekules, V. (eds.), *Medieval Art and Architecture at Gloucester Cathedral*, Transactions of the Annual Conference of the British Archaeological Association 7, Leeds, 1–5, at 1.

13 Re surveying, see Fernie, *Norwich*, 13. Medieval architectural drawings only survive from after the late 12th century, and it might

be argued that they were brought into use because the buildings were becoming more complex. The pier forms of 13th-century churches are certainly more complicated than those of earlier centuries, but I find it impossible to believe that cathedrals such those of Canterbury and Durham were built without a plan. What changed around 1200 is much more likely to be that they started to make and retain copies, as part of the revolution in record-keeping of the late 11th and 12th centuries.

14 I am grateful to Paul Bennett for the information on the plan of Lanfranc's Canterbury, and to John Schofield for the figures for St Paul's.

15 Fernie, E., 1998, 'The Romanesque Church of Bury St Edmunds Abbey', in Gransden, A. (ed.), *Medieval Art and Architecture at Bury St Edmunds*, Transactions of the Annual Conference of the British Archaeological Association 20, Leeds, 1–15.

16 Gem, R., 1983, 'The Romanesque Cathedral of Winchester: Patron and Design in the Eleventh Century', in Heslop, T. A. and Sekules, V., *Medieval Art and Architecture at Winchester Cathedral*, Transactions of the Annual Conference of the British Archaeological Association 6, Leeds, 1–12.

I should explain my reasons for choosing the points I have selected for measuring between, and hence the lengths provided in the tables. They are not overall lengths: Norman Winchester is 162 m (531 ft) long from end to end, much greater than the 133 m (436 ft) of my lists. The lengths are to do with comparability: they are measures taken between the ends of the high roofs, so that, for example, the length of apse, ambulatory and axial chapel is separated from the core size of the building at the east end as a porch would be at the west end. St Albans, without an ambulatory and radiating chapels, can thus be compared with Winchester which has those features.

It should be noted that the figures given in Tables 2, 3 and 4 are different from those I have published elsewhere (e.g. Fernie, *Architecture of Norman England*, 304–7). This is because those were taken to the west end of the nave rather than the interior of the façade as here. I had two reasons for making the change, first to see if the pattern holds, which it does, and second because it separates the St Peter's group more clearly from the four earlier buildings of 1070–77.

17 Mention should be made of the megalomaniac abbot at Fulda in the time of Charlemagne who used the dimensions of the transept of St Peter's for that part of his church: Krautheimer, R., 1942, 'The Carolingian Revival of Early Christian Architecture', *Art Bulletin* 24, 1–38.

18 Kubach, H. and Haas, W., 1972, *Der Dom zu Speyer*, Munich.

19 Bates, *William the Conqueror*, 499–500.

20 Bates, *William the Conqueror*, 389–96; 409: 'For all that Bishop Walchelin was ultimately responsible for the cathedral's design, it was most assuredly William and his conception of rule that he had in mind when he embarked on such a huge project.'; 509: 'The trend towards the construction of extremely large cathedrals and monastic churches drawing on inspirations that were not in Normandy was present from the earliest period of conquest. Here William's personal insistence on grandeur and display must have been a powerful influencing factor'.

21 Bates, D., 2006, 'William the Conqueror's Wider Western European World', *HSJ* 15, 73–87, at 78. Bates carefully notes that Hugh would have been grateful to William for funding his pilgrimage to Jerusalem, perhaps causing him to overstate the case. This is likely to be true, but good flattery has to be credible. The article also cites (75) the evidence for William in 1074 entering the Confraternity of Cluny, joining many of the kings and queens of Europe, and the emperor.

22 On the marriage negotiations see Castiñeiras, M., 2010, *Compostela and Europe: The Story of Diego Gelmírez*, Santiago de Compostela and Milan, 38, and Bates, *William*, 330, 393. On the conspiracy, Falque Rey, E. (ed.), 1988, *Historia Compostellana*, Turnhout, 15: I, 2, lines 245–7, and Fernie, 'Three Romanesque', 1–22.

23 Castiñeiras, *Compostela and Europe*; Nicolai, B. and Rheidt, K. (eds.), 2015, *Santiago de Compostela: Pilgerarchitectur und bildliche Repräsentation in neuer Perspektive*, Berne, Berlin, Brussels, Frankfurt am Main, New York, Oxford, Vienna.

24 Walker, R., 2016, *Art in Spain and Portugal from the Romans to the Early Middle Ages*, Amsterdam, 311.

25 Rollason, D., 1989, *Saints and their Relics in Anglo-Saxon England*, Oxford and Cambridge (Mass), 223–4. Bates, *William the Conqueror*, 430–31, notes that William's intervention in Wales in 1081 was described by a contemporary source as a pilgrimage: 'this illustrates William once more showing deference to a prestigious saint [David], a phenomenon that we have already observed in the cases of St Edmund, St Cuthbert, and St Etheldreda.' There were instances where Anglo-Saxon saints' cults were suppressed; see for example Browett, R., 2016, 'The Fate of Anglo-Saxon Saints After the Norman Conquest of England: St Æthelwold of Winchester as a Case Study', *History* 101, 183–200.

26 The Normans' overall intention was nonetheless clear as, of the 18 bishops appointed between 1070 and 1089, at least 16 were Norman by birth or training (Loyn, H. R., 1982, *The Norman Conquest*, (1965), London, Melbourne, Sydney, Auckland, Johannesburg, 158).

27 Gem, R., 1978, 'Bishop Wulfstan II and the Romanesque Cathedral Church of Worcester', in Popper, G. (ed.), *Medieval Art and*

Architecture at Worcester, Transactions of the Annual Conference of the British Archaeological Association 1, Leeds, 15–37.

28 Klukas, A., 1984, 'The Architectural Implications of the *Decreta Lanfranci*', *ANS* 6, 136–71.

29 Liess, R., 1967, *Der Frühromanischen Kirchenbau des 11. Jahrhunderts in der Normandie*, Munich; Baylé, M. (ed.), 1997, *L'architecture normande au Moyen Age*, 2 vols., Caen; Morgenstern, J., 2003, 'Jumièges, église Notre-Dame', *Congrès Archéologique de France. Rouen et Pays de Caux*, 79–96.

30 Brown, R. A., 1982, 'William of Malmesbury as an Architectural Historian', in *Mélanges d'archéologie et d'histoire médiévale en l'honneur du Doyen Michel de Boüard*, Geneva, 9–16. Edward erected the church 'in a new style of architecture' (*ecclesiam aedificationis genere nouo fecit*), and 'in that style which he was the first in England to use' (*quam ipse illo compositionis genere primus in Anglia edificauerat*), while in William of Malmesbury's own day you could see everywhere churches 'built after a style unknown before' (*nouo edificandi genere consurgere*). Fernie, E., 2009, 'Edward the Confessor's Westminster Abbey', in Mortimer (ed.), *Edward the Confessor, the man and the Legend*, 139–50; Woodman, F., 2015, 'Edward the Confessor's Church at Westminster: An Alternative View', in Rodwell, W. and Tatton-Brown, T. (eds.), *Westminster, I. The Art, Architecture and Archaeology of the Royal Abbey*, Transactions of the Annual Conference of the British Archaeological Association 39, Leeds, 61–8.

31 Reilly, L., 1997, 'Durham Cathedral: The Emergence of Anglo-Norman Architecture', *ANS* 19, 335–51; Thurlby, M., 2015, 'The Anglo-Saxon Tradition in Post-Conquest Architecture and Sculpture', in Woodman and Brett (eds.), *The Long Twelfth-Century View*, 307–58; Fernie, 'The Effect', 72–7; Fernie, 'Architecture', 111–15; Fernie, *Architecture of Norman England*, 34, 273.

32 Gem, R., 1984, 'L'architecture pré-romane et romane en Angleterre: problèmes d'origine et de chronologie', *Bulletin monumental* 142, 233–72: English text: 'Pre- Romanesque and Early Romanesque Architecture in England: Problems of Origin and Chronology', in Gem, R., 2004, *Studies in English Pre-Romanesque and Romanesque Architecture*, London, 356–416 (394–416); Fernie, 'The Effect', 77–85; Fernie, 'Architecture', 106–15.

13 The aristocracy of conquered England

1 *DP.*

2 Keats-Rohan, K. S. B., 1992, 'The Bretons and Normans of England 1066–1154: The Family, the Fief and the Feudal Monarchy', *Nottingham Medieval Studies* 36, 42–78. For the Flemings, see

Oksanen, E., 2012, *Flanders and the Anglo-Norman World 1066–1216*, Cambridge, chapter 6.

3 Keats-Rohan, K. S. B., 2003, 'Le Rôle des élites dans la colonisation de l'Angleterre (vers 1066–1135)', in Bouet, P. and Gazeau, V. (eds.), *La Normandie et l'Angleterre au Moyen Age*, Caen, 39–60.

4 Blair, J., 'D'Oilly, Robert (d.c.1092)', *ODNB*.

5 Wareham, A., 'Bigod, Roger (I) (d.1107)', *ODNB*.

6 Tsurushima, H., 1992, 'The Fraternity of Rochester Cathedral Priory about 1100', *ANS* 14, 313–37.

7 Brown, R. A., 1973, *The Origins of English Feudalism*, London, 72–82.

8 Reynolds, S., 1994, *Fiefs and Vassals: The Medieval Evidence Reinterpreted*, Oxford; Abels, R., 2009, 'The Historiography of a Construct: "Feudalism" and the Medieval Historian', *History Compass* 7/3, 1008–31; for the old view see, for example, Brown, *Origins of English Feudalism*, introduction.

9 Green, *The Aristocracy*, chapter 2.

10 Garnett, *Conquered England*.

11 Maddicott, *Origins of the English Parliament*, 80–6.

12 Lieberman, M., 2015, 'A New Approach to the Knighting Ritual', *Speculum* 90, 391–423.

13 Cowdrey, H. E. J., 1969, 'Bishop Ermenfrid of Sion and the Penitential Ordinance Following the Battle of Hastings', *JEH* 20, 225–42.

14 Gillingham, J., 1994, '1066 and the Introduction of Chivalry into England', *Law and Government in England and Normandy in the Middle Ages*, Garnett, G. and Hudson, J. (eds.), Cambridge, 31–55.

15 Crouch, *The English Aristocracy*, 40–48.

16 For the transition, see now Sharpe, R., 2016, 'The Earliest Norman Sheriffs', *History* 101, 485–94.

17 Stenton, F. M., 1961 (2nd ed.), *The First Century of English Feudalism*, Oxford, 80–114; Crouch, *The Image of Aristocracy*, 106–14. The process by which some lordships came to be known as baronies evolved over time. One criterion used was payment of £100 as a relief or succession payment. For a succinct description see Roffe, D., 2000, *Domesday: The Inquest and the Book*, 44–5.

18 The term was used in the address clauses of royal documents.

19 Hollister, C. W., 1987, 'The Greater Domesday Tenants-in-Chief', in Holt, J. C. (ed.), *Domesday Studies*, Woodbridge, 219–48.

20 Roffe, D., 2012, 'English Lords in Post-Conquest Lincolnshire and Beyond', in Roffe, D. (ed.), *The English and their Legacy 900–1200: Essays in Honour of Ann Williams*, Woodbridge, 205–28.

21 Arnold, T. (ed.), 1882–5, Symeon of Durham, *Historia Regum* in *Opera omnia*, 2 vols., Rolls Series, London, ii, 188; JW, iii, 10.

22 Dalton, P., 1994, *Conquest, Anarchy and Lordship. Yorkshire, 1066–1154*, Cambridge; Green, *Forging the Kingdom*, 235–6.

23 Harvey, S. P. J., 1988, 'Domesday England', in Hallam, H. E. (ed.), *The Agrarian History of England and Wales: Volume 2, 1042–1350*, Cambridge, 45–136.

24 Moore, J. S., 1989, 'Domesday Slavery', *ANS* 11, 191–220.

25 *GR*, i, 362.

26 Pelteret, D. A. E., 1995, *Slavery in Early Medieval England: From the Reign of Alfred until the Twelfth Century*; Wyatt, D., 2009, *Slaves and Warriors in Early Medieval Britain and Ireland, 800–1200*, Leiden and Boston.

27 Pelteret, *Slavery in Early Medieval England*, chapter 10.

28 Faith, R., 1997, *The English Peasantry and the Growth of Lordship*, London, chapter 8.

29 Hyams, P. R., 1980, *Kings, Lords and Peasants in Medieval England: The Common Law of Villeinage in the Twelfth and Thirteenth Centuries*, Oxford; Hatcher, J., 1981, 'English Serfdom and Villeinage: Towards a Reassessment,' *Past and Present* 90, 3–39.

30 Stafford, P., 1998, 'Review of Faith, *English Peasantry*', *History* 83, 701–2.

31 Williamson, T., 2003, *Shaping Medieval Landscapes: Settlement, Society, Environment*, Oxford. See further Oliver Creighton's chapter in this volume.

32 David Roffe, for instance, has stressed that king's thegns before 1066 were comparable with barons, and their powers of sake and soke over lesser thegns were transferred to their Norman successors: Roffe, *Domesday*, 30–1; Roffe, D., 1990, 'From Thegnage to Barony: Sake and Soke, Title and Tenants-in-Chief', *ANS* 12, 157–76.

33 The classic discussion of the honour in Norman England was that by Stenton, *First Century of English Feudalism*, 42–83. For criticism, see Crouch, D., 1995, 'From Stenton to McFarlane: Models of Societies of the Twelfth and Thirteenth Centuries', *TRHS* 6th ser., 5, 179–200. For lords' courts see Hudson, *Oxford History of the Laws of England*, 284–8.

34 Davison, B., 1961, 1962–3, 'Sulgrave', *Medieval Archaeology* 5, 329; 6–7, 333.

35 Liddiard, *Castles in Context*; and Liddiard, R., 2000, *Landscapes of Lordship: Norman Castles and the Countryside in Medieval Norfolk, 1066–1200*, BAR, British Series, 309.

36 Fleming, *Kings and Lords*; cf. Green, *The Aristocracy*, chapter 2.

37 Stenton, F. M., 1971 (3rd ed.), *Anglo-Saxon England*, Oxford, 626.

38 Dalton, *Conquest, Anarchy and Lordship*, chapter 1.

39 Williams, A., 2016, 'Hunting the Snark and Finding the Boojum: The Tenurial Revolution Revisited', in Roffe, D. and Keats-Rohan, K. S. B. (eds.), *Domesday Now: New Approaches to the Inquest and the Book*, Woodbridge, 155–68.

40 Green, *The Aristocracy*, chapter 4.

41 Green, *The Aristocracy*, chapter 5.
42 Harvey, S. P. J., 1983, 'The Extent and Profitability of Demesne Agriculture in England in the Later Eleventh Century', in Aston, T. H., Coss, P. R., Dyer, C. and Thirsk, J. (eds.), *Social Relations and Ideas: Essays in Honour of R. H. Hilton*, Cambridge, 45–72; Hamshere, J. D., 'Domesday Book: Estate Structures in the West Midlands', in Holt (ed.), *Domesday Studies*, 155–82.
43 Matthew, D. J. A., 1962, *Norman Monasteries and their English Possessions*, Oxford.
44 Golding, B., 1986, 'Anglo-Norman Knightly Burials', in Harper-Bill, C. and Harvey, R. (eds.), *The Ideals and Practice of Medieval Knighthood*, Woodbridge, 35–48; Cownie, *Religious Patronage*, 201–6 and Appendix, 212–15.
45 Holt, J. C., 1982–5, 'Feudal Society and the Family in Early Medieval England', Presidential Addresses to the Royal Historical Society, *TRHS* 5th ser., 32, 193–212; 33, 193–220; 34, 1–25; 35, 1–28.
46 Holt, J. C., 1972, 'Politics and Property in Early Medieval England', *Past & Present* 57, 3–52.
47 Green, *The Aristocracy*, chapter 11. For the situation before the Conquest, see Stafford, P., 1994, 'Women and the Norman Conquest', *TRHS* 6th ser., 4, 221–49.
48 Fenton, K., 2008, *Gender, Nation and Conquest in William of Malmesbury's Gesta Regum Anglorum*, Woodbridge.
49 Bartlett, R., 1994, 'Symbolic Meanings of Hair in the Middle Ages', *TRHS* 6th ser., 4, 43–60; Stafford, P., 2005, 'The Meanings of Hair in the Anglo-Norman World: Masculinity, Reform and National Identity', in Dijk M. van and Nip, R. (eds.), *Saints, Scholars and Politicians: Gender as a Tool in Medieval Studies. Festschrift in Honour of Anneke Mulder-Bakker on the Occasion of her Sixty-Fifth Birthday*, Turnhout, 153–71; Darlington, R. R. (ed.), 1928, *The Vita Wulfstani of William of Malmesbury*, Camden Society 3rd ser., 40, 23.
50 *GR*, i, 456–61.
51 *GR*, i, 558–60.
52 *GR*, i, 558.
53 Sykes, *The Norman Conquest: A Zooarchaeological Perspective*; Sykes, N., 2010, 'Deer, Land, Knives and Halls: Social Change in Early Medieval England', *Antiquaries Journal* 90, 175–93; Hagger, M., 2012, 'Lordship and Lunching: Interpretations of Eating and Food in the Anglo-Norman World, 1050–1200, with reference to the Bayeux Tapestry', in Roffe (ed.), *The English and their Legacy*, 229–44.
54 Sykes, *The Norman Conquest: A Zooarchaeological Perspective*, 34, 42, 65, 68, 86–93.
55 Sykes, *The Norman Conquest: A Zooarchaeological Perspective*, 76–85.

56 Sykes, *The Norman Conquest: A Zooarchaeological Perspective*, 28, 34, 42, 60–69, 87–91; Williamson, T., 2007, *Rabbits, Warrens and Archaeology*, Stroud; Aston, M., 1988, *Medieval Fish, Fisheries and Fishponds in England*, BAR, 182.

57 Richard II was mentioned as hunting at Vernon by William of Jumièges, *GND*, ii, 10. William the Conqueror enjoyed falconry, *GG*, 24. Early ducal charters contain relatively few references to *forestae*, Jørgensen, D., 2010, 'The Roots of the English Royal Forest,' *ANS* 32, 114–28, at 117–21.

58 Almond, R., 2003, *Medieval Hunting*, Stroud, 73–89.

59 ASC 'E', 1086 (Swanton (ed. and trans.), 221).

60 Green, J. A., 2013, 'Forest Laws in England and Normandy in the Twelfth Century', *HR* 86, 416–31. Details in Domesday Book about the New Forest in Hampshire reveal that whilst two royal manors and their hunting grounds were at the heart of the forest, other land had been brought within its bounds: Mew, K., 2001, 'The Dynamics of Lordship and Landscape as Revealed in a Domesday Study of the *Nova Foresta*', *ANS* 23, 155–66.

61 This subject has been neglected, but see now Jones, G., 2010, '"A Common of Hunting": Forests, Lordship and Community before and after the Conquest' in Langton, J. and Jones, G. (eds.), *Forests and Chases of Medieval England and Wales c.1000–c.1500*, Oxford, 37–67 at 39.

62 The situation before 1066 seems to have been that described in Cnut's second lawcode, clause 80, Liebermann, F. (ed.), 1903–16, *Die Gesetze der Angelsachsen*, 3 vols., Halle, i, 367–8. The hostility to King William's actions was expressed forcefully by the author of the 'E' version of the Anglo-Saxon Chronicle, Jurasinski, S., 2004, 'The *Rime of King William* and its Analogues', *Neophilologus* 88, 131–44.

63 Gautier, A., 2007, 'Game Parks in Sussex and the Godwinesons', *ANS* 29, 51–64.

64 ASC 'E', 1088 (Swanton (ed. and trans.), 223).

65 Thomas, *The English and the Normans*.

66 Bates, *The Normans and Empire*.

67 Golding, B., 1994, *Conquest and Colonization: The Normans in Britain 1066–1100*, Houndmills; West, F. J., 1999, 'The Colonial History of the Norman Conquest', *History* 84, 219–36.

68 Sharpe, R., 2011, 'Peoples and Languages in Eleventh- and Twelfth-Century Britain and Ireland: Reading the Charter Evidence', in D. Broun et al. (eds.), *The Reality behind Charter Diplomatic*, Glasgow, 1–119.

69 Garnett, G., 1985, '*Franci et Angli*: The Legal Distinction between Peoples after the Norman Conquest', *ANS* 8, 109–37.

70 Short, I., 1992, 'Patrons and Polyglots: French Literature in Twelfth-Century England', *ANS* 14, 229–49.

71 Matarasso, P. (ed.), 1993, 'John of Ford, "Life of Wulfric of Haselbury"', in *The Cistercian World: Monastic Writings of the Twelfth Century*, London, 243–4.
72 OV, ii, 256.
73 *GR*, i, 716.
74 Rule (ed.), Eadmer, *Historia Novorum*, 224.
75 Tyler, E. M., 2011, *Conceptualizing Multilingualism in Medieval England, c.800–c.1250*, Turnhout; O'Brien, B., 2011, *Reversing Babel: Translation Among the English During an Age of Conquests, c.800 to c.1200*, Newark; Treharne, E., 2012, *Living through Conquest: The Politics of Early English, 1020–1220*, Oxford.
76 Latimer, P., 2010, 'Assimilation in North-Western England from the Norman Conquest to the Early Thirteenth Century: The Kirkby, Pennington and Copeland Families', *Northern History* 47, 49–66.
77 Molyneaux, *Formation*.
78 Wareham, A., 2005, *Lords and Communities in Medieval East Anglia*, Woodbridge.
79 Green, *Forging the Kingdom*, 222–4.
80 Crouch, *English Aristocracy*, chapters 6–8.

14 1066 and the landscape

1 See Thomas, *The English and the Normans*.
2 Rippon, S. J., 2008, *Beyond the Medieval Village: The Diversification of Landscape Character in Southern Britain*, Oxford, 7; for a regional view of the Norman Conquest, see McClain, A., 2017, 'Rewriting the Narrative: Regional Dimensions of the Norman Conquest', in Dyer and Hadley (eds.), *The Archaeology of the 11th Century*, 203–28.
3 OV, ii, 214–15.
4 Dyer and Hadley (eds.), *The Archaeology of the 11th Century*.
5 McClain, 'Rewriting the Narrative', in Dyer and Hadley (eds.), *The Archaeology of the 11th Century*, 203–28.
6 Oksanen, E., 2012, *Flanders and the Anglo-Norman World, 1066–1216*, Cambridge, 11–17, chapter 6.
7 Le Patourel, *The Norman Empire*, 26.
8 Eales, R., 2014, 'Castles and Borders in England After 1066', *Château-Gaillard* 26, 149–57, at 154.
9 ASC 'E', 1092, (Swanton, 227).
10 Baring, F., 1898, 'The Conqueror's Footprints in Domesday', *EHR* 13, 17–25; Palmer, J. J. N., 1995, 'The Conqueror's Footprints in Domesday', in Ayton, A. and Price, J. L. (eds.), *The Medieval Military Revolution State, Society and Military Change in Medieval and Early Modern Europe*, London, 23–44.

11 Wightman, W. E., 1975, 'The Significance of "Waste" in the Yorkshire Domesday', *Northern History* 10, 55–71.

12 Palliser, D. M., 1993, 'Domesday Book and the "Harrying of the North"', *Northern History* 29, 1–23.

13 See, for example, Allerston, P., 1970, 'English Village Development: Findings from the Pickering District of North Yorkshire', *Transactions of the Institute of British Geographers* 51, 95–109; Sheppard, J., 1974, 'Metrological Analysis of Regular Village Plans in Yorkshire', *Agricultural History Review* 22.2, 118–35; Sheppard, J., 1976, 'Medieval Village Planning in Northern England: Some Evidence from Yorkshire', *Journal of Historical Geography* 2, 3–20.

14 McClain, 'Rewriting the Narrative', 203–28.

15 Bates, *William the Conqueror*, 313–21.

16 Dolley, R. H. M., 1966, *The Norman Conquest and the English Coinage*, London, 39; Palliser, 'Domesday Book and the "Harrying of the North"', 7–8.

17 Matthews, J. S., 2003, 'William the Conqueror's Campaign in Cheshire in 1069–70: Ravaging and Resistance in the North-West', *Northern History* 40, 53–70.

18 Creighton, O. H., *Castles and Landscapes*.

19 Fleming, R., 1993, 'Rural Elites and Urban Communities in Late-Saxon England', *Past & Present* 141, 3–37.

20 Harfield, C. G., 1991, 'A Hand-List of Castles Recorded in Domesday Book', *EHR* 106, 371–92, at 373.

21 Leary, J., Canti, M., Field, D., Fowler, P., Marshall, P. and Campbell, G., 2013, 'The Marlborough Mound, Wiltshire. A Further Neolithic Monumental Mound by the River Kennet', *Proceedings of the Prehistoric Society* 79, 137–63.

22 Eales, R., 1990, 'Royal Power and Castles in Norman England', *Medieval Knighthood* 3, 49–78.

23 See Creighton, O. H. and Wright, D. W., 2016, *The Anarchy: War and Status in Twelfth-Century Landscapes of Conflict*, Liverpool, chapter 4.

24 Marshall, P., 2016, 'Some Thoughts on the Use of the Anglo-Norman Donjon', in Davies et al. (eds.), *Castles and the Anglo-Norman World*, 147–58.

25 Gregory, J. and Liddiard, R., 2016, 'Visible from Afar? The Setting of the Anglo-Norman Donjon', in Davies et al. (eds.), *Castles and the Anglo-Norman World*, 159–74.

26 For an overview, see Creighton, *Castles and Landscapes*, chapter 8.

27 Higham, R. and Barker, P., 2000, *Hen Domen, Montgomery: A Timber Castle on the English-Welsh Border*, Exeter, 173–80.

28 Mayes, P. and Butler, L., 1983, *Sandal Castle Excavations 1964–1973, a Detailed Archaeological Report*, Wakefield. For summary, see Creighton, *Castles and Landscapes*, 27–33.

29 Beresford, G., 1987, *Goltho: The Development of an Early Medieval Manor c.850–1150*, London. The dating is much discussed: for a summary, see Creighton, *Castles and Landscapes*, 21 –7.

30 Gardiner, M., 2017, 'Manorial Farmsteads and the Expression of Lordship Before and After the Norman Conquest', in Dyer and Hadley (eds.), *The Archaeology of the 11th Century*, 88–103, at 99–100.

31 Armitage, E., 1912, *The Early Norman Castles of the British Isles*, London, 85.

32 Aston, M. A., 2000, *Monasteries in the Landscape*, Stroud, 74–8.

33 Knowles, D., 1963 (2nd ed.), *The Monastic Order in England: A History of its Development From the Times of St Dunstan to the Fourth Lateran Council, 940–1216*, Cambridge, 153.

34 Creighton and Wright, *The Anarchy*, 196–208.

35 See, for example, McClain, A., 2007, 'Medieval Cross Slabs in North Yorkshire: Chronology, Distribution, and Social Implications', *Yorkshire Archaeological Journal* 79, 155–93; McClain, A., 2011, 'Local Churches and the Conquest of the North: Elite Patronage and Identity in Saxo-Norman Northumbria', in Petts, D. and Turner, S. (eds.), *Early Medieval Northumbria: Kingdoms and Communities, AD 450–1100*, Turnhout, 151–78.

36 Craig-Atkins, E., 2017, 'Seeking "Norman Burials": Evidence for Continuity in Funerary Practice Following the Norman Conquest', in Dyer and Hadley (eds.), *The Archaeology of the 11th Century*, 139–58, at 150–2.

37 Creighton, *Castles and Landscapes*, 122–3.

38 Shapland, M. G., 2017, 'Anglo-Saxon Towers of Lordship and the Origins of the Castle in England', in Dyer and Hadley (eds.), *The Archaeology of the 11th Century*, 104–19, at 106–8.

39 Rollason, D., 2016, *The Power of Place: Rulers and their Palaces, Landscapes, Cities, and Holy Places*, Princeton and Oxford, 136–67.

40 Liddiard, R., 2003, 'The Deer Parks of Domesday Book', *Landscapes* 4, 4–23, at 7.

41 Rackham, O., 1986, *The History of the Countryside*, London, 125–7.

42 Mileson, S. A., 2009, *Parks in Medieval England*, Oxford, 121; Cantor, L. M. and Hatherly, J., 1979, 'The Medieval Parks of England', *Geography* 64, 71–85, at 78.

43 Cantor and Hatherly, 'The Medieval Parks', 79.

44 Muir, R., 2005, *Ancient Trees, Living Landscape*, Stroud, 122–4.

45 For examples, see Creighton, O. H., 2009, *Designs upon the Land: Elite Landscapes of the Middle Ages*, Woodbridge, 157–8.

46 See Creighton, *Designs upon the Land*, 214–15. For a different view, see Liddiard, R. and Williamson, T., 2008, 'There by Design? Some Reflections on Medieval Elite Landscapes', *The Archaeological Journal* 165, 520–35.

47 Davis, R. H. C., 1987, 'The Warhorses of the Normans', *ANS* 10, 67–82.

48 Sykes, *The Norman Conquest: A Zooarchaeological Perspective*, 79–80; Sykes, N., 2007, 'Animal Bones and Animal Parks', in Liddiard, R. (ed.), *The Medieval Park: New Perspectives*, Bollington, 58–9.

49 Sykes, N. and Carden, R. F., 2011, 'Were Fallow Deer Spotted (OE **pohha/*pocca*) in Anglo-Saxon England? Reviewing the Evidence for *Dama dama* in Early Medieval Europe', *Medieval Archaeology* 55, 139–62, at 149–50.

50 Sykes, *The Norman Conquest: A Zooarchaeological Perspective*, 80–4.

51 Rackham, O., 2011, 'Forest and Upland', in Crick and van Houts (eds.), *A Social History*, 46–55.

52 Green, J. A., 2013, 'Forest Laws in England and Normandy in the Twelfth Century', *HR* 86, 416–31.

53 Bond, J., 1994, 'Forests, Chases, Warrens and Parks in Medieval Wessex', in Aston, M. and Lewis, C. (eds.), *The Medieval Landscape of Wessex*, Oxford, 115–58, at 121–3.

54 Rahtz, P., 1979, *The Saxon and Medieval Palaces at Cheddar: Excavations 1960–62*, BAR, British Series, 65, Oxford.

55 Winchester, A. J. L., 2004, 'Moorland Forests of Medieval England', in Whyte, I. D. and Winchester, A. J. L. (eds.), *Society, Landscape and Environment in Upland Britain*, Society for Landscape Studies Supplementary Series 2, Birmingham, 21–36, at 22, 34.

56 Creighton, O. H. and Rippon, S. J., 2017, 'Conquest, Colonisation and the Countryside: Archaeology and the Mid-11th- to Mid-12th-Century Rural Landscape', in Dyer and Hadley (eds.), *The Archaeology of the 11th Century*, 57–87, at 60.

57 Jørgensen, D., 2010, 'The Roots of the English Royal Forest', *ANS* 32, 114–28.

58 Bond, 'Forests, Chases, Warrens and Parks in Medieval Wessex', 122.

59 Darby, H. C. and Campbell, E. M. J., 1962, *The Domesday Geography of South-East England*, Cambridge, 337–8.

60 Palliser, D. M., Slater, T. R. and Dennison, E. P., 2000, 'The Topography of Towns 600–1300', in Palliser, D. M. (ed.), *The Cambridge Urban History of Britain Volume 1: 600–1540*, Cambridge, 160, 153–86, at 173–4.

61 Williams, *The English*, 3.

62 Fleming, *Kings and Lords*, 210.

63 Fleming, *Kings and Lords*, 124–5.

64 Searle, E., 1974, *Lordship and Community: Battle Abbey and its Banlieu, 1066–1538*, Toronto, 49.

65 Welldon Finn, R., 1971, *The Norman Conquest and its Effects on the Economy: 1066–86*, London, 4.

66 Baxter, S., 2011, 'Lordship and Labour', in Crick and Van Houts (eds.), *A Social History*, 98–114, at 107.

67 See, for example, Thomas, *The English and the Normans*, 166.
68 Mortimer, R., 1981, 'The Beginnings of the Honour of Clare', *ANS* 3, at 119–41, at 133–4.
69 Witney, K. P., 1989, 'Development of the Kentish Marshes in the Aftermath of the Norman Conquest', *Archaeologia Cantiana* 107, 29–50.
70 Faith, R., 1997, *The English Peasantry and the Growth of Lordship*, Leicester, 215–18; Dyer, C., 2002, *Making a Living in the Middle Ages: The People of Britain 850–1520*, New Haven and London, 89.
71 Faith, *The English Peasantry*, 209–14.
72 Creighton and Rippon, 'Conquest, Colonisation and the Countryside', 69–71; Jervis, B., Whelan, F. and Livarda, A., 2017, 'Cuisine and Conquest: Interdisciplinary Perspectives on Food, Continuity and Change in 11th-Century England', in Dyer and Hadley (eds.), *The Archaeology of the 11th Century*, 244–62, at 247–51.
73 Jervis et al., 'Cuisine and Conquest', 248–53.
74 Unwin, T., 1991, *Wine and the Vine: An Historical Geography of Viticulture and the Wine Trade*, London and New York, 158.
75 Kapelle, W. E., 1979, *The Norman Conquest of the North: The Region and its Transformation, 1000–1135*, London, 213–25.
76 Creighton, O. H., 2005, 'Castles and Castle-Building in Town and Country', in Dyer, C. and Giles, K. (eds.), *Medieval Town and Country 1100–1500*, Society for Medieval Archaeology Monograph 22, Leeds, 275–92; see also Creighton, *Castles and Landscapes*, 103, 157.
77 Gelling, M., 1978, *Signposts to the Past: Place-Names and the History of England*, London: Dent, 237–8; Williams, *The English*, 211.
78 Smith, A. H., 1964, *The Place-Names of Gloucestershire, Volume 1*, English Place-Name Society vol. 38, Cambridge, 129–30.
79 Barker and Higham, *Hen Domen*, 12.
80 Gelling, *Signposts to the Past*, 238.
81 Weetch, R., 2017, 'Tradition and Innovation: Lead-Alloy Brooches and Urban Identities in the 11th Century', in Dyer and Hadley (eds.), *The Archaeology of the 11th Century*, 263–82, at 264.
82 See Meeson, R. A. and Welch, C. M., 1993, 'Earthfast Posts: The Persistence of Alternative Building Techniques', *Vernacular Architecture* 24, 1–17.
83 For an overview, see Taylor, C. C., 1983, *Village and Farmstead: A History of Rural Settlement in England*, London. For a recent view that many villages in Midland England attained their historic nucleated forms only in the 11th and 12th centuries, see Williamson, T., Liddiard, R. and Partida, T., 2013, *Champion: The Making and Unmaking of the English Midland Landscape*, Liverpool.

84 See, for example, Rippon, *Beyond the Medieval Village*.
85 Creighton and Rippon, 'Conquest, Colonisation and the Countryside', in Dyer and Hadley (eds.), *The Archaeology of the 11th Century*, 71–7.
86 For an overview, see Beresford, M. and Hurst, J., 1990, *Wharram Percy: Deserted Medieval Village*, London.
87 Stamper, P. A. and Croft, R. A., 2000, *Wharram: A Study of Settlement on the Yorkshire Wolds. Vol. 8, The South Manor Area*, York, 197–8.
88 Darby, H. C., 1977, *The Domesday Geography of England*, Cambridge, 337; Williams, *The English*, 196–7.
89 Harfield, 'A Hand-List of Castles', 374, 375–6, 381.
90 Harfield, 'A Hand-List of Castles', 377, 380.
91 For a summary and examples, see Creighton, O. H. and Barry, T., 2012, 'Seigneurial and Elite Sites in the Landscape', in Christie, N. and Stamper, P. (eds.), *Rural Medieval Britain and Ireland, AD800–1600: Settlements, Landscape and Regions*, Oxford, 70–4.
92 Faith, *The English Peasantry*, 225, and see also 225–9; for examples, Taylor, *Village and Farmstead*, 138–47; Creighton and Wright, *The Anarchy*, 234–6.
93 Creighton and Wright, *The Anarchy*, 236–40.
94 King, D. J. C. and Spurgeon, J., 1965, 'Mottes in the Vale of Montgomery', *Archaeologia Cambrensis* 114, 69–86.
95 Harfield, 'A Hand-List of Castles', 374, 375–6, 377.
96 Creighton and Wright, *The Anarchy*, 235.
97 Carver, M. O. H., 1979, 'Three Saxo-Norman Tenements in Durham City', *Medieval Archaeology* 23, 1–80, at 71.
98 Creighton and Rippon, 'Conquest, Colonisation and the Countryside', 76–7.
99 Birks, H. J. B., 1965, 'Pollen Analytical Investigations at Holcroft Moss, Lancashire, and Lindow Moss, Cheshire', *Journal of Ecology* 53, 299–314.
100 Fleming, R., 2011, 'Land Use and People', in Crick and van Houts (eds.), *A Social History*, 15–37, at 37.

15 Writing about William the Conqueror

1 The notes to this essay have been kept to a minimum and are largely restricted to publications that have appeared since *William the Conqueror* was published and to earlier ones that are central to this article's arguments. Recent publications include other biographies, Davy, G., 2014, *Guillaume le Conquérant: le bâtard de Normandie*, Paris; Morris, *William I*, and a major treatment of William's life in German, Peltzer, J., 2016, *1066: Der Kampf um Englands Krone*, Munich. I am grateful to all who have attended

lectures and presentations I have given about *William* and to all those with whom I have discussed the themes of this article.

2 Bates, *The Normans and Empire*.

3 On this, see Bates, D., 2009, 'Lucien Musset et la Normandie au XIe siècle: un point de vue d'Outre-Manche', in Gazeau, V. and Neveux, F. (eds.), *Postérité de Lucien Musset*, Caen, 35–42, at 35–6.

4 *Acts of William I*, 2.

5 For a post-1066 William charter not in *Acts of William I*, see Allen, R., 2009, '"A Proud and Headstrong Man": John of Ivry, Bishop of Avranches and Archbishop of Rouen, 1060–79', *HR* 82, 1–39, at 21–7. For a charter dating from 1066, see Allen, R., 2017, 'Un nouvel acte de Guillaume le Bâtard, duc de Normandie (18 juin 1066)', *Bibliothèque de l'Ecole des Chartes* 171, 517–38.

6 Rozier, Roach, Gasper and van Houts (eds.), *Orderic Vitalis*; Thomson, Dolmans, and Winkler (eds.), *Discovering William of Malmesbury*; Winkler, *Royal Responsibility*; Tyler, *England in Europe*.

7 The general complexities are well set out in Ashe, *The Oxford English Literary History*, chapters 1 and 2.

8 Wood, I., 2013, *The Modern Origins of the Early Middle Ages*, Oxford.

9 In addition to works already cited, Treharne, *Living Through Conquest*; Green, *Forging the Kingdom*; Hagger, *Norman Rule in Normandy* and Barrow, *The Clergy in the Medieval World* are very important books that fall into this category.

10 A further important contribution published since *William* appeared is Lambert, T., 2017, *Law and Order in Anglo-Saxon England*, Oxford.

11 For an essay on the paradoxes I have in mind, see Nelson, J. L., 1997, 'Kings with Justice, Kings without Justice: An Early Medieval Paradox', in *La giustitzia nell'alto medioevo (secoli IX-XI): Settimane di Studio del Centro Italiano di Studi sull'Alto Medioevo* 44, ii, 797–826. See also Kershaw, P. J. E., 2011, *Peaceful Kings: Peace, Power, and the Early Medieval Political Imagination*, Oxford, 262–8; Koziol, G., 1992, *Begging Pardon and Favor: Ritual and Political Order in Early Medieval France*, Ithaca and London.

12 Malegam, J. Y., 2013, *The Sleep of Behemoth: Disputing Peace and Violence in Medieval Europe, 1000–1200*, Ithaca and London, 6.

13 Van Houts, 'The Norman Conquest through European Eyes' will always be for me the seminal essay on this subject, even if here and in *William* I want to either nuance or adjust the contexts in which some of the opinions were expressed.

14 Hadley and Dyer (eds.), *The Archaeology of the 11th Century*.

15 McDougall, S., 2017, *Royal Bastards: The Birth of Illegitimacy, 800–1230*, Oxford, with William's case treated at 116–20.

16 Van Houts, E., 2016, 'Orderic and his Father, Odelerius', in Rozier et al. (eds.), *Orderic Vitalis*, 17–26.

17 Licence, 'Edward the Confessor and the Succession Question'.

18 Tyler, *England in Europe*, 260–94, with Matilda discussed at 273–8.

19 Bates, D., [forthcoming], 'William the Conqueror and Wessex'.

20 Williams, A., 2017, 'Of Danes and Thegns in Domesday Book: Scandinavian Settlement in Eleventh-Century Berkshire', *ANS* 39, 219–35, at 225–8.

21 Browett, R., 2016, 'The Fate of the Anglo-Saxon Saints after the Norman Conquest: St Æthelwold of Winchester as a Case Study', *History* 101, 183–200.

22 Lucas-Avenel, M.-A., 2018, 'Écrire la conquête: une comparaison des récits de Guillaume de Poitiers et de Geoffroi Malaterra', in Bates, D'Angelo and van Houts (eds.), *People, Texts and Artefacts*, 153–70, at 159–63.

23 *GG*, 102–3 (*Conuenit etiam externus miles in auxilium copiosus, uerum omnes iustae causae fiducia contraxit*); ASC 'D', 1066.

24 *GG*, 162–5; ASC 'D', 1066.

25 O'Donnell, T., 2017, 'The *Carmen de Hastingae Proelio* and the Poetics of 1067', *ANS* 39, 151–67, with the quotation at 167.

26 Dalton, 'William the Peacemaker', with 'intimidate' at 25.

27 For relevant recent and forthcoming studies, see Sharpe, R., 2016, 'The Earliest Norman Sheriffs', *History* 101, 485–94; Bates, D., 2018, 'Guillaume le Conquérant et les abbés anglais', in Bauduin, P., Combalbert, G., Dubois, A., Garnier, B., and Maneuvrier, C. (eds.), Sur les pas de Lanfranc du Bec à Caen: Recueil d'études en hommage à Véronique Gazeau, Cahiers des Annales de Normandie, no. 37, Caen, 335–42.

28 Bates, *Normans and Empire*, 13–14.

29 McClain, A., 2017, 'Rewriting the Narrative: Regional Dimensions of the Norman Conquest', in Hadley and Dyer (eds.), *The Archaeology of the 11th Century*, 203–28, opens up the subject in important new ways.

30 Savill, B., 2017, 'Prelude to Forgery: Baldwin of Bury Meets Pope Alexander II', *EHR* 132, 795–822.

31 Plassmann, A., 2018, 'Bede's Legacy in William of Malmesbury and Henry of Huntingdon', in Bates, D'Angelo and van Houts (eds.), *People, Texts and Artefacts*, 171–92.

32 Winkler, *Royal Responsibility*, 214. For his treatment of William, see 124–8, 190–93, 222–5. For the Anglo-Saxon Chronicle, 90–4.

33 *GP*, i, 90–7, with Malmesbury's comment on his earlier *Gesta Regum* at 94–5. See further, Kemp, R., 2017, 'Advising the King: Kingship, Bishops and Saints in the Works of William of Malmesbury', in Thomson et al. (eds.), *Discovering William of Malmesbury*, 65–79, at 69–70.

34 Bates, D., [forthcoming], 'Lives, Identities, and the Historians of the Normans'.

35 Thus, on the Harrying of the North, cf. OV, ii, 230–3; *GR*, i, 462–5.

36 Malegam, *The Sleep of Behemoth*, 61–75.

37 Pössel, C., 2009, 'The Magic of Early Medieval Ritual', *EME* 17, 111–25, at 117.

38 For valuable reflections, see Stafford, P., 2006, 'Writing the Biography of Eleventh-Century Queens', in Bates, D., Crick, J. and Hamilton, S. (eds.), *Writing Medieval Biography, 750–1250: Essays in Honour of Professor Frank Barlow*, Woodbridge, 99–109.

39 Brownlie, S., 2013, *Memory and Myths of the Norman Conquest*, Woodbridge. For my own efforts, see Bates, D., 2005, '1066: Does the Date Still Matter?', *HR* 78, 443–64, at 446–7. A study day organised by The Wuffing Education Study Centre at Sutton Hoo on 14 October 2017 made an especially enjoyable and informative contribution to this topic.

40 Gazeau, V., 2014, 'Imagining the Conqueror: The Changing Image of William the Conqueror, 1830–1945', *HSJ* 25, 245–64; Golding, B., 2017, 'Remembering the Battle of Hastings: Memorialization, Le Souvenir Normand, and the Entente Cordiale', *ANS* 39, 65–79.

41 Thus, for example, Wood, *The Modern Origins of the Early Middle Ages*; Matthews, D., 2015, *Medievalism: A Critical History*, Woodbridge; Fazioli, K. P., 2017, *The Mirror of the Medieval: An Anthropology of the Western Historical Imagination*, New York and Oxford.

42 McKitterick, R., 2008, *Charlemagne: The Formation of a European Identity*, Cambridge, 1–7.

43 Bates, 'William the Conqueror and Wessex'.

44 Thus, for example, Vincent, N., 2011, 'More Tales of the Conquest', in Crouch and Thompson (eds.), *Normandy and its Neighbours*, Turnhout, 271–301.

45 Lebouteiller, S., 2017, 'Le meurtre de Mathilde de Flandre par Guillaume le Conquérant: itinéraire d'une légende dans la littérature islande médiévale', *AN* 67, 15–41.

46 Bates, D., [forthcoming], 'Migration, Conquest and Identity: England in the Eleventh and Twelfth Centuries', in *Le Migrazioni nell'Alto Medioevo: Settimane di Studio del Centro Italiano di Studi sull'Alto Medioevo 66*.

Select bibliography

This bibliography contains the published primary sources and the secondary sources which have been frequently referred to in this book and those which are recommended as further reading for those wishing to explore the book's subject in greater depth. For further reading, attention must also be drawn to the articles that appear in the annual publications based on the proceedings of the Battle Conference on Anglo-Norman Studies, the Haskins Society conference, and the conferences held in Normandy at Cerisy-la-Salle. Many of the individuals mentioned in the articles have entries in the *Oxford Dictionary of National Biography*. With a small number of exceptions, the contents of this bibliography have been limited to books and to English language publications. All the items included in the bibliography appear in shortened form in the notes to the articles in which they are cited.

Published primary sources

Barlow, F. (ed. and trans.), 1992 (2nd ed.), *The Life of King Edward who Rests at Westminster, Attributed to a Monk of Saint-Bertin*, OMT, Oxford

Barlow, F. (ed. and trans.), 1999, *The Carmen de Hastingae Proelio of Guy Bishop of Amiens*, OMT, Oxford

Bates, D. (ed.), 1998, *Regesta Regum Anglo-Normannorum: The Acta of William I (1066–1087)*, Oxford

Blake, E. O. (ed.), 1962, *Liber Eliensis*, Camden 3rd ser., 92 (Fairweather, J. (trans.), 2005, *Liber Eliensis: A History of the Isle of Ely from the Seventh Century to the Twelfth*, Woodbridge)

Brown, R. A., 1984, *The Norman Conquest*, Documents of Medieval History, 5, London

Burgess, G. S and Holden, A. J. (eds.), 2002, *The History of the Norman People: Wace's Roman de Rou*, translated by Glyn S. Burgess with the text of Anthony J. Holden, and notes by Glyn S. Burgess and Elisabeth van Houts, Société Jersiaise, St Helier

Chibnall, M. (ed. and trans.), 1969–80, *The Ecclesiastical History of Orderic Vitalis*, 6 vols., OMT, Oxford

Clover, H. and Gibson, M. (ed. and trans.), 1979, *The Letters of Lanfranc, Archbishop of Canterbury*, OMT, Oxford

Darlington, R. R. and McGurk, P. (eds.), 1995–8, *The Chronicle of John of Worcester*, 2 vols. (vols. ii and iii), OMT, Oxford

Davis, R. H. C. and Chibnall, M. (ed. and trans.), 1998, *The Gesta Guillelmi of William of Poitiers*, OMT, Oxford

Douglas, D. C. and Greenaway, G. W. (eds.), 1981 (2nd ed.), *English Historical Documents, vol. II: 1042–1189*, London

Erskine, R. W. H. (ed.), 1986, *Great Domesday Book*, London

Farley, A. (ed.), 1783, *Domesday Book, seu Liber Censualis Willelmi Primi*, 2 vols., London

Fauroux, M. (ed.), 1961, *Recueil des actes des ducs de Normandie de 911 à 1066*, Mémoires de la Société des Antiquaires de Normandie, vol. xxxvi, Caen

Greenway, D. (ed. and trans.), 1996, Henry, Archdeacon of Huntingdon, *Historia Anglorum: The History of the English People*, OMT, Oxford

Harmer, F. E., 1952, *Anglo-Saxon Writs*, Manchester

Hilbert, K. (ed.), 1979, 'Adelae Comitissa', in *Baldricus Burgulensis, Carmina*, Heidelberg, 149–87 (Otter, M. (trans.), 2001, 'Baudri of Bourgueil, "To Countess Adela"', *The Journal of Medieval Latin* 11, 60–141)

Licence, T. (ed. and trans., with the assistance of Lockyer, L.), 2014, *Herman the Archdeacon and Goscelin of Saint-Bertin, Miracles of St Edmund*, OMT, Oxford

Morris, J. et al. (eds.), 1975–92, *Domesday Book*, Chichester

Morton, C. and Muntz, H. (eds. and trans.), 1972, *The Carmen de Hastingae Proelio of Guy Bishop of Amiens*, OMT, Oxford

Mynors, R. A. B., Winterbottom, M. and Thomson, R. M. (eds. and trans.), 1998–9, William of Malmesbury, *Gesta regum Anglorum: The History of the English Kings*, 2 vols., OMT, Oxford

Rule, M. (ed.), 1884, *Eadmer, Historia Novorum*, Rolls Series, London (Bosanquet, G. (trans.), 1964, *Eadmer's History of Recent Events in England: Historia Novorum in Anglia*, London)

Sawyer, P. H., 1968, *Anglo-Saxon Charters: An Annotated List and Bibliography*, London (updated at www.esawyer.org.uk)

Swanton, M. J. (ed. and trans.), 1996, *The Anglo-Saxon Chronicle*, London

van Houts, E. M. C. (ed. and trans.), 1992–5, *The Gesta Normannorum Ducum of William of Jumièges, Orderic Vitalis, and Robert of Torigni*, 2 vols., OMT, Oxford

van Houts, E. M. C. (ed. and trans.), 1999, 'The *Breuis Relatio de Guillelmo nobilissimo comite Normannorum*, written by a Monk of Battle Abbey', in van Houts, E., *History and Family Traditions in England and the Continent*, chapter VII; reprinted here, with a translation added, from van Houts, E., 1997, in *Camden Miscellany*, 5th ser., x, Cambridge, 1–48

van Houts, E. M. C., 2000, *The Normans in Europe*, Manchester

van Houts, E. M. C. and Love, R. (eds. and trans.), 2013, *The Warenne (Hyde) Chronicle*, OMT Oxford

Whitelock, D. (ed.), 1979 (2nd. ed.), *English Historical Documents, vol. I, c.500–1042*, London

Whitelock, D., Brett, M. and Brooke, C. N. L., 1981, *Councils and Synods with Other Documents Relating to the English Church, 1066–1204*, 2 vols., Oxford

Williams, A. and Martin, G. (eds.), 2000, *Little Domesday Book*, 3 vols., London

Winterbottom, M. and Thomson, R. M. (eds. and trans.), 2002, William of Malmesbury, *Saints' Lives: Lives of Ss. Wulfstan, Dunstan, Patrick, Benignus and Indract*, OMT, Oxford

Winterbottom, M. and Thomson, R. M. (eds. and trans.), 2007, William of Malmesbury, *Gesta pontificum Anglorum: The History of the English Bishops*, 2 vols., OMT, Oxford

Secondary sources

Aird, W. M., 1998, *St Cuthbert and the Normans: The Church of Durham, 1071–1153*, Woodbridge

Aird, W. M., 2008, *Robert Curthose, Duke of Normandy, c.1050–1134*, Woodbridge

Ashe, L. 2017, *The Oxford English Literary History, Volume 1, 1000–1350: Conquest and Transformation*, Oxford

Barlow, F., 1997 (2nd ed.), *Edward the Confessor*, New Haven and London

Barrow, J., 2015, *The Clergy in the Medieval World: Secular Clerics, Their Families and Careers in North-Western Europe, c.800 to c.1200*, Cambridge

Bartlett, R., 1993, *The Making of Europe: Conquest, Colonization and Cultural Change 950–1350*, London

Bartlett, R., 2000, *England Under the Norman and Angevin Kings, 1075–1225*, Oxford

Bates, D., 1982, *Normandy Before 1066*, London and New York

Bates, D., 2013, *The Normans and Empire: The Ford Lectures Delivered in the University of Oxford During Hilary Term 2010*, Oxford

Bates, D., 2016, *William the Conqueror*, New Haven and London

Bates, D., D'Angelo, E. and van Houts, E. (eds.), 2018, *People, Texts and Artefacts: Cultural Transmission in the Medieval Norman Worlds*, London

Bauduin, P., 2004, *La première Normandie (Xᵉ–XIᵉ siècles). Sur les frontières de la haute Normandie: identité et construction d'une principauté*, Caen

Bauduin, P., 2009, *Le monde franc et les Vikings VIIIe–Xe siècle*, Paris

Baxter, S., 2007, *The Earls of Mercia: Lordship and Power in Late Anglo-Saxon England*, Oxford

Baxter, S., 2009, 'Edward the Confessor and the Succession Question', in Mortimer (ed.), *Edward the Confessor*, 77–118

Blair, J., 2005, *The Church in Anglo-Saxon Society*, Oxford

Bouet, P., Levy, B. and Neveux, F. (eds.), 2004, *The Bayeux Tapestry: Embroidering the Facts of History*, Caen

Burton, J., 1994, *Monastic and Religious Orders in Britain, 1000–1300*, Cambridge

Campbell, J., 1986, *Essays in Anglo-Saxon History*, London and Ronceverte

Campbell, J., 2000, *The Anglo-Saxon State*, London and New York

Chibnall, M., 1986, *Anglo-Norman England, 1066–1166*, Oxford

Clarke, P. A., 1994, *The English Nobility Under Edward the Confessor*, Oxford

Coulson, C., 2003, *Castles in Medieval Society: Fortresses in England, France, and Ireland in the Central Middle Ages*, Oxford

Cownie, E., 1998, *Religious Patronage in Anglo-Norman England*, Royal Historical Society Studies in History, Woodbridge

Creighton, O. H., 2005, *Castles and Landscapes: Power, Community and Fortification in Medieval England*, London

Creighton, O. H., 2009, *Designs Upon the Land: Elite Landscapes of the Middle Ages*, Woodbridge

Crick, J. and van Houts, E. (eds.), 2011, *A Social History of England, 900–1200*, Cambridge

Crouch, D., 2002, *The Normans: The History of a Dynasty*, London and New York

Crouch, D., 2011, *The English Aristocracy 1070–1272: A Social Transformation*, New Haven and London

Crouch, D. and Thompson, K. (eds.), 2011, *Normandy and its Neighbours, 900–1250: Essays for David Bates*, Turnhout

Dalton, P., 1994, *Conquest, Anarchy and Lordship: Yorkshire 1066–1154*, Cambridge

Dalton, P., 2015, 'William the Peacemaker: The Submission of the English to the Duke of Normandy, October 1066–January 1067', in Dalton, P. and Luscombe, D. (eds.), 2015, *Rulership and Rebellion in the Anglo-Norman World, c.1066–c.1216: Essays in Honour of Professor Edmund King*, Farnham and Burlington VT, 21–44

Davies, J. A., Riley, A., Levesque, J.-M. and Lapiche, C. (eds.), 2016, *Castles and the Anglo Norman World: Proceedings of a Conference Held at Norwich Castle in 2012*, Oxford and Philadelphia

Davies, R. R., 1991, *The Age of Conquest: Wales, 1063–1415*, Oxford

Douglas, D. C., 1964 and 1999 (new ed.), *William the Conqueror: The Norman Impact on England*, London (1964) and New Haven and London (1999)

Dyer, C. C. and Hadley, D. (eds.), 2017, *The Archaeology of the 11th Century: Continuities and Transformations*, Society for Medieval Archaeology Monograph 38, London and New York

Fernie, E., 2000, *The Architecture of Norman England*, Oxford

Fleming, R., 1991, *Kings and Lords in Conquest England*, Cambridge

Fleming, R.,1998, *Domesday Book and the Law: Society and Legal Custom in Early Medieval England*, Cambridge

Foot, S., 2011, *Æthelstan: the First King of England*, New Haven and London

Foys, M. K., Overbey, K. E. and Terkla, D. (eds.), 2009, *The Bayeux Tapestry: New Interpretations*, Woodbridge

Gameson, R., 1999, *The Manuscripts of Early Norman England (c.1066–1130)*, Oxford

Garnett, G., 2007, *Conquered England: Kingship, Succession, and Tenure, 1066–1166*, Oxford

Gillingham, J., 2000, *The English in the Twelfth Century: Imperialism, National Identity and Political Values*, Woodbridge

Gillingham, J., 2015, *William II: The Red King*, London

Green, J. A., 1990, *English Sheriffs to 1154*, London

Green, J. A., 1997, *The Aristocracy of Norman England*, Cambridge

Green, J. A., 2017, *Forging the Kingdom: Power in English Society, 973–1189*, Cambridge

Hagger, M., 2012, *William: King and Conqueror*, London and New York

Hagger, M., 2017, *Norman Rule in Normandy, 911–1144*, Woodbridge

Hallam, E. M., 1986, *Domesday Book through Nine Centuries*, London

Harper-Bill, C. and van Houts, E. (eds.), 2003, *A Companion to the Anglo-Norman World*, Woodbridge

Harvey, S., 2014, *Domesday: Book of Judgement*, Oxford

Hicks, C., 2006, *The Bayeux Tapestry: the Life-Story of a Masterpiece*, London

Higham, N. J., 1997, *The Death of Anglo-Saxon England*, Stroud

Higham, N. J., 1998, *The Norman Conquest*, Stroud

Holt, J. C. (ed.), 1987, *Domesday Studies*, Woodbridge

Holt, J. C., 1997, *Colonial England, 1066–1215*, London and Ronceverte

Hudson, J., 2012, *The Oxford History of the Laws of England, volume II: 871–1216*, Oxford

Impey, E. (ed.), 2008, *The White Tower*, New Haven and London

Keats-Rohan, K. S. B. , 1999, *Domesday People. A Prosopography of Persons Occurring in English Documents, 1066–1166. 1. Domesday Book*, Woodbridge

Lawson, M. K., 2002/2016, 2002, *The Battle of Hastings 1066*, Stroud; 2016: https://archive.org/details/LawsonBattleofHastings3rdedn

Le Patourel, J., 1976, *The Norman Empire*, Oxford

Lewis, M. J., Owen-Crocker, G. R. and D. (eds.), 2011, *The Bayeux Tapestry: New Approaches. Proceedings of a Conference at the British Museum*, Oxford

Licence, T. (ed.), 2014, *Bury St Edmunds and the Norman Conquest*, Woodbridge

Licence, T., 2017, 'Edward the Confessor and the Succession Question: A Fresh Look at the Sources', *ANS* 39, 113–27

Maddicott, J. R., 2010, *The Origins of the English Parliament 924–1327*, Oxford

Mason, E., 2004, *The House of Godwine. The History of a Dynasty*, London and New York

Mayr-Harting, H. R. E., 2011, *Religion, Politics and Society in Britain, 1066–1272*, Harlow

Molyneaux, G., 2015, *The Formation of the Kingdom of the English in the Tenth Century*, Oxford

Morillo, S., 1994, *Warfare Under the Anglo-Norman Kings, 1066–1135*, Woodbridge

Morillo, S., 1996, *The Battle of Hastings: Sources and Interpretations*, Woodbridge

Morris, M., 2016, *William I: England's Conqueror*, London

Mortimer, R. (ed.), 2009, *Edward the Confessor: the Man and the Legend*, Woodbridge

Nelson, J. L., Reynolds, S. and Johns, S. M. (eds.), 2012, *Gender and Historiography: Studies in the Earlier Middle Ages in Honour of Pauline Stafford*, London

O'Brien, B. R., 1999, *God's Peace and King's Peace: the Laws of Edward the Confessor*, Philadephia

Oksanen, E., 2012, *Flanders and the Anglo-Norman World 1066–1216*, Cambridge

Owen-Crocker, G. R. (ed.), 2005, *King Harold II and the Bayeux Tapestry*, Woodbridge

Pastan, E. C. and White, S. D., with Gilbert, K., 2014, *The Bayeux Tapestry and its Contents: A Reassessment*, Woodbridge

Pohl, B., 2015, *Dudo of Saint-Quentin's* Historia Normannorum: *Tradition, Innovation and Memory*, Woodbridge

Roach, L., 2013, *Kingship and Consent in Anglo-Saxon England, 871–978: Assemblies and the State in the Early Middle Ages*, Cambridge

Roach, L., 2016, *Æthelred the Unready*, New Haven and London

Roffe, D. (ed.), 2012, *The English and their Legacy, 900–1200: Essays in Honour of Ann Williams*, Woodbridge

Roffe, D. and Keats-Rohan, K. S. B. (eds.), 2016, *Domesday Now: New Approaches to the Inquest and the Book*, Woodbridge

Rowley, T., 2013, *The Man Behind the Bayeux Tapestry: Odo, William the Conqueror's Half-Brother*, Stroud

Rozier, C. C., Roach, D., Gasper, G. E. and van Houts, E. (eds.), 2016, *Orderic Vitalis: Life Works and Interpretations*, Woodbridge

Stafford, P., 1997, *Queen Emma and Queen Edith: Queenship and Women's Power in Eleventh-Century England*, Oxford

Strickland, M. (ed.), 1992, *Anglo-Norman Warfare*, Woodbridge

Strickland, M., 1996, *War and Chivalry: The Conduct and Perception of War in England and Normandy, 1066–1217*, Cambridge

Stringer, K. J. and Jotischky, A. (eds.), 2013, *Norman Connections: Connections, Continuities and Contrasts*, Farnham and Burlington VT

Sykes, N., 2007, *The Norman Conquest: A Zooarchaeological Perspective*, Oxford

Thomas, H. M., 2003, *The English and the Normans: Ethnic Hostility, Assimilation, and Identity, 1066–c.1220*, Oxford

Thomas, H. M., 2014, *The Secular Clergy in England, 1066–1216*, Oxford

Thomson, R. M., Dolmans, E. and Winkler, E. A. (eds.), 2017, *Discovering William of Malmesbury*, Woodbridge

Treharne, E., 2012, *Living Through Conquest: The Politics of Early English, 1020–1220*, Oxford

Tyler, E., 2017, *England in Europe: English Royal Women and Literary Patronage, c.1000–c.1150*, Toronto, Buffalo and London

van Houts, E., 1995, 'The Norman Conquest Through European Eyes', *EHR* 110, 832–53 (reprinted in van Houts, E., *History and Family Traditions*, chapter VIII)

van Houts, E., 1999, *History and Family Traditions in England and the Continent 1000–1200*, Aldershot

Walker, I. W., 1997, *Harold: The Last Anglo-Saxon King*, Stroud

Williams, A., 1995, *The English and the Norman Conquest*, Woodbridge

Williams, A., 1999, *Kingship and Government in pre-Conquest England*, Basingstoke and London

Williams, A., 2009, *The World Before Domesday: The English Aristocracy 900–1066*, London

Winkler, E. A., 2017, *Royal Responsibility in Anglo-Norman Histories*, Oxford

Wormald, P., 1999, *Legal Culture in the Early Medieval West: Law as Text, Image and Experience*, London

Index

The index below is almost entirely an index of personal and place-name. Subjects are only indexed when they have a clear and direct bearing on the book's theme. The words 'Anglo-Saxons' and 'Normans' have not been indexed, because they appear on almost every page of the book.